Property Practice & Land Law

Property Practice & Land Law

Fourth edition

Mark Richards
Solicitor and Visiting Lecturer in Law
at the University of Westminster

OXFORD
UNIVERSITY PRESS

OXFORD
UNIVERSITY PRESS

Great Clarendon Street, Oxford, OX2 6DP,
United Kingdom

Oxford University Press is a department of the University of Oxford.
It furthers the University's objective of excellence in research, scholarship,
and education by publishing worldwide. Oxford is a registered trade mark of
Oxford University Press in the UK and in certain other countries

First edition 2021
Second edition 2022
Third edition 2023

Published in the United States of America by Oxford University Press
198 Madison Avenue, New York, NY 10016, United States of America

British Library Cataloguing in Publication Data
Data available

Library of Congress Control Number: 2024937658

ISBN 978-0-19-893301-4

For Robin and Freddie, Alfred and Bertie

Thank you to Professor Robert Abbey for his assistance in the development of this manual

Acknowledgements

Some content under Crown copyright regarding different court structures is reproduced by kind permission under the Open Government Licence (http://www.nationalarchives.gov.uk/doc/open-government-licence/).

Grateful acknowledgement is made to the Solicitors Regulation Authority for copyright material which appears in this book.

For the latest version of the SRA Standards and Regulations, please visit their website (https://www.sra.org.uk/solicitors/standards-regulations/).

Every effort has been made to trace and contact copyright holders prior to going to press. If notified, the publisher will undertake to rectify any errors or omissions at the earliest opportunity.

Contents

Table of Cases

Table of Legislation

Table of Statutes

Table of Statutory Instruments

Table of European Law

Table of Professional Conduct Codes, Rules and Regulations

Exam Technique

A.1 Introduction

The functioning legal knowledge (FLK) assessments for SQE 1 comprise two assessments of 180 questions each.

The FLK assessments will cover the following subject areas:

1 Business Law and Practice; Dispute Resolution; Contract; Tort; Legal System of England and Wales; Constitutional and Administrative Law; and EU Law and Legal Services.

2 Property Practice; Wills and the Administration of Estates; Solicitors Accounts; Land Law; Trusts; Criminal Law and Practice.

The objective of the assessments, which is linked to the Statement of Solicitor Competence, is to assess the depth and breadth of your knowledge of the law of England and Wales. The assessments are not just about nuggets of knowledge but about demonstrating how well you can apply that knowledge to demonstrate the threshold competence required of a newly qualified solicitor on day one of practice.

In practice, the reality is that you will often look up information which you need to know either to confirm your thinking, to refresh your memory or, indeed, to find out about an issue with which you are unfamiliar. However, the FLK assessments are closed book. This means that, without reference to books and notes, you are answering the questions based upon your knowledge derived from your prior learning, including that provided and supported through these manuals, and through the practise questions.

Each question in the assessment contributes to the overall validity of the assessment; that is, it allows you the opportunity to demonstrate your knowledge and understanding about the application of the law. Therefore, it should be possible to infer that a successful candidate has demonstrated their competence to meet the threshold and is thus capable of being a solicitor.

The purpose of this chapter is to talk you through the assessment questions: how they are structured, what to look for and what to avoid. Be encouraged; the questions in the assessments and the questions in the question bank are written by human beings so bear in mind that the same thinking process which has been used to generate the question can be used by you to determine the correct answer. Questions are not written in a way purposefully to catch you out, as the point of a question is to assess what you *do* know, not what you *do not* know. If you have prepared thoroughly, you should be in a position to respond positively to the assessment.

A.2 Question structure

To begin, let us take a question from the SRA SQE 1 FLK sample questions published on 16 December 2019. These sample questions were published to give a guide as to what might be expected in the live assessment, and frequent reference will be made to them throughout this chapter.

The question is split into three parts, as illustrated in **Figure A.1**:

- the context;
- the stem; and
- the options.

In the course of a trial various arguments are put to the judge as to the exact meaning of a particular section of a relevant statute. When deciding the case, the judge first looks at the natural ordinary meaning of the words used. However, such an interpretation of those words results in an absurd meaning being given to the section.The judge, therefore, in coming to his decision, interprets the words in a different way which does not result in an absurd meaning. — **Context**

What method of statutory interpretation has the judge used? → **Stem**

A. The literal rule.
B. The mischief rule.
C. The extrinsic evidence rule.
D. The golden rule.
E. The intrinsic evidence rule.

— **Options**

FIGURE A.1 Example of question structure (SRA sample question 15)

A.2.1 **The context**

The context may be objective, for example, just a couple of generalised sentences before the stem, which puts the question to be answered and which aims to capture a particular piece of knowledge. SRA sample question number 6 demonstrates an objective context:

EXAMPLE

A decision is made by the Court of Appeal (Civil Division) in favour of the claimant. The defendant wishes to obtain permission to appeal.

Which of the following courts have the power to grant permission to appeal?

Or, as in question 15, the context may be subjective and contain more scene-setting for the question which follows, providing details about where, who and why something happened, as represented in **Figure A.2**.

You should read the context carefully because it will contain clues which have been laid by the question writer to help you answer the question.

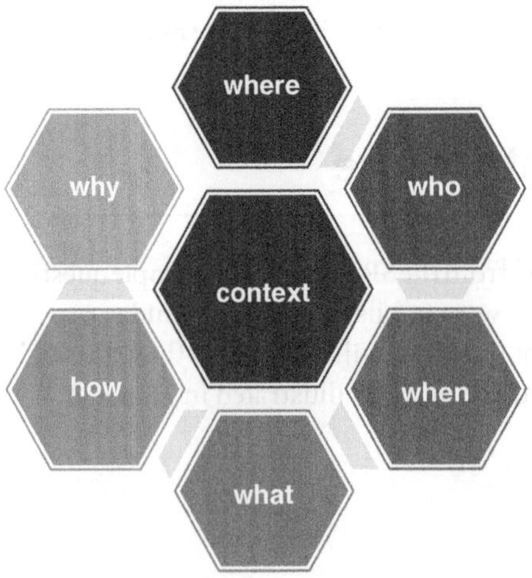

FIGURE A.2 Subjective context

Here is the question 15 context again with highlighted relevant sections which give a good idea as to what is in the question writer's mind—the rules of statutory interpretation:

> **EXAMPLE**
>
> In the course of a trial various arguments are put to the judge as to the *exact meaning* of a particular section of a relevant statute. When deciding the case, the judge first looks at the *natural ordinary meaning of the words* used. However, such an interpretation of those words *results in an absurd meaning* being given to the section. The judge, therefore, in coming to his decision, *interprets the words* in a different way which *does not result in an absurd meaning.*
>
> What method of statutory interpretation has the judge used?

In this particular question, the stem itself also tells you that the question is about statutory interpretation but the stem might not always be quite so helpful. You may have to consider the facts carefully to establish which area of knowledge is being assessed; each assessment covers multiple subject areas, so you will not know what kind of question you are attempting until you read it. Having read the context carefully, you should be in the right mental zone as the context contains all of the relevant facts which are needed to give the correct answer to the stem which follows and which supports the answer.

A.2.2 **The stem**

Look at the stem very carefully—after all, it is the link to the correct answer. Given its importance, the stem should be absolutely clear, should be connected to the context and include as much information as possible to be precise about what is being asked. Stems, properly written, should pass what is known as the *cover test*. The cover test means that the correct answer should, without seeing any of the options, pop into your head as soon as you read the stem. This is a very useful step to take as it prompts your memory to offer up the right answer without being conflicted by any distracting options. If you think of what you believe to be the correct answer and then, to your surprise, you do not see it in the options, double-check that you have read the stem correctly!

> **TIP**
>
> When you use the practise question bank, get into the habit of using the *cover test* as a technique as it is good for revision and will improve your recollection. A good habit to have! Having read the stem thoroughly, take a moment to pause and think what answer you expect to see amongst the options. When you read through the options, if that answer appears, you know you might be on the right track but pause again before you enthusiastically tick the box and move on to the next question! Check what you believe to be the answer very carefully to make sure that it matches what you had expected to see, then look through the other options to be doubly sure that you are correct in your selection. This is especially important in relation to single best answer questions which are discussed more fully later in the chapter; bear in mind that the 'best' answer might be very close to the second best answer giving you all the more reason to look carefully at all options. Only when this process is complete should you make your selection.

A.2.2.1 Types of question

The SQE 1 FLK assessment contains what are described as single best answer questions. They are likely to be of two types. The stems for each are different although both lead to the selection of a single correct or a single best answer:

- a traditional multiple-choice question leading to a single correct answer; and
- a single best answer question leading to a single best answer.

A.2.2.2 Traditional multiple-choice questions (MCQ)

For this type of question, there must be *only one unambiguously correct answer*. The answer is supported by the stem which will be worded in such a way that it can only lead to that one correct answer and is a heavy hint that you are looking for that one correct answer. As there is just one correct answer, these questions are an ideal way to practise using the cover test (see **A.2.2**).

Stem examples:

- Which of the following . . .
- What must X do . . .
- By when . . .
- What is the next step which should be taken . . .
- What is the correct advice to give . . .
- What is the correct procedure to . . .
- What is the accurate description of . . .

In question 15, the stem is worded: 'What method of statutory interpretation has the judge used?' The language is very precise: 'What method . . .'. It is an MCQ as there can only be one unambiguously correct answer.

A.2.2.3 Single best answer questions (SBA)

A single best answer question may need a little more unravelling than a traditional MCQ. For an SBA, a range of responses might be possible or reasonable within the context of the question. However, only one will be the star option as it is the most preferable, reasonable and appropriate as the *single best answer* in the circumstances as provided by the context.

The context, here, is particularly important and is likely to require evaluation in order to determine what course of action is for the best. As there is no immediate stand-out correct answer, as for a traditional MCQ, the possible solutions require an evaluative judgement as to what is best to do in the situation. Each judgement-based option may be represented visually; see **Figure A.3** which shows how the options may be ranged from least suitable or worst option to the best option. Note that there is only *ONE* best option. You should bear in mind that the least suitable option, here B, may simply be wrong which is explanation in itself as to why it is the least suitable option!

In **Figure A.3**, A is identified as the best option on a given set of facts; B and E are identified as the least suitable options on the same set of facts with C and D somewhere in between. D is clearly challenging A for the star option spot but there is no provision to choose both options and so there will be a particular reason on the facts why option A trumps the other options.

As you can see, more thought is needed to work through and determine the best option in an SBA. The options are likely to be carefully nuanced and these types of questions demonstrate a higher degree of application in a professional context. For example, you can envisage a circumstance in which a solicitor needs to advise a client in the client's best interests. All options might present possible and plausible advice which might be given, although one option might definitely not be in the client's interests while another is recognisably the *best* advice.

Stem examples:

- Which of the following is the most appropriate ground upon which . . .
- Which of the following represents the best advice which might be given . . .

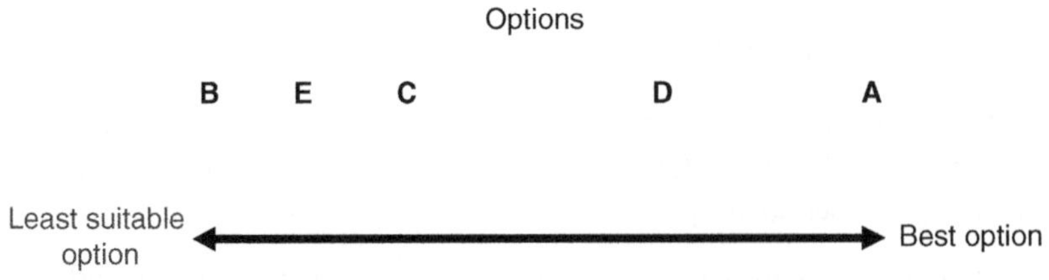

FIGURE A.3 Range of responses

- What is the best course of action to recommend in these circumstances?
- How is the court most likely to determine the claimant's application?
- What approach is the most sensible to adopt on these facts?

TIP

As you work through the practise questions in the question bank, familiarise yourself with the stem types and see how the options differ so that you are best prepared. Remember that identifying the type of question you are being asked naturally links to the type of answer which is expected. If the stem looks to be an MCQ, then the expected answer should be an unambiguously correct response; if the stem looks to be an SBA, then the expected answer will be what is best in the circumstances. The feedback which is provided to the practise questions will help you to understand why a particular best option has been identified on the facts of the question.

A.2.3 **The options**

After the stem come the five options lettered (A–E) from which you are to select your answer. Rest assured that the options will always include the right answer so there is some comfort in that! If the question has been carefully written, the answer should not stand out as being the correct answer, it should have been carefully embedded within the options which should all offer plausible alternatives to sway your choice. If you consider that the purpose of the question is to be able to infer competence, it is clear why it is unlikely that the right answer will stand out.

The remaining options are known as *distractors*, which is an apt description as they are there to distract you from the right answer. The distractors are likely to be plausibly based on common misconceptions or misunderstandings and be compatible with, and flow from, the stem. A distractor may look very similar to the right answer but will differ in a small but significant way, for example:

EXAMPLE

Which of the following is the correct explanation to provide about an unless order requiring filing and service of the defendant's list of documents by 4 pm on 21 May?

A. That unless by 4 pm on 21 May the defendant has filed and served its list of documents, the claim will be struck out.

B. That unless by 4 pm on 21 May the defendant has filed and served its list of documents, the defence will be struck out.

In this example there is a one-word difference between A and B. In the rush to answer and move on to the next question, the temptation may be to plump immediately for the first answer because it looks about right but, of course, it is wrong.

A distractor may also offer the wrong explanation for a definitive answer.

EXAMPLE

If the stem asks simply: 'Is the client entitled to take this course of action, and for what reason?', you know that the expected answer will be unambiguously correct because this is a traditional MCQ. The options might be presented as three 'Yes' options each followed by a different reason, one of which is correct, and two 'No' options each followed by a different reason.

A. Yes, because . . .

B. Yes, because . . .

C. Yes, because . . .

D. No, because . . .

E. No, because . . .

In some ways, these questions are quite helpfully structured because you might readily be able to eliminate the two 'no' options but you must still look carefully through the three remaining options to ensure that you home in on the correct reason for the 'yes' response.

> **TIP**
>
> If there are three positive options and two negative options, *do not immediately discount the negative options* and assume that one of the positive options is bound to be the right answer; the imbalance might be trying to lull you into a false sense of safety in numbers and prompt you to select a positive answer. Only eliminate options if you are sure that they are wrong.

The best distractors will also look similar to the answer in construction and length: they have symmetry. This is demonstrated in SRA sample question 15 where the options are given as:

A. The literal rule.

B. The mischief rule.

C. The extrinsic evidence rule.

D. The golden rule.

E. The intrinsic evidence rule.

A distractor must work hard to distract you from the correct answer. In the same way that a stand-out correct answer does little to assess competence, a stand-out wrong option is also unhelpful to assessors because it can be eliminated from the running and so increases the chances of a candidate getting the question right without actually knowing the answer! In the FLK assessments, there are five options and you have a 1 in 5 chance of getting the answer correct even if you guess (more on this in **A.4.1**). If two of the options are implausible, the probability of selecting the correct answer increases to 1 in 3.

In SRA sample question 6 about appeals, these are the options:

A. The Court of Appeal only.

B. The Supreme Court only.

C. The House of Lords only.

D. The Court of Appeal and the Supreme Court.

E. The Court of Appeal and the House of Lords.

There are two stand out options here, C and E, which can be eliminated as they are plainly wrong because they contain a reference to the House of Lords rather than the Supreme Court. The choice has now reduced to A, B and D.

Notice that A and B include the word 'only'. Be wary of such limiting phrasing and ask yourself whether this could possibly be correct in the context.

> **TIP**
>
> It is worth bearing in mind that options which include 'always' and 'never' are (almost) always wrong and never right. Do not discount them without some thought as such phrasing may be appropriate for the context, but bear in mind that such absolute phrasing often hints that the option is likely to be incorrect as it is inflexible and allows for no exceptions. This is often too rigid an approach in the field of law.

By this process of elimination, A and B include the word 'only' which is too absolute for the reality of those options. Therefore, only option D remains and that is the correct answer to the question.

The words 'must' and 'may' are frequently encountered in MCQs. Bearing in mind that the stem supports the answer and connects to the distractors, look carefully at whether either of those words appear in the options.

EXAMPLE

What is the likely costs order which the judge will make?

If any of the options contains the word 'must', for example:

A. The judge *must* make an order for the claimant to pay the defendant's costs in any event

think carefully; costs are discretionary and, therefore, you would expect the correct answer to read:

A. The judge *may* make an order for the claimant to pay the defendant's costs in any event'.

TIP

Through use of the cover test technique, you will hopefully have in mind what you believe to be the answer and may mentally benchmark an option as soon as you see it. Do not bank that option too soon until you have reviewed the other options; use it as the measure against which the other options are considered as being correct/incorrect or better/worse. Then, eliminate options to narrow your choice further. Think logically, analyse the wording carefully and eliminate options based upon the *specific facts* you are given and not the general law, practice or procedure. The majority of questions will have a specific set of facts and the correct answer depends on those. If, after that analysis, you are still persuaded that your initial thought was correct, go ahead and bank the option!

A.3 **Worked examples**

Now that you understand how a question is constructed, you can see that there are four simple steps to take to approach each question:

Step 1. Read the context carefully, taking note of key words to identify which topic area the question is about.

Step 2. Read the stem and identify whether this is an MCQ or SBA.

Step 3. From the stem, conduct the cover test.

Step 4. Read the options and identify the distractors.

Using these steps, have a look through these worked examples and try to think one step ahead.

WORKED EXAMPLE: DISPUTE RESOLUTION

A claimant, in proceedings in which they had raised a claim and a defence to counterclaim, does not attend court on the first day of trial.

What order should the defendant ask the court to make?

A. To adjourn the trial.
B. To give judgment on the counterclaim.
C. To make a wasted costs order.
D. To strike out the claim.
E. To strike out the claim and the defence to counterclaim.

Step 1: Review the context.

A claimant, in proceedings in which *they had raised a claim and a defence to counterclaim, does not attend court* on the first day of *trial.*

Your first thoughts might be that this is a very short fact-pattern and so unlikely to be a tricky question but it packs in a considerable amount of detail. The key words have been highlighted: we know that the claimant pursues a claim but is also defending a counterclaim, and does not attend court for the trial. Of those key words, perhaps the most significant is the presence of a counterclaim, which is a claim in its own right pursued by the defendant against the claimant and which can alter the dynamic between the parties. Having got a grip on the facts, read the stem.

Step 2: Read the stem and identify whether this is an MCQ or SBA.

What order should *the defendant* ask the court to make?

Is this an MCQ or an SBA? You might be thinking that this looks like an MCQ as it begins 'What order . . .' as if only one precise and correct answer is possible. However, look again; this is an SBA. The use of the word 'should' is a hint here. It is more or less asking: what is the best thing to do in these circumstances if you were the defendant. Note that the use of the word 'should' might also appear in an MCQ to indicate what should be done correctly in the circumstances—close reading of the fact-pattern and the stem will help you to decide what you are being asked. There is also a shift of context here: the fact-pattern sets up the scenario from the claimant's perspective but the question itself is asked from the defendant's perspective.

Step 3: From the stem, conduct the cover test.

Before looking at the options, try the cover test: what pops into your head as to what order the defendant should be seeking? Anything? Do not worry if not as we can now take a look at the options.

Step 4: Read the options and identify the distractors.

Read through all of the options once. This may provide an immediate prompt as to which of the options might possibly be the answer.

A. To adjourn the trial.
B. To give judgment on the counterclaim.
C. To make a wasted costs order.
D. To strike out the claim.
E. To strike out the claim and the defence to counterclaim.

Now go back and begin the process of elimination taking each option in turn and thinking from the defendant's perspective:

A cannot be right as, although a defendant can, of course, ask the court to adjourn the trial, there is no reason for a defendant to ask the court to adjourn the trial as the court may proceed with the trial in the absence of the claimant. Why would a defendant give up the opportunity to succeed against the claimant in their absence? B looks like a possibility, but this would not dispose of the claimant's claim, only the counterclaim; but something is beginning to emerge here as to what might be best for the defendant. C seems like a good idea to make the claimant pay but this is going down the wrong track because costs orders are consequential upon an event. Some event must occur first on which to hang the costs order. Also, there is something here that is not quite right as a wasted costs order is made against the legal representatives and there is nothing on the facts to suggest that the claimant's legal representatives are at fault. Let us look at D. This does not look right as it would leave the counterclaim live so let us look closely at E: asking for an order to strike out the claim and the defence to counterclaim looks to be a good answer on these facts as although the court may proceed with the trial in the absence of a party, if the claimant does not attend the trial, the court may strike out the claim and any defence to counterclaim. Got to the best answer, E, in the end!

WORKED EXAMPLE: PROPERTY LAW

A solicitor is acting for the buyer of a house which has a registered title. The house was first registered in 2004 following a sale. The house was the subject of a further sale which was registered in 2012. The house is built on land which is near the church within a Church of England parish. There is no entry in the register as to chancel repair liability.

Which one of the following correctly describes whether the buyer's solicitor needs to carry out a chancel repair liability search?

A. No, because the title was registered under the Land Registration Act 2002.

B. Yes, because chancel repair liability takes effect as an overriding interest.

C. No, because there has been a registered transfer on sale subsequent to first registration of title.

D. No, because no entry has been made in the register in respect of any chancel repair liability.

E. Yes, because there has been no registered transfer on sale after 12 October 2013.

Step 1: Review the fact pattern.

A solicitor is acting for the buyer of a house which has a *registered* title. The house was first registered in *2004* following a sale. The house was the subject of a *further sale* which was registered in *2012*. The house is built on land which is near the church within a *Church of England* parish. There is no entry in the register as to *chancel repair liability.*

This fact-pattern sets the context for the question, which relates to a purchase of a house with registered title which is near a church. The key words and dates have been highlighted and these identify the issue—which is whether the house could be subject to chancel repair liability—and provide the important details which will be relevant to this issue. Those details include both dates and facts, so this should flag up to you that you will need to consider not just what events have taken place, but how the timing of those events could affect the outcome. With this in mind, you can now look at the stem.

Step 2: Read the stem and identify whether this is an MCQ or SBA.

Which one of the following correctly describes whether the buyer's solicitor needs to carry out a chancel repair liability search?

Is this an MCQ or an SBA? The key words here are 'correctly' and 'needs', which indicate that this is an MCQ rather than an SBA. Although the focus of the question is on whether a search is considered necessary, the determining factor is objective; that is, it is based on the underlying law rather than subjective judgement as to which of several courses of action might be 'best' in the circumstances.

Step 3: From the stem, conduct the cover test.

Before looking at the options, try the cover test: what pops into your head as to whether a search might be necessary? Anything? If so, apply this when considering your answer, but do not pre-empt your conclusion until you have read the options. Do not worry if nothing occurs to you at this stage, as we can now take a look at the options.

Step 4: Read the options and identify the distractors.

Read through all of the options once. This may provide an immediate prompt as to which of the options might possibly be the correct answer.

A. No, because the title was registered under the Land Registration Act 2002.

B. Yes, because chancel repair liability takes effect as an overriding interest.

C. No, because there has been a registered transfer on sale subsequent to first registration of title.

D. No, because no entry has been made in the register in respect of any chancel repair liability.

E. Yes, because there has been no registered transfer on sale after 12 October 2013.

Now go back and begin the process of elimination taking each option in turn and thinking from the solicitor's perspective:

A. can be discounted because although the title was first registered in 2004, after the 2002 Act came into force, at that time chancel repair liability continued to be an overriding interest in the same way as it had previously.

B. superficially looks as though it might be correct—chancel repair liability *was* originally within the list of overriding interests. But the key word here is 'was'—it ceased to be within the list after 12 October 2013. So, again, this option can be discounted.

C. is a technical point where timing comes into play. Consider this option in conjunction with option B: when did chancel repair liability cease to be an overriding interest? In 2013—so if this transfer took place in 2009, the liability will have been binding on the transferee because it was an overriding interest at that time.

D. looks, on the face of it, as though it could be a correct option: if chancel repair liability is no longer an overriding interest and there is no entry in the register as to any liability, will the buyer not take free of it? But again, remember the importance of timing here—the buyer has not yet completed their purchase, so is there still a risk? Bear in mind that just because chancel repair liability ceased to be an overriding interest in 2013, this did not mean the liability automatically ceased to exist.

E. raises a technical point where again timing comes into play. Although there is currently no entry in the register and chancel repair liability no longer takes effect as an overriding interest after that date, the property remains subject to any existing liability until the next transfer on sale is registered. Consider whether there is a risk, at this stage of the transaction, that an application could still be made to register any such liability and the buyer would then be bound by it if they proceeded with their purchase.

Having evaluated the options, go back to the stem and check exactly what the question is asking. With this in mind, confirm the results of your evaluation and select the option you consider to be correct. In this instance, the correct option is E.

WORKED EXAMPLE: BUSINESS LAW

A woman has been appointed to the board of directors of a private limited company (with unamended model articles). It is her first directorship and she wants to understand the legal requirements relating to decisions taken by the board of directors.

Which one of the following correctly describes the requirements of the company's articles and/or the Companies Act 2006 in respect of decisions taken by the board of directors of the company?

A. Only the directors can attend board meetings.

B. If the director cannot attend a board meeting, she can appoint a proxy.

C. The directors may take decisions by way of written resolution.

D. The directors can vote at board meetings on either a show of hands or by a poll vote.

E. Minutes of the board meetings must be filed with the Registrar of Companies.

Step 1: Review the context.

A woman has been appointed to the board of directors of *a private limited company* (with unamended model articles) and seeks your advice. It is her first directorship and she wants to understand the legal requirements relating to *decisions taken by the board of directors.*

When you look at the context, you will see that this is one of those generalised style questions which seeks to test your understanding of a particular topic. The key words have been highlighted for you: we are told that the woman is seeking advice about the requirements relating to decisions taken by the board of directors of a private limited company. It is important to recognise that the question focuses entirely on board decisions. This question is not asking about shareholder decisions so you should already be thinking about the difference in formalities and procedure of the two. It is also significant that we are told about this company's constitution: it has unamended model articles. Now that you have understood the context, you must read the stem.

Step 2: Read the stem and identify whether this is an MCQ or SBA.

Which one of the following correctly describes the requirements of the company's articles and/or the Companies Act 2006 in respect of decisions taken by the board of directors of the company?

Is this an MCQ or an SBA? The clue here is the use of the words 'Which one of the following' and 'correctly'. It is an MCQ as there can only be one correct answer. This stem does not ask you to advise the woman which is the best course of action when taking a decision as a director, but rather to confirm which one of the statements is a correct option.

Step 3: From the stem, conduct the cover test.

Before looking at the options, try the cover test: what pops into your head about the requirements for the decisions of the board of directors of private limited companies? What rules governing the taking of board decisions do you expect to see amongst the options? Now, move on to look at the options.

Step 4: Read the options and identify the distractors.

Carefully read through all of the options once. This may provide an immediate prompt as to which of the options might possibly be the answer.

A. Only the directors can attend board meetings.
B. If the director cannot attend a board meeting, she can appoint a proxy.
C. The directors may take decisions by way of written resolution.
D. The directors can vote at board meetings on either a show of hands or by a poll vote.
E. Minutes of the board meetings must be filed with the Registrar of Companies.

Now go back and begin the process of elimination, taking each option in turn.

A cannot be correct as others—for example, a company secretary, the company's lawyers or accountants—may also attend board meetings. Whilst they do not have a right to vote, they may attend. This option needs to be eliminated. This option also includes the word 'only'. Be alert to the use of this word as it is creating an exclusive category. It may be appropriate for a context but here it is clearly not appropriate as others may attend the meetings.

At first glance B might look like a correct answer; however, this is where a solid understanding of the differences between board decisions and shareholder decisions is important. If the director cannot attend a board meeting, she could, if the articles of association allow (and the model articles do not), appoint an alternate director to attend in her place. A proxy is the term used for someone who attends a shareholders' meeting on behalf of the shareholder, so this is not a correct option and this option needs to be ruled out. Furthermore, this option uses the word 'can'. Again, be alert to this. 'Can' means the same as to be able to do something but bear in mind that just because you can do something does not mean that you should or that it is the correct thing to do. Here, although the option is worded that the director 'can appoint a proxy' and, literally, she can do that, it would be the wrong thing to do in her position to meet requirements.

How about C? The model articles do allow the directors to take decisions either at a board meeting or in writing. This looks like it is a correct option. If you think that C is the correct answer, pause before you select the option and move on to the next question. Look through the final two options to be doubly sure that you are correct in your selection. The word 'may' is used in this option which is an expression of possibility and means that a choice may be exercised to do something or not to do something; there is no obligation to do a specific thing. Here, the directors have a choice as they may take decisions either at a board meeting *or* in writing and so C looks like a good contender for the correct answer as the option provides that the directors may take decisions by way of written resolution.

D is incorrect as directors can only vote for or against the resolution by a show of hands. A poll vote is an alternative way of voting at a general meeting of shareholders. Again, this is where a good understanding of the differences between board decisions and shareholder decisions is important. Here, again, we meet use of the word 'can'. In this context, just because the directors are physically able to vote by a show of hands does not mean that they should or that it is the correct thing to do to meet requirements.

Finally, E is incorrect as the minutes are a private record of the decisions taken by the board and there is no requirement under either the articles or the Companies Act 2006 for them to be filed with the Registrar of Companies. The use of the word 'must' creates an obligation, a necessity or requirement to do something. It may be appropriate to a given context but be alert to it being a categorical answer; there is no doubt or any choice but to do something.

Having carefully considered each of the options, go back to the stem and check exactly what the question is asking. Apply the results of your evaluation and select the option you considered to be correct. In this instance, the correct option is C.

A.4 Time management

Each FLK assessment is likely to allow five hours and six minutes to answer 180 questions; just 1.7 minutes per question. So, it is clearly important to practise your time management. You can use the practise questions however you wish but to get the most from them you might:

- use the questions to support your learning as you work through the manuals. You might read a section or a chapter of the manual and then try your hand at answering some of the questions to reinforce your learning;
- come to the questions fresh and try your hand at a random selection of questions to keep you on your toes and to embed learning over a period of time and to highlight where you may need to look again at a topic to deepen your understanding. The feedback on each question and cross-referencing with the manual will be helpful here;
- practise the questions against the clock to replicate the assessment time constraint and to be sure that you can complete the assessment within the allocated time.

A.4.1 Blind guessing against making an educated choice

This chapter would be incomplete without facing down the old chestnut that you can guess your way through a multiple-choice assessment. Statistically speaking, it has a basis in truth. Simply, there are five options and, by making a selection, you have a 1 in 5 chance of getting the answer correct. But blind guessing is a risky strategy to deploy throughout an assessment. Think of it this way: for every question answered by guessing, you have 4 chances in 5 of getting it wrong! Statistically, that would be 144 out of 180 questions wrongly answered on an FLK assessment. You may also have heard that selecting option C consistently is bound to improve your chances. This is not true. Options are often randomised so option C is no more likely to be correct than A, B, D or E.

It is far better to make an educated guess which may be necessary where you are struggling either against time, in the closing minutes of the assessment, or against a mental blank which is blocking progress. Making an educated guess involves narrowing down the options by the process of elimination leaving perhaps a choice between two or three options. You now have, respectively, a 1 in 2 or 1 in 3 chance of selecting the right answer, which has significantly improved the odds. But let us be realistic. Under time pressure, you may temporarily be at a loss even to make an educated guess. Your memory has not been prompted by reading the stem and nothing stands out when you read through the options. What should you do? Be positive and hold your nerve; recognise that this is a temporary block and there are other questions which need your attention which you will be able to answer—so get a move on to the next question. You may even find that, in working through the other questions, your memory suddenly gives up the answer which had eluded you before. Near the end of the assessment, go back to any missed questions and make an educated guess; there is no negative marking in the assessment, that is losing a mark for an incorrect answer, but, as a certainty, skipping a question loses you the chance to gain a mark.

A.5 Summary

You will now appreciate that there is a method to the process of answering questions; just as there is a method to writing them. A methodical approach brings calm to the process; knowing that there is a structured approach to the creation of a question helps you to know that the question can also be deconstructed. An understanding of how that can be done, and the step-by-step process which has been outlined, will be a guide on your shoulder when you are either working your way through the question bank or working your way through the exam paper.

Of course, 'knowing your stuff' will provide the required bedrock of functioning legal knowledge, which is at the heart of the SQE assessments. The manuals, the question banks and your own preparation and practise will help put you into the best possible position to respond to the questions in the assessments.

TIP

This tip applies throughout the entire preparation process building up to sitting the FLK assessments. From studying the manual materials, going over a tricky area of law or procedure which you do not grasp at first, practising the questions until you know (and understand) why the answer is as given, to sitting the assessment: preparation and perseverance are key. *Remember, giving up assures a fail but the difference between failing and succeeding is trying one more time!*

Good luck!

Ethics, Professional Conduct and Client Care

FUNCTIONING LEGAL KNOWLEDGE

Candidates are required to demonstrate their ability to act honestly and with integrity, and in accordance with the SRA Standards and Regulations as follows:

- the purpose, scope and content of the SRA Principles
- the purpose, scope and content of the:
  - SRA Code of Conduct for Solicitors, Registered European Lawyers and Registered Foreign Lawyers
  - SRA Code of Conduct for Firms in relation to:
    - managers in authorised firms
    - compliance officers

AUTHORITIES UNDERPINNING PRACTICE

The key authorities that underpin this area of practice are listed below. Note that for legislation you are linked to legislation.gov.uk.

Although much of the legislation on this government website is available in its amended form, the incorporation of new amendments into the text of legislation can be delayed. You should refer to legal databases to ensure you are referencing the most up-to-date legislation.

- SRA Code of Conduct 2019 for Solicitors, REL's and RFL's
  https://www.sra.org.uk/solicitors/standards-regulations/code-conduct-solicitors/
- Solicitors Regulation Authority Standards and Regulations
  https://www.sra.org.uk/solicitors/standards-regulations
- Criminal Finances Act 2017
  http://www.legislation.gov.uk/ukpga/2017/22/contents
- Data Protection Act 2018
  http://www.legislation.gov.uk/ukpga/2018/12/contents/enacted
- Legal Services Act 2007
  http://www.legislation.gov.uk/ukpga/2007/29/contents
- Money Laundering, Terrorist, Financing and Transfer of Funds (Information on the Payer) Regulations 2017 (SI 2017/692)
  http://www.legislation.gov.uk/uksi/2017/692/contents/made
- Proceeds of Crime Act 2002
  https://www.legislation.gov.uk/ukpga/2002/29/contents
- Terrorism Act 2000
  https://www.legislation.gov.uk/ukpga/2000/11/contents

B.1 Introduction

This chapter introduces ethics, professional conduct and client care in relation to solicitors and law firms. A practical understanding of ethics and professional conduct are fundamental to being a good solicitor; indeed, it is paramount that solicitors act with integrity and honesty while recognising the need to be guided by certain moral principles. Client care is covered within this chapter because it is important for all businesses, even more so for law firms. As a solicitor, you have an obligation to take care of your clients, though these are not always thought of as ethical concerns. Clients are usually facing challenging life circumstances when they contact a solicitor and they need to have trust and confidence in them to be able to deal with their matter well, whether it is part of their ethical obligations or in addition to them.

B.2 Introduction to ethics and professional conduct

Ethical principles have been recognised by the solicitors' profession for centuries. Many have argued the need to ensure a neutral partisanship: this holds that a solicitor must pursue a legal end for any client by any legal means. It is difficult, however, to balance the ethical conflicts between professional and personal morality. Ethics which arise by virtue of a solicitor's professional status are identified as professional or legal ethics. These ethics may at times be incompatible with what is morally required of non-professionals.

The Law Society was founded in 1825. At the Law Society's inception, the organisation was both the representative body and regulatory body for solicitors in England and Wales. It was only in 1960, however, that an actual text incorporating principles was published. It was called *A Guide to the Professional Conduct and Etiquette of Solicitors* and was written by the Law Society. The Solicitors' Practice Rules were then established in 1990 and were adhered to by solicitors until 1 July 2007, when the Code of Conduct 2007 was implemented.

The Solicitors Regulation Authority (SRA) is now the independent regulatory body overseeing the regulation of solicitors on behalf of the Law Society in England and Wales. It was created in January 2007, in anticipation of the Legal Services Act 2007 but also due to conflict within the profession and in an attempt to restore public trust in solicitors, which was an issue around that time. The SRA supports solicitors who are faced with moral dilemmas that arise in practice by setting out the principles and code of conduct which all solicitors and law firms in England and Wales must regulate and uphold. In the event of a conflict, the principles which safeguard the wider public interest take precedence over those relating to an individual client's interests. Solicitors should, where relevant, inform their client of the circumstances in which their duty to the court and other professional obligations will outweigh their duty to them. At the present time, the Code of Conduct 2019 is guided by trust, confidence and the protection of the public interest. It is as much about ethical values as moral principles.

B.2.1 Changes to the Code of Conduct

Since the first Code of Conduct was implemented in 2007 there have been two updates, one in October 2011 and the second, most recently, in November 2019. These are discussed in more detail later.

B.2.2 Code of Conduct 2007

The Code of Conduct 2007 was a lengthy and prescriptive code, supported by guidance. Along with the Code, there were also the Solicitors' Account Rules 1998, the SRA Recognised Bodies Regulations and the Client Financial Protection Requirements, which formed the regulatory authority to which solicitors had to adhere. Clearly, this was a lot of information placed in a number of different sources, and so it was time-consuming for solicitors to be able to understand and consult these when faced with an ethical dilemma.

B.2.3 **Code of Conduct 2011 and SRA Handbook**

The Code of Conduct 2011 was contained in the SRA Handbook which came into force for all firms on 6 October 2011. The purpose of the Handbook was to provide an accompanying set of rules and regulations which supported the standards and requirements which all law firms, in-house legal departments and alternative business structures were expected to uphold. There were ten Principles. They were all-pervasive and underpinned all of the Handbook requirements. The Code of Conduct chapters showed how the Principles would apply in certain contexts and focused on the quality of the service a solicitor was delivering to a client, using outcomes and indicative behaviours to generate what is known as 'outcomes focused regulation'. The 2011 Code was shorter and less prescriptive. The SRA hoped that this would offer greater flexibility as solicitors would need to use greater professional judgement to ensure compliance with the SRA. It was more detailed in some areas than others, which created uncertainty and led to some criticism. However, it did reflect the overall aim of the SRA which was to focus on the quality of what a solicitor was delivering to a client rather than prescribing how the solicitor had reached that stage.

B.2.4 **Code of Conduct 2019**

The SRA Standards and Regulations came into effect on 25 November 2019 and replaced the SRA Handbook. They can be found on the SRA website and, as they are published online only, they can be updated and amended regularly, so it is important to keep up to date with the website as there may have been changes since this manual was published. As well as making it easier to update, publishing the Standards and Regulations online was intended to make access to a solicitor or barrister easier for members of the public.

There was a change in this Code from a focus on indicative behaviour to one on ethical conduct, and there are now seven Principles rather than ten. There are also two types of Code of Conduct in the 2019 set of SRA Standards and Regulations.

Code of Conduct for Solicitors, Registered European Lawyers (RELs) and Registered Foreign Lawyers (RFLs) applies to those individuals who are authorised by the SRA to provide legal services.

Code of Conduct for Firms which applies to all bodies authorised by the SRA to provide legal services.

One of the reasons for creating a code for individual solicitors and another for firms is that the onus is now on a firm's management team to establish processes, structures and controls to ensure uniformity across the firm.

In light of the UK's withdrawal from the European Union (Brexit), the SRA's guidance on RFLs, initially published on 23 July 2019, was updated on 24 March 2021. See SRA Guidance: Registered Foreign Lawyers.

B.2.4.1 The Principles

The Principles, alongside the Code of Conduct, are the basis of ethical behaviour which the SRA expects individual solicitors as well as law firms, managers and employees, to uphold. The Principles were established by the SRA Enforcement Strategy which underpins all the requirements set out in the Principles, Codes, and rules and regulations. It provides a detailed explanation of the approach to taking regulatory action in the public interest. If the Principles come into conflict, those which safeguard the wider public interest and public confidence in solicitors take precedence over an individual client's interest. It is important to explain this potential situation to a client.

EXAMPLE

To demonstrate how the Principles can come into conflict, suppose a solicitor is asked to allow a witness to give evidence in support of their client, in the knowledge that the evidence is untrue. The solicitor would have to refuse to do this as the wider public interest and public confidence take precedence over the client.

The Principles are mandatory, and so a breach of these Principles may constitute professional misconduct which could result in a warning, a financial penalty, a referral to the Solicitors Disciplinary Tribunal or some level of control or disqualification from acting in certain roles. When faced with an ethical dilemma in practice, the Principles are where a solicitor should look initially for guidance.

The seven current Principles are as follows.

1 To act in a way that upholds the constitutional principle of the rule of law, and the proper administration of justice.
2 To act in a way that upholds public trust and confidence in the solicitors' profession and in legal services provided by authorised persons.
3 To act with independence.
4 To act with honesty.
5 To act with integrity.
6 To act in a way that encourages equality, diversity and inclusion.
7 To act in the best interests of each client.

EXAMPLE

In a corporate firm, a solicitor may be approached by a firm of brokers to refer all clients to them. They may be offered a large financial incentive to do this. This, however, would compromise their independence and so would not comply with the Principles above, apart from where certain conditions are met (Code of Conduct paras 5.1–5.3)). In particular to act with independence and to act in the best interests of each client. The solicitor would usually need to decline to act and suggest that the brokers provide a list of corporate firms in the area or link to the Law Society Find a Solicitor webpage, to allow the client to decide who they wished to instruct. This would avoid any risk of compromising the solicitor's independence and would allow them to continue to act in the best interests of each client who instructed them.

B.2.4.2 SRA Regulation

In line with the SRA Enforcement Strategy, the SRA seeks to:

- ensure a strong, competitive, and highly effective legal market
- ensure a focus on quality and client care
- promote a culture in which ethical values and behaviours are embedded

The SRA have a number of regulatory tools which are used in order to support compliance from law firms. The SRA Enforcement Strategy lists these as including:

- conducting thematic reviews of areas of risk
- publishing a risk outlook highlighting our priority risks
- providing advice and support through our Professional Ethics helpline and a range of toolkits and guidance
- SRA Innovate, a service which helps legal services providers to develop their business in new ways

In addition to the regulatory requirements set by the SRA Codes, Principles, rules and regulations, the SRA monitor and enforce the requirements relating to referral fees set out in s56 of the Legal Aid, Sentencing and Punishment of Offenders Act 2012. They also look at provisions relating to anti-money laundering which is mentioned at **B.3**.

B.2.5 **Compliance officers**

There are two different types of compliance officers. Compliance officers for legal practice (COLPs) and compliance officers for finance and administration (COFAs). All practices authorised by the SRA must appoint a COLP and a COFA. They are both a fundamental part of a law firm's compliance and governance arrangements as well as the culture of compliance within the firm. They have a broad number of responsibilities and may be liable for regulatory action if they fail to meet them. The Law Society Practice Note on Compliance Officers sets out a full list of the compliance officer roles, and best practice as to how breaches should be recorded and monitored.

COLPs and COFAs have a duty to report a serious breach of compliance to the SRA. This may go against the wishes of the managers of the practice. They have a duty to keep records of all breaches in order to recognise when one may be a serious breach. Managers are, however, responsible for their firm's compliance with the Code of Conduct. This responsibility is joint and several, if they share management responsibility with other managers of the firm.

EXAMPLE

A potential new solicitor applies to a firm for a job and in his additional paperwork he gives details of a physical disability which will require various reasonable adjustments to be made by his employer. The day after he submits this paperwork, the firm withdraws the job offer, giving only a brief explanation as to the reasons behind this decision. The solicitor makes a formal complaint to the firm, alleging disability discrimination.

The firm's COLP has a duty to investigate the complaint and write a report with their conclusion. If the COLP is satisfied that there is no regulation issue, then they would not need to report this.

If the COLP is, however, concerned about being misled by any staff involved in the decision then this must be reported, as a regulatory concern has arisen regarding potentially being given misleading information relating to the job offer being withdrawn.

B.2.6 Complaints and the Legal Ombudsman

If a client believes that their solicitor has not treated them fairly or professionally, they are entitled to complain. The main issues they may complain about are the way the case was handled or the costs for the services. If a client does complain then they will have been provided with details of how to complain by the law firm. The first step is usually to contact the solicitor to explain what the issue is and how it may be resolved. In most situations where a client complains, the matter will be resolved internally, and the complaint and file could be closed.

If the complaint has not been dealt with to the client's satisfaction or within eight weeks, then the client is entitled to complain to the Legal Ombudsman. The Legal Ombudsman deals with complaints across the entire legal profession, not just solicitors. There is a £400 fee potentially payable by the law firm which is being complained about. The aim of the Ombudsman is to use speed and informality to try and come to an agreement between the parties. If an agreement cannot be reached, then a decision is made by an officer of the Ombudsman. There are several remedies which may be available if the Ombudsman finds in favour of the complainant. There are also time limits (revised on 1 April 2023) which need to be adhered to by the client and the Ombudsman. Further details on remedies, limitations and the Legal Ombudsman can be found on the Law Society's website.

EXAMPLE

A client believes that his solicitor has not been honest with him about his chances for success and has not acted in his best interests. He feels that the solicitor encouraged him to take a matter to litigation and pay a large amount in legal fees; he subsequently lost the case and was told by the judge that he did not have a strong case in the first place. The client can lodge a complaint to the law firm but, if not satisfied with their response, then he could take it to the Legal Ombudsman.

If the client believes that a solicitor has breached the SRA Code of Conduct then they may contact the SRA direct in order to report it. Examples of breaches which a client may be concerned about include discrimination, fraud and dishonesty.

EXAMPLE

If a solicitor refused to continue acting for a client due to their religious belief, this would be a form of discrimination and thus a breach of the SRA Code of Conduct. The client could make a complaint to the law firm but, again, if not satisfied with their response then they could take it to the Legal Ombudsman and/or to the SRA.

B.2.7 **Conflicts of interest**

A solicitor has a duty to act in the best interests of their client and to make sure that these interests do not conflict with each other. This is a key area within ethics and professional conduct as it is important for public protection and for acting in relation to the client's best interests. There will be occasions when you find that your firm already acts for a client whose interests conflict with a potential new client. When this happens, then it is almost impossible to be able to act for both in their best interests. The Code of Conduct 2019 (paras 6.1–6.2) prevents a solicitor acting where a conflict of interest exists, apart from in very limited circumstances.

As the SRA Guidance on Conflicts explains (SRA Case Studies: Conflict of Interest) there are two types of conflict of interest situations. The first is a conflict between two or more clients, known as a 'conflict of interest'. The second is a conflict between the client's interests and the solicitor's interests, known as an 'own interest conflict'.

A solicitor can never act in an 'own interest conflict'; however, in certain circumstances they can act in a 'conflict of interest' situation. The best interests of the clients continuously need to be considered. There is also another conflict to consider which relates to Principle 1, to uphold the law, as solicitors are also officers of the court. There could be occasions where there is a conflict between acting in the best interests of your client (Principle 7) and your duty as an officer of the court. This is more common when conducting litigation. In this situation, a person's duty to the court would outweigh their duty to the client. An example of this is calling a witness to give evidence when the solicitor knows they are lying.

Paragraph 6.2 of the Code of Conduct 2019 outlines the circumstances where a solicitor may be able to act in a 'conflict of interest' situation:

> You do not act in relation to a matter or particular aspect of it if you have a conflict of interest or a significant risk of such a conflict in relation to that matter or aspect of it, unless:
>
> - the clients have a substantially common interest in relation to the matter or the aspect of it, as appropriate; or
> - the clients are competing for the same objective,
> - and the conditions below are met, namely that:
> - all the clients have given informed consent, given or evidenced in writing, to you acting;
> - where appropriate, you put in place effective safeguards to protect your clients' confidential information; and
> - you are satisfied it is reasonable for you to act for all the clients.

In practice, it is important to carry out a conflict check as soon as possible. Ideally, this information should be obtained from the client before the interview:

- name, address and telephone number;
- area of law on which advice is needed (eg crime, property, contract);
- name and address of any potential opponent or other involved (if applicable).

If this information is not obtained in advance of the interview, a conflict check should be done when the client arrives at the office and then the interview may progress if there is no conflict of interest. On occasions a client may not understand who the other parties are in their case and so once you recognise who they are then a conflict check must be carried out as soon as practicable. Money laundering regulations (discussed in more detail at **B3.3**), also demand information being taken into account, which supports the notion of conflict checks.

The SRA provides a helpful case study—see SRA Case Studies: Conflicts of Interest: Solicitors Regulation Authority.

EXAMPLE

There are many ways in which a conflict can arise in practice and some areas of law have more likelihood of a conflict than others. In a family law situation, a person may come to a law firm for advice when they are thinking about leaving a relationship, despite the other person being unaware of it. The advice provided could simply be a one-off appointment. A conflict would arise if at a later date the other person in the relationship came to the law firm for advice. In criminal law, a conflict could be where the criminal department of a firm represents someone accused of assaulting their wife and the wife attends the family department for advice on separation. In both instances, a solicitor would have to decline the instructions and provide details of other solicitors in their area who could assist in that area of law and/or provide them with the Law Society Find a Solicitor webpage.

B.2.8 **Confidentiality**

Confidentiality between a solicitor and client is one of the most important parts of their relationship. It is significant in the area of ethics and professional conduct as it is an area in which it is important that the solicitor receives all of the information from the client in order to provide the best advice, and that the client is confident that their solicitor will not release this to the public. The duty of confidentiality remains when the client retainer is terminated and even on the death of the client. Paragraphs 6.3–6.5 of the Code of Conduct (2019) state that a solicitor must keep the affairs of clients and former clients confidential apart from in limited situations. The main situations are if the client consents to the disclosure or if permitted by law.

Paragraph 6.2 the Code of Conduct (2019) outlines the situation when a solicitor may limit the information provided to a client:

> Where you are acting for a client on a matter, you make the client aware of all information material to the matter of which you have knowledge, except when:
>
> - the disclosure of the information is prohibited by legal restrictions imposed in the interests of national security or the prevention of crime;
> - your client gives informed consent, given or evidenced in writing, to the information not being disclosed to them;
> - you have reason to believe that serious physical or mental injury will be caused to your client or another if the information is disclosed; or
> - the information is contained in a privileged document that you have knowledge of only because it has been mistakenly disclosed.

Paragraph 6.5 of the Code of Conduct (2019) explains the limited circumstances when you can act for a client who has an adverse interest and where you hold confidential information:

> You do not act for a client in a matter where that client has an interest adverse to the interest of another current or former client of you or your business or employer, for whom you or your business or employer holds confidential information which is material to that matter, unless:
>
> - effective measures have been taken which result in there being no real risk of disclosure of the confidential information; or
> - the current or former client whose information you or your business or employer holds has given informed consent, given or evidenced in writing, to you acting, including to any measures taken to protect their information.

EXAMPLE

There are many ways in which an issue around confidentiality can arise in practice. In a criminal law firm, a person may come to a law firm for advice and you may overhear them on the telephone planning to sell drugs. In this case, in order to prevent a crime you would have to disclose this information to the police and would therefore be breaching confidentiality.

In a private client firm, a solicitor may have drafted a will for a lady who has now died. If her son contacts the solicitor after she has passed to ask if he has been left anything, then because of the duty of confidentiality the solicitor would be unable to tell him without the consent of the personal representatives of the will.

B.2.9 **Undertakings**

An undertaking made by a solicitor is a commitment to do or not do something that someone places reliance upon. An undertaking is binding and does not necessarily have to be made by a solicitor or use the word 'undertake'. It is often made to clients or third parties in a matter. Once the undertaking has been relied upon, then it cannot be withdrawn without the agreement of both parties.

Many areas of practice, such as conveyancing and litigation, rely on the giving and receiving of undertakings to progress matters. The solicitor giving the undertaking needs to be careful and is not obliged to give undertakings. If an undertaking is breached, then the solicitor could be sued personally for the money which was promised within the undertaking. The solicitor would have also breached the Code of Conduct and disciplinary proceedings would likely follow.

The SRA's Guidance on Undertakings, given by, or on behalf of, incorporated practice explains your obligations when undertakings are provided, by or on behalf of incorporated practices. This is because the Supreme Court decision in *Harcus Sinclair v Your Lawyers* [2021] UKSC 32 confirmed that the courts have no jurisdiction to enforce undertakings against incorporated practices. However, an incorporated practice could still face regulatory proceedings as there might have been a breach of our rules.

EXAMPLE

A solicitor is acting for a client in relation to debt matters and one large debt of £80,000 is owed by him to Jones Construction, who have written to ask for payment of the full amount within ten days. The client is in the process of selling a flat at auction, which has been valued at £100,000. The auction is in seven days and the solicitor provides an undertaking to Jones Construction to pay the £80,000 from the proceeds of sale from the flat.

The flat is only sold for £70,000 and Jones Construction has demanded the £80,000 from the solicitor. The solicitor must perform the undertaking and pay the full amount of £80,000. Failure to do so could be considered a breach of professional conduct.

In hindsight, what the solicitor should have done was to draft the undertaking but state that the payment would be limited to the amount received from the auction sale, or make it clear that they were not accepting responsibility for any personal liability.

B.2.10 **Alternate Business Structures (ABSs)**

It is worth noting that all of these regulations also bind ABSs. ABSs were introduced by the Legal Services Act 2007 and the SRA began accepting applications from prospective ABSs in January 2012. This allowed non-lawyers to own or invest in a law firm, when previously only lawyers could seek to create and operate a law firm. At the time, this was seen to be a huge change in the way law firms could function. They are still overseen by the SRA and the SRA decides whether a firm or business can become an ABS.

There are two key distinct ABS roles, those which entail the appointment of a recognised lawyer and those which do not require a qualified lawyer. There was a great deal of scepticism by many in the legal profession when the ABS was introduced. It was feared that big businesses would reduce the quality of legal work provided and that 'Tesco Law'-type businesses would emerge.

B.3 **Money laundering**

Money laundering is an illegal practice in which money generated from criminal activities is disguised and made to appear to have come from a legitimate source, in order to make it easier to spend the money and avoid suspicion. There are a wide variety of activities in which money may be attempted to be laundered. Examples of these are fraud, prostitution, robbery and the trafficking of drugs or people.

The purpose of anti-money laundering legislation is because solicitors' firms are often targeted in order to assist with money laundering. They can legitimise a transaction, have access to financial markets and often advise on property and business deals. It is therefore important for solicitors to understand the legislation, remain vigilant and to have the right training and processes in place in order to avoid the risk of facilitating this crime.

The Legal Sector Affinity Group (LSAG)'s Anti-Money Laundering Guidance for the legal profession, published in 2021, provides detailed guidance in this area.

Ensuring that solicitors do not facilitate money laundering is, of course, as much an ethical issue as a financial one. For more detail on money laundering regulations, see the financial services chapter in *Public Law, Legal Services & the Legal System.*

B.4 **Client care**

Client care is a fundamental part of the role of a solicitor. A client is required to be given information in a way that they understand and allows them to make decisions about the services they need, how their case will be handled and the options which are available to them (para 8.6 of the 2019 Code). They are also required to be provided with information about costs both at the time of engagement and as the matter progresses (para 8.7 of the 2019 Code). Most complaints from clients are either regarding not being updated about how the matter is progressing or with issues about costs.

B.4.1 **General Data Protection Regulation**

The UK General Data Protection Regulation (GDPR) sets out key principles, rights and obligations when processing personal data. It sits alongside the Data Protection Act 2018 and incorporates the EU GDPR, but, following Brexit, it allows the UK government the flexibility to review and amend its provisions. Personal data is essentially data that allows a living person to be directly or indirectly identified from information that is available. All solicitors hold personal data relating to both clients and employees. It is therefore crucial to be able to comply with the regulations. Knowing what personal data you have is the first step in compliance.

Further detailed guidance on the GDPR for solicitors can be found on the Law Society website.

B.4.2 **The first interview**

Some practical considerations are necessary in relation to client care and when meeting the client for the first time, it is important to be fully prepared. Clients may have a range of emotions depending on the areas of law you are advising on. It is important that the client is reassured, offered an appointment promptly and also that the solicitor is fully prepared for the first interview.

Before the interview, the Law Society, in its client information requirements practice note, advises that when the client attends the interview the following information must be explained to them and confirmed in writing:

- name and status of the solicitor or other person conducting the interview;
- information on the costs for the interview;
- details of who to contact if they have a complaint including the right to complain to the Legal Ombudsman, the time frame and the contact details.

This information can be prepared in a pro forma document in advance. It is important to keep a copy on file.

In the first interview, you must remember to cover all of the professional conduct issues, money laundering regulations, the GDPR and legal issues as well as to obtain the basic details from the client.

B.4.3 Client care letter

This letter is used by most law firms to set out the necessary client care information to a client. It is usually the first piece of correspondence you will send to your client and it is therefore an extremely important document. It must have certain regulatory information in it in order to comply with the Code of Conduct. It is usually also the retainer or contract between you and your client and is the beginning of the solicitor/client relationship. The Consumer Contracts (Information, Cancellation and Additional Charges) Regulations 2013 (SI 2013/2014) apply when you enter into a retainer with a consumer client who you have not met. This is often known as a distance contract.

B.4.4 Fees and costs

In most circumstances, you will have a direct retainer with the client and the client will be responsible for paying your costs. In certain areas of law, this may be different such as criminal law, family law and personal injury. In those areas, a client may be eligible for Legal Aid or there may be a 'no win, no fee' arrangement. Legal aid is the provision of assistance to people who are unable to afford legal representation and/or access to the court system. Firms must have a legal aid contract in order to be able to offer this service to clients and legal aid is only available in certain areas of law (usually family law and criminal law) and for clients who, in most cases, have a low income. More information regarding legal aid and how it is assessed can be found on the Gov.uk website.

'No win, no fee', often called a conditional fee agreement, is a legal fee arrangement whereby the client agrees to pay only if they win their case and is generally used in personal injury law. A damages-based agreement is another legal fee arrangement under which the client agrees to pay the solicitor a set percentage of the compensation they receive if they win the case.

In the situation where a client is paying your costs, there are several options available regarding how to charge a client for work. The main two ways of charging a client are by hourly rates or a fixed fee arrangement. Whichever way you do charge, it is essential to communicate this to the client and to provide the client with a likely overall cost of the matter. If the likely overall cost changes then it is important to advise the client of this as soon as possible in order to avoid any issues which may give rise to a complaint or a potential breach of the Code of Conduct.

B.4.5 Advertising

A solicitor cannot make an unsolicited approach to members of the public regarding the advertising of its legal services, but this does not apply to current or former clients. Any potential client referred to the firm by a current or former client will be seen as a member of the public (para 8.9 of the Code of Conduct for Solicitors, RELs and RFLs).

KEY POINT SUMMARY

- Ethics and professional conduct are fundamental to being a good solicitor.
- The Code of Conduct 2019 and the Principles provide the most up-to-date set of standards and requirements expected of solicitors, RELs and RFLs, and you should refer to them frequently.
- Breach of the Code of Conduct may constitute professional misconduct and could result in being fined, lead to criminal proceedings and/or being struck off from the roll of solicitors.
- It is crucial that solicitors have knowledge and understanding of the GDPR, money laundering and client care.

PART A
Basic Fundamentals

CHAPTER 1
Introduction to Property Practice and Land Law

1.1 The purpose and context of this manual

This manual presents a discussion and explanation of the topics of property practice and land law, which comprise the functioning legal knowledge required for the SQE 1 assessments. Essentially it covers all aspects of the process that is known as conveyancing, which is how legal practitioners arrange the **transfer** of property ownership from seller to buyer. This manual has been written to assist you in the study of this process, the purpose of which is the handover of legal **title** to property. Use the glossary at the end of the manual to assist in your understanding of key terms.

1.1.1 The foundations of property practice

Property practice rests upon three foundations: land law, contract law and equity and trusts. It also concerns itself with several other areas of the law, such as company and partnership law, succession, planning law and several parts of tax law. It is this diversity that can make property practice a complicated subject to command. Arising out of this diversity is a split or divide in the profession in the way conveyancing practitioners handle residential and commercial transactions. However, a brief look at the three main foundations will help you get to grips with a complete perspective on this extensive subject that will support both commercial and residential viewpoints.

1.1.2 Land law

As you might expect, a durable understanding of land law is critical for success in property practice. If you are unsure of the fundamentals of land law you will surely have trouble in mastering conveyancing. Please read **Chapter 2** of this manual carefully; it gives you an overview of land law in general and its most important principles. Do bear in mind, however, that land law is a vast subject in its own right. If you require further detail on the substantive law relating to land then *A Textbook on Land Law* by Aruna Nair (19th edn, Oxford University Press, 2023) is recommended as a clear and direct guide to the fundamentals of this important foundation to property practice.

In the context of assessment, a clear understanding of land law is a fundamental prerequisite of property practice. However, you should also have prior knowledge and understanding of the formation of contracts, formalities of written contracts, misrepresentation and remedies for breach of contract. Accordingly, you will appreciate that there may be questions in examinations that will test not just your knowledge of the conveyancing process, but also the foundations of land law and contract law upon which property practice is built.

1.1.3 Contract law

Contract law is considered to be as important for students of property practice as land law. When you consider that conveyancing is about the transfer of title and these transfers are in the main made by contract, then you will appreciate why contract law plays such an important part. Should you end up being a property practitioner, you would do well to actively maintain your knowledge of the fundamentals of contract law, as you will regularly encounter transactions concerned with it. Each **conveyance** on sale involves the preparation of a written contract. Indeed, land law tells you that without a written contract containing all the terms of the agreement there is no deal (see s2 Law of Property (Miscellaneous Provisions) Act 1989).

In these circumstances it is not difficult to anticipate questions in property practice that will test and examine your understanding of contract law as well as its application in conveyancing. However, it goes further than just the formation of valid contracts. You will also need to know about misrepresentation and, in particular, remedies for breach of contract. It is clear that these areas are of particular interest to examiners and a thorough grounding in both topics is advisable if you wish to do well in your SQE assessment.

1.1.4 Equity and trusts

Then there is the potentially difficult foundation subject of equity and trusts. This important stanchion to property practice is not so obviously relevant as land law and contract law, but it is nevertheless a pervasive element, certainly as far as assessment is concerned. Why is this? Frankly, it is because this complex area provides challenging questions that are ripe for a subject assessment question. For example, the topic of third party rights is a fertile and attractive location for your examiner to find questions that will concern equity and trusts in the context of the conveyancing process. **Co-ownership**, however, is the ideal topic for the kind of challenging questions set by examiners. You will therefore need to be absolutely clear on the law relating to trusts, and in particular trusts of land. You will need to understand the differences between tenants in common and joint tenants and their relevance to joint ownership in property. Finally, you will need to remind yourself about the equitable remedies that are available. It is one thing to understand their availability in theory but it is another to actually apply them to a practical situation. Property practice is an area that will give rise to the application of those equitable remedies.

1.1.5 Blending your knowledge

So, the key to understanding the nature of property practice in the context of assessment is to appreciate how it calls upon and involves these differing strands of the law. In doing so, it brings together other parts of the law that you should have encountered and that you will now need to apply on a practical basis. You will need to integrate these other areas into your knowledge and understanding of the conveyancing process. It means that you must disregard a discrete or compartmentalised approach to learning and applying this area of the law. Property practice requires you to apply your blended knowledge and many of these elements apply to both domestic as well as commercial properties. As such, you need to understand the fundamentals of both areas of practice to enable you to be prepared for SQE assessments and subsequent practice. If you work through this manual thoroughly and methodically, you will be well on the way to completing that important preparation. The SQE series has been designed to blend your learning across all of the assessed subjects; your learning from one manual will complement another.

1.1.6 Ethics, professional conduct and client care

As well as blending your knowledge, you must also have regard to the important pervasive area of ethics, professional conduct and client care which is a key element of the SQE. The SRA Principles and SRA Standards and Regulations for Solicitors are referred to throughout this manual as many professional conduct issues can arise during the course of a property transaction. Breaching the SRA Principles and SRA Standards and Regulations is a serious matter that may lead to disciplinary proceedings. The SRA Principles which most impact on property practice are that you should act:

- in a way that upholds public trust and confidence in the solicitors' profession;
- with honesty;
- with integrity;
- in the best interests of each client.

We shall examine specific ethical and professional conduct issues as they arise in the chapters ahead, but do pay particular attention to the commentary in **Chapter 3** as conduct issues play an important part when taking instructions from a client at the beginning of a conveyancing transaction (see **3.8**). Throughout the manual you will also find useful conduct point feature boxes.

1.2 An outline of a conveyancing transaction

Property practice (a label that covers conveyancing) is not just about the transfer of title; it is the process as a whole that enables that transfer to take place. In the subsequent chapters, each part of the process will be considered and the procedure has been deconstructed to reveal its constituent parts. However, in this introductory chapter we look at the conveyancing process as a whole through an outline of a typical conveyancing transaction. **Figure 1.1** provides an overview of the structure of this process and will appear throughout the manual to aid your understanding of where certain sections or stages fall within the conveyancing timeline.

Pre-exchange					Exchange & pre-completion				Completion & post-completion		
Stage 1 Taking instructions & advising client	**Stage 2** Draft contract	**Stage 3** Pre-contract searches, enquiries & planning	**Stage 4** Title	**Stage 5** Mortgage (applies throughout process)	**Stage 6** Exchange of contracts	**Stage 7** Purchase deed	**Stage 8** Pre-completion searches and requisitions	**Stage 9** Financial statements	**Stage 10** Completion	**Stage 11** SDLT & registration	**Stage 12** Delays and remedies

FIGURE 1.1 Conveyancing timeline

1.2.1 A transaction in outline

Table 1.1 is a general conveyancing overview of the process that applies in most residential cases and many commercial transactions. For example, when a property investor buys a commercial investment property, that investor will need to complete the same steps listed in the table, as would a first-time buyer of a residential property.

Table 1.1 makes several assumptions, the most important of which will be readily obvious, which is that there may not be any borrowings (**mortgages**) involved for either party. However, the principles are sound and set out a clear overview. You will find chapters on these various steps within this manual. If you want to understand how a transaction progresses then it may be best to understand the process as a series of stages as set out next.

TABLE 1.1 General conveyancing: outline of a simple conveyancing transaction

Seller	Buyer
Take instructions	Take instructions and consider financial arrangements for purchase
Prepare and issue draft contract (sometimes with a draft **purchase deed**)	Make all necessary pre-contract searches and enquiries
Deduce (prepare and issue copies of the) **title**	**Investigate title** Approve draft contract
Exchange contracts	Exchange contracts (arrange insurance) Prepare purchase deed
Approve purchase deed	Make all necessary pre-completion searches
Prepare for completion	Prepare for completion
Completion	Completion
Post-completion procedures (including accounting to the client)	Post-completion procedures (including paying **stamp duty land tax** and title registration)

There are six main stages in a conveyancing transaction, as follows:

1 Pre-market (**Energy Performance Certificate** (EPC)).
   - Obtaining an EPC before sale on behalf of the seller.
2 Pre-contract (draft contract/investigate title)
   - Seller's conveyancer prepares the contract, having checked seller's **deeds** or registered title.
   - Buyer's conveyancer checks the contract, investigates title, carries out searches and raises enquiries.
3 Contract (first key date—a legally binding agreement and a **deposit** paid)
   - Buyer now has an equitable interest in the property. The contract may require the buyer to insure.
4 Pre-completion (final checks and preparation)
   - Buyer's conveyancer carries out final **Land Registry** or land charges priority searches.
   - Seller's conveyancer checks transfer deed signed in readiness for completion.
   - Both conveyancers will prepare **completion statements**.
5 Completion (second key date—money changes hands)
   - Buyer becomes legal owner of the property.
6 Post-completion (administration time)
   - Buyer's conveyancer deals with stamp duty land tax, return filing and payment of tax.
   - Buyer's conveyancer deals with the registration of title.
   - Seller's conveyancer accounts to the client for the sale proceeds.

Table 1.2 is an overview of the main differences in the conveyancing process between registered and unregistered titles. (You will probably be aware that a registered title is a title recorded at the Land Registry whereas an unregistered title is one recorded in the title deeds of the property.) **Table 1.1** and **Table 1.2** demonstrate that you need to have a holistic approach to your understanding of property practice. This means that you need to appreciate the complete picture to enable you to successfully deconstruct the process. In this way, you will understand the mechanics of the conveyancing process more clearly by understanding the way they all come together to make a property transaction.

1.2.2 Energy Performance Certificates

Before a property can be marketed, the seller must obtain for prospective buyers an Energy Performance Certificate (EPC). This shows a property's energy efficiency. In particular, an EPC contains information about a property's energy use and typical energy costs along with recommendations about how to reduce energy use. It will also give a property an energy efficiency rating from A (most efficient) to G (least efficient) and it is valid for ten years. Alternatively, it can take the form of a Predicted Energy Assessment for newly built homes, which are usually marketed before they are built. This should be replaced by a full EPC when the home is built. (Listed buildings, usually buildings of special historical or architectural merit, are exempt from EPC requirements.)

1.2.3 The Land Registry Portal

The way a **registered land** conveyancing transaction is progressed is greatly affected by the Land Registry Portal, a secure website platform from which all existing and future Land Registry electronic services will be launched. The portal provides instant access to the land register and, in particular, to more than 25 million computerised registers of title. (Registered land in England and Wales makes up roughly 86 per cent of the total land in the country.) It is an electronic gateway that enables all Registry customers to access systems from a single central point. The portal can be adjusted to the needs of an individual customer. It provides Land Registry services to users

TABLE 1.2 Outline of main differences between registered and unregistered conveyancing

Steps taken	Unregistered	Registered
Taking instructions	No real difference	No real difference
Draft contract	No real difference	No real difference
Pre-contract searches	**Preliminary enquiries** of seller	Same
	Local land charges search	Same
	Water and drainage search	Same
	Inspection of the property	Same
	Search of public **index map**	Not needed
	Search in Central Land Charges Department	Not needed
	Environmental search	Same
Deduce (prepare and issue the) title	By abstract or copies of title deeds and production of originals at or shortly before completion	By official copies of the registered title and plan
Investigate title	By perusing abstract or copies of title deeds and checking them against the originals	By checking official copies, the title plan and any **overriding interests**
Exchange of contracts	No basic difference	No basic difference
Preparation and approval of purchase deed	To be drafted by buyer's solicitor	To be prepared by buyer's solicitor on basis of prescribed forms of transfer
Pre-completion search	Central Land Charges Department	Land Registry Office
Prepare for completion	No basic difference	No basic difference
Complete	Title deeds and transfer handed to buyer. Legal **estate** passes	Only the transfer handed to buyer. Legal estate does not pass yet
Post-completion matters	Buyer registered as proprietor on **first registration**	Buyer registered as proprietor. Legal estate passes

electronically, including the online viewing of title plans and title registers. Facilities available through the portal include:

- online **official searches** of complete titles with immediate priority;
- online land charges searches;
- online official title copy applications;
- immediate access to computerised registers with the ability to print working copies of on-screen information;
- online home rights searches;
- the facility to apply for a search of the index map; and
- online registration applications.

With regard to their e-services, as at March 2023 the Land Registry confirmed that 99 per cent of service requests (eg searches etc) are lodged electronically, as are 76 per cent of registration applications and 80 per cent of mortgage discharges.

The portal can now be used for the electronic registration of most types of applications (e-DRS). Registered organisations will control their own access permissions. These permissions will be administered and maintained by a designated person called an administrator.

1.2.4 The Law Society Conveyancing Quality Scheme

The Law Society has produced a Conveyancing Quality Scheme (CQS), the aim of which is to provide a recognised quality standard for residential conveyancing practices. The Law Society states that the scheme enhances the reputation of conveyancing solicitors, provides reassurance about integrity and practice standards and creates a trusted conveyancing community that deters fraud whilst providing a more effective service for clients. The scheme utilises the Conveyancing Protocol and adopts guiding principles that include status checks (criminal record checks) for individual conveyancers and firms, consistent processes and standards across participating solicitors, a client charter that aims to ensure quality of service delivery and monitoring of members, who may be subject to spot checks and audits. There are fees payable on applying and for membership. Members are able to display the scheme logo on their stationery and in their offices. Alongside the introduction of this scheme, the Law Society has also issued a fifth edition of its standard form of conveyancing contract (see **Chapter 4**) and a revised Code for Completion by Post (see **Chapter 11**).

1.2.5 Future developments

What lies ahead for the future of conveyancing? It is clear that the process of first registration of land will continue until most, if not all, of England and Wales is registered. There will be a declining amount of **unregistered land** but, while it remains, conveyancers will need to be able to deal with unregistered titles. With the increasing predominance of registered land will come the increasing use of online resources for checking the title via the Land Registry Portal, for carrying out searches and enquiries and for applying for registration of title and the transfer of title. Indeed, the whole process will be case managed on practitioner computers and could take place over the internet, with communications by email and by online transactions in 'transaction rooms'. Eventually e-conveyancing will be fully supported by the Land Registry and by the banking system. At that point, the current paper-based system will come to an end. The Registry has suggested in its latest strategy for end-to-end digital conveyancing that secure paperless buying and selling of property 'could be the norm' by 2024–25. With this aim in mind, it will seek to encourage the property market to adopt new technology such as digital identity verification and e-signatures, which are seen as essential to the paperless process.

KEY POINT SUMMARY

- The key foundations of property practice lie in land law, contract law and equity and trusts.
- Learn the basic steps of a conveyancing transaction before studying each aspect of the transaction in detail later in this manual.
- Understand the key differences between registered conveyancing and unregistered conveyancing.
- Understand how the Land Registry Portal system assists the registered conveyancing process.
- Use the glossary at the end of the manual to assist your understanding of key terms.

PART B
Land Law and Conveyancing

CHAPTER 2
Principles of Land Law

FUNCTIONING LEGAL KNOWLEDGE

This chapter covers the following functioning legal knowledge required to pass the SQE 1 assessments:

Principles of land law:

- nature of land
- **title** to land
- **co-ownership** and trusts
- proprietary rights
- **leases**

AUTHORITIES UNDERPINNING PRACTICE

The key authorities that underpin this area of practice are listed below. Note that for legislation you are linked to legislation.gov.uk.

Although much of the legislation on this government website is available in its amended form, the incorporation of new amendments into the text of legislation can be delayed. You should refer to legal databases to ensure you are referencing the most up-to-date legislation.

- Law of Property Act 1925
  https://www.legislation.gov.uk/ukpga/Geo5/15-16/20/contents
- Trustee Act 1925
  https://www.legislation.gov.uk/ukpga/Geo5/15-16/19/contents
- Landlord and Tenant (Covenants) Act 1995
  https://www.legislation.gov.uk/ukpga/1995/30/contents
- Law of Property (Miscellaneous Provisions) Act 1989
  https://www.legislation.gov.uk/ukpga/1989/34/contents
- Trusts of Land and Appointment of Trustees Act 1996
  https://www.legislation.gov.uk/ukpga/1996/47/contents
- Land Registration Act 2002
  https://www.legislation.gov.uk/ukpga/2002/9/contents

2.1 Introduction

Land law is an important foundation for the study of property practice and this chapter will provide a useful summary of the fundamental principles that you should have studied at an academic stage of training. Please be aware that this commentary is not exhaustive, and for more substantive coverage of the law you should consult a specialist text such as *A Textbook on Land Law* by Aruna Nair (19th edn, Oxford University Press, 2023).

2.2 Estates and interests in land

2.2.1 Legal estates and interests

An **estate** is a right to own and enjoy land for a particular length of time (although in the case of a **freehold estate** the time can last indefinitely). An interest is a right affecting someone else's land. The Law of Property Act 1925 (LPA 1925) reduced the number of legal *estates* to two—freehold and leasehold; and the number of legal *interests* to five, the three most important of which are:

- legal **easements** and profits;
- a legal rentcharge; and
- a **charge** by way of legal **mortgage**.

2.2.2 Equitable interests

Any interest in land that is not classified as a legal estate or legal interest is known as an equitable interest (s1(3) LPA 1925). Equitable interests include:

- the benefit of a restrictive **covenant** or contract;
- the interest of a beneficiary under a trust.

Only legal estates and interests are capable of being registered under the Land Registration Act 2002 (LRA 2002). Equitable interests are not capable of substantive registration at the **Land Registry**, but may be protected on the register by notice or registration (see **2.8**).

2.3 Trusts and co-ownership

2.3.1 Introduction

Where two or more persons are entitled to possession of land at the same time, there is a **trust of land** governed by the Trusts of Land and Appointment of Trustees Act 1996. The legal estate is vested in the trustees, and the persons with co-ownership rights are known as the beneficiaries. The trustees hold the legal estate but the beneficiaries as owners in equity are effectively the 'real' owners. Very often the trustees and beneficiaries are one and the same, for example husband and wife or unmarried couples. Trusts can be created expressly or may be implied by law.

2.3.2 Implied trusts

Co-ownership may arise in favour of someone even though that person's name does not appear on the register of title or in the **deeds**. This is known as an implied trust. It arises where someone acquires an interest in land, for example by contributing to the purchase price or paying for improvements to the property. There are essentially two types of implied trust—the resulting trust and the constructive trust.

2.3.3 Resulting trusts

A resulting trust occurs typically where the legal estate is transferred into the name of one person following the payment of some or all of the purchase price by another person. For example, in *Bull v Bull* [1955] 1 QB 234 property was conveyed into Mr Bull's name but the purchase price for the property was provided by both Mr Bull and his mother. Mr Bull therefore held the legal estate on resulting trust for himself and his mother.

2.3.4 Constructive trusts

A constructive trust arises where it would be unconscionable for the legal owner of the land to deny the equitable interest of another. There needs to be evidence of a common intention between the parties that the property will be jointly owned and that the non-legal owner relied on that agreement to their detriment (see *Lloyds Bank v Rosset* [1991] 1 AC 107).

2.3.5 Overreaching

Payment of capital money to at least two trustees will **overreach** the interests of the beneficiaries under the trust. This means that a buyer or **mortgagee** making the payment will not be bound by the interests of the beneficiaries, as those interests will attach to the proceeds of sale (see *Williams & Glyn's Bank v Boland* [1981] AC 487 and *City of London Building Society v Flegg* [1988] AC 54).

Once overreaching has occurred, the beneficiaries will no longer be entitled to remain in possession of the land. Instead, they will obtain an interest in the proceeds of sale which will be held on trust for them by the trustees, for instance the sellers of the legal estate.

2.3.6 Co-ownership

There are two types of co-ownership—**joint tenancy** and **tenancy in common**. The legal estate can be held under a joint tenancy but not a tenancy in common. The beneficiaries holding the equitable estate can hold either under a joint tenancy or a tenancy in common.

The crucial distinction between these two types of co-ownership is that the survivorship principle applies to a joint tenancy but not to a tenancy in common. This means that on the death of a joint tenant the land immediately passes to the surviving joint tenant(s); it does not pass under the deceased's will or **intestacy**. Conversely, under a tenancy in common the survivorship principle does not apply and the deceased's share passes under their will or intestacy.

2.3.7 Joint tenancy

Under a joint tenancy, the co-owners own the whole of the land together and all joint tenants have the same interest in the land irrespective of their respective contributions to the purchase price. Four unities must be present as between the co-owners:

1 unity of possession (ie all joint tenants are entitled to possess every part of the land);
2 unity of interest (eg the land is all freehold or all leasehold);
3 unity of title (ie title acquired under the same document or transaction);
4 unity of time (ie all co-owners acquired their interest at the same time).

2.3.8 Tenancy in common

As already mentioned, only the equitable estate can be held as a tenancy in common, not the legal estate. Each co-owner owns specific shares in the land, either equally or unequally. Only unity of possession is necessary for a tenancy in common. Where co-owners of **registered land** hold as tenants in common, the Land Registry will enter the following restriction in the proprietorship register of the title:

> No disposition by a sole proprietor of the registered estate (except a trust corporation) under which capital money arises is to be registered unless authorised by an order of the court.

2.3.9 Severance of a joint tenancy

A joint tenancy in equity can be severed and thereby converted into a tenancy in common. In this case, the right of survivorship no longer applies. If there are more than two joint tenants, **severance** operates only on the share of the party effecting the severance. The other parties remain as joint tenants as between themselves.

The different methods of severance are:

- written notice under s36(2) of the LPA 1925 given by one or more joint tenants to all the other joint tenants;
- selling or charging the beneficial interest (including a charging order made by a court);
- bankruptcy—the bankrupt's severed beneficial interest vests in the trustee in bankruptcy.

Remember that a legal estate cannot be held as a tenancy in common, so notwithstanding severance of an equitable joint tenancy the legal estate will remain as a joint tenancy.

The maximum number of trustees of the legal estate permitted by statute is four (s34(2) Trustee Act 1925). Where more than four are named in the deed, the property vests in the first four who are of full age.

EXAMPLE

Mark co-owns a freehold house with his very elderly mother who still lives in the property. The registered title shows a restriction in the proprietorship register stating that no disposition by a sole proprietor of the registered estate (except a trust corporation) under which capital money arises is to be registered unless authorised by an order of the court. This restriction indicates that Mark and his mother hold the property as tenants in common in equity. When Mark's mother dies, it will be unwise for a buyer to pay the purchase monies to one person, so a second trustee must be appointed to sell with Mark thereby overreaching the equitable interests under her estate. On the death of his mother, Mark will hold his mother's share on trust for the beneficiary as shown in his mother's will.

2.4 Easements

2.4.1 Introduction

An easement is a right attached to one piece of land (the **dominant tenement**), which gives the owner of that land a right to use another person's land (the **servient tenement**). The owners of the dominant and servient tenements must both have estates in the land. Examples of easements are rights of way or drainage, and the rights of tenants to use common parts in a block of flats.

2.4.2 Characteristics of an easement

A right can only be capable of being an easement if it satisfies the four characteristics laid down in *Re Ellenborough Park* [1956] Ch 131.

1. There must be a dominant and a servient tenement. Note that a public right of way is not an easement because it does not benefit specific land (ie there is no dominant tenement).
2. The dominant and servient tenements must be owned or occupied by different persons.
3. The right must benefit the dominant tenement, namely (ie it cannot be purely a personal right in favour of the occupier).
4. The right must be capable of forming the subject matter of a grant (ie granted by deed and sufficiently definite. In addition, no exclusive possession must be conferred).

This four-pronged test was recently confirmed by the Supreme Court in *Regency Villas Title Ltd and others v Diamond Resorts (Europe) Ltd and others* [2018] UKSC 57.

2.4.3 Creation of an easement

If the right satisfies the *Re Ellenborough Park* test, it does not become an easement unless it is created either through a grant or a **reservation**. A grant is where an easement is given to a buyer over land that is retained by a seller, for example a right of way or drainage. A reservation occurs where an easement is retained by a seller over land that is sold to a buyer.

A grant may be either express (ie by deed), or be implied by various methods (see later), or it may be presumed (ie by prescription). A reservation may be either express or implied by necessity or common intention only (see **2.4.4**).

An express easement may be legal (if it is created by deed) or equitable (if it complies with s2 of the Law of Property (Miscellaneous Provisions) Act 1989; that is, it is in writing, contains all the agreed terms and is signed by the parties).

An easement created impliedly or by prescription is a legal easement.

2.4.4 Implied grants

An implied grant may be created by the following:

1 necessity, for example where land is landlocked (see *Nickerson v Barraclough* [1981] Ch 426). Mere inconvenience is insufficient to create an easement of necessity;

2 common intention of the parties (see *Liverpool City Council v Irwin* [1977] AC 239);

3 on a sale of part—namely, where some land is sold off—the rule in *Wheeldon v Burrows* [1879] 12 Ch D 31 applies if the following conditions are met:
   - one person owned and occupied the whole of the land;
   - the owner previously exercised a quasi-easement over the land;
   - the right is continuous and apparent (ie obvious);
   - the right is necessary for the reasonable enjoyment of the land;

4 s62 of the LPA 1925. This converts mere permissions into easements if the following conditions are met:
   - there should usually be diversity of ownership and occupation (eg landlord and tenant);
   - there was a '**conveyance**' (ie a transfer of legal title to the occupier, eg a lease (see *Wright v Macadam* [1949] 2 KB 744)).

To avoid uncertainty, it is standard conveyancing practice for the parties to agree to exclude the operation of the implied grant rules. If any easements are required by the buyer, then they should be granted expressly in the **transfer** deed.

EXAMPLE

Meena had a lease of a property from her landlord Adil who lives in the house next door. During the lease, Adil allowed Meena to use a barn at the rear of his property for storage. Adil has recently renewed Meena's lease by deed for a further eight years. Adil has asked Meena to stop using the barn as he wants to convert into it a garage. Provided Meena's right can be recognised as an easement under the principles in *Re Ellenborough Park*, when the second lease was granted her informal right to use the barn crystallised into a legal easement by virtue of s62 of the LPA 1925. In those circumstances, it would be binding on Adil for the remainder of the lease.

2.4.5 Implied reservations

If an easement is not expressly reserved, it can only be implied by necessity or common intention; namely, not by the rule in *Wheeldon v Burrows* or s62 of the LPA 1925. However, courts are generally reluctant to imply reservations of easements on the basis that a seller should not derogate from its grant (see *Walby & another v Walby & another* [2012] EWHC 3089 (Ch)).

2.4.6 Presumed or prescriptive easements

This is the grant of an easement through long usage. It applies only to freehold land, except for easements of light. It can be acquired in three ways: at common law; through the fiction of 'lost modern grant' or under the Prescription Act 1832.

In addition, a claimant must satisfy the following criteria:

- the easement must have been exercised as of right; that is, not by force, not in secret and not with permission;
- there must have been continuous and unbroken use of the easement for the prescribed period; and
- the use was by a freehold owner of the dominant tenement against a freehold owner of the servient tenement.

Grant of easements (in favour of buyer)—methods of creation

- Express.
- Implied (necessity, common intention, the rule in *Wheeldon v Burrows* or s62 LPA 1925), presumed (ie prescription).

Reservation of easements (in favour of seller)—methods of creation

- Express.
- Implied (necessity or common intention only).

2.4.7 Easements in registered land

Registration of title includes the benefit of any appurtenant easements, whether or not expressly referred to on the register.

Section 27(2)(d) of the LRA 2002 provides that an express easement over registered land must be completed by registration. This applies even in respect of estates not capable of substantive registration, for example a lease for a term not exceeding seven years. In this case, the easement must be registered even though the lease itself cannot be registered. The easement is not a legal easement until it has been registered; namely, it takes effect only in equity.

2.4.8 Easements that are overriding interests

Under Sch 3 to the LRA 2002, since 13 October 2006 any legal easement arising through implied grant or reservation or prescription is an **overriding interest** binding on a buyer, only if:

- it is known to the buyer; or
- it would have been obvious to the buyer on a reasonably careful inspection; or
- it has been exercised in the 12 months prior to the disposition.

In registered land, equitable easements can be protected by the entry of a notice under s34 of the LRA 2002. In **unregistered land**, equitable easements can be protected by registering a class D(iii) land charge against the name of the estate owner.

2.4.9 Profits à prendre

A ***profit à prendre*** is different from an easement in that it is a right for one person to remove something from land belonging to another person, such as wood, grass or fish. The person enjoying the profit does not need to own land that is benefited by the profit. This is known as a profit 'in gross'.

Profits can be created in the same way as easements except that they cannot be acquired by implied grant or reservation. The benefit of a profit in gross is capable of substantive registration under the LRA 2002.

2.5 Freehold covenants

2.5.1 Introduction

Covenants affecting freehold land can be either restrictive or positive in nature. A restrictive covenant restricts a person's use of land (eg not to build or not to run a business). A positive covenant imposes an obligation to perform a specific act and normally involves doing work or spending money (eg erecting and maintaining a boundary wall). Courts will consider the substance of the covenant in determining whether it is positive or negative. So 'not to allow land to become infested with rabbits' requires positive action, such as shooting the rabbits, and is therefore a positive covenant.

The person with the benefit of the covenant is known as the **covenantee** and the person with the burden of the covenant is known as the **covenantor**. The benefit and burden of restrictive covenants can run with the land. The benefit of positive covenants can run with the land but the burden of positive covenants cannot run with the land either at common law or in equity. This is now explained.

2.5.2 Enforcing covenants

A covenant is always enforceable between the original parties because of privity of contract (X and Y in **Figure 2.1**). But if either piece of land is sold there is no longer privity of contract between the current owners of the two pieces of land. Whether the covenant can be enforced will now depend on whether the benefit of the covenant has passed to the buyer of the benefiting land (A in the figure) and the burden of the covenant has passed to the buyer of the burdened land (B in the figure).

2.5.3 The benefit at common law

The benefit of the covenant will run at common law if the following requirements are satisfied:

1. the covenant 'touches and concerns' the land of the covenantee; that is, it benefits the land and is not purely personal;
2. the covenantee owns the legal estate in the land to be benefited when the covenant is made so that the benefit can attach to it;
3. the original parties intended that the covenant should run;
4. the **assignee** derives title from the original covenantee.

2.5.4 The burden at common law

The burden of the covenant will not run at common law (*Rhone v Stephens* [1994] 2 AC 310). However, this rule can be circumvented by:

- a chain of **indemnity covenants** in which each successive buyer agrees to indemnify their predecessor in title (see **4.9**);
- the conveyance containing the covenant reserves a rentcharge with a right of entry to make good any breach of covenant;

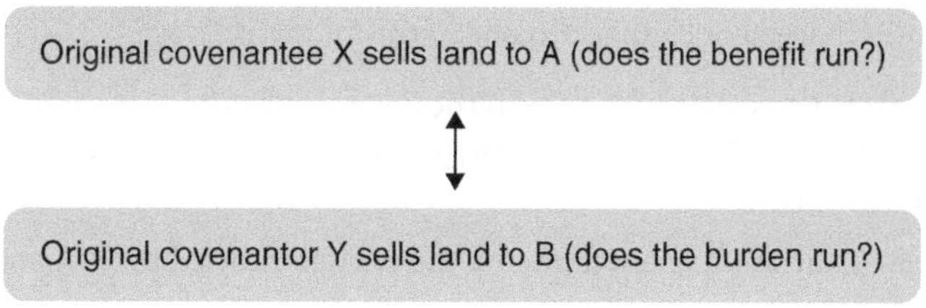

FIGURE 2.1 Enforcing covenants

- the rule in *Halsall v Brizell* [1957] Ch 169, which says a person cannot take a benefit unless they observe a related obligation (eg to use a road provided they contribute towards its maintenance);
- creating commonhold land.

2.5.5 **The benefit in equity**

The benefit of the covenant may run in equity in one of three ways:

- annexation of the covenant to the land. This is implied by s78 of the LPA 1925;
- express **assignment** of the covenant to the buyer of the benefiting land;
- through a building scheme (see *Elliston v Reacher* [1908] 2 Ch 374).

2.5.6 **The burden in equity**

The burden of the covenant will run in equity if the rules derived from *Tulk v Moxhay* (1848) 2 Ph 774 are satisfied:

- the covenant is restrictive in nature (see **2.5.1**);
- the original parties intended that the burden should run. This is implied by s79 of the LPA 1925;
- the covenantee owned land capable of benefiting from the covenant at the time it was created;
- the party to be bound has notice of it, namely if created after 1925, the covenant has been protected by registration either as a notice in registered land (s34 LRA 2002) or a class D(ii) land charge in unregistered land.

Importantly, where the burden passes in equity, a buyer of the benefiting land must show that the benefit has passed in equity as well. In these circumstances, it is not enough to show that the benefit passes merely at common law.

EXAMPLE

Lee is buying a freehold property for commercial use as an acupuncture clinic. The title to the property is unregistered. The deeds state that the property is not to be used for any trade or business. The property is an Edwardian semi-detached house and is in a redeveloped area of town where several properties are currently used for professional or commercial purposes. As the title is unregistered, to be enforceable the burden of the covenant must have been registered as a class D(ii) land charge. A search of the Land Charges Registry will establish whether this is the case. If the person having the benefit of the covenant still owns land capable of being benefited by the covenant or if the land has been sold and the benefit has passed on, then the covenant may still be enforceable. However. this is less likely if the covenant is very old which appears to be the case here. Lee could consider indemnity insurance against any claims. (The issue of planning consent is another consideration—see **Chapter 7**.)

2.5.7 **Discharge or variation of covenants**

A covenant may be discharged or changed in one of the following ways:

1. Lands Tribunal Order (s84(1) LPA 1925) if the covenant has become obsolete or impedes the reasonable use of the land (see *Derreb Ltd v Blackheath Cator Estate Residents Ltd and others* [2017] UKUT 209 (LC));
2. deed of release or variation entered into by the parties entitled to the benefit and burden of the covenant;

3 where both the benefited and burdened land has come into common ownership (unless the covenant remains enforceable under a building scheme);
4 where the covenant is void for non-registration as a class D(ii) land charge.

2.6 Leases

2.6.1 Introduction

A lease (or tenancy) is a right for a person to occupy and use land for a term with a fixed commencement date and a fixed maximum duration. This includes fixed-term leases and periodic tenancies that automatically renew themselves at the end of each period of the tenancy.

2.6.2 Formalities

A legal lease must be made by deed. However, a legal lease may be created orally or in writing if it is for a term of three years or less and takes effect immediately, reserving the best rent reasonably obtainable (s54(2) LPA 1925). If not legal, the tenant will have an equitable interest provided the lease complies with s2 of the Law of Property (Miscellaneous Provisions) Act 1989; namely, it is in writing, contains all the agreed terms and is signed by the parties.

The tenant (or **lessee**) must hold a term that is shorter than that held by the landlord (or **lessor**). Although quite normal, payment of rent is not an essential element of a lease.

The tenant must have exclusive possession; that is, the right to use the premises to the exclusion of all others, including the landlord (*Street v Mountford* [1985] 2 All ER 289). If not, the agreement will not create a legal interest in land and be merely a **licence**.

A lease for a term of more than seven years is compulsorily registrable at the Land Registry. If such a lease is granted on or after 19 June 2006 it must contain prescribed clauses (see **14.2.1** for further details).

2.6.3 Leasehold covenants

Leasehold covenants are the obligations of the landlord and tenant under the lease. Typical landlord covenants are to allow the tenant quiet enjoyment of the premises and to repair and maintain the exterior of a building where part of it is let. Typical tenant covenants include payment of rent, not to assign the lease without the landlord's consent and not to use the premises except as authorised by the lease.

There is privity of contract between the original parties to the lease (L1 and T1 in **Figure 2.2**) so there is little problem with enforcement if the lease or **reversion** has not been assigned. However, if assignment of the lease or reversion has taken place, then one set of rules applies to 'old' leases granted before 1 January 1996 (LPA 1925) and another set of rules applies to 'new' leases granted on or after that date (Landlord and Tenant (Covenants) Act 1995).

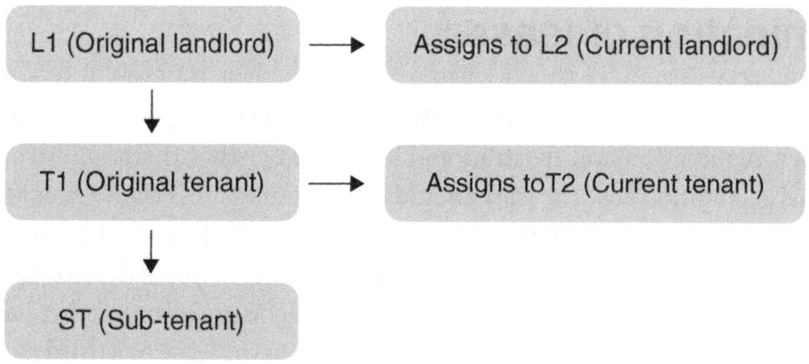

FIGURE 2.2 Leasehold covenants

2.6.4 Rules for 'old leases'

An assignee of an old lease (T2) is liable for breaches of covenant under the principle of 'privity of estate' (ie the relationship between the current landlord and the current tenant). For the burden to run, however, the covenant must 'touch and concern' the land (ie relate to the land itself (*Spencer's Case* (1583) 5 Co Rep 16a)). This applies to most tenants' covenants in leases.

The original tenant (T1) will remain liable throughout the term of the lease for any breach of covenant by their successor (T2). Thus, the original tenant can still be sued by the landlord even after the original tenant has assigned their lease. If the current tenant has disappeared or been made bankrupt, the landlord can therefore pursue the original tenant.

The original landlord (L1), after assigning its reversion, also continues to remain liable under the landlord's covenants.

2.6.5 Rules for 'new leases'

Under privity of estate rules for new leases, the 'touch and concern' test no longer applies. The burden of all covenants will pass to the assignee of the lease (T2) unless in the lease the covenants are expressed to be personal only.

The key difference for new leases is that once the original tenant (or assignee) has assigned their lease they are released from the tenant's covenants and cannot be sued by the landlord. However, the landlord may, where the landlord's consent to the assignment is required, require the tenant to enter into an **authorised guarantee agreement** (AGA) under s16 of the 1995 Act. Under an AGA the tenant agrees to guarantee their immediate assignee's performance of the covenants.

Unlike tenants of new leases, landlords are not released automatically from their covenants when they assign their reversion. However, they can apply to their tenant to be released or, failing that, to the court.

EXAMPLE

You act for Bill who assigned a **commercial lease** to Stan last year. The lease was granted in 2013. Stan has gone bankrupt and the landlord is now pursuing Bill for Stan's unpaid rent. Unless Bill gave an authorised guarantee agreement to the landlord when he assigned the lease to Stan, the landlord cannot pursue Bill as the Landlord and Tenant (Covenants) Act 1995 released Bill from the tenant's covenants on assignment.

2.6.6 Sub-leases

There is no privity of contract or privity of estate between a head landlord (L1) and a sub-tenant (ST) so on the face of it neither can sue the other directly. However, restrictive covenants in a head-lease may be enforced against a sub-tenant if the sub-tenant has notice of them. This is based on the old doctrine of notice (*Tulk v Moxhay* (1848) 2 Ph 774).

2.6.7 Termination of leases

Leases can be brought to an end by **forfeiture**, effluxion of time (or expiry), notice to quit, surrender, merger, disclaimer, repudiation and frustration. Do remember that the landlord's right to forfeit a lease is not implied at common law. The lease should contain an express clause providing for forfeiture on breach of a tenant's covenant. Surrender occurs when the tenant, with the landlord's agreement, gives up the **leasehold estate** to the landlord. Surrender can be by express deed or operation of law (eg the lessor takes back possession and agrees that the lessee will be under no further liability). A merger takes place when the lessee acquires the immediate reversion to the lease or a third party acquires both the lease and the reversion. The lease effectively 'merges' into the reversionary estate. The detail of the law relating to disclaimer, repudiation and frustration goes beyond the scope of this manual.

2.7 Mortgages

2.7.1 Introduction

A mortgage is a right of a lender (mortgagee) over land that guarantees the payment of a debt. The borrower is known as the **mortgagor**. Mortgages can be created expressly or arise under statute. They can be either legal or equitable. A legal mortgage must be by deed. An equitable mortgage will normally arise inadvertently due to some defect in a legal mortgage, such as where the document has not been executed as a deed. Equitable mortgages are quite rare so we shall confine ourselves to the law relating to legal mortgages.

2.7.2 Registered land

A legal mortgage of registered land must be completed by registration if the mortgagee wishes to exercise its statutory powers, including the power of sale. Once registered, it has priority over other interests unless they are protected on the register or are overriding interests.

2.7.3 Unregistered land

A mortgagee with a first mortgage will hold the title deeds as security. A first mortgage protected in this way has priority over all other mortgages. Second and subsequent mortgagees should protect their mortgages by registering them as class C(i) land charges.

2.7.4 Company mortgagor

Mortgages by companies must be registered at the Companies Registry within 21 days of creation of the mortgage. If not, the mortgage will not bind the liquidator or creditors if the company subsequently goes into liquidation.

2.7.5 Rights of the mortgagor

The mortgagor has the following important protections:

1 Undue influence. The court can set aside a mortgage that has been obtained through undue influence on the mortgagor. The principal ground for setting aside a transaction is the notice that the mortgagee had or ought to have had of the undue influence (see *Barclays Bank plc v O'Brien* [1994] 1 AC and *CIBC Mortgages plc v Pitt* [1994] 1 AC 200). In *Royal Bank of Scotland v Etridge (No 2)* [2002] 2 AC 773, the House of Lords gave guidance to lenders as to the steps they should take to guard against the risk of being affected with notice of undue influence (see **8.10**).

2 The Consumer Credit Act 2006 allows the court to reopen a credit agreement to do justice between the parties, for example if the interest rate is extortionate.

3 There must be no clog or fetter on the mortgagor's right to redeem the mortgage. Thus, any provision in the mortgage that prevents the mortgagor from redeeming is ignored by equity and is void (see *Jones v Morgan* [2002] 1 EGLR 125).

4 There must be no postponement of the right to redeem that would effectively make it impossible to redeem the mortgage (see *Fairclough v Swan Brewery Co Ltd* [1912] AC 565).

5 There must be no collateral advantage to the mortgagee, for example where an owner of a public house agrees to buy all their beer from a brewery mortgagee. (See generally *Noakes & Co Ltd v Rice* [1902] AC 24 and *Kreglinger v New Patagonia Meat & Cold Storage Co Ltd* [1914] AC 25.)

2.7.6 Rights of the mortgagee

The mortgagee has the following rights against the mortgagor:

1 to sue for the debt;
2 to take possession of the property;
3 foreclosure. This is the judicial procedure by which the mortgagee acquires the land free from the interests of the mortgagor. It is now rarely used;
4 to appoint a receiver to manage or sell the property. This is more common in commercial mortgages. The receiver acts as the agent of the mortgagor;
5 to sell the property; namely, the mortgagee's power of sale. This is the right most frequently used by a mortgagee. It may sell if:
   - the power of sale exists. This is implied in a mortgage made by deed unless, unusually, the deed expressly excludes it;
   - the power of sale has arisen. This occurs once the contractual date for redemption of the mortgage has passed (usually about six months after creation of the mortgage);
   - the power of sale has become exercisable. Under s103 of the LPA 1925, this occurs when:
     - interest payments are more than two months in arrears; or
     - there has been a written request for repayment of the capital and three months have elapsed without payment; or
     - there has been a breach of some other term of the mortgage.

The mortgagee can choose when to sell and the mode of sale but must obtain the best price reasonably obtainable (*Cuckmere Brick Co v Mutual Finance Ltd* [1971] Ch 949). This is why sales by mortgagees are often held at auction; that is, to demonstrate that they are getting the best price.

A sale by mortgagee is subject to any prior mortgages but will be free of the mortgagor's interests and of any estates or interests over which the mortgagee has priority (s104(1) LPA 1925), such as subsequent mortgages.

2.7.7 Application of sale proceeds

Under s105 of the LPA 1925, after paying off any prior mortgages the money received from the buyer must be held on trust by the selling mortgagee to pay:

- all expenses incidental to the sale;
- itself the principal sum, interest and costs due under its mortgage;
- any surplus to the next mortgagee in line or, if none, to the mortgagor.

EXAMPLE

Richard bought a leasehold flat last year with the aid of a loan from Sharks Moneylenders Ltd who took a first legal charge on the property. Clause 5 of the mortgage deed states that Richard cannot repay the loan during the first ten years of the mortgage. Unfortunately, Richard recently lost his job and cannot keep up his mortgage repayments. He wishes to sell up, repay the loan and move into rented accommodation. In law, he is free to repay the loan at any time as clause 5 amounts to a clog on the **equity of redemption** and is void.

2.8 Third party rights, overriding interests and the register of title

2.8.1 Introduction

In registered land, a registrable disposition for valuable consideration, such as a transfer on sale, has priority over any third party right that is not protected in one of the ways prescribed by the LRA 2002.

The means of protection of third party rights are either by an entry on the register (eg notice or restriction) or by virtue of the right's status as an overriding interest. An overriding interest will not appear on the register but will bind a buyer irrespective of notice (see **2.8.4**).

2.8.2 Notices

A notice is the appropriate way to protect rights that are intended to bind third parties (s32 LRA 2002). It may be either an agreed notice (ie with the consent of the **registered proprietor**) or a unilateral notice. Examples of interests that may be protected by notice are:

- a restrictive covenant;
- an easement;
- a right of occupation under the Family Law Act 1996;
- a lease affecting a reversionary title;
- charging orders made against a sole registered proprietor.

2.8.3 Restrictions

A restriction regulates the circumstances in which a disposition of a registered estate or charge may be the subject of an entry in the register (s40(1) LRA 2002). Examples of situations in which restrictions may be used are:

- to ensure that purchase monies are paid to at least two trustees or a trust corporation in order to overreach interests under the trust. Such a restriction will be entered where co-owners hold the beneficial estate as tenants in common (see **2.3.8**);
- to show any limitation on the powers of a corporation or other body;
- to ensure that any necessary consents to a disposition are obtained.

2.8.4 Overriding interests

Overriding interests are those interests that bind a purchaser of a legal estate despite not being protected by an entry on the register. The LRA 2002 distinguishes between interests that override **first registration** (set out in Sch 1 LRA 2002) and those that override registered dispositions (set out in Sch 3 LRA 2002). There is, however, much overlap between the two.

In relation to property practice, the most important overriding interests are:

- leases for a term of seven years or less;
- the interest of a person in actual occupation of the land, unless enquiry was made of that person who failed to disclose the interest. Such an interest will not be overriding in registered land where the buyer of the land had no actual knowledge of the interest or the occupation was not obvious on a reasonably careful inspection of the land;
- legal easements and profits (subject to limitations: see **2.4.8**).

2.8.5 The register of title

The register of title is the official record of ownership of a piece of registered land and the other interests that are registrable under the LRA 2002. A new edition of the register is prepared whenever a register entry is created or removed. Section 66 of the LRA 2002 allows anyone to inspect or make copies of the register and title plan and any document kept by the Registrar that either is referred to in the register or relates to an application. Anyone may apply for **official copies of the register** (s67 LRA 2002) that are, of course, commonly used in conveyancing.

An example of a registered title appears in **Appendix 2**. There are three parts to the register:

1 Property register. This provides a description of the property, including a statement of estate, namely, whether it is a freehold or leasehold. If leasehold, the statement of estate will also include the date of the registered lease, its term, parties and the start date. Rights of way and all other easements for the benefit of the property can also be detailed in this register. For all properties, reference will also be made to the title plan of the registered property. The title plan shows the location of the property together with adjoining property. The title plan shows general boundaries only unless the exact line of the boundary has been determined (which is rare).

2 Proprietorship register. This includes the class of title (see **2.8.6**) followed by the name and address of the registered proprietor. Notices and restrictions will appear within this register.

3 Charges register. This lists the registered charges affecting the property and these are listed in order of priority. The charges register also includes adverse interests, such as restrictive covenants, to which the property may be subject. Leases that do not comprise overriding interests will also be noted on the charges register of the superior title.

2.8.6 Classes of title

On first registration, the registered title will be given one of the following classes of title.

2.8.6.1 Absolute title

An absolute title is the best class of title available, either freehold or leasehold. Almost all freehold titles are registered with absolute title. Section 9(2) of the LRA 2002 provides that a person may be registered with absolute freehold title if the Registrar considers that the title is such as a willing buyer could properly be advised by a competent professional advisor to accept. Even if the title is defective, the Registrar may still grant absolute title if they consider that the defect will not cause the holding under the title to be disturbed (s9(3)).

The legal estate is vested in the proprietor together with all the interests subsisting for the benefit of the estate, such as easements (s11(3)). As far as burdens are concerned, the proprietor takes subject only to the interests set out in s11(4) affecting the estate at the time of first registration.

These are:

(a) interests which are the subject of an entry in the register in relation to the estate (these can be registered charges, notices and restrictions, and pre-13 October 2003 cautions and inhibitions);

(b) unregistered interests which fall within any of the paragraphs of Sch 1 (ie interests which override first registration);

(c) interests acquired under the Limitation Act 1980 of which the proprietor has notice.

Registration with an absolute leasehold title has the same effect as registration with an absolute freehold title, except that the estate is vested in the leaseholder, subject to implied and express covenants, obligations and liabilities incident to the estate (s12(3), (4)). These will be apparent from an inspection of the lease (eg lessee's covenants). When the Registrar issues an absolute leasehold title, the State is guaranteeing not just that there is a legal leasehold but also that the lease has been validly granted out of the reversionary title. Clearly, the Registrar can only do this if the reversionary title has been disclosed to the Registry to confirm that the lessor has the power to grant the lease.

Where the superior title, usually the freehold, is already registered with an absolute class of title, this is sufficient to confer the same class of title on the leasehold.

2.8.6.2 Possessory title

A possessory title will be given either where the applicant's title is based on adverse possession or where title cannot be proven because the title deeds have been lost or destroyed. The LRA 2002 provides that possessory title will be appropriate where the applicant is either in actual possession, or in receipt of rents and profits, and there is no other class of title with which they may be registered (s9(5)). Registration with a possessory freehold title has the same effect as registration with an absolute title, except that it does not affect the enforcement of any estate, right or interest adverse to, or in derogation of, the proprietor's title subsisting at the time of registration or then capable of arising (s11(7)). A possessory title can be upgraded to absolute if missing deeds are found or if the title has been registered with possessory title for 12 years and the proprietor is still in possession (s2(4)).

2.8.6.3 Qualified title

A qualified title is very rare. It will be given where the Registrar considers that the applicant's title can only be established for a limited period, or subject to certain reservations that are such that the title is not a good holding title (s9(4)). An example of this might be where the transfer to the applicant was made in breach of trust. Registration with a qualified freehold title has the same effect as registration with an absolute title except that it does not affect the enforcement of any estate, right or interest which appears from the register to be excepted from the effect of registration (s11(6)).

2.8.6.4 Good leasehold title

A proprietor of a good leasehold title is in the same position as a proprietor of an absolute leasehold title, except that the registration is such that there is no guarantee that the lease has been validly granted. The Registry will issue this class of title when the superior title—the reversionary title—has not been seen and approved by the Registrar. If the lessor was not entitled to grant the lease in the first place, then clearly the Registry would not have all the details to enable it to guarantee the validity of the lease. Consequently, a good leasehold title will be issued in place of the more desirable absolute leasehold title. Some mortgagees will not accept good leasehold title as security, and the lender's requirements should always be considered. A good leasehold title can be upgraded to an absolute title if the Registrar is satisfied as to the superior title (s62(2)), for example where the superior title is itself registered for the first time.

EXAMPLE

Aaron owns a registered freehold house and wants to know how he can find out the extent of the property he owns, what rights he has over other people's land, who has rights over his own land and what restrictions and charges affect his land. He needs to read his registered title. The description of his land is shown in the property register and the extent of his land is edged red on the title plan. Any rights for the benefit of his property over other land are also contained in the property register. Any rights which burden his property will be shown in the charges register; and any restrictions on his property such as restrictive covenants and charges will be also shown in the charges register.

KEY POINT SUMMARY

- Learn the differences between estates and interests in land, both legal and equitable.
- Understand the nature of implied trusts and the concept of overreaching.

- Appreciate the difference between the two ways of co-owning property, namely joint tenancy and tenancy in common.
- Understand the characteristics of easements and how they are created.
- Understand freehold covenants, how they are enforced and how their benefit and burden can pass to successors.
- Understand the concept of a lease and the rules for enforcing covenants in 'new' and 'old' leases.
- Learn how a mortgage operates and the rights of mortgagors and mortgagees.
- Understand third party rights in registered land, overriding interests and the constituent parts of the register of title.
- Understand the different classes of title in registered land.

PART C
Pre-Exchange

CHAPTER 3
Taking Instructions and Advising the Client

FUNCTIONING LEGAL KNOWLEDGE

This chapter covers the following functioning legal knowledge required to pass the SQE 1 assessments:

Co-ownership and trusts
Law Society Conveyancing Protocol

Finance:

- sources of finance for a property transaction
- types of **mortgage**

Stamp duty land tax (and **land transaction tax** in Wales)

Capital gains tax:

- basis of charge
- private residence relief

AUTHORITIES UNDERPINNING PRACTICE

The key authorities that underpin this area of practice are listed below. Note that for legislation you are linked to legislation.gov.uk.

Although much of the legislation on this government website is available in its amended form, the incorporation of new amendments into the text of legislation can be delayed. You should refer to legal databases to ensure you are referencing the most up-to-date legislation.

- Environment Act 1995
  https://www.legislation.gov.uk/ukpga/1995/25/contents
- Taxation of Chargeable Gains Act 1992
  https://www.legislation.gov.uk/ukpga/1992/12/contents
- Stamp Duty Land Tax Act 2015
  https://www.legislation.gov.uk/ukpga/2015/1/contents
- SRA Principles and Code of Conduct 2019
  https://www.sra.org.uk/solicitors/standards-regulations/code-conduct-solicitors/
- Proceeds of Crime Act 2002
  https://www.legislation.gov.uk/ukpga/2002/29/contents
- Money Laundering, Terrorist Financing and Transfer of Funds (Information on the Payer) Regulations 2017
  https://www.legislation.gov.uk/uksi/2017/692/contents
- Law Society Conveyancing Protocol
  https://www.lawsociety.org.uk/en/topics/property/conveyancing-protocol

Pre-exchange					Exchange & pre-completion				Completion & post-completion		
Stage 1 Taking instructions & advising client	**Stage 2** Draft contract	**Stage 3** Pre-contract searches, enquiries & planning	**Stage 4** Title	**Stage 5** Mortgage (applies throughout process)	**Stage 6** Exchange of contracts	**Stage 7** Purchase deed	**Stage 8** Pre-completion searches and requisitions	**Stage 9** Financial statements	**Stage 10** Completion	**Stage 11** SDLT & registration	**Stage 12** Delays and remedies

FIGURE 3.1 Conveyancing timeline

3.1 Introduction

The first interview will enable you to gather essential facts, but it should also be used, where necessary, to furnish the client with important advice on how to proceed. It gives you the opportunity to instil confidence in the client of your abilities as a conveyancer. Ultimately, it is likely to be the high level of service that impresses clients more, not the low level of fees; and a satisfied client is one who will return to you with future instructions. Always remember to note down basic information such as the client's name, address, email address and contact telephone numbers. Remember who pays stamp duty (the buyer), who pays the estate agent's commission account (the seller) and who pays any capital gains tax (the seller). Remember that giving **survey** advice to a buyer is essential and the type of survey you recommend will depend primarily on the age of the property. Regarding mortgage advice, these days endowment mortgages should generally be avoided at all costs, with the usual recommendation being a repayment mortgage, especially for first-time buyers who are looking for the cheapest option in terms of monthly outlay.

The Money Laundering, Terrorist Financing and Transfer of Funds (Information on the Payer) Regulations 2017 require you to obtain satisfactory evidence of the client's identity when you establish a business relationship with the client, for example at the first interview. Strictly speaking, you should not even open a file or prepare a client care letter until the client's identity has been verified (see **3.8.2**).

3.2 Advice on co-ownership

When giving advice to joint buyers on co-ownership, explain the differences between a **joint tenancy** and a **tenancy in common** simply, clearly and without using legal jargon.

3.2.1 Joint tenancy

Under a joint tenancy, the purchasers own collectively the whole of the equitable **estate** with each other—they do not own individual shares. Accordingly, a 'share' in the property cannot be left by will, because upon death the deceased's 'share' passes automatically to the survivor(s). This is known as the right of survivorship. A joint tenancy is normally suitable for a married couple or cohabitees in a stable relationship, but not for those who have children from a previous relationship (see the next paragraph).

3.2.2 Tenancy in common

A tenancy in common is the opposite to a joint tenancy in that the buyers do own separate shares that may be left by will, or pass on **intestacy** in the event of no will, or may even be disposed of *inter vivos*. A tenancy in common should be recommended where the buyers are neither married nor in a stable relationship, where they have contributed in unequal proportions to the purchase price or where they are business partners. It would also be appropriate for couples where one or both have children from a previous relationship, so that those children (and possibly any grandchildren) can be provided for.

3.2.3 Trust declaration and making wills

Where purchasers buy as tenants in common you should, on or before completion of the purchase, prepare a declaration of trust, signed by the parties, setting out their respective financial contributions and agreeing their share of the beneficial interest in the property. The declaration can also deal with other matters, such as the proportions each will pay towards the mortgage (if any) and other household expenditure, and the procedures for a later sale if one wishes to sell and the other does not.

The declaration of trust should be kept safely and referred to in the event of any later dispute as its express terms are unlikely to be overturned by a court. **Land Registry** Form JO may be used by joint owners to declare their interests. Without a trust declaration, uncertainty may arise in the event of a later dispute between the co-owners over the distribution of future sale proceeds. The court has a wide discretion to assess their shares in the property, having regard to the conduct and contributions of each party (*Oxley v Hiscock* [2004] EWCA Civ 546), but a purchase of domestic property in the joint names of cohabitants will establish a prima facie case of joint and equal beneficial interests until the contrary is proved (see *Stack v Dowden* [2007] UKHL 17 and *Jones v Kernott* [2011] UKSC 53). Because the survivorship rule does not apply to a tenancy in common, tenants in common should also be advised to make wills.

Failure to give proper advice in this area may result in a negligence claim against you if a client suffers loss as a result. The classic mistake is for a conveyancer to advise a joint tenancy where a tenancy in common is clearly appropriate; for instance, where unmarried co-purchasers contribute in unequal shares to the purchase price.

3.2.4 Establishing whether owners are joint tenants or tenants in common

You may need to know whether clients who already own property are joint tenants or tenants in common, for instance if one owner dies or if the property is to be sold and the proceeds split. You can find out as follows.

3.2.4.1 Registered land

If the **title** is registered, you should consult the proprietorship register of the title to see whether a joint proprietorship restriction has been entered in the following terms: 'No disposition by a sole proprietor of the registered estate (except a trust corporation) under which capital money arises is to be registered unless authorised by an order of the court' (you may come across earlier versions). The presence of such a restriction tells you that the owners are tenants in common. The absence of such a restriction tells you that they are joint tenants.

3.2.4.2 Unregistered land

If the title is unregistered, you should consult the most recent **conveyance** to the present owners, which should state whether they (ie the purchasers in the conveyance) are joint tenants or tenants in common.

EXAMPLE

Robin acts for Michael and Laurie who are on their second marriage and are buying a house together. Michael has children from a previous marriage and Laurie has none. On his death, Michael wishes to provide for his children in his will and the house will be his only substantial asset. If Michael and Laurie hold the property as joint tenants in equity, upon the first death, the equitable interest of the deceased will pass automatically to the survivor and will not pass under the deceased's will. Robin therefore advises them to hold the property as tenants in common so that their individual shares will pass in accordance with their wills upon death. He advises them to enter into a declaration of trust recording their equitable ownership. Following completion of the purchase, the Land Registry will enter a co-ownership restriction in the proprietorship register, thereby preventing a sole survivor from disposing of the property alone.

3.3 Advice on survey

3.3.1 General considerations

A buyer should always be advised to have a survey of the property carried out before **exchange of contracts** because of the ***caveat emptor*** principle ('let the buyer beware'). It is for the buyer to discover any physical defects in the property and these may not be apparent from the client's own inspection. A client is sometimes reluctant to incur the additional expense of a survey fee so it is your job to reassure the client that this is money well spent. Failure on your part to give this advice could amount to negligence. For a case on the dangers of not having a survey, see *Hardy v Griffiths* [2014] EWHC 3947 (Ch).

A physically defective property may, of course, be unsafe to occupy, but there are financial implications for the purchaser as well. The market value of a property will be reduced if it is in poor condition and so the purchaser may be paying more than they should for it. It may also adversely affect the purchaser's ability to mortgage the property or sell it at a later date. These are all considerations that must be drawn to the client's attention.

3.3.2 Different types of survey

There are currently three types of survey widely available.

3.3.2.1 Basic valuation

This is the simplest and cheapest form of survey but it does no more than establish the property's value on the open market. A prospective **mortgagee** will normally commission this type of survey in order to verify whether the property being charged is adequate security for the proposed loan. The mortgagee's surveyor owes a duty of care not only to the lender but also to the borrower who relies on the report (*Smith v Eric S Bush* [1990] 1 AC 831). A copy of the report should be made available to the borrower.

Unless the property has been built within the last ten years, and has the benefit of a National House Building Council (NHBC) guarantee, clients should be advised to seek a survey that is more detailed than the basic valuation. Even for new properties, a basic survey should be recommended.

3.3.2.2 Home buyer's valuation and survey report

This is more detailed than the basic valuation but not as comprehensive as the full structural survey. It is popular amongst house buyers who, reluctant to incur the costs of a full structural survey, seek a compromise that gives more information than a basic valuation. The small print should be read carefully though; the conditions will often reveal just how superficial the report can be. Invariably, the surveyor will not inspect unexposed or inaccessible areas, for instance the roof space or below floorboards.

A buyer who opts for this type of survey should be advised to contact the buyer's mortgagee to request that the mortgagee's surveyor carries it out instead of—not in addition to—the basic valuation. This will generally be acceptable to the mortgagee and means that the client will avoid incurring two survey fees.

3.3.2.3 Full structural survey

A full survey ought in theory to reveal the true state and condition of the property, but this is not always the case and the small print of the conditions of survey should be checked for exclusions. You would generally advise the client to have a full structural survey if the property is old (say, more than 80 years) or is of high value or if the client has plans to alter the property structurally. The survey fee is obviously more (usually in excess of £750), but for this the client should at least get peace of mind (as long as the survey is favourable). If physical defects are revealed, then the client should be advised either to withdraw from the transaction or to seek from the seller a reduction in the purchase price. A lender may also withdraw the mortgage offer in the case of serious physical defects.

3.3.2.4 External wall survey (for apartment blocks)

Following the Grenfell Tower fire tragedy in June 2017, external wall survey certificates (known as EWS1 forms) have been required by members of UK Finance or the Building Societies Association since December 2019, for any mortgage applications for leasehold properties in residential buildings over 18 metres in height (approximately six storeys). The RICS guidance concerning EWS1 forms states: 'The EWS process, and resulting form, is a set way for a building owner to confirm to valuers and lenders that an external cladding system on residential buildings in scope above 18m in height (approx. 6-storeys) has been assessed by a suitable expert. Not every building in scope above 18m will require an EWS form—only those with some form of combustible cladding or combustible material on balconies.'

Completing an EWS1 form is not a legal requirement, despite information coming from various lenders insisting that they must be completed. However, the requirement for an EWS1 form is now a widespread condition being imposed on mortgage applicants by prospective lenders. There are thousands of affected properties across the UK and lengthy delays are starting to build due to the shortage of professionals who are suitably qualified to complete an EWS1 form and who also have a suitable level of professional indemnity insurance.

3.3.3 Special considerations

3.3.3.1 Neighbouring property

There will be occasions when a survey of neighbouring property will be necessary, for example on the purchase of a flat or property that is structurally attached to the neighbouring property. In this case, the surveyor should be instructed to inspect the main structure of the building and the adjoining property (if possible), as well as the subject property. The poor physical condition of the building of which a flat forms part will inevitably lead to increased levels of **service charge** payable by the occupiers of the flats (see **Chapter 16** regarding service charges in **leases**).

3.3.3.2 Drainage

You should consider whether the subject property is served by mains drainage, maintainable at the public expense (this will be revealed by the water search: see **5.5**). If not, and the drainage system is privately owned, it would be prudent to commission an expert's report on its condition, because your client buyer may incur future costs of maintenance.

3.3.3.3 Electric wiring

If the electric wiring in the property has not been checked for many years, then an inspection by an expert should be considered.

3.3.3.4 Commercial premises

The acquisition of commercial premises will usually necessitate a thorough inspection and survey, the extent of which will depend on the nature and location of the property and the terms of any relevant lease. This is considered again in **Chapter 18**. One particular area of concern today is the potential liability for expensive 'clean-up costs' under the Environmental Protection Act 1990 and the Environment Act 1995. The detail of these statutes is outside the scope of this manual, but the point must be stressed that any purchaser (and mortgagee) of land for development should consider the desirability of an environmental survey to check for contamination by hazardous substances (eg industrial waste).

Under the Environment Act 1995, local authorities are required to identify contaminated land within their areas and to serve a remediation notice requiring clean-up works to be carried out where necessary. The 'appropriate person' upon whom the notice is served is the original polluter but, if that person cannot be found, then the appropriate person will be the 'owner or occupier' of the land.

For further information concerning the important topic of contaminated land, refer to *A Practical Approach to Commercial Conveyancing and Property* by Abbey and Richards (Oxford University Press, 2016).

EXAMPLE

Sarina acts for Robert who is buying for £1.5 million a former vicarage in the small village of Winterslow. The property was built in 1825. In view of the property's great age as well as the high price he is paying, Sarina will advise Robert to commission a full structural survey to reveal the full state and condition of the property.

3.4 Estate agents

Most sellers will use an estate agent to market their properties and to negotiate on the sale price. The agent normally charges the seller a percentage of the selling price as commission. This becomes due on exchange of contracts but is paid out of the sale proceeds on completion. By the time the seller first contacts the conveyancer, the seller usually will have secured a buyer at an agreed price. The estate agent should continue to assist the client throughout the transaction by speaking directly to other parties to resolve outstanding non-legal issues.

3.5 Capital gains tax: will the seller have to pay it?

3.5.1 Private Residence Relief

Capital gains tax (CGT) is prima facie payable on the disposal of an interest in land. The disposal for tax purposes occurs at exchange of contracts (when the beneficial interest passes to the buyer), not on completion. Nevertheless, CGT is rarely payable in the context of residential conveyancing because of the availability of Private Residence Relief (PRR). The disposal (ie sale) of an individual's private residence, including grounds of up to 0.5 hectares, is exempt from CGT. Although this will apply in most domestic transactions, the practitioner should always check the client's situation carefully to ensure that PRR does in fact apply in each case.

3.5.1.1 Only or main residence

In the first place, it should be established whether the seller has lived anywhere else since the subject property was acquired, because the exemption states that the seller must have lived in the house as their only or main residence throughout the period of ownership. Certain periods of absence are disregarded, in particular the following cumulative periods:

- non-residence during the last nine months of ownership;
- the first 12 months of ownership;
- any period of absence in employment overseas;
- up to four years' absence if a condition of employment;
- any period up to three years in total throughout the period of ownership.

3.5.1.2 Exclusive business use

Secondly, the client's confirmation should be obtained that no part of the private residence has been used exclusively for business purposes; otherwise a proportion of the relief may be lost in respect of the business use area. The word 'exclusively' is emphasised because if the business room (or rooms) is shared with other members of the household, this should qualify as 'duality of user', enabling the full relief to apply.

3.5.1.3 Half a hectare limit

The practitioner should establish how much land is being sold along with the private residence. If the grounds exceed half a hectare (5,000 square metres or 1.235 acres) there could be a tax liability on the excess unless the excess is proved to be necessary for the reasonable enjoyment of the house, for example if a large house with a large garden is being sold. Where ownership of the house is retained but land alone is sold, the land enjoys the benefit of the PRR provided the land sold does not exceed half a hectare.

3.5.1.4 Other matters

Check whether the client owns another house. Married couples are only entitled to one PRR. If a married couple own more than one house, then they should elect which house is to take the benefit of the exemption. This election is revocable if they wish to change their minds. Finally, check that the client's house was not originally purchased in the name of a company, otherwise the PRR will not apply.

3.5.1.5 Losses and allowances

Even if the PRR does not apply, either in full or in part, any chargeable gain on the sale of the property could be reduced or possibly wiped out altogether if certain allowable deductions are available and taken into account. For example, losses from previous assessment years can be carried forward and set off against gains. Also, each individual has an annual allowance for CGT, which was £12,300 for tax year 2022/23. However, this allowance was reduced to £6,000 for tax year 2023/24 and is reduced to £3,000 for tax year 2024/25. Chargeable gains are treated as the top slice of an individual's combined gains and income. Any part of a taxable gain exceeding the upper limit of the income tax basic rate band (£37,700 for 2024/25) is taxed at 28 per cent. Below that, the rate is 10 per cent. Rates are subject to change by the government and should be checked by visiting the relevant government website. Any UK resident must inform HM Revenue and Customs about the capital gain and pay the tax due within 60 days from completion.

3.5.1.6 Advising buyers

Advice on CGT is, of course, primarily of importance to a client who is selling a property. However, a client who is intending to buy a property that will not qualify for PRR should be advised of any potential liability for CGT on a subsequent disposal.

EXAMPLE

Natalie acts for Sandra who is an osteopath in Wimbledon. Sandra has instructed Natalie in relation to the sale of her residential house for £875,000. She bought the house 25 years ago for £220,000. Throughout that period, she has used one downstairs room of the house exclusively as a surgery to treat her patients. Natalie will advise her that as the room was used exclusively for business use, on sale she will lose a proportion of her private residence relief and CGT will therefore be chargeable on her capital gain.

3.6 Stamp duty land tax: will the buyer have to pay it?

Where the price for the property exceeds a certain threshold figure (currently £250,000 for residential properties and £150,000 for non-residential and mixed-use properties), the buyer is required to pay a government tax known as stamp duty land tax (SDLT). In Wales, it is simply known as land transaction tax (LTT). Before 4 December 2014, SDLT was charged at a single rate for the entire price of the property. Since 4 December 2014, SDLT is charged at increasing rates for each part of the price.

For residential properties the purchaser will pay:

- zero on the first £250,000;
- 5 per cent on the next £675,000;
- 10 per cent on the next £575,000;
- 12 per cent on the rest (above £1.5 million).

EXAMPLE

If a purchaser who is not a first-time buyer (see later) buys a residential property for £325,000, they will pay SDLT of £3,750. This is calculated as follows:

- zero on the first £250,000;
- £3,750 (5 per cent) on the remaining £75,000

The HM Revenue and Customs calculator for SDLT is a useful resource to help work out how much your client will pay: https://www.tax.service.gov.uk/calculate-stamp-duty-land-tax/#!/intro.

For non-residential and mixed-use properties, the purchaser pays the following rates of SDLT:

- property price, premium or value up to £150,000 (annual rent no greater than £1,000) = zero
- properties between £150,001 and £250,000 = 2%
- properties over £250,000 = 5%

Since 1 April 2016, there has been a 3 per cent SDLT surcharge when an additional residential property in England, Wales or Northern Ireland is bought by someone who already owns a home; that is second homes and 'buy to let' properties. The higher rates are 3 per cent above the current SDLT residential rates. They are charged on the portion of the value of the property that falls into each band; that is:

Band	Existing residential SDLT rates	Additional property SDLT rates
£0–£250,000	0%	3%
£250,000–£925,000	5%	8%
£925,000–£1.5 million	10%	13%
£1.5 million and above	12%	15%

To assist people moving home, if a purchaser buys an additional dwelling before selling their main dwelling, they will have 36 months after buying the new property in which to dispose of their previous main residence and claim a repayment of the 3 per cent SDLT surcharge.

The higher residential rates of LTT in Wales increased by 1 per cent across all bands on 22 December 2020. This applies to sales of second homes and buy-to-let properties as opposed to the main residential home.

First-time buyers paying £425,000 or less for a residential property will pay no SDLT. First-time buyers paying between £425,001 and £625,000 will pay SDLT at 5 per cent on the amount of the purchase price in excess of £425,000. A first-time buyer is defined as an individual or individuals who have never owned an interest in a residential property in the UK or anywhere else in the world and who intends to occupy the property as their main residence. First-time buyers purchasing property for more than £625,000 will not be entitled to any relief and will pay SDLT at the normal rates.

From 1 April 2021, all non-UK residents buying residential property pay a 2 per cent surcharge on top of any stamp duty already chargeable on their purchase.

If the price is just over the threshold for SDLT, you should consider apportioning the price between the land and any contents included in the sale (eg carpets and curtains). This could reduce the price for the land below the threshold and thus reduce or avoid SDLT altogether. However, you should take care that the price for the contents is a proper reflection of their value. Any overvaluation in these circumstances may constitute a fraud against HM Revenue and Customs (by both you and the client), and could also make the contract for sale unenforceable by action (see *Saunders v Edwards* [1987] 1 WLR 1116). You will also be in breach of the Principles in the SRA Standards and Regulations, namely acting with integrity and behaving in a way that maintains the trust the public places in you.

HM Revenue and Customs has issued guidance as to items it regards as chattels where apportionment is allowable, and items it regards as fixtures where apportionment is not allowable:

- *chattels*: carpets, curtains, light shades, pot plants, free-standing kitchen white goods and portable electric or gas fires;
- *fixtures*: fitted bathroom sanitary ware, central heating systems, plants growing in the soil and gas fires connected to a piped gas supply.

Any reduction in the purchase price of the property should also be reported to and first approved by the client's prospective mortgagee (if any). The mortgagee may possibly decide to reduce the amount it is prepared to lend.

To assist you in filling out the SDLT return following completion, ask the buyer for their National Insurance number when taking instructions and keep it on file.

SDLT rates are subject to change by the government and should be checked by visiting the relevant government websites for the UK and Wales.

CONDUCT POINT

Client care procedures and advice on costs are important aspects of the SRA Code of Conduct for Solicitors 2019 (the Code), which came into force on 25 November 2019. Full details of the Code can be found on the Solicitors Regulation Authority website.

3.7 Client care and advice on costs

The SRA Transparency Rules came into force on 6 December 2018 and require practitioners to give clients the best possible information, both at the time of engagement and when appropriate as their matter progresses, about the likely overall cost of their matter. This should include a breakdown between fees, VAT and disbursements. At the start of a conveyancing transaction, it should be possible to agree an estimate for the whole transaction. Remember that this will also have to include your fee for acting for the client's lender (if any). You should also advise the client of VAT payable on top of your profit costs, together with other expenses such as possible stamp duty, Land Registry fees, search fees and bank transfer fees. If you forget to mention VAT, the client may assume that the quoted figure is inclusive of it (s89 Value Added Tax Act 1994). There is a useful Law Society practice note on the SRA Transparency Rules.

Once you have settled an estimated figure, it is sensible to inform the client that you reserve the right to increase your charges should the transaction prove to be unduly complicated or protracted. In this way, you are not binding yourself to a fixed, unalterable fee. You may reassure the client, however, by saying that in the vast majority of cases no increase is usually necessary. You should also discuss how and when the costs are to be met. This is done usually at the conclusion of the transaction, although most firms expect clients to pay money on account of disbursements (eg search fees) at the beginning of the transaction; typically around £300. You should confirm the estimate to the client in writing, and you must also advise the client immediately in writing if the figure is to be revised. Care is needed here because if you go further than giving an estimate—by committing yourself to a fixed (or 'agreed') fee—then you will not be permitted to charge more even if circumstances change.

The SRA Transparency Rules require firms to publish price and service information on their websites, or to provide it to prospective clients on request if they do not have a website, for specific legal services including conveyancing. Firms are required to publish the total cost of services (or the average costs or range of costs), the basis of charges, key stages of the matter and likely time frames, any likely disbursements (and whether they include VAT) and the experience and qualifications of anyone carrying out the work.

3.7.1 Complaints handling and client care generally

The SRA Transparency Rules require clients to be informed in writing at the outset of the matter of their right to complain and how complaints can be made. Firms should deal with clients' complaints promptly, fairly, openly and effectively. Firms should therefore operate a written complaints procedure, and ensure that all staff are made aware of it. In particular, the firm's written complaints procedure should:

- be brought to the clients' attention at the outset of the matter;
- be easy for clients to use and understand, allowing for complaints to be made by any reasonable means;
- be responsive to the needs of individual clients, especially those who are vulnerable;
- enable complaints to be dealt with promptly and fairly, with decisions based on a sufficient investigation of the circumstances;
- provide for appropriate remedies; and
- not involve any charges to clients for handling their complaints.

Clients should be provided with a copy of the written complaints procedure upon request and, in the event that a client makes a complaint, the client should be provided with all necessary information concerning the handling of the complaint. Clients should be informed in writing, both at the time of engagement and the conclusion of the solicitors' complaints procedure, of their right to complain to the Legal Ombudsman, the time frame for doing so and full details of how to contact the Legal Ombudsman. The Law Society has issued a useful complaints management practice note to help solicitors achieve good practice in this area. (https://www.lawsociety.org.uk/support-services/advice/practice-notes/handling-complaints/).

In relation to client care generally, the following action by practitioners is recommended:

- agreeing an appropriate level of service with your client, for example the type and frequency of communications;
- explaining your responsibilities and those of the client; and
- ensuring that the client is told, in writing, the name and status of the person(s) dealing with the matter and the name and status of the person responsible for its overall supervision.

A practitioner must decide what is appropriate for an individual client taking into account the client's particular needs and circumstances. For example, it may be inappropriate to give full information in certain cases, for example when acting for a regular client for whom repetitive work is done where the client has already been provided with the relevant information. It follows that the indicative behaviours mentioned above are of particular importance when taking instructions from a new or non-established client.

At some stage during the first interview, you should advise the client of the future action to be taken to progress the matter, the likely timescale of the transaction and when you will next contact the client. If the client is unfamiliar with the conveyancing process, it is good practice to offer a brief explanation of the procedures involved and to estimate when exchange of contracts and completion are likely to take place. All relevant client care information, including advice on costs, must be confirmed to the client in writing.

EXAMPLE

Maria is an established client of your firm and has made an appointment to see her solicitor, James, regarding her proposed sale, and a purchase of shop premises where she wishes to run a business. She has already received a mortgage offer on her purchase of the shop and so does not require any mortgage advice. She has a mortgage on the property she is selling. She will be living in rented accommodation, which has been arranged. As Maria is an established client there is no need for her solicitor to give full client care advice or to verify her identity. However, he should inform her that he will have the day-to-day running of the files and give her the name of the partner with overall responsibility. He notes down her contact details, such as telephone number and email address, and details of the estate agents involved. He asks her to confirm the agreed sale and purchase price, whether she has paid any preliminary **deposit** and whether any other terms have been agreed, for example purchase of goodwill and fixtures and fittings if she is acquiring an existing business with the shop premises. He informs her of his firm's fees plus VAT and any other relevant expenses, such as stamp duty land tax. He asks whether anyone else occupies the sale property. He could give her the Property Information Questionnaire for her to complete and return. He prepares a brief financial statement for her in respect of both sale and purchase and gives her an indication of any likely shortfall she must find in order to complete. He tells her he will write to her existing mortgagee, requesting the **deeds** (if any) and asking for confirmation of the loan currently outstanding (**redemption statement**). He asks for her mortgage account number. On the sale, he checks that the principal private dwelling exemption applies for CGT purposes. On the purchase, he establishes the age of the property and gives appropriate advice on survey. She may require specialised advice in respect of the new business and it may be worth referring her to another lawyer in the firm who specialises in business law and practice. He concludes the interview by informing her of the next steps and that he will be writing to confirm his advice. He gives her some indication of how long the whole conveyancing process is likely to take (on average about two months).

3.8 **Professional conduct**

3.8.1 **General considerations**

The SRA Principles and SRA Code of Conduct ('the Code') are intended to make it clear to consumers what outcomes they should expect from their legal service providers. Practitioners need to consider how best to achieve the right outcomes for their clients taking into account the way that the practitioner works and their client base. Breaching the SRA Principles or Code are serious matters that may lead to disciplinary proceedings. Many conduct issues may arise during the course of a conveyancing transaction. On exchange of contracts and completion, professional **undertakings** will be given; there are rules governing practitioners' handling of clients' money; there are recommendations to follow regarding **contract races** (see **4.4**). In this section, we will consider client **confidentiality**, money laundering and acting for more than one party in a property transaction, all key issues when taking instructions from a client.

3.8.2 **Client confidentiality and money laundering**

3.8.2.1 Confidentiality

Paragraphs 6.3–6.5 of the Code deal with confidentiality and disclosure. A practitioner must keep the affairs of clients confidential except where disclosure is required or permitted by law or the client consents. Where your duty of confidentiality to one client comes into conflict with your duty of disclosure to another client, your duty of confidentiality takes precedence. Thus, client affairs are confidential and must never be disclosed to a third party without the client's consent, even where the practitioner is no longer acting for the client.

EXAMPLE

Aaron acts for borrower Hardeep and lender Nationwide Building Society in relation to Hardeep's acquisition of a freehold house. Hardeep tells him that she intends to run a business from the premises, in breach of a mortgage condition. Aaron cannot continue to act because there is a **conflict of interest**, but neither can he tell Nationwide the reason why he can no longer act—this would be a breach of confidentiality to the borrower Hardeep.

3.8.2.2 Money laundering

One exception to the confidentiality rule that is of importance in the context of conveyancing concerns money laundering. The National Crime Agency (NCA) has highlighted the prevalence of property transactions as a means of laundering criminal funds, and the high risk of exposure of professionals offering conveyancing services to the public. The Criminal Justice Act 1993 and the Proceeds of Crime Act 2002 introduced criminal offences for *failing to disclose* to the authorities (ie the NCA) knowledge or suspicion of others who are involved in laundering the proceeds of a crime, drug trafficking or terrorism. Thus, if you have such knowledge or suspicion, you must report it to your firm's nominated officer (see shortly) as soon as practically possible prior to the transaction taking place (subject to any legal professional privilege, see later). For a case where a firm of solicitors failed to perform its anti-money laundering obligations, see *Purrunsing v A'Court & Co (a firm) & Anor* [2016] EWHC 789 (Ch).

The Law Society has issued very useful anti-money laundering guidance and leaflets obtainable from the Law Society's website alerting solicitors to likely circumstances which could amount to assisting in money laundering. Two examples in relation to property practice in particular are:

- unusual instructions, such as clients instructing you to buy a property from the other end of the country when they could be using a local firm;
- unusual settlement requests, such as paying for a property with large sums of cash.

3.8.2.3 'Tipping off'

It is an offence to 'tip off' the client that you have made a disclosure to the authorities, or that the authorities are investigating a possible laundering offence. This rule is also contrary to the normal solicitor–client relationship of confidentiality. The duty of disclosure extends to any party (not just your client) suspected of being involved, so this covers the other side's client as much as suspicion about your own client.

3.8.2.4 Legal professional privilege

The case of *Bowman v Fells* [2005] EWCA Civ 226 has altered how conveyancers should approach reporting issues, and careful attention should be paid to the Law Society guidance on its website about the implications of this decision. Essentially, if a conveyancer forms knowledge or suspicion of money laundering, they should first consider whether the information on which that knowledge or suspicion is based was received in legally privileged circumstances. If it was, they cannot make a report to the NCA without the client's authority. In these circumstances, conveyancers should consider whether they would prefer not to act for the client. Advice on a case-by-case basis can be obtained from the Law Society's Professional Ethics helpline (0370 606 2577).

3.8.2.5 The Money Laundering, Terrorist Financing and Transfer of Funds (Information on the Payer) Regulations 2017

These money laundering regulations apply to all legal professionals acting in any real property transaction and extend to the proceeds of any criminal activity. For more details, see the chapter on financial services in the *Public Law, Legal Services & Legal Systems* manual.

EXAMPLE

Charley acts for new clients of her firm, Abby and William, who are buying their first flat. Before she can start acting for them she will require verification of their identity. She must have sight of their original passports or photocard driving licences together with proof of address in the form of a bank statement or utility bill which is not more than three months old.

3.8.3 Acting for seller and buyer

Practitioners should have effective systems and controls in place to help identify and assess conflicts of interest. Accordingly, it is for the practitioner to decide whether acting for both buyer and seller in a particular conveyancing transaction will amount to a client conflict. You should consider various factors such as whether:

- the clients' interests are different;
- your ability to give independent advice to the clients may be fettered;

- there is a need to negotiate between the clients;
- there is an imbalance in bargaining power between the clients; and
- any client is vulnerable.

Clearly, acting for buyer and seller in the same matter carries a high risk of conflicts of interest and the SRA has indicated that it will not expect solicitors to act routinely for buyer and seller. Accordingly, acting for a buyer (including a **lessee**) and seller (including a **lessor**) in a transaction relating to the **transfer** of land for value is likely to show that a practitioner has not acted with integrity (SRA Principle 5) or in the best interests of each client (SRA Principle 7).

Paragraph 6(2)(a) of the Code of Conduct states that you can act for more than one party even if there is a client conflict where the clients have a substantially common interest in relation to a matter or a particular aspect of it. However, importantly, acting for two or more clients where a seller is transferring property to a buyer may tend to show that you have not acted in the best interests of each client. In the light of this, best practice is to decline to act for buyer and seller in the same transaction where the land is being transferred for value. However, it may be possible to act for both parties where the land is being gifted or being transferred between parties who are related by blood, adoption, marriage, civil partnership or living together. Similarly, in a commercial context, it may be possible to act where the parties are associated companies (eg subsidiaries of the same holding company). However, if a conflict were to arise during the course of the transaction, you would have to cease acting for at least one of the clients and could only continue to act for the other client if the duty of confidentiality to the former client were not put at risk.

Any decision to act for both buyer and seller should be of benefit to both clients, rather than in the practitioner's own commercial interests. This accords with SRA Principle 5, which requires the practitioner to act with integrity. You should also bear in mind SRA Principle 3 (acting with independence) and SRA Principle 7 (acting in the best interest of each client).

Confidentiality may also become an issue in relation to acting for both parties. For example, a seller may want certain information kept confidential, but this information may be material to the buyer. As the duty of confidentiality takes precedence over the duty of disclosure, you would have to consider ceasing to act for the buyer.

3.8.4 Acting for joint buyers or joint sellers

You can act for joint buyers or joint sellers provided no conflict of interest exists or is likely to arise between them. In most cases, the interests of the joint buyers or sellers are the same, so there is rarely a problem. You should obtain instructions (or verification of instructions) directly from each client, rather than simply relying on the word of the other(s). This allows you to clarify the client's exact requirements and to ensure that the instructions are not tainted by undue influence or duress.

3.8.5 Acting for lender and borrower

This is considered in **Chapter 8** dealing with mortgages. Generally speaking, acting for both a borrower and an institutional lender, for example a bank or building society, in the same transaction is permitted because both parties have a common interest in ensuring that the property is good and marketable. However, you should be aware of possible conflicts of interest that may arise and which would prevent you from acting for both parties (see **8.5**).

3.8.6 Conveyancing and cybercrime

Conveyancing firms must be alert to the risk of cybercrime, in particular fraudsters hacking into their email accounts and intercepting emails between practitioners and clients, or between practitioners and their counterparts in conveyancing transactions. There have been cases where sellers have emailed their solicitor to ask for the sale proceeds to be transmitted to a named account, but in fact the client's email account had been hacked by fraudsters and the sale monies ended up going into the fraudsters' account. This has happened in reverse too—clients being duped into sending money to fraudsters who had hacked into the solicitor's email account.

Always advise your clients of the potential risk of email fraud and the importance of their email accounts being made secure (eg regular password changes). Any confidential information, such as bank details, should not be sent by email unless the email is encrypted, or alternatively a password-protected portal is used. Bank account details should also be confirmed in person or by telephone (including a security question). Be especially cautious if, partway through a transaction, you are asked to send money to a different bank account.

3.9 Law Society Conveyancing Protocol

3.9.1 General considerations

The Law Society introduced the National Conveyancing Protocol in 1990 to help speed up the process of residential conveyancing. There is no compulsion to use the Protocol, but solicitors for the seller and buyer should agree whether or not it will be used. In practice, the seller's solicitor usually takes the decision and the buyer's solicitor normally goes along with it. The Protocol has been made compulsory for solicitors' practices that are part of the Conveyancing Quality Scheme. If one party will not adopt it, this does not prevent it being used by the other party. The Law Society recommends that conveyancers use the Protocol preferred practice in all domestic conveyancing transactions. However, the obligation to act in the best interests of the client will take precedence over the Protocol.

Reference will be made to the Protocol throughout this manual as the various stages in the conveyancing process unfold. The latest edition of the Protocol (2019) can be accessed via the link in **Appendix 1**. It is worth consulting at regular intervals during the transaction to refresh your memory of what exactly is required under the Protocol.

3.9.2 Advising the client about the protocol

You should explain the use and purpose of the Protocol to the client when taking instructions. Its use will generally be beneficial to the client but there is one area that may cause difficulty—the requirement to keep the other side informed of the client's situation in any related sale or purchase. This should be discussed with the client because it could be contrary to the client's best interests to disclose this information. For instance, if you inform the seller's solicitor that your client has not found a buyer for their own property, the seller may decide to sell to someone else who is in a better position to proceed (eg buyer found or no property to sell). If the client declines to offer information about a related sale or purchase, the practitioner must, of course, respect this wish in accordance with the duty of confidentiality to the client.

3.9.2.1 Seller's Property Information Form

If your client is selling and you have decided to use the Protocol, you can save time by asking the client to complete the Property Information Form during the first interview. This form raises standard questions about the property such as whether the owner is aware of any boundary disputes, or whether the owner has received any notices concerning the property from the local authority. The Property Information Form is discussed in more detail in **Chapter 5**.

3.9.3 Commercial transactions

The full terms of the Protocol are generally not appropriate in the context of commercial conveyancing for the simple reason that the standard forms adopted by the Protocol contemplate the sale of a dwelling. Nevertheless, the spirit behind the Protocol is usually adopted in that the seller will provide the buyer with a pre-contract package, which will include a draft contract, replies to pre-contract enquiries and evidence of title (see **Chapter 18** regarding commercial conveyancing).

A commercial developer selling new houses on an estate should also provide a comprehensive pre-contract package to the individual purchaser's solicitors. Although the properties are dwellings, the full terms of the Protocol are, as already discussed, generally inappropriate because the properties very often have not been physically completed before contracts are exchanged (see **Chapter 13** regarding new properties).

3.10 Advice on finance

3.10.1 General considerations

You should ensure that sufficient funds will be available both to complete the purchase and to pay for the costs and disbursements, including Land Registry fees and stamp duty land tax. The funding would be achieved either directly from the client's own resources or, more usually, through a combination of the client's own resources, a mortgage loan and the proceeds of any related sale (unless, of course, the client is a first-time buyer).

It is helpful for the client if, while taking instructions, you can prepare a brief financial statement showing the expected payments and receipts on the sale and/or purchase. In this way, you can calculate how much extra money the client may need to find, either from the client's own resources or by mortgage loan, in order to complete the transaction(s).

Before proceeding with the conveyancing process, it is obviously important to check that:

- the client understands all the financial implications and can afford to go ahead; and
- sufficient funds are or will be available to finance the total expenditure.

If the client has a related sale and purchase, the net proceeds of sale will normally be used to assist the funding of the purchase price:

3.10.1.1 Calculating the net sale proceeds (a)

You can calculate roughly how much will be available from the sale by deducting from the total sale price the following:

- amount to be repaid under any existing mortgage(s) on the sale property (the client should be able to guide you on this, and you can verify the exact figure direct with the mortgagee);
- if estate agents are involved, their commission fee, including VAT;
- your costs on the sale, plus VAT and disbursements;
- rarely, any capital gains tax payable on the sale.

You should also consider whether any person other than your client has a claim to any part of the sale proceeds that would reduce the amount available to your client, such as someone who contributed towards the purchase price when the property was bought.

3.10.1.2 Calculating the full cost of purchase (b)

You will add to the purchase price:

- the price agreed for any chattels or other extras included in the purchase;
- any stamp duty land tax payable;
- your costs on the purchase, plus VAT and disbursements (including search fees).

To calculate how much the client must find either from the client's own resources or by mortgage loan, simply deduct the net sale proceeds (a) from the full cost of purchase (b). **Completion statements** are more fully explained at **10.9**.

If the client is only selling (without a related purchase), you should confirm to the client calculation (a). If the client is just buying (without a related sale), you should confirm to the client calculation (b).

It is also prudent to remind the client of other possible expenditure that the client will have to settle personally before completion, for example the surveyor's fee on a purchase (see **3.3**) and furniture removal costs.

Advice may be required on potential liability to capital gains tax (see **3.5**).

3.10.2 **Deposit payable on exchange of contracts**

A buyer will normally be required to pay a deposit on exchange of contracts. The deposit acts as part-payment as well as a guarantee, which the seller can **forfeit** if the buyer defaults on the contract. The deposit is usually 10 per cent of the purchase price, although sometimes the parties agree less. Your client buyer will need to place you in funds for the deposit before exchange and you should advise the client of this now. Many clients believe mistakenly that their mortgage advance will cover the deposit but the advance is, of course, not available until shortly before completion (ie after exchange).

3.10.2.1 Financing the deposit

If the client does not have funds available, you will need to explore other ways of financing the deposit. If the client has a related sale, it may be possible to utilise the deposit you receive on the sale towards the purchase deposit. This will depend on the terms of the contract. Alternatively, the deposit guarantee scheme could be considered or, if the client has a related sale, short-term bridging finance (see **9.2.2**). The last two methods will incur cost for the client and these should be explained. A common form of financing the deposit is a gift from parents who should be advised to obtain independent advice before signing any waiver of rights document which is usually a requirement of lenders.

3.10.3 **Mortgages**

Mortgages are considered in **Chapter 8**.

EXAMPLE

A firm has been instructed to act for Stuart Rush and his wife Harriet Rush in the sale of 'Saxifrage' and the related purchase of 'Bentley Lodge'. A principal has passed their solicitor the two files from which they note the following:

- The sale price of Saxifrage is £175,000.
- The purchase price of Bentley Lodge is £185,000.
- The clients have an endowment mortgage on Saxifrage securing a loan of £120,000.
- The clients have received a mortgage offer on Bentley Lodge of £130,000. There is a retention of £30,000 on the mortgage advance until essential repairs have been carried out to the roof and chimney stacks.
- The clients wish to complete the purchase before the sale as Harriet's mother lives with them and they wish to carry out the repairs before they all move.
- The clients' bank has offered them a **bridging loan** of £30,000 to enable them to complete the purchase before the sale.
- The bank will only release the bridging loan upon receipt of a solicitor's undertaking to pay the net sale proceeds of Saxifrage to the bank.
- The estate agent's particulars relating to Saxifrage have arrived in this morning's post.

Before considering the advice, it may be helpful to prepare a brief financial statement:

Sale price	175,000
less mortgage redemption	120,000
Sale proceeds	55,000
Purchase price	185,000
less net mortgage advance	100,000
	85,000
Sale proceeds	55,000
add bridging loan	30,000
	85,000

The purchase price is below the stamp duty threshold and, at first glance, the calculations appear to be correct but a careful analysis of the clients' instructions will reveal that they have overlooked the following matters.

- The amount required to redeem the Saxifrage mortgage will not be exactly £120,000. This is the initial loan and does not take into account any outstanding interest charges, administration fees or redemption penalties. You must obtain an up-to-date redemption figure. (As the mortgage is an endowment rather than a repayment, the principal sum will not have been reduced.)
- We are told there are estate agents on the sale so the clients will be liable to pay their commission plus VAT.
- They must pay legal fees on the sale and purchase, plus VAT and disbursements (eg Land Registry and search fees). They must also pay their surveyor's fee.
- The bridging loan will incur interest charges and probably an arrangement fee.

In the light of this, the clients should be advised that the net sale proceeds of Saxifrage would be insufficient to repay the bridging loan. Their solicitor cannot advise them to proceed unless they can increase their bridging loan or find additional funds. An alternative solution would be to try and negotiate a reduction in the purchase price of Bentley Lodge.

The Rush's solicitor will advise the clients that they will need to fund the 10 per cent deposit on the purchase, payable on exchange of contracts. They could seek to utilise the deposit you receive on the sale (this is permitted under a contract incorporating the **Standard Conditions of Sale**), but this would still leave a shortfall of £1,000. The clients would have to find this from their own resources or seek a further bridging loan. Alternatively, the owners of Bentley Lodge could be asked to accept a reduced deposit. Saxifrage appears to be the clients' principal private dwellinghouse but if this is not the case then they must be advised of their potential liability to CGT.

CONDUCT POINT

Breach of a solicitor's undertaking is professional misconduct and will result in disciplinary action. If Mr and Mrs Rush's bridging loan (see above) proceeds, you must consider several matters before giving an undertaking to the bank.

- Can you trust the clients and are they creditworthy?
- The clients must give you an express and irrevocable authority in writing to give the undertaking.
- The undertaking should be in writing and signed by a partner of the firm.
- You must be sure that you can comply absolutely with the terms of the undertaking. To this end, the wording must be clear, unambiguous and wholly capable of performance by your firm.
- Are you satisfied that the anticipated net sale proceeds will be sufficient to discharge the bridging finance plus interest?
- In your undertaking, you would state the sale price and itemise the anticipated deductions (eg mortgage redemption, agent's commission and legal fees) to calculate the approximate net proceeds of sale.
- As the undertaking is one to pay money, you would make it clear in the wording that payment by your firm of the net sale proceeds of Saxifrage will be made only if and when the sale proceeds are received by your firm. This safeguards against the possibility of you never receiving the proceeds of sale (eg because of client bankruptcy), but still being obliged to repay the bank.
- Ideally, the undertaking should not be given until after exchange of contracts. However, as the clients will require a synchronised exchange you would in practice give it shortly before the point of exchange, provided there are no unresolved issues.

KEY POINT SUMMARY

- Obtain client's full name, address, email address and contact telephone numbers.
- Has your firm acted for the client before (relevant to client care advice)?
- Is it necessary to check client's identity (relevant to money laundering and mortgage fraud)?
- Confirm address of property and tenure.
- Is it a residential or commercial property?
- Obtain details of any estate agents involved. Obtain copy of agent's particulars. Any preliminary deposit paid to agents?
- If it is a commercial transaction, have the parties agreed heads of terms? If so, what are they?
- Obtain details of solicitors acting for other side.
- Price agreed.
- Other terms agreed, for example sale of chattels, likely **completion date**?
- Which fixtures will remain or be removed?
- Does client have a related sale or purchase, which has to be synchronised with this transaction?
- Who occupies the property (relevant to third party rights and vacant possession)?
- If it is a **commercial lease**, are there any sub-leases?
- Is property near river or railway or in unusual location (relevant to searches and enquiries)?
- How much deposit will be paid or received on exchange? Traditionally 10 per cent of purchase price but less could be negotiated.
- If you are dealing with a lease, is it the grant of a new lease or the **assignment** of an existing one?
- Is there anything additional you need to know from the client or upon which the client requires your advice, which may be relevant to this particular transaction?
- Advise the client how long it should all take and what the next steps will be.
- How will purchase price be financed? If client requires a mortgage, consider mortgage advice.
- How will deposit payable on exchange be financed? In whole or part from deposit received on related sale?
- If more than one buyer, advise on co-ownership.
- Confirm proposed use of property (relevant to planning and any restrictions in the title).
- Advise the buyer client whether stamp duty land tax is payable. Can you apportion the price between land and chattels to reduce or eradicate stamp duty?
- If buyer client is presently in rented accommodation, advise on giving landlord notice to end tenancy.
- Explain to prospective co-buyers the differences between a joint tenancy (where the buyers collectively own all the property) and a tenancy in common (where the buyers own separate shares in it).
- Explain the principle of survivorship in a joint tenancy.
- Failure to give correct co-ownership advice may result in negligence.
- If buying as tenants in common, the buyers should make a declaration of trust and consider making wills.
- For tenants in common, the Land Registry will enter a co-ownership restriction in the proprietorship register to prevent a sole survivor from disposing of the land alone.
- If this restriction is absent from the register, you know that the registered owners are joint tenants.
- For residential property, advise buyer on three different types of survey: basic valuation, home buyer's, full structural.
- Full structural survey is preferable for older or high-value properties.

- Commercial premises may require a more comprehensive survey.
- When buying a flat, consider a survey of the whole building because of service charge liability etc.
- Private Residence Relief (PRR) means that clients selling their only or main home will usually be exempt from CGT.
- For this to apply, the seller must have lived in the house as their only or main residence throughout the period of ownership, although certain periods of absence are disregarded.
- Part of the CGT relief may be lost for large gardens over 0.5 hectares or if part of the house is used exclusively for business purposes.
- PRR does not apply to second homes, although an election can be made; that is, the client can choose which home is exempted.
- Advise buyers of potential CGT in the future if they are not buying a main residence.
- Give the client a legal costs estimate and remember to include VAT, disbursements and any stamp duty land tax.
- Advise the client of your firm's complaints procedure, who will have the day-to-day running of the file and the name of the partner or other fee earner in overall charge.
- Advise the client of the future action to be taken and the likely timescale of the transaction.
- Confirm everything in writing to the client.
- Become familiar with the SRA Code of Conduct, in particular client care.
- Ensure that sufficient funds will be available both to complete the purchase and to pay for the costs and disbursements, including Land Registry fees and stamp duty land tax.
- Prepare a brief financial statement showing the expected payments and receipts on the sale and/or purchase.
- Remind the client of other expenditure that the client will need to settle personally before completion, for example the surveyor's fee on a purchase and furniture removal costs.
- It may be necessary to give generic advice on mortgages (see **Chapter 8**).
- Where are the title deeds? If property is mortgaged, obtain full name and address of first mortgagee plus mortgage account number, so you can write to mortgagee requesting deeds on loan. In **registered land**, there are no traditional title deeds as such, so official copies of the registered title should be obtained from the Land Registry.
- Are there any second or subsequent mortgages? Acting for seller, obtain details of *all* outstanding mortgages on property, including names and addresses of lenders and amounts outstanding.
- Did you act for seller client when the property was bought? If yes, it may be helpful to get the old file from store.
- What are seller client's instructions regarding sale proceeds?
- If Protocol is being used, client to complete Property Information Form.
- Advise seller client not to stop mortgage repayments or cancel building insurance until completion.
- On an assignment of a commercial lease, has the client approached the lessor for consent to assign (if required)?
- Generally do not act for both buyer and seller in a conveyancing transaction for value.
- Keep your client's affairs confidential.
- Be aware of potential money laundering. Verify your client's identity and do not accept large sums of cash.
- You can normally act for joint sellers or joint buyers.
- You can normally act for buyer and lender provided it is an institutional mortgage on standard terms.
- Be aware of the dangers of cybercrime, for example email hackers.

CHAPTER 4
The Draft Contract

FUNCTIONING LEGAL KNOWLEDGE

This chapter covers the following functioning legal knowledge required to pass the SQE 1 assessments:

Legal formalities required to create and transfer interests and estates in land

Key conditions contained in the:

- **Standard Conditions of Sale**
- Standard Commercial Property Conditions of Sale

Purpose of, and matters covered by, special conditions in the draft contract

Methods of holding adeposit:

- stakeholder
- agent

In a sale of part transaction, the significance of proprietary rights such as **easements** and **covenants**

AUTHORITIES UNDERPINNING PRACTICE

The key authorities that underpin this area of practice are listed below. Note that for legislation you are linked to legislation.gov.uk.

Although much of the legislation on this government website is available in its amended form, the incorporation of new amendments into the text of legislation can be delayed. You should refer to legal databases to ensure you are referencing the most up-to-date legislation.

- Section 2 of the Law of Property (Miscellaneous Provisions) Act 1989
  https://www.legislation.gov.uk/ukpga/1989/34/contents
- Section 62 of the Law of Property Act 1925
  https://www.legislation.gov.uk/ukpga/Geo5/15-16/20/contents
- SRA Code of Conduct for Solicitors
  https://www.sra.org.uk/solicitors/standards-regulations/code-conduct-solicitors/

Pre-exchange					Exchange & pre-completion				Completion & post-completion		
Stage 1 Taking instructions & advising client	**Stage 2** Draft contract	**Stage 3** Pre-contract searches, enquiries & planning	**Stage 4** Title	**Stage 5** Mortgage (applies throughout process)	**Stage 6** Exchange of contracts	**Stage 7** Purchase deed	**Stage 8** Pre-completion searches and requisitions	**Stage 9** Financial statements	**Stage 10** Completion	**Stage 11** SDLT & registration	**Stage 12** Delays and remedies

FIGURE 4.1 Conveyancing timeline

4.1 Introduction

Acting for the seller, you will draft the contract and send it in duplicate to the buyer's practitioner. Before drafting the contract, you should obtain the seller's title **deeds** and, if the **title** is registered, apply for official copies from the **Land Registry**. If the property is leasehold, you will need the original **lease** too. The title to the property should be checked carefully. This is to ensure primarily that the seller's duty of disclosure is satisfied because you have to disclose any **encumbrances** in the contract. In addition, you must also check that the seller actually owns the legal estate and/or is otherwise entitled to sell it. You can also check for any discrepancies on the title plan, for example if any land is missing from it. Investigating your own client's title will enable you to identify any defects in the title and to anticipate (and hopefully remedy) the questions (or requisitions) that the buyer's practitioner is likely to raise. The Law Society's Conveyancing Protocol requires that if there is an error in the title, for example a name change has not been recorded on the register, the seller's solicitor should rectify this rather than wait for the buyer's solicitor to raise it.

4.2 Occupiers and tenancies

Be careful to check with the seller who occupies the property. This is important because to fulfil a contractual obligation to give vacant possession, the seller must be satisfied before contracts are exchanged that all occupiers will vacate the property on or before the contractual **completion date**. In respect of a non-owning spouse, civil partner or other adult occupier, always obtain a written release of any rights in the property together with an agreement to vacate.

CONDUCT POINT

The occupier(s) must be informed that their rights may be affected by giving such consent and that they should obtain independent advice from another practitioner before signing the release.

If the property is to be sold subject to tenancies, full details of these must be disclosed in the contract. Standard Condition (SC) 3.3 deals with leases affecting the property. It says that the seller is obliged to provide full particulars of lettings with copies of any documents relating thereto so as to ensure the buyer enters into the contract 'knowing and fully accepting those terms'. To give effect to this provision, the seller should supply, with the draft contract, a copy of any relevant lease or **tenancy** agreement along with any deeds or documents that are supplementary to them, such as a deed of variation. The seller must inform the buyer of any lease or tenancy termination after exchange but before completion, as well as to act as the buyer reasonably directs, with the buyer indemnifying the seller against any consequent loss or damage. Similarly, the conditions prohibit the seller from agreeing any changes to the lease terms and require the seller to advise the buyer of any proposed or agreed changes. If there are tenants but the property is to be sold with vacant possession, then the seller must take steps to terminate the tenancies and ensure that the tenants vacate.

4.3 Seller's duty of disclosure

The seller is obliged to disclose in the contract all latent encumbrances and defects in title. This duty does not extend to physical defects in the property, to which ***caveat emptor*** ('let the buyer beware') applies. However, wilful concealment of a physical defect may give rise to a claim in the tort of deceit (see *Gordon v Selico Co Ltd* [1986] 1 EGLR 71, which concerned the covering up of dry rot). A breach of the seller's duty of disclosure will normally permit the buyer to rescind the contract and claim damages.

A latent encumbrance is one that is not apparent from an inspection of the property (a restrictive covenant is an example of a latent encumbrance). However, there is some doubt about the precise meaning of 'latent'. In *Yandle and Sons v Sutton* [1922] 2 Ch 199, a right of way across land was held to be a latent encumbrance that the seller should have disclosed. The seller's conveyancer will therefore ensure that all non-physical defects and encumbrances that are known to the seller are disclosed in the contract. This includes matters apparent from an inspection of the title deeds, thus underlining the importance of a full title investigation by the seller's conveyancer.

4.4 Formalities

Section 2 of the Law of Property (Miscellaneous Provisions) Act 1989 lays down the requirements for the creation of land contracts created on or after 27 September 1989. It provides that the contract must be in writing and incorporate all the agreed terms, either in one document or by reference to another document. The written contract must be signed by or on behalf of each party to the contract although, where contracts are to be exchanged, both sides need sign only their respective parts, not both parts. This formality does not apply to auction contracts.

EXAMPLE

Martin and Derek shook hands on a deal for Derek to buy Martin's house for £200,000 and Derek paid Martin £1,000 as a deposit. Section 2 of the Law of Property (Miscellaneous Provisions) Act 1989 applies to a contract for the sale of an interest in land. It states that the contract must be made in writing, incorporate all agreed terms in one document (or in each of two identical documents where contracts are exchanged) and be signed by or on behalf of both parties. So neither the handshake nor the deposit payment is sufficient to create a binding contract between Martin and Derek.

CONDUCT POINT

A **contract race** arises when a seller decides to deal with more than one prospective buyer, thus creating a 'race' by the buyers to see who can secure the property by being first to exchange contracts. A contract race raises an issue of professional conduct for the seller's practitioner. Paragraph 1.2 in the Code of Conduct requires you to refrain from abusing your position by taking unfair advantage of clients or others with whom you deal. Accordingly, if you act for a seller of land, you must inform all buyers immediately of the seller's intention to deal with more than one buyer. Telephone conversations should be confirmed by letter or email. However, in line with your duty of **confidentiality** to the client, the seller's confirmatory instructions should be obtained before such disclosure is made. If the seller refuses to consent to the disclosure, you must immediately cease to act for the seller.

4.5 Contents of the contract

As well as the formal parts, such as names and addresses of the parties, the contract will comprise the particulars of sale and the conditions of sale. The particulars describe the physical extent of the property being sold and its tenure; that is, freehold or leasehold. The property may be described using a simple postal address, provided the land is easily identifiable from it. If not, a more detailed description is necessary, referring to a scale plan and/or measurements. This applies particularly on a sale of part of an existing title where a new description will be required. For **registered land**, the description in the property register of the title can be used and the title number quoted, together with the class of title (absolute, good leasehold, etc). For **unregistered land**, the description in the previous **conveyance** to the seller can usually be used, although its accuracy should always be verified. A misdescription may, of course, entitle the buyer to rescind the contract or seek an abatement in the purchase price.

Due to the complexity of the common law rules concerning land contracts (known as the 'open contract rules'), property lawyers have devised their own standardised general conditions of sale. These are periodically updated, and the current edition is the fifth edition of the Standard Conditions of Sale. There is also a set of conditions for commercial property known as the Standard Commercial Property Conditions (3rd edn) (SCPCs). The general conditions cover a variety of areas, such as time limits for submission and approval of the draft **purchase deed**, proof of title and remedies. The Standard Commercial Property Conditions (3rd edn) are examined in detail at **16.1.1**.

In addition, there are special conditions that are specific to the transaction in question. If the parties agree to delete or modify a general condition, this is done by an appropriate special condition. Some special conditions almost invariably apply in every transaction, and for convenience they are printed on the last page of the Law Society standard form of contract. It should be noted that one of the alternatives in Special Condition 4 must be deleted depending on whether the property is to be sold with vacant possession or subject to tenancies. Special Condition 6 states that neither party can rely on any representation made by the other, unless made in writing by the other or their conveyancer, but this does not exclude liability for fraud or recklessness. This is a sensible provision that effectively prevents reliance on oral statements, which are difficult to prove.

In every transaction the practitioner must consider whether any additional special conditions are necessary, over and above those on the printed form. This is particularly so in sales of part of an existing title, where the parties often agree to create new easements and covenants, the precise terms of which should properly be expressed in the special conditions (see later). The Law Society's Conveyancing Protocol states that additional special conditions should not be added unless it is necessary to accord with current law, or specific and informed instructions have been given by the seller that inclusion of such clauses are necessary and are required for the purposes of the particular transaction.

4.6 Deposit

The deposit, payable on **exchange of contracts**, is normally 10 per cent of the purchase price (although the parties sometimes agree less). The Standard Conditions provide for the deposit to be held as stakeholder except where the seller before completion agrees to buy another property in England or Wales for their residence (ie the seller has a related purchase). In this situation, the seller may use all or any part of the sale deposit as a deposit on the related purchase provided it is used only for this purpose (SC 2.2.5). Effectively, this permits a deposit to be passed along a chain of transactions and assists the operation of a telephonic exchange under Law Society Formula C (see **Chapter 9**).

The buyer should be wary of allowing the deposit to be held as agent for the seller. This would mean that once exchange has taken place the seller's practitioner is free to release the deposit to the seller. But if this release occurs, there is an inherent risk for the buyer if the seller defaults. This is because although the buyer will be legally entitled to the return of the deposit if the seller defaults, the buyer may have practical difficulty in actually recovering the deposit from the seller (eg because the seller is bankrupt or cannot be traced).

EXAMPLE

Claire exchanged contracts to buy Dorita's flat and paid £150,000 as a deposit. The contract stated that the deposit was to be held by Dorita's solicitors 'as agent for the seller'. On exchange, Dorita instructed her solicitors to remit the deposit monies direct to her bank account which they did. Thereafter Dorita failed to complete on the contractual completion date. She has disappeared and is thought to have gone to South America with the deposit monies. Even if Claire can rescind the contract, in practical terms she may have difficulty in recovering the deposit. If the contract had provided for the deposit to be held by Dorita's solicitors 'as stakeholder', it would still be in their stakeholder account.

4.7 Completion

Where your client has a related sale and purchase, you should seek to ensure that the agreed completion dates for both transactions are the same. If synchronisation is not possible, the client must be advised before exchange in writing of the implications, financial or otherwise. By completing the sale first, the client may have to move into temporary accommodation and incur other expenses such as furniture storage fees. By completing the purchase first, the client will almost certainly require a **bridging loan** and the consent of the buyer's **mortgagee**.

If the seller has met all deadlines during the transaction and the buyer fails to pay the balance of the purchase price on the contractual completion date, the buyer will be liable to pay the seller interest on the amount outstanding (see SC 7.2.2 and SCPC 10.3.2). Interest is calculated at the 'contract rate' specified in the contract (normally 4 per cent above the base rate of a high street bank). Care must be exercised where the client has a related sale and purchase. The practitioner should ensure that the contract rate in the purchase contract is no higher than the contract rate in the sale contract. Imagine a situation in which the contract rate on the sale is 4 per cent above base while the contract rate on the purchase is 5 per cent above base. If the client is dependent on the sale proceeds to finance the purchase but the client's buyer completes late, the client will as a consequence be forced to complete the purchase late. The compensation the client has to pay under the purchase contract will be 1 per cent more than the compensation receivable under the sale contract; the client will therefore be out of pocket.

4.8 Title guarantee

The contract should state what title guarantee (if any) the seller is giving to the buyer. The seller must decide whether to give a full title guarantee, a limited title guarantee or no title guarantee at all. The importance of the title guarantee is that covenants for title on the part of the seller are implied into the purchase deed. By definition, a limited guarantee will imply less extensive covenants for title than a full guarantee, and no guarantee will imply none. A full title guarantee is given normally where the seller owns the whole legal and equitable interest in the property. A limited title guarantee is given normally where the legal owner/seller is a **personal representative**, or a trustee holding on trust for others. It is usual to give no title guarantee where the seller has little or no knowledge of the property or the title history, or if the disposition is by way of gift.

4.9 Indemnity covenants

Under privity of contract, an owner of land may continue to be liable under a covenant affecting the land even after the control of the land has passed to someone else, namely the buyer or buyer's successor in title. In this situation, the seller's practitioner must ensure that the buyer gives the seller an **indemnity covenant** against any future breaches of the covenant because the seller could in future be sued for breach of contract. As the property continues to change hands, a chain of indemnity covenants will be built up between successors in title.

Standard Condition 4.6.4 provides that if, after completion, the seller will remain bound by any obligation affecting the property, the buyer will indemnify the seller against any future breach as well as perform the obligation. The indemnity covenant itself is given in the purchase deed. To determine whether your client seller requires an indemnity from the buyer, you need to ask yourself two questions:

- Did your client previously give any new covenants?
- When your client acquired the land, did they give the previous owner an indemnity covenant?

You can discover the answers to these questions as follows. If the land is unregistered, simply read the covenants (if any) given by your client in the most recent conveyance, namely the one to your client. If the land is registered, inspect the **charges** register for details of any covenants given by the proprietor (ie your client) and inspect the Proprietorship Register for evidence of any indemnity covenant given by the proprietor. (If the proprietor is the first **registered proprietor**, it may be necessary to inspect the last pre-registration conveyance, ie the one to the present proprietor.) If the answer to either of the two questions is yes, your client seller will require an indemnity covenant from the current buyer. So when you later approve the draft purchase deed after exchange, you will have to check that the buyer's practitioner has included the indemnity covenant in the draft (see **Chapter 10**).

EXAMPLE

Ted bought a new house five years ago and covenanted with the builder/seller not to add any large extensions to the house without the builder's consent. When Ted sold to Marion last year under SC 4.6.4, he was entitled to an indemnity covenant from Marion to observe and perform the covenant with the builder. When Marion sells to Asif this year under SC 4.6.4, she will likewise be entitled to an indemnity covenant from Asif. This arrangement has created a chain of indemnity covenants.

4.10 Sales of part

The issues we have considered generally in relation to the draft contract apply equally to sales of part. However, sales of part are generally more complex transactions than sales of whole and special considerations apply. First, it will be necessary to draft an entirely new description of the land being sold off, and for this purpose reference to a scaled plan is essential. The plan should be of sufficient size and scale to enable the boundaries to be easily identified. A plan on a scale of 1:1,250 should be adequate in most cases, but a larger scale may be necessary for sales of flats or the division of buildings into separate units. It is customary that the land being sold should be edged red on the plan, while the land being retained by the seller (normally defined in the contract as 'the retained land') should be edged blue. Other features should also be clearly marked so that, for instance, if a right of way is being granted or reserved, the route would be shown by a broken line of a different colour or, if appropriate, by hatching.

On a sale of part the buyer may acquire certain rights over the seller's retained land by virtue of s62 of the Law of Property Act 1925 and the rule in *Wheeldon v Burrows* (1879) 12 Ch D 31. As the nature and extent of these implied rights is not always clear, it is prudent for the seller's practitioner to exclude the effect of the rules and set out expressly the rights and **reservations** required by the parties. If implied rights of light or air were granted to the buyer, this could hinder any future plans of the seller to develop the retained land.

The seller's practitioner should always consider the covenants, if any, that the seller may wish to impose on the buyer, for instance regarding the future use of the land being sold off. The buyer's practitioner in turn must determine whether the seller should enter into any new covenants, for example not to obstruct access to the property being sold or possibly a fencing obligation. Both practitioners should ensure that they discuss with their clients any proposed new covenants and that the covenants are not too onerous on their clients.

If the seller has a **mortgage**, the mortgagee's consent to the sale of part should be obtained as soon as possible. The lender may require all or part of the proceeds of sale to be paid to it before it is willing to release the part being sold from the mortgage. In registered land, the release will be effected by Form DS3, together with a plan showing the extent of the land being released. In unregistered land, the lender will execute a deed of release in respect of the land being released from the mortgage.

The form of purchase deed on a sale of part is Land Registry Form TP1 (see **10.3**). Where the part being sold is a plot on a new building estate, the draft purchase deed will usually be prepared by the seller and attached to the draft contract as part of the seller's standard documentation (see **13.1**).

EXAMPLE

Ayesha acts for the owner of 151 Langley Way, Torquay, registered with title absolute under title number BT12345. Her client is selling part of the garden as a building plot with **planning permission** to a property developer and has given you the following instructions:

- Access to the building plot will be along the client's driveway, which runs along the side of the garden. The client will share the use of the driveway with the buyer.
- The buyer can lay new drains and sewers and connect them into the client's existing drains and sewers ('the existing services'). The existing services in turn connect into the mains drainage and sewage systems in Langley Way.
- Once the buyer's connection is made, the buyer can share the use of the existing services and come on to the seller's retained land to carry out any necessary maintenance or repairs to the services.
- There is a greenhouse on the building plot. Once the sale is legally binding on the buyer, the seller will relocate it in the part of the garden he is keeping.
- The client does not want to be overlooked, so the new building must be no more than one storey high. The seller will also want to see and approve the plans for the new property before it is built.
- The buyer will put up a suitable fence along the boundary between the plot and the land the seller is keeping, and the buyer will maintain the fence.

4.10.1 Recommended clauses for the draft contract above (with commentary)

The following 'new' description of the land being sold is suggested:

> All that freehold land ('the Property') more particularly delineated and shown edged red on the plan annexed ('the Plan') forming part of 151 Langley Way Torquay registered at HM Land Registry with Title Absolute under title number BT12345. The land being retained by the Seller is more particularly delineated and shown edged blue on the Plan ('the Retained Land').

The following special condition is suggested regarding the grant of easements:

> *The* ***Transfer*** *to the Buyer shall contain the following rights in favour of the Buyer and the Buyer's successors in title:*
>
> a) *A free and uninterrupted right of way at all times and for all purposes with or without vehicles over the accessway shown hatched black on the Plan ('the Accessway') leading across the Retained Land subject to the Buyer paying a fair proportion according to user of the cost of maintaining repairing and renewing the Accessway;*
>
> b) *A right to lay maintain and use for all proper purposes connected with the Property a new drain and sewer ('the New Services') under the Retained Land along the route marked with a broken orange line on the Plan;*
>
> c) *A right to connect into the Seller's existing drain and sewer ('the Existing Services') on the Retained Land and to use the Existing Services in common with the Seller subject to the Buyer paying a fair proportion of the cost of maintaining, repairing and renewing the Existing Services and making good any damage caused to the satisfaction of the Seller;*
>
> d) *A right on giving reasonable notice and at reasonable times (except in the case of emergencies) to enter the Retained Land for the purpose of inspecting maintaining and repairing the New Services and the Existing Services, the person exercising such right causing as little damage as possible and making good any such damage caused.*

The seller has been protected by the provision for the buyer to make good any damage caused to the seller's retained land and for repairs to be carried out only upon prior notice, save in the case of an emergency. The route of the new services has also been specified so as to avoid any unnecessary intrusion on to the seller's retained land.

A special condition highlighting the negation of implied grants of easements would also be appropriate and the following clause can be used for this purpose:

> The Transfer to the Buyer shall contain an agreement and declaration that the Buyer shall not by implication or otherwise become entitled to any rights of light or air that would restrict or interfere with the free use of the Retained Land for building or other purposes.

From the instructions, it appears that the only reservation the seller will require is the right to remove the greenhouse. The following special condition would cover the point:

> The Seller reserves the right to remove the greenhouse on the Property provided that the Seller shall exercise this right before completion and shall cause no unnecessary damage to the Property.

The right to remove the greenhouse could be taken care of by mentioning it on the Fixtures, Fittings, and Contents Form.

The seller has imposed some specific conditions and each one will be the subject of a new covenant imposed on the buyer. Although not mentioned in our instructions, it would be prudent in addition to:

- restrict the use of the new property to residential only (this is probably a condition of the planning permission anyway);
- prohibit the buyer from obstructing the driveway; and
- impose a general covenant against causing a nuisance or annoyance to the owners and occupiers of the seller's retained land.

The following special condition is suggested:

> The Buyer shall in the Transfer enter into a covenant with the Seller to the intent that the burden of such covenant shall run with and bind the Property and every part thereof and that the benefit of such covenant shall be annexed to and run with the Retained Land and every part thereof to observe and perform the following:
>
> a) *Not to erect on the Property any building or other structure other than one bungalow and garage for residential use and occupation by one family in accordance with plans previously approved in writing by the Seller or the Seller's successors in title;*
>
> b) *Within three months from the date of completion to erect and forever thereafter maintain a closeboarded fence not less than two metres in height along the boundary between the Retained Land and the Property between the points marked A and B on the Plan;*
>
> c) *Not to park vehicles on or otherwise obstruct or cause or permit to be obstructed the Accessway;*
>
> d) *Not to do or permit to be done on the Property anything that may be or grow to be a nuisance or annoyance to the owners or occupiers of the Retained Land.*

4.11 Option agreements

A typical option agreement is a contract in which the grantee of the option (the buyer) is able, within a fixed period, to serve notice on the owner requiring the latter to transfer the land to the buyer. The option is a particularly useful tool for developers wishing to acquire several pieces of land from different owners in order to develop a larger site. Once the developer has secured options over all the pieces of land, it has effectively gained control of the development site and can safely apply for planning permission. Then, once planning permission is obtained, the developer can exercise all the options to ensure that it owns every part of the proposed development site.

The option agreement should state that, title having been **deduced**, the grantee shall not raise any requisition or objection to it. The agreement should provide for a completion date for the purchase, such as ten working days after service of the buyer's notice exercising the option. The method of service of the notice should also be made clear, for example 'notice in writing served on the grantor on or before . . .'. As with ordinary contracts, the agreement should also provide for the incorporation of general conditions of sale, for example the latest Standard Commercial

Property Conditions. The grantee may require a warranty from the owner that it will not encumber the land without the grantee's consent.

Owners who grant options must, of course, appreciate that the land will be tied up for the length of the option period and any sale of the land by the owner will be subject to the rights under the option (provided the option is registered). Consequently, an option is an **estate contract** and as such the grantee must protect it by registration. This is done either by lodging an agreed or unilateral notice in registered land or, in unregistered land, registering a class C(iv) land charge. Only registration of the option will make it binding on any subsequent purchaser of the land; actual notice of the option by a subsequent purchaser will be irrelevant (*Midland Bank Trust Co Ltd v Green* [1981] AC 513).

EXAMPLE

Fortuna Developments Ltd want to acquire farmland in Wales for development. Three farmers own the extent of the land in question under three separate registered titles. The company will take option agreements from each of the three farmers and protect those options by registering unilateral notices against the registered titles. The company will then apply for planning permission for housing development on the land. Once planning permission has been granted, the company will exercise the options, complete the purchase of the entirety of the land from the three farmers and commence the housing development.

4.12 Conditional contracts

A conditional contract may be proposed (usually by the buyer) where the parties are ready to exchange but an important matter is still outstanding, for example where the buyer is still waiting for a satisfactory local search, mortgage offer or planning permission. If the contract is created conditional upon the buyer's receipt of a satisfactory local search, this is a condition precedent to the performance of the contract. It means there can be no binding contract unless and until the condition is satisfied. Accordingly, a seller would normally be advised to resist such a condition for the obvious reason that it would allow the buyer to walk away from the contract if the condition remained unfulfilled.

Conditional contracts should never be used where either party has a related unconditional sale or purchase. For example, suppose your client is buying and selling, with each transaction being dependent on the other in the normal way. You exchange on the purchase as usual (ie an unconditional contract) and contemporaneously you exchange a conditional contract on the sale (eg subject to the buyer receiving a satisfactory mortgage offer). If the buyer's mortgage offer is not forthcoming, your client will end up with two properties.

Another danger with conditional contracts is that the law in this area is complex and unless great care is taken in drafting the conditions a court may declare the condition void for uncertainty. In *Lee-Parker v Izzett (No 2)* [1972] 1 WLR 775, a contract expressed to be 'subject to the purchaser obtaining a satisfactory mortgage' was held to be void for uncertainty because the condition was too imprecise.

KEY POINT SUMMARY

- Obtain the deeds from the mortgagee or seller. The mortgagee will require your **undertaking** to hold the deeds to order pending redemption.
- If the property has registered title, apply for official copies of title online or on Form OC1 plus copies of other documents referred to on the title (Form OC2).
- **Investigate** the seller's title and, if the title is unregistered, carry out the necessary **land charges searches** against the previous estate owners (unless valid searches are already with the deeds).
- Check that the contract implies that the seller is selling free from incumbrances. It is important to disclose in the draft contract all latent incumbrances and defects in title.

- Obtain details of occupiers of the property. In particular, is there a non-owning spouse or civil partner? The contract will imply that home rights are released. Obtain from the occupiers release of any rights of occupation and an agreement to vacate on completion.
- Check the seller's capacity to sell. What conditions, if any, need to be satisfied before the seller can deal with the property?
- If the Protocol is being used, the contract should be drafted on the Law Society Standard Form of Contract incorporating the current edition of Standard Conditions of Sale.
- Ensure that the contract contains all agreed terms to satisfy s 2 of the Law of Property (Miscellaneous Provisions) Act 1989.
- Check that the description of property is accurate and any plan is to scale.
- Consider special conditions generally.
- Where the sale is dependent on a related purchase, ensure that the terms of the two contracts are consistent and protect your client.
- Will the deposit be held as agent or stakeholder? Under the special conditions, a sale deposit can be utilised towards a related purchase deposit.
- What title guarantee will be given by the seller, if any?
- Check whether the seller will need an indemnity covenant from the buyer.
- The seller must obtain consent of any existing mortgagee. How much money will the mortgagee require on completion?
- Lastly, on a sale of part of the seller's land consider the following:
  - Draft the new accurate description of the part being sold by reference to a scale plan; define the seller's retained land.
  - Draft any new easements and covenants expressly as special conditions (do not rely on special conditions, SCPCs or implied rights under common law or statute).
  - What express easements will the buyer wish to be granted over the land being retained by the seller? (The seller should negate any implied rights in favour of the buyer.)
  - What express easements will the seller wish to reserve over the land being sold to the buyer? (Remember that, unlike for buyers, no implied rights are reserved in favour of the seller.)
- Possible easements to consider:
  - Are there any rights of way? With or without vehicles? At certain times only? Who will be responsible for repairs and maintenance? Specify the route on the contract plan.
  - Is there a right to lay new drains, pipelines, cables? Is there a right to connect into and use existing drains, pipelines, cables? Who will be responsible for repairs and maintenance?
  - Is there a right to enter adjoining land to inspect and repair above? If so, when? Is there any notice to be given? Do you need to make good any damage caused? Specify the route on the contract plan.
  - The seller should negate any implied grant of easements in favour of the buyer.
  - What new covenants do the parties wish to impose?
- Possible covenants to consider:
  - use of the land;
  - restriction on new buildings;
  - avoiding nuisance;
  - maintenance and repair of buildings;
  - restriction against parking on or blocking right of way; and
  - fencing.
- For precedent clauses, see the worked example in this chapter.
- Remember that sale of part contract issues are also relevant on the sale of a new property on a new estate (see **Chapter 13**).

CHAPTER 5
Pre-Contract Searches and Enquiries

FUNCTIONING LEGAL KNOWLEDGE

This chapter covers the following functioning legal knowledge required to pass the SQE 1 assessments:

Pre-contract searches and enquiries:

- range and purpose of making searches and raising enquiries
- who will make the searches and raise enquiries
- results of searches and enquiries

AUTHORITIES UNDERPINNING PRACTICE

The key authorities that underpin this area of practice are listed below. Note that for legislation you are linked to legislation.gov.uk.

Although much of the legislation on this government website is available in its amended form, the incorporation of new amendments into the text of legislation can be delayed. You should refer to legal databases to ensure you are referencing the most up-to-date legislation.

- Section 24 of the Land Charges Act 1969
  https://www.legislation.gov.uk/ukpga/1969/59/section/24
- Localism Act 2011
  https://www.legislation.gov.uk/ukpga/2011/20/contents
- Environmental Protection Act 1990
  https://www.legislation.gov.uk/ukpga/1990/43/contents
- Building Safety Act 2022
  https://www.legislation.gov.uk/ukpga/2022/30/contents

Pre-exchange					Exchange & pre-completion				Completion & post-completion		
Stage 1 Taking instructions & advising client	**Stage 2** Draft contract	**Stage 3** Pre-contract searches, enquiries & planning	**Stage 4** Title	**Stage 5** Mortgage (applies throughout process)	**Stage 6** Exchange of contracts	**Stage 7** Purchase deed	**Stage 8** Pre-completion searches and requisitions	**Stage 9** Financial statements	**Stage 10** Completion	**Stage 11** SDLT & registration	**Stage 12** Delays and remedies

FIGURE 5.1 Conveyancing timeline

5.1 Introduction

The topics covered by this chapter seem to the casual observer to be straightforward. However, as is usually the case with conveyancing, topics that seem simple generally turn out to be quite complex. The main difficulty for you will be the broad variety of problems and issues that solicitors and conveyancers can expect to encounter in their search results and replies to enquiries. This chapter will first look at pre-contract searches and then enquiries. Searches are requests for information about the subject property made by conveyancers that are sent to various agencies that hold that information, like local authorities. Enquiries are, of course, questions about the subject property that are sent to a seller to answer. These are interesting and important subjects within the conveyancing process and cover a lot of topics that can be of considerable consequence to a buyer. So far as enquiries are concerned, they have been greatly affected by changes brought in by the Law Society's Conveyancing Protocol. You should acquaint yourself with the contents of the old-style pre-printed traditional forms of enquiries before contract as well as the newer Property Information Forms introduced by the Protocol. You will also need to be aware of the different enquiries required in commercial transactions. You will need to appreciate how the residential system has been streamlined with the adoption of the Protocol approach. Finally, there is some overlap between enquiries and planning in that there should always be planning enquiries in most transactions. You should be aware of this and be able to demonstrate your knowledge of this possible combination of topics. Basic planning matters are covered in **Chapter 6**. Furthermore, all three items—searches, enquiries and planning—will be important to both sides of property practice, namely commercial and residential.

Finally, there is set out in **Figure 5.2** a decision tree that covers all of the topics considered in this chapter but in diagrammatic format. This should help you to understand the topics from the perspective of an overview and enable you to make selections according to the nature of a particular transaction, be it commercial or residential.

5.2 Pre-contract searches

Caveat emptor ('let the buyer beware') remains a cornerstone of conveyancing in England and Wales. As such, a buyer will need to find out as much as possible about the subject property before contracts are exchanged. This being so, it will inevitably lead to a buyer's practitioner making all appropriate pre-contract searches and detailed pre-contract enquiries. The reason being that failure to make an appropriate search or to raise an apt enquiry could lead to a claim in negligence against the practitioner concerned.

CONDUCT POINT

Failure to carry out the appropriate searches in a property purchase may amount to a breach of the SRA Code of Conduct. You must act in the best interests of each client and you must provide a proper standard of service to your clients.

5.2.1 The National Land Information Service

The modernisation of the process of applying for pre-contract searches has been ushered in with the creation of the National Land Information Service (NLIS). The idea behind the NLIS is to create an environment over the internet that will allow speedy and simple access to a wide range of land and property information, held on the databases of many different public and private sector groups. The aim of the service is that this wide range of data will be available from a single point of enquiry. This is because it brings together in one point of enquiry almost all the different agencies involved in a **conveyance**, such as the local authority, the **Land Registry**, the local water companies, Companies House, the Environment Agency and the Coal Authority. The NLIS is now fully operative (having first gone live in February 2001) in all of England and Wales through NLIS licensed channels, the name for companies providing search facilities via NLIS. Practitioners can set up facilities to carry out searches via these companies. NLIS has processed over 24 million searches and around 290,000 searches are being completed monthly. Eventually the NLIS will use Britain's first comprehensive gazetteer of addressable properties: the National Land and Property Gazetteer (NLPG). All addresses will be given a unique identifier, called a 'Unique Property Reference Number' (UPRN), which will be used to cross-reference data for conveyancing searches.

Q.1 Is the property registered?	
Yes Go to Q.2	No Do a map index search and, if you have title details, a land charges search
Q.2 Is the property in an urban area?	
Yes Go to Q.3	No If it is rural or on the edge of town or a recent development, do a commons registration search question
Q.3 Have you checked the location in the Coal Mining Directory and is it affected?	
Yes Complete a coal mining search	No Go to Q.4
Q.4 Are you buying from a company?	
Yes Complete a company search	No Go to Q.5
Q.5 Have you completed an environmental search?	
Yes Go to Q.6	No Check your client's instructions and always advise that one is necessary
Q.6 Have you completed a local authority search, a water company search?	
Yes Go to Q.7	No Do them now. Both searches should be made in all transactions
Q.7 Have you advised your client to inspect the property prior to exchange?	
Yes Go to Q.8	No This should be done to check the state of the property, whether there are any unlawful occupiers, etc
Q.8 Have you checked for other location-dependent searches?	
Yes Go and do something else	No Complete all other such searches, eg tin mining in Cornwall or brine extraction in Cheshire

FIGURE 5.2 Searches decision tree

Indeed, there is already a section in the latest edition of the **local authority search** form for practitioners to insert the NLPG UPRN to assist in identifying a subject property. The main data providers of interest to conveyancers are now available to practitioners via NLIS as listed below:

- local authority search (LLC1, CON29R, CON29O);
- Land Registry (a wide range of searches are available);
- water utilities (drainage and water CON29DW);
- Coal Authority (mining and brine extraction);
- Environment Agency (flooding);

- Forestry Commission;
- Highways Agency (road building and maintenance);
- electricity (national grid);
- gas (pipelines);
- telecommunications (cabling);
- London Transport (London Underground and Docklands Light Railway);
- Civil Aviation Authority (airports);
- Canal and River Trust (canals);
- Ordnance Survey (maps and plans);
- specialty searches (radon, clay, tin mining, limestone, gypsum, Cheshire brine, Cornish tin, chancel repairs);
- company searches.

At the time of publication, there were five search providers called NLIS channels: 'BigPropertyData', 'IndexPI', 'Legalinx', 'SearchFlow' and 'Thames Water Property Searches'.

5.3 Why do searches?

A seller has a common law duty to disclose latent defects, defects in **title** and land charges affecting the property (s24 Land Charges Act 1969). Technically, **local land charges** also fall within this duty of disclosure. Under the terms of the **Standard Conditions of Sale** (5th edn) a property is sold subject to **encumbrances** specified in the contract, or discoverable by inspection of the property, or that the seller does not reasonably know about as well as entries in public registers (except those at the Land Registry, the Land Charges Registry and Companies House) and public requirements. Many sellers put a special condition in the contract that the subject property is sold subject to all matters that would have been revealed by searches and enquiries that a prudent buyer would make before entering into the contract (subject to the exclusion of monetary **charges** or encumbrances). The effect of this is to allocate to the buyer the responsibility of making all appropriate searches.

Acting for the seller, you should be aware of the dangers of falling foul of the Consumer Protection from Unfair Trading Regulations 2008 (SI 2008/1277) as amended by the Consumer Protection (Amendment) Regulations 2014 (SI 2014/870). The aim of these regulations is to prohibit trading practices that are unfair to consumers and, as such, arguably change the traditional role that *caveat emptor* has played in conveyancing practice. As a consequence, seller's practitioners may need to consider disclosing (with their client's consent) adverse matters affecting the property of which they have knowledge, even physical defects. See the Law Society practice note on consumer protection regulation in conveyancing online.

A seller's duty of disclosure and the documentation arising from that duty will not satisfy a buyer's needs regarding the investigation of the title and other relevant factors about a possible purchase of a property. A buyer needs to know all the matters that affect the property, either positively or negatively, before exchanging contracts for the purchase. Because the buyer needs to be fully aware of all of these matters before committing themselves to a purchase, the buyer must carry out all pre-contract searches.

5.4 The seller's Energy Performance Certificate

A seller must provide an **Energy Performance Certificate** (EPC)/Predicted Energy Assessment (PEA). A seller is required to make reasonable efforts to secure the EPC within 28 days of marketing the property. If there is a pre-existing EPC it will remain valid for ten years. A buyer should always ask to see an EPC to inform their view of how energy efficient the property they are buying might be. A PEA is utilised when the subject property is about to be built and is sold as a newly developed property; see **Chapter 13** on new properties. From 9 January 2013, no EPC will be required when listed properties are sold or rented. (Listing a property highlights a building's special architectural and historic interest. It also brings it under close consideration within the planning system so that some care must be taken when considering possible future alterations or additions to the listed structure.)

5.5 What searches should you do and when?

In the context of pre-contract searches, the first question for a practitioner is: have I completed all the searches I need to for a particular property? **Figure 5.2** should assist.

This approach can apply to both commercial and residential properties. As to when the searches should be completed, the answer is as soon as possible following confirmation that a buyer's offer has been accepted and full details of the property have been provided, including a sample scale plan. In addition to appropriate enquiries of the seller's solicitors and an inspection of the property, the following searches should be considered, all or some of which may be required prior to an **exchange of contracts**:

(a) *Local authority search incorporating a* ***commons registration search***. This search is of such importance that no conveyancing matter, be it commercial or residential, should proceed without one. The search is made in two parts: first, of the local land charges register and, secondly, by submitting a list of standard enquiries of the local authority. A practitioner will need to carefully review both the results of the search on the local land charges register (Form LLC1) and the replies to standard enquiries completed by the local authority (Form CON29). There are two parts to the enquiries; the first part is made up of standard enquiries (CON29) and the second part lists options questions (CON29O).

The search application is, of course, sent to the local authority for the subject property. If it cannot be easily identified by the postal address, then the application needs to include a site plan. The Land Registry is to become the sole registering authority for local land charges (LLC) in England and Wales and the sole provider of official search results. The Infrastructure Act 2015 provides for the transfer of responsibility for LLC from local authorities to the Land Registry. Unofficial searches of the LLC register will continue, as now, to be provided by personal search companies where required. Eventually, it could be that the proposed change leads to the situation where the Land Registry provides search results of the LLC register but replies to CON29 requests will still be dealt with by the local authority, which in effect means that for any conveyancer there will be two search requests as against one currently. The Land Registry says that there are over 20 million records to be put on the LLC database and this will be done by one local authority after another; that is area by area. Presently, rules are being drafted to give effect to the scheme and local authorities should be on the LLC database soon (the City of London Corporation began migrating its data to the central system in December 2017). A search fee will be payable and there is VAT on that fee. Accordingly, the intention is that through the local land charges programme, the Land Registry will deliver a single, digital local land charges register, standardising the cost, speed and format of results. The Registry will do this by centralising and digitising the current local land charges registers of all local authorities in England, held in a range of formats, and replacing them with a single digital register, available online. The Registry is hoping to complete building work on a digital register for local land charges by 2024. However, the Land Registry has acknowledged that migration of data is going slower than expected.

The Law Society launched revised CON29 forms in July 2016. Some new enquiries have been added to the forms, for example concerning the Community Infrastructure Levy and assets of community value as well as a section on public rights of way. Regarding assets of community value, this creation of statute means communities can ask their local council to list certain assets as being of value to the community. If an asset is listed and then comes up for sale, a new right will give communities that want it six months to put together a bid to buy it.

Forms LLC1 and CON29 together are accepted in practice as constituting the local authority search result. With regard to a commons registration search, there is a question in the optional enquiries (question 22) that may be sent to the local authority; this is of particular relevance when buying a new property. This commons registration search now forms part of the local authority search as an additional optional question that can be asked of the local authority in part 2 of the enquiries section. An answer from the council may disclose if the land in question is a village green or a common. If a registration is disclosed, the buyer should be informed. This is because if the land is subject to a commons registration, it could mean that no development or fencing off of the subject property will be possible.

Regarding the first part of the search (Form LLC1), the burdens in the register are set out in the search in 12 parts of the register. They are:

1 General financial charges.
2 Specific financial charges.
3 Planning charges.
4 Miscellaneous charges.
5 Fenland ways maintenance charges.
6 Land compensation charges.
7 New towns charges.
8 Civil aviation charges.
9 Open-cast coal mining charges.
10 Listed buildings charges.
11 Light obstruction notices.
12 Drainage scheme charges.

The list highlights the kind of information that will be disclosed in the search result. This includes various financial charges that will affect the property, planning consents concerning the property and compulsory purchase orders, as well as tree preservation orders. Additionally, other registrations of consequence will be revealed, such as whether or not the property is within a conservation area or smoke control zone. In the case of this last kind of restriction, the client will need to be advised of the restrictive nature of the registration and how it might affect the property and its neighbourhood. Any entry disclosure should be carefully considered and where necessary disclosed to the client and any **mortgagee** that might be affected by the entry. Once the search result is issued, it should be appreciated that there is no **priority period** for the result, or indeed any other form of protection given by the search. (This means that changes to the results could be made the day after the result was issued and there would be no protection from this for the buyer.)

In relation to the second part of the search, Form CON29 should always accompany the local land charge search request. The questions in themselves are straightforward. They cover topics including how the property may be affected by planning and **building regulations**, nearby road schemes, railway schemes and traffic schemes. It will also disclose any notices affecting the subject property, if it is in a conservation area, subject to a compulsory purchase order and whether it might be affected by contaminated land or radon gas. There are also questions on drainage schemes (sustainable urban drainage schemes, or SuDS). These systems are a natural approach to managing drainage in and around properties and other developments. SuDS work by slowing and holding back the water that runs off from a site, allowing natural processes to break down pollutants.

CON29O covers optional enquiries that include questions about public paths, houses in multiple occupation, noise abatement, hedgerow notices and, as mentioned previously, commons registration. Each question must be selected for an answer so far as the question or questions relate to the subject property. In the main, all that is sent to the applicant by the local authority is a rather confusing list of 'Yes' and 'No' answers adjacent to the number of the question concerned. This therefore means that practitioners must either memorise the questions or, more practically, have a reminder list to hand when looking at the usually dislocated answers. Caution should be exercised, as familiarity with the form may induce a cursory look at the answers that might result in an important answer being overlooked. Answers in the positive must always be investigated.

It is possible to make a personal search of the register called a 'regulated search'. These searches are normally more expensive and are carried out by experts who work for professional search companies. They may request further information, or recommend that it be sought; to be sure that the property being acquired is not affected by anything adverse. Regulated searches also have insurance policies attached to them. If you are not happy with the company, and your complaint is not dealt with satisfactorily, you can make an independent complaint to the Property Ombudsman. Professional search companies also ensure that searches are as useful as possible by standardising the search results and summarising the most pertinent information required by practitioners, so there is less chance that important information may be overlooked. The standard non-personal search used by most conveyancing practitioners is known as a 'council search' and is carried out by staff employed by the local authority.

EXAMPLE

Ari acts for Joshua who is buying a house served by an unmade road and there is a private road sign at the entrance to the road. Ari should check the following matters. The unmade road appears to be privately owned in which case it is not adopted and maintained by the local authority but Ari's enquiries of the local authority will confirm if this is the case. He needs to ensure that Joshua has an adequate right of way (ie an **easement**) to use the road, both on foot and with vehicles. Ari can check the official copies of the title (assuming it is registered) and make enquiries of the seller's conveyancer regarding use. He will also need to check any associated maintenance obligations and costs by making enquiries of the seller.

After completion, Joshua wants to cut down a large copper beech tree in the middle of the garden to allow more light to the house. The **land charges search** will confirm whether the tree is subject to a tree preservation order (TPO). If a TPO is in place then it would be a criminal offence to lop or fell the tree without the consent of the local authority.

(b) *Water company search and enquiries*. This provides details about water and drainage services to the subject property. It is completed on Form CON29 (DW) and it covers details on water supply, metering and the proximity of a public sewer. Once again, this will be of relevance to all types of conveyancing cases. Commercial property searches should be carried out on the specific commercial Form CON29 (DW). It is an important search as it will reveal matters such as whether there is a public sewer within the boundaries of the property or whether the property has foul drainage and surface water drainage to the public sewer. The search answers could disclose possible future financial liabilities for the owner of the subject property and therefore full details for the search result should be explained to the buyer/client.

(c) *Coal mining search*. This affects all types of conveyancing cases when they are located in an area currently or previously affected by coal mining. The subject property might be a victim of subsidence or could be a potential victim. A buyer needs to know this before deciding on the merits of the proposed purchase. You can check if there is a need to complete this search by using the postcode search facility available at the Coal Authority's website. In May 2018, the Law Society published best practice guidance on coal mining searches which lists the affected areas of England and Wales. The search is submitted either to the Coal Authority or, alternatively, the Law Society in 2018 licensed a non-public body, Terrafirma, as a CON29M report producer. Terrafirma satisfies all Law Society best practice guidance and provides expert interpretation and improved risk screening. It claims that 95 per cent of its reports will be delivered within 24 hours and its report automatically includes additional data and interpretation at no extra cost.

(d) ***Index map*** *search*. This search must be carried out when buying **unregistered land** to check that the land has not been registered. It goes to the Land Registry and is used particularly to see if the title to the subject property is partially or completely registered and, if so, what tenures are registered. It is made on Land Registry Form SIM and a fee may be payable. A plan to scale should be supplied by you to the Registry. The Land Registry has launched a free MapSearch service, a searchable online version of the index map. It allows applicants to locate any registered property in England and Wales without having to apply to the Registry for the information. (It should be noted that this search is not covered by the Land Registry indemnity scheme. If this cover is required then a SIM search is necessary.)

(e) *Land charges search*. This is of use in unregistered land only when you have seen all the title before exchange and you are taking the prudent step of checking for undisclosed encumbrances at an early stage in the transaction. The search is against the names of title owners and will give details of all land charges affecting the title and registered against current and previous **estate** owners from 1926 onwards. Accordingly, restrictive **covenants**, easements and options affecting the subject property can all be revealed by this search result. More detailed information regarding this search can be found in **Chapter 10**.

(f) *Company search*. This search is relevant if you are buying from a company. It is particularly important when buying an unregistered title and where you want to make sure that the company is properly registered at Companies House and is not subject to any winding-up or liquidation proceedings. The search will also reveal any fixed or floating charges entered into by the company. As company charges need only be registered within 21 days of creation, you should note that a search may not disclose a very recently created charge. The search is made either in person or through an agent by attendance at the Companies Registration office or online. A company search will also be required where the property is leasehold and there is a management company involved in the leasehold relationship.

(g) Other searches, dependent upon the location of the property. See the discussion on extra searches at **5.5.1**.

(h) *Physical search or inspection of the property.* This is to check the condition of the property just before exchange and to make sure that any contents or fixtures and fittings mentioned in the contract are where they should be at the time the contract becomes binding. Accordingly, when considering searches it is always appropriate for domestic conveyancing, and probably for many types of commercial conveyancing matters, to advise the buyer to inspect the subject property prior to exchange. In detail, the reasons for the inspection are fivefold and are to check:

- the state and condition of the property;
- who is in actual occupation of the property;
- the boundaries;
- any rights and easements affecting or benefiting the property; and
- that the fixtures and fittings contracted to be sold are in the subject property just prior to exchange.

(i) *Environmental searches (including flooding).* The need for this search has arisen out of recent legislation making landowners responsible for contamination remediation of land that they own. An environmental search result should reveal if the subject property is affected by contamination whether directly or indirectly. Failure to discover contamination could lead to liability under the Environmental Protection Act 1990 and this liability can rest with the current owner. Similarly, the recent increase in the frequency of the flooding of property has affected the insurability of some premises located near to or adjacent to sources of flooding. Accordingly, in every transaction a conveyancer must consider whether contamination or flooding might be a relevant issue. Searches and enquiries should be made about these environmental concerns in all transactions, both domestic and commercial, hence the need for environmental searches, including enquiries about flooding. There are several commercial organisations prepared to provide environmental search results for properties in England and Wales. The Law Society has produced a practice note to help solicitors protect clients from flood risk.

The Environment Agency has made maps available on the internet that show areas potentially liable to flooding. This is a free service and can be accessed using a property postcode. The government has been working with insurers to construct a scheme to help homeowners of properties which are uninsurable because of a substantial flooding risk. Flood Re is a not-for-profit flood re-insurance scheme run by the insurance industry. The scheme offers assistance to those at high risk of flooding. When the insurer identifies the property as high risk, it will cede that part of the policy to Flood Re. In the event of a flood claim, the insurers pay the customer and recoup the cost from Flood Re. Homes built after 1 January 2009 will not be covered. Commercial properties, including commercial leasehold properties, will not be included. Leasehold blocks with three residential units or fewer are eligible for Flood Re, providing the freeholder responsible for purchasing the buildings insurance lives in the block and the building meets the other required eligibility criteria.

(j) *Chancel repairs liability search.* A chancel is the part of a church containing the altar and is usually separated from the nave by a screen. The subject property may be in a parish with a medieval church and, if so, there can be a liability to contribute to the cost of repairs to the chancel of that church (see *PCC of Aston Cantlow v Wallbank* [2003] UKHL 37 in [2003] 7 PLC 47). The Land Registration Act 2002 took away from chancel repairs the status of an **overriding interest** (by abolishing s 70(1)(c) LPA 1925). As a transitional provision, the Land Registration Act 2002 (Transitional Provisions) (No 2) Order 2003 (SI 2003/2431) extends the overriding status for a transitional period of ten years. Since 13 October 2013, chancel repairs have had to be protected by an entry on the register. Potential liability will continue to remain until the subject property is sold. If there is no protective entry then the property will be sold free of this liability. To see if there is any such liability a buyer can, through a commercial search provider, obtain a report that establishes if a property is located within the boundary of a 'risk parish' that could charge for chancel repairs. 'Chancelcheck' is available at http://www.clsl.co.uk. Where potential risk is identified, the same company offers indemnity insurance.

5.5.1 Extra pre-contract searches

In addition, you should also appreciate that other searches may be necessary and you can only decide what others are required by looking closely at the address and location of the subject property. England and Wales can be viewed as a patchwork of exclusive localities. Consequently, each exclusive locality can have a speciality, a peculiarity, all to itself. This being so, searches can be specialised or localised depending on the location of the subject property. An examiner could quite easily place a subject property in the Greater Manchester area and ask about pre-contract searches. In doing so, you would be expected to know that coal mining and brine extraction might affect the property and, consequently, searches would be required to address these potential concerns. Examples of some of these less common localised searches are:

1. *Limestone mining searches.* If the property is located in Dudley, Sandwell, Walsall or Wolverhampton, a search should be sent to the local council asking about limestone mining. The result will reveal the presence, or indeed absence, of disused underground workings that could cause subsidence.
2. *Clay mining searches.* If the property is located in Devon or Cornwall, a search should be sent to English China Clay Company asking about clay mining. The result will reveal the presence or absence of any operations that could cause subsidence.
3. *Brine extraction searches.* If the property is located in Cheshire or Greater Manchester, a search should be sent to Groundsure requesting a Cheshire Salt Search report. This report will reveal any brine-extraction works in the locality and the presence or absence of old workings that could cause subsidence.
4. *Tin mining searches.* If the property is located in Devon or Cornwall, a search should be sent to Cornwall Consultants Limited asking about tin mining. The search result will reveal the presence or absence of disused mines that could cause subsidence. (In fact, a search will disclose if there has been tin, copper, lead, silver or iron mining that might affect the subject property.)

5.6 Pre-contract enquiries

This topic covers questions asked by the buyer to the seller to find out as much as possible about the subject property. It will span questions raised in Protocol cases, as well as those where traditional conveyancing procedures are used. In Protocol cases, this involves Property Information Forms, and in traditional cases the forms are called 'enquiries before contract'. Consideration is then given to specific enquiries that are preferred for commercial transactions, namely the Commercial Property Standard Enquiries.

5.7 Why raise pre-contract enquiries?

The buyer must carry out all appropriate enquiries before entering into a binding contract to purchase the subject property. If a buyer makes all necessary enquiries of the seller, and gets sensible answers, an informed decision can then be taken about the nature and suitability of the property based on all the information obtained prior to exchange. So a buyer will need to find out as much as possible about the subject property before contracts are exchanged. The simple yet compelling reason for this is that the buyer must take the property in whatever condition it is in, at the point when there is a binding contract for the purchase. Consequently, the law imposes a clear obligation upon the buyer to find out as much about the property as possible because the common law recognises that the seller has only a limited duty of disclosure.

CONDUCT POINT

Failure to carry out appropriate enquiries in a property purchase may amount to a breach of the SRA Code of Conduct. You must act in the best interests of each client and you must provide a proper standard of service to your clients.

5.8 What enquiries should you raise and when?

Pre-contract enquiries, otherwise called **preliminary enquiries**, can, in domestic transactions, take two different forms. The first type is the orthodox traditional form in the style of a list of far-reaching questions aimed at the seller and intended to seek out as much detail as possible via the seller's solicitor. In commercial transactions, traditional lists of questions are always used, as specific questions are always required for non-domestic transactions, because commercial properties will usually be more complicated than a house or flat and, in many cases, will involve leaseholds that require particular enquiries about the nature of the **tenancy**.

The second more modern style of form emanates from changes made by the Law Society. Preliminary enquiries have been greatly affected by procedural changes brought in by the Law Society's Conveyancing Protocol. It can be useful to acquaint yourself with the contents of the old-style printed traditional forms of enquiries before contract, as well as with the new Protocol Property Information Forms. By doing this, you will come to appreciate the ways in which the forms differ and how the conveyancing process has been, to a limited extent, streamlined with the adoption of the Protocol approach.

The old-style preliminary enquiry forms have been replaced by client questionnaires that form an integral part of the Protocol. The latest edition of the Protocol brought with it a revision of these questionnaires. The forms are listed here with their form reference number:

- TA6 Property information form;
- TA7 Leasehold information form;
- TA8 New home information form;
- TA9 Commonhold information form;
- TA10 Fittings and contents form;
- TA13 Completion information and **requisitions on title**

Some specimen versions of these forms are available to download on the Law Society website.

Many conveyancing practitioners have adopted the Protocol 'enquiry' forms even when they are not actually using the full Protocol process. They will also use the Protocol forms specifically dedicated to leaseholds. However, others remain traditionally minded and use pre-printed forms or their own in-house preliminary enquiry forms. These questions, sometimes actually entitled preliminary enquiries and sometimes enquiries before contract, are listed in duplicate and submitted to the seller. (Two copies are issued as a convenient and helpful practice, enabling the seller's practitioner to retain a copy of the questions with replies as a file copy.) Whatever form is used, the intention remains the same: to seek out answers from the seller about any matters that affect or could affect the subject property.

Of the Protocol forms listed, the two likely to be used the most are TA6 and TA7. TA6 is a single set of questions required in almost all transactions, while TA7 will be used with TA6 but TA7 is meant to cover leasehold information. When using Protocol forms, there still remains the difficulty of reconciling the professional obligation on the buyer's conveyancing practitioner to make all proper and reasonable enquiries on behalf of their client with the aim of the Protocol, that of streamlining the enquiry process. The difference between this aspect of the Protocol procedures and the buyer's conveyancing practitioner's overriding duty to the client now appears to be very slender. It seems inevitable that either the printed Protocol forms will continue to expand or they will be accompanied by copious extra enquiries raised by anxious or perhaps prudent conveyancing practitioners. It is only natural for them to incline towards more rather than fewer questions. This is, of course, in the perhaps vain hope that, notwithstanding the Property Information Forms, by asking as many questions as possible, practitioners might be able to avoid negligence claims by dissatisfied clients. Form TA7 includes a section on building safety to assist transactions affected by the Building Safety Act 2022, including questions about remediation work, known defects that create a building safety risk, building ownership and management and details of the seller if it is a company.

It is clear that when a conveyancer is involved in the buying or selling of tenanted properties, the heavier burden rests with the buyer's practitioner. This is because the buyer will want to have full details of the title approved, as well as details of the tenancy or tenancies affecting the subject property. A buyer will expect a good and marketable title to the subject property, as well as a letting that is upon terms that the buyer deems acceptable. This will, of course, centre on the rental due, but will also cover other terms of the tenancy or letting. Therefore, this form of conveyancing transaction in particular requires extra care when raising preliminary enquiries. This is also the case when looking at the title and when raising requisitions.

In summary, the following matters should always form the subject of preliminary enquiries:

- *Disputes.* No buyer would willingly buy a property that is subject to an ongoing dispute. Furthermore, it is incumbent upon a seller to advise a buyer of any dispute, particularly one that involves a neighbour.
- *Notices.* A buyer will want to know about notices served upon the seller from, say, the local authority or central government of the landlord of the subject premises.
- *Boundaries and fences.* Where adjoining properties meet should be clearly delineated, to avoid subsequent disputes. It should be remembered that the Land Registry title plan only shows general boundaries not the exact line of boundaries.
- *Services and conducting media.* Does the property have the benefit of all the main services such as gas and electricity? Is there main drainage or does the property have a private drainage arrangement?
- *Exclusive facilities.*
- *Shared facilities.*
- *Occupiers.* This might cover tenants as well as licensees.
- *Use and planning.* Has there been a permitted change of use or are there any planning issues affecting the subject property?
- ***Service charges.*** This can cover both leaseholds and **freeholds** paying an estate rentcharge and will therefore cover both commercial and residential properties.
- *Insurance arrangements.* It is always important to check on insurance arrangements especially if the property is leasehold.
- *Covenants.* On the title and possibly in a **lease**.
- *Flooding and general environmental concerns.*

There will be a need for additional core topics for leasehold matters. For example, it is a great help for the buyer and the buyer's conveyancer if the seller can accurately confirm the names and addresses of the **lessor**, any superior lessor, the superior lessor's managing agent, if any, and the superior lessor's solicitors. If there is a management company mentioned in any of the leases of the subject property, full details of the management company, its officers, agents and solicitors should be requested. Finally, with leasehold properties full details of insurance arrangements will be necessary, along with similar details for service charges.

The Localism Act 2011 provides for a scheme called 'assets of community value'. It requires a local council to maintain a list of 'community assets'. Nominations for community assets can be made by parish councils or by groups with a connection with the community. Individuals cannot nominate community assets. If the nomination is accepted, the group will be given time to come up with a bid for the asset when it is sold. It would therefore seem prudent to make enquiries about whether this might apply to your subject property.

The Law Society has issued a conveyancing form called LPE1. It is intended to be used for collecting information about a subject property where that information is held by landlords, management companies and managing agents. The information that the form will gather will normally be about ground rent, insurance and service charges. The sections within the form cover contact details, **transfer** and registration details, ground rent service charge and insurance information, and lists required documents such as service charge accounts for the last three years. This form should be used when a lessor or management company must be contacted to obtain information from them about a leasehold property that is in the process of being sold.

Form LPE1 includes questions aimed to reduce the need for additional enquiries, for example with regard to any transfer fees payable on sale. It also asks whether any documents have been served in relation to the sale of the property or remedial works and if there is any outstanding enforcement action. A buyer's leasehold information summary form (LPE2) has also been introduced. It seeks to inform the buyer of the buyer's key financial responsibilities such as ground rent, service charges, insurance premiums and possible future costs arising out of these.

EXAMPLE

Jeremiah acts for Robin and Alfred who are in the process of buying together a detached house known as Haven Lodge situated on the edge of a village in Derbyshire. His clients have raised several questions:

1. Who owns the field behind the house and is the field likely to be built on?
2. Robin has been told there used to be a coal mine in the area and is worried about possible mine shafts located nearby.
3. Is the seller leaving white goods, carpets, curtains and the garden shed?
4. How old is the central heating boiler and is it in good condition?

Regarding the field behind the house, Jeremiah can carry out a search of the index map (SIM) to find out if the land is registered or unregistered. If registered, the title number will enable him to apply for official copies. Otherwise his enquiries of the seller might reveal who the owner is. He can also carry out a commons registration search as an additional enquiry of the local authority to discover if the land in question is registered as common land. He will carry out a local authority search and enquiries against Haven Lodge but this will not necessarily reveal plans for neighbouring land and the search result is only valid as at the date of issue. Jeremiah could advise Robin and Alfred to speak to the local planning office about this.

Regarding the mining question, as the property is in Derbyshire you will as a matter of course carry out a coal mining search which will reveal details of any past mining in the area and any subsidence claims.

The fittings and contents form (TA10) will specify which fittings and contents are included, excluded or offered for sale. The property information form (TA6) includes questions about the central heating system (eg type, dates of installation and last service, whether in good working order, copies of any guarantees, CORGI completion certificate, service reports).

5.9 Commercial property enquiries

The Commercial Property Standard Enquiries (CPSEs) is a set of documents that have been drafted by members of the London Property Support Lawyers Group under the sponsorship of the British Property Federation (BPF). Contributions were also made by a number of other firms and individuals. The CPSEs are endorsed by the BPF and it is anticipated that they might become industry standard pre-contract enquiries for commercial property conveyancing. Form CPSE.1 is designed to cover all commercial property transactions and will (together with any additional enquiries relevant to the particular transaction) be sufficient if the transaction deals only with a freehold sold with vacant possession. Form CPSE.1 was updated in February 2014 to include enquiries relating to concealment of planning breaches, assets of community value and the Community Infrastructure Levy and was again subject to minor revisions in 2015 and 2016. The supplemental enquiries forms listed here are intended to be used in conjunction with CPSE.1. Which particular additional form or forms will be required will depend upon the individual circumstances of each transaction. The following supplemental forms are available:

- CPSE.2: where the property is sold subject to existing tenancies.
- CPSE.3: where a lease of a property is being granted.
- CPSE.4: where the property being sold is leasehold.
- CPSE.5: enquiries before surrender of a rack rent **commercial lease**.
- CPSE.6 and CRC enquiries. These new enquiries are necessary to deal with issues arising under the Carbon Reduction Commitment Energy Efficiency Scheme 2010 (CRC). CPSE.6 can be utilised when a commercial property is subject to a residential tenancy.

- The enquiries themselves are in the main quite lengthy. To address this potential difficulty CPSE.7 (version 1.0) general short-form pre-contract enquiries for all property transactions were issued in July 2015 and are a reduced set of enquiries that can be selected in place of the longer set comprising CPSE.1.

The enquiries set out in CPSE.1 cover the following topics, all of which will normally be of concern when buying a commercial property and can therefore be used whether the property is subject to a letting or not:

1. Boundaries and extent.
2. Party walls.
3. Rights benefiting the property.
4. Adverse rights affecting the property.
5. Title policies.
6. Access to neighbouring land.
7. Access to and from the property.
8. Physical condition.
9. Contents.
10. Utilities and services.
11. Fire safety and means of escape.
12. Planning and building regulations.
13. Statutory agreements and infrastructure.
14. Statutory and other requirements.
15. Environmental.
16. Occupiers and employees.
17. Insurance.
18. Rates and other outgoings.
19. Notices.
20. Disputes.
21. Community Infrastructure Levy (CIL).
22. Commonhold.
23. **Stamp duty land tax** (SDLT) on **assignment** of a lease.
24. Deferred payment of SDLT.
25. Value added tax (VAT) registration information.
26. Transfer of a business as a going concern (TOGC).
27. Other VAT treatment.
28. Standard-rated supplies.
29. Exempt supplies.
30. Zero-rated supplies.
31. Transactions outside the scope of VAT (other than TOGCs).
32. Capital allowances.

Finally, as a general word of warning, the seller and the seller's solicitor should be aware of the risks of qualifying a reply to an enquiry with words like 'not so far as the seller is aware' or 'not to our knowledge but no warranty can be given'. These and similar phrases are treated by the courts as an implied representation that the seller and the seller's solicitors have no actual knowledge of a matter and that they have made all the investigations that a prudent conveyancer would be expected to have made (*William Sindall plc v Cambridgeshire County Council* [1994] 1 WLR 1016). Clearly, an answer of this type is intended to avoid making the effort to research the true answer. The decision makes it clear that the answer will infer that the work was done, even if in reality it was not.

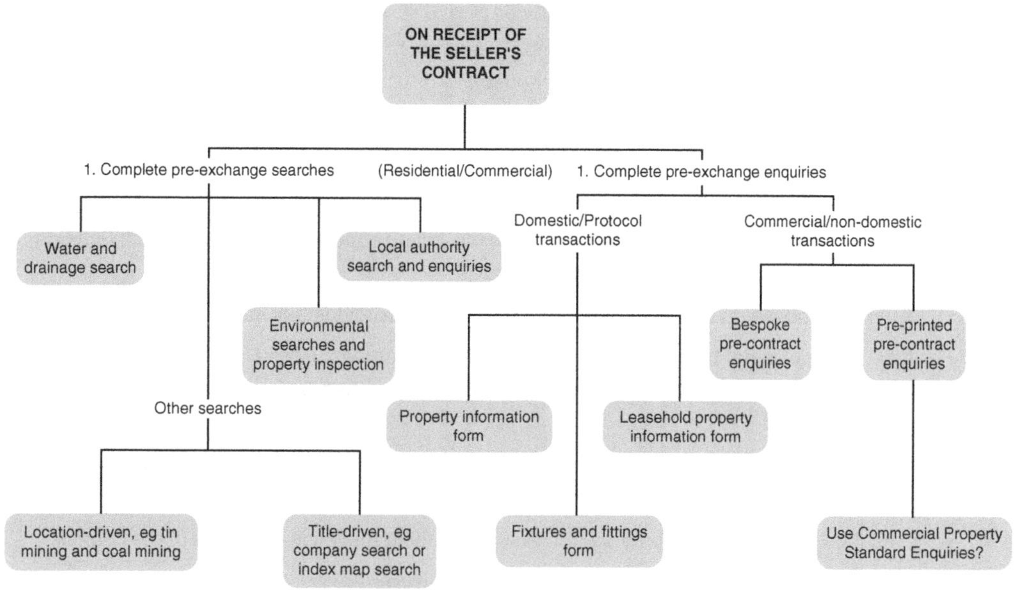

FIGURE 5.3 Pre-contract searches and enquiries

5.10 A pre-contract decision tree

See **Figure 5.3** for the different branch decisions and selections you need to make for pre-contract searches and enquiries. There are two clear strands to the diagram and each represents the approach you will need to consider for each part covered by this chapter. The decision tree can apply equally to commercial as well as domestic property transactions.

KEY POINT SUMMARY

- Unless otherwise agreed in writing, the conveyancer acting for the buyer should always make a local search and a water search.
- Reflect on the location of the subject property to enable you to decide which other searches are relevant to this particular property.
- Location is also crucial when considering the necessity for a coal mining search and other unusual searches.
- On receipt of the local authority search, always check the result. Read the land charges disclosed in the result and then check all answers provided by the local authority.
- Always advise clients of any onerous or unusual replies or results to any of the searches and request their written instructions in response.
- Consider an environmental search and make such a search in all cases both residential and commercial. On receipt of the result, always check to see if the subject property might be affected by flooding and, if it is, report the findings to the client and check the position regarding the availability of insurance.
- Consider the need for a chancel repairs liability search.
- Is the property rural or urban, and is a plan required?
- If not sure, or newly built, do a commons registration search.
- If rural, or on the edge of a town or village, do a commons registration search.
- Check to see if the property is in an area of current or previous coal mining and do a coal mining search if necessary.

- Is the seller a company? If so, do a company search, possibly online at https://www.gov.uk/government/organisations/companies-house.
- If the property has an unregistered title, carry out an index map search and a land charges search.
- Has the property been physically inspected and, if so, with what result?
- Are any minor searches required, for example for a property in Cornwall, a clay-mining search?
- Is the Protocol being adopted; and if it is, will the seller provide any searches?
- If the Protocol is not being used, buyer must do all searches. If the Protocol is being used, buyer must do all necessary searches, having ascertained a response to the previous checklist item.
- When issuing a local authority search request, decide on which extra pre-printed questions should be asked in Part II of the form.
- In relation to the local authority search result, including replies to enquiries of the council:
  - check all local land charges disclosed and always advise clients of any onerous or unusual replies or results, and request the clients' written instructions in response;
  - check all replies to enquiries and always advise clients of any onerous or unusual replies or results, and request the clients' written instructions in response;
  - always make a file note of the date of dispatch of the searches made on a specific property file and do not exchange contracts until all search results are in and approved, and the client has seen and approved full details.
- Is the Protocol being adopted, and if it is, has the seller provided a full set of completed Protocol-style enquiry forms?
- If the Protocol is being adopted and if the seller has provided a set of completed Protocol-style enquiry forms, are there any specific additional enquiries you need to raise?
- If the Protocol is not being utilised, which forms are you using; or should you use Protocol or not, pre-printed or not, core and/or additional?
- If the Protocol is not being utilised, what extra questions need to be asked that are specific to the subject property?
- What specific enquiries should you raise consequent on any particular instructions you may have received from the client?
- Consider the need for a specific enquiry about flooding.
- Always advise your client of any onerous or unusual replies or results to any of the preliminary enquiries, and request written instructions in response.
- Always make a file note of the date of dispatch of the enquiries made on a specific property file, and do not exchange contracts until all enquiries have been answered satisfactorily and the client has seen and approved full details.
- If the transaction involves commercial property, consider using the Commercial Property Standard Enquiries (CPSE).
  - Which forms should you use—Protocol or not, pre-printed or not, core and/or additional?
  - What extra questions need to be asked that are specific to the subject property?
  - Always advise your client of any onerous or unusual replies to any of the preliminary enquiries and request written instructions in response.
  - Acting for seller, remember the effect of the decision in *William Sindall plc v Cambridgeshire County Council* [1994] 1 WLR 1016 and never give vague, evasive or generalised-type answers.

CHAPTER 6
Planning Law

FUNCTIONING LEGAL KNOWLEDGE

This chapter covers the following functioning legal knowledge required to pass the SQE 1 assessments:

Planning law:

- statutory definition of 'development'
- matters that do not constitute 'development'
- matters that do not require express **planning permission**
- building regulations control
- enforcement: time limits and the range of local planning authority's enforcement powers

AUTHORITIES UNDERPINNING PRACTICE

The key authorities that underpin this area of practice are listed below. Note that for legislation you are linked to legislation.gov.uk.

Although much of the legislation on this government website is available in its amended form, the incorporation of new amendments into the text of legislation can be delayed. You should refer to legal databases to ensure you are referencing the most up-to-date legislation.

- Sections 55, 57, 174 and 183 of the Town and Country Planning Act 1990
  https://www.legislation.gov.uk/ukpga/1990/8/contents
- Town and Country Planning (Use Classes) Order 1987
  https://www.legislation.gov.uk/uksi/1987/764/contents/made
- Town and Country Planning (Use Classes) (Amendment) (England) Order 2005
  https://www.legislation.gov.uk/uksi/2005/84/contents/made
- Town and Country Planning (Use Classes) (Amendment) (England) Order 2013
  https://www.legislation.gov.uk/uksi/2013/1101/made
- Town and Country Planning (Use Classes) (Amendment) (England) Order 2015
  https://www.legislation.gov.uk/uksi/2015/597/contents/made
- Town and Country Planning (General Permitted Development) Order 1995
  https://www.legislation.gov.uk/uksi/1995/418/contents
- Town and Country Planning (General Permitted Development) (Amendment) (No 2) (England) Order 2008
  https://www.legislation.gov.uk/uksi/2008/2362/contents/made
- Energy Performance of Buildings (Certificates and Inspections) (England and Wales) Regulations 2007
  https://www.legislation.gov.uk/uksi/2007/991/contents
- Community Infrastructure Levy Regulations 2010
  https://www.legislation.gov.uk/uksi/2010/948/contents/made
- Section 36(6) of the Building Act 1984
  https://www.legislation.gov.uk/ukpga/1984/55/contents

- Building (Amendment) Regulations 2002
  https://www.legislation.gov.uk/uksi/2002/440/contents/made
- Localism Act 2011
  https://www.legislation.gov.uk/ukpga/2011/20/contents
- Town and Country Planning (General Permitted Development) (England) (Amendment) Order 2021
  https://www.legislation.gov.uk/uksi/2021/428/contents/made

Pre-exchange					Exchange & pre-completion				Completion & post-completion		
Stage 1	**Stage 2**	**Stage 3**	**Stage 4**	**Stage 5**	**Stage 6**	**Stage 7**	**Stage 8**	**Stage 9**	**Stage 10**	**Stage 11**	**Stage 12**
Taking instructions & advising client	Draft contract	Pre-contract searches, enquiries & planning	Title	Mortgage (applies throughout process)	Exchange of contracts	Purchase deed	Pre-completion searches and requisitions	Financial statements	Completion	SDLT & registration	Delays and remedies

FIGURE 6.1 Conveyancing timeline

6.1 Introduction

Town and country planning legislation seeks to control the development of land and buildings (see s57(1) Town and Country Planning Act 1990). In particular, this section stipulates that 'planning permission is required for the carrying out of any development of land'.

Development is defined by s55 of the 1990 Act as being of two kinds:

1 'the carrying out of building, engineering, mining or other operations in, on, over or under land'; and

2 'the making of any material change in the use of any buildings or other land'.

Types of use for planning purposes are defined within the Town and Country Planning (Use Classes) Order 1987 (SI 1987/764), as amended, which lists 16 separate classes, and these are considered at **6.3**. (There are in fact additional use classes, with others having been introduced after 1987.) Therefore, there are two main elements of town and country planning: first, the obtaining of planning permission for new developments and, secondly, the change of use of existing properties. Both of these will be considered in **6.2**.

6.1.1 Development under the Town and Country Planning (General Permitted Development) Order 1995 (SI 1995/418 as amended)

This Order grants extensive permission for certain kinds of specific development of a somewhat limited nature. Examples include the erection of fences. This is a development that will not (subject to height restrictions) require express planning consent. Similarly, the exterior painting of a property is covered by the Order, subject to the painting not amounting to advertising.

Perhaps the most important blanket approval is that for small extensions to an existing dwellinghouse. These small extensions, such as a rear kitchen extension, are subject to restrictions on size and position but otherwise can be made without the necessity for express planning permission.

Planning authorities can exclude the effect of all or part of the Order if they deem it expedient to do so. This is known as an Article 4 Direction. The purpose of this restrictive provision is to allow a planning authority to control all aspects of development in great detail. This permits the authority to control even minor development activities such as the installation of double glazing or a plastic front door where it is appropriate to do so, say in a conservation area.

In the Chancellor's 2023 Autumn Statement, it was announced that the government would consult on a new permitted development right to allow a house to be converted into two flats provided the exterior remains unaffected. The intention is that this reform will be implemented in late 2024 following the period of consultation.

EXAMPLE

Edith acts for Harriet and Montana who are buying a house in Swanage, Dorset. The house has an attractive conservatory which was added to the property last year. Edith will need to check that the conservatory's dimensions fall within the size and volume limits of the Town and Country Planning (General Permitted Development) Order 1995. If it does, then express planning permission would not have been required for the conservatory. However, Edith should also check the result of their **local authority search** to ensure that the Order has not been excluded in whole or part in Swanage by an Article 4 Direction.

6.2 **Obtaining planning permission**

If a client intends to carry out development in the manner defined by the 1990 Act, then planning permission, a planning consent, will be required. This can be obtained in one of two ways:

- by a permission deemed to have been given as a consequence of the effects of the Town and Country Planning (General Permitted Development) Order 1995 and the Town and Country Planning (General Permitted Development) (Amendment) (No 2) (England) Order 2008 (SI 2008/2362); or
- by a formal application for planning permission submitted to the local planning authority. If the Town and Country Planning (General Permitted Development) Order 1995 does not apply, then an express application will be needed.

An applicant for express permission has the choice of making an application either for outline planning permission or for full planning permission. An outline application will elicit a response from the planning authority without the expense of having to prepare a comprehensive application involving full plans. The planning authority can impose conditions attaching to the outline consent. If outline consent is granted, it can be expressed to be subject to 'reserved matters', thereafter being resolved to the satisfaction of the planning authority. Reserved matters will relate to the detail of the application, such as the external appearance of the property, means of access to it and landscaping. If there are reserved matters, it will mean that a full application will be necessary to obtain approval for the applicant's proposals in relation to the reserved matters. This must be made within three years of the outline consent. The work itself must start within two years from approval of the reserved matters, otherwise the planning consent will lapse. The planning authority may prescribe alternative time limits if it deems it appropriate on planning grounds. The alternative to an application for outline approval is a full planning application. The planning authority can impose conditions attaching to the full planning consent. Moreover, the work itself must start within three years from the date of the full planning consent, otherwise the planning consent will lapse.

You should also be aware that general permissions for change across different use classes are authorised by the Town and Country Planning (General Permitted Development) Order 1995 and the Town and Country Planning (General Permitted Development) (Amendment) (No 2) (England) Order 2008 (SI 2008/2362). Perhaps the most important blanket approval is that for small extensions to an existing dwellinghouse. These small extensions, such as a rear kitchen extension, are subject to restrictions on size and position but otherwise can be made without the necessity for express planning permission. The scope of this general permission covers the enlargement, improvement or other alteration of a dwellinghouse, changes to the roof (such as a minor loft conversion) and the erection of a porch.

The government has recently implemented a series of changes to permitted development rights. In summary, the following additional permitted development rights are available from 31 August 2020:

1 permitted development rights allowing the demolition and rebuilding of 'vacant and redundant' office and light industrial buildings into dwellings, without planning permission.

2 permitted development rights to enable the upward extension, by up to two storeys, of existing postwar-built homes. These rights will also be extended to the creation of new homes above terraces, offices and shops, without planning permission.

The above rights require prior approval from the local authority prior to commencement of the development. This includes approval in respect of traffic and highway matters, air traffic and defence asset impacts, contamination risks, flood risk, the external appearance of the building, the provision of adequate natural light in all habitable rooms of the new dwellings, impact on amenity of the existing building and neighbouring premises including overlooking, privacy and loss of light, and the impact on any protected views.

The upward extension rights will only apply to existing residential dwellings or purpose-built, detached blocks of flats. Mixed-use buildings will not benefit from these new rights.

EXAMPLE

Joe is buying a freehold house in Brighton, which benefits from a large outhouse in the back garden. One of his main interests is repairing electric bikes and once he moves in he intends to expand this hobby into a business using the outhouse as his business premises. With the growth in electric bikes, he is hopeful that the business will become successful in which case he intends to extend the outhouse at ground level to about twice its current size.

Joe should be advised that a change of use from residential to business is 'development' (s55 Town and Country Planning Act (TCPA) 1990) and he would require planning permission to carry on a business in the outhouse (s57 TCPA 1990). Extending the outhouse would also be 'development' (s55 TCPA 1990). There is deemed permission for certain kinds of development under the Town and Country Planning (General Permitted Development) Order (GPDO) 1995 (as amended). The GPDO 1995 sets out detailed limitations on the size and volume of any **permitted development** and Joe's proposals appear to be extensive enough to fall outside those limits. Joe could be advised to speak to the local authority's planning department for more detailed advice but it would seem that he would need to apply for express planning permission.

6.3 **Use classes**

Types of use are defined in the Town and Country Planning (Use Classes) Order 1987, which lists 16 separate classes. From 21 April 2005, there were changes to the use classes that were created by the 1987 Order. That order was amended by the Town and Country Planning (Use Classes) (Amendment) (England) Order 2005 (SI 2005/84), which substitutes for the former A3 (food and drink) three new use classes mentioned next.

The following classes are of greatest importance. Changes of use *within* a class do not require planning consent, while changes *between* classes may do:

- *Class A1 shops*: this class includes post offices, travel agencies, internet cafes, hairdressers, dry cleaning agencies and the retail sale of goods *other than* hot food.
- *Class A2 financial and professional services*: this allows property to be used for the provision of financial services or professional services (not being health or medical services), or any other service appropriate to a shopping area where such services are intended for visiting members of the public. This class does not include betting offices or payday loan shops.
- *Class A3 food and drink*: this class has been amended since 21 April 2005, and is now restricted to restaurants and cafes. The class will therefore not cover pubs, takeaways and

bars. Drinking establishments (pubs and bars) are covered by A4, and hot-food takeaways are in Class A5.

- *Class B1 business*: this class covers offices other than those covered by A2, for research and development of products or processes or for any other industrial process.
- *Class B2 general industrial*: this is the class that permits any use for the carrying on of an industrial process not covered by B1, or by other provisions in the Order covering special industrial processes (eg alkaline works and other types of heavy industry that tend to emit noxious fumes or effluent).
- *Class C1 hotels and hostels*: this class clearly covers the use of buildings as hotels or hostels, and will include boarding houses and guesthouses.
- *Class C2 residential institutions*: this class covers buildings used for the provision of personal care or treatment, and residential educational facilities.
- *Class C3 dwellinghouses*: this class will allow the use of property for the accommodation of a family, as well as the coming together of up to six individuals as a single household.
- *Class C4 houses in multiple occupation*: this class covers small, shared dwellinghouses occupied by between three and six unrelated individuals, as their only or main residence, who share basic amenities such as a kitchen or bathroom.

The Town and Country Planning (General Permitted Development) (Amendment) (England) Order 2013 (SI 2013/1101) has amended the position regarding changes of use. This permits certain changes of use between Classes A, B, C and D including, for a time-limited period, the change from B1 (offices) to C3 (dwellinghouses).

As a consequence of the Town and Country Planning (General Permitted Development) (England) Order 2015 (SI 2015/596), a number of new permitted development rights have been allowed, examples of which are:

- the conversion of retail premises to restaurants/cafes (Class C);
- the existing permitted development to convert a shop to a deposit-taker is replaced by a wider right to convert a shop (or a betting office) to a premises providing financial and professional services (Classes D and F);
- the conversion of retail premises to assembly and leisure (Class J);
- the conversion of casinos or amusement arcades to dwellinghouses (Class N);
- the conversion of premises used from storage or distribution centre uses to dwellinghouses (Class P).

Changes to Use Classes from 1 September 2020

The Town and Country Planning (Use Classes) (Amendment) (England) Regulations 2020 (SI 2020/757) amend the Town and Country Planning (Use Classes) Order 1987 and introduce significant changes to the system of use classes.

In force since 1 September 2020, the core changes include the recalibration of the classification of uses of property. Classes A, B1 and D1, applicable to retail, office and non-residential institutions and assembly and leisure uses respectively, are removed and new use classes introduced in their place. The new Class E encompasses commercial, business and service, while the new F.1 and F.2 apply to learning and non-residential institutions and local community use respectively.

In addition, some uses which were previously given their own use class have been moved into the 'sui generis' category, meaning they now belong to no specific class. Changes to and from these uses will be subject to full local consideration through the planning application process. The new list of sui generis uses includes:

- Pubs, wine bars and other drinking establishments (including those with expanded food provision)
- Hot food takeaways
- Live music venues
- Cinemas, concert halls, bingo halls and dance halls.

The residential (C classes), general industrial (B2) and storage and distribution (B8) use classes remain unchanged, except for a new cross-reference in the B2 class to the new Class E 'commercial' use class.

The table below provides a brief summary of how uses have been reclassified from 1 September 2020:

Use	Use class until 31 August 2020	Use class from 1 September 2020
Shops	A1	E
Financial & Professional Services	A2	E
Food & Drink (mainly on the premises)	A3	E
Business (office, research and development and light industrial process)	B1	E
Non-residential institutions (medical or health services, crèches, day nurseries and centres)	D1	E
Assembly and Leisure (indoor sport, recreation or fitness, gyms)	D2	E
Non-residential institutions (education, art gallery, museum, public library, public exhibition hall, places of worship, law courts)	D1	F.1
Shop no larger that 280sqm (selling mostly essential goods and at least 1km from another similar shop); community hall, outdoor sport/recreation area, indoor or outdoor swimming pool, skating rink	A1	F.2
Public House, wine bar, drinking establishment	A4	Sui generis
Hot Food Takeaway	A5	Sui generis
Cinema, Concert Hall, Bingo Hall, Dance Hall, Live music venue	D2	Sui generis

The 2020 changes were made to enable a repurposing of buildings on high streets and town centres. The new Class E allows for a mix of uses to reflect changing retail requirements. It allows a building to be used flexibly by having a number of uses taking place concurrently or by allowing different uses to take place at different times of the day. Changes to another use, or mix of uses, within this class will not require planning permission.

The new concept of 'Local Community' uses—Class F.2—has been introduced to ensure important community facilities are protected through the planning system. Again, changes of use within this class do not require planning permission.

Changes to Use Classes from 1 August 2021

With the aim to increase housing stock, the Town and Country Planning (General Permitted Development) (England) (Amendment) Order 2021 (SI 2021/428) introduced new Class MA. This allows for a change of use from Class E (Commercial business and service) to Class C3 (Residential). The unit to be converted must have been in Class E for a continuous period of at least two years, been vacant for at least three months and must not exceed 1,500 square metres of floorspace. Although express planning permission is not required for a change of use permitted by Class MA, the applicant must still apply to the local planning authority for prior approval. The authority will assess the proposal for transport and parking issues, contamination, flooding, availability of natural light and any noise from nearby commercial premises.

In addition, new Class ZA allows for the demolition of either a single, purpose-built, detached block of flats or a single, detached building and its replacement with either a single, purpose-built block of new flats or a single, purpose-built house with up to two additional storeys for the new structure in the airspace. Change of use under Class ZA also requires prior approval from the local planning authority.

6.4 Other planning-related issues

Sellers, **lessors** and builders must all provide an **Energy Performance Certificate** (EPC) to prospective buyers and prospective **lessees**. The EPC gives details of the energy efficiency of the subject property on a range from A to G, with G being the least efficient and A being the most. In commercial property, they must be shown on request to any possible lessee. The EPC is required by reason of the Energy Performance of Buildings (Certificates and Inspections) (England and Wales) Regulations 2007 (SI 2007/991) and replaces previous **building regulations** in this area. Since 9 January 2013, no EPC is required when listed properties are sold or rented.

After 1 April 2008, any newly built residential property requires a sustainability certificate. This relates to the promotion of higher environmental standards in the construction of residential units. These are a requirement for sellers to obtain when marketing a property.

The Community Infrastructure Levy (CIL) is a planning charge, introduced by the Planning Act 2008 as a tool for local authorities in England and Wales to help deliver infrastructure to support the development of their area. It came into force on 6 April 2010 through the Community Infrastructure Levy Regulations 2010 (SI 2010/948). Development may be liable for a charge under the Community Infrastructure Levy if a local planning authority has chosen to set a charge in its area. Once planning permission is granted, collecting authorities will issue applicants with a levy liability notice. Applicants should then assume liability to pay the levy charge prior to commencement of development. The levy charge becomes due when development commences.

6.5 Breaches of planning control and enforcement

If the local planning authority becomes aware of a breach of planning control, it has the power to issue and serve an enforcement notice. Failure to comply with an enforcement notice can amount to a criminal offence, for which magistrates can impose an unlimited fine.

Where enforcement action is contemplated, it must be taken within four years of any operational development (ie such as the erection of a new building). The four-year period runs from when the operations were substantially completed. Similarly, a four-year period for enforcement operates for changes of use of any building to use as a single dwellinghouse, running from when the fresh use commenced. In the case of any other breach of planning law, the enforcement action period is ten years from the date of any breach. Any other breach will be a breach, including a change of use other than operational development or a change of use to a single dwellinghouse. The four-year rule therefore applies to the change of use of a building to a single dwellinghouse. The four-year rule also applies to building works such as a flat conversion. If a notice is validly served, then the recipient can appeal to the Secretary of State on one or more of the grounds for appeal set out in s174 of the Town and Country Planning Act 1990. These grounds include indicating that planning permission ought to be granted and that the proposals, if they occur, do not constitute a breach of planning control.

While an enforcement notice is under appeal it has no effect. The consequence of this is that the alleged improper use can continue. If the authority wishes to terminate the use forthwith upon service of an enforcement notice, then they must also issue and serve a stop notice. The planning authority can rely upon s183 of the Town and Country Planning Act 1990, which empowers them to issue stop notices that effectively prohibit any use or activity contained or mentioned in the allied enforcement notice. A stop notice will not prohibit the use of any building as a dwellinghouse (s183(4) Town and Country Planning Act 1990). Accordingly, a stop notice will arise only in the context of an enforcement notice.

EXAMPLE

Kumar is thinking of buying a semi-detached house on a small residential estate. The house is on the edge of the estate occupying a corner site near a side road. Kumar likes this particular house because the present owner built a garage five years ago at the bottom of the garden and fronting onto the side road. Since that time, the owner has been using the garage for his business of repairing motorcycles. Kumar wishes to take over and run the business. When Kumar asked the owner about planning permission, he said he did not think it was a problem and anyway no one had objected.

You should advise Kumar that there has been a material change of use of the garage from residential to business use. This would have required planning permission which was not granted. There is a ten-year time limit for the service of an enforcement notice by the local planning authority and, in these circumstances, it could serve an enforcement notice requiring the business use to cease. The local authority search on the property would reveal the existence or otherwise of an enforcement notice. Failure to comply with an enforcement notice is a criminal offence. So far as the building of the garage is concerned, the time limit of four years has passed so no enforcement notice can be served requiring its demolition. Consider also whether building regulations approval would have been required (see below).

6.6 **Building regulations**

Building regulations set standards for design and construction that apply to most new buildings and many alterations to existing buildings in England. Accordingly, whenever any meaningful building works are carried out to a property they must comply with a range of building regulations. These regulations are in place to ensure adequate standards of building work, and impose minimum standards covering a variety of areas, including energy conservation and health. For example, electrical works may require building regulations compliance.

You need to appreciate that this is an entirely separate requirement from planning matters. There is a requirement for plans to be filed with the local authority which will, on satisfactory completion of the works, issue a final certificate called a certificate of compliance. Consequently, there may be an extensive history of building regulations matters affecting a subject property going back many years.

It should be noted that in *Cottingham v Attey Bower & Jones (A firm)* [2000] EGCS 48, Rimmer J held the solicitors for the claimants to have acted negligently by failing to take all reasonable steps to obtain copies of building regulations consents. The judge mentioned in his judgment that injunction proceedings under s36(6) of the Building Act 1984 enable a local authority to take enforcement proceedings at any time after the works have been carried out. This provision, in effect, creates an unlimited obligation on conveyancers to seek copy building regulations approvals. Alternatively, Countrywide Legal Indemnities has available a 'Lack of Building Regulation Consent' insurance. The policy offers cover up to a tiered number of limits of indemnity, at least in respect of any works carried out at the subject property, provided they were fully completed 12 months prior to the date cover is taken out. The government is currently consulting on a number of changes to the building regulations regime in England.

CONDUCT POINT

Failure to carry out appropriate planning enquiries on behalf of a client may amount to a breach of the SRA Code of Conduct. You must act in the best interests of each client and you must provide a proper standard of service to your clients.

6.7 Typical planning enquiries

The Law Society's Conveyancing Protocol states that where the seller has completed some alterations to the subject property, then planning permissions and/or building regulations consents and completion certificates should be supplied by the seller to a buyer. The following is a list of topics that should prompt pre-contract enquiries of a seller and could well apply to both commercial and residential transactions:

- *Alterations and additions*: a prudent buyer will want to know if there have been any alterations and/or additions and, if so, when they were made. By obtaining this information, a buyer can decide if all appropriate consents are available for these works.
- *User*: the seller should be asked to confirm two points: first, the nature of the current use (and when this commenced); and, secondly, that this is the permitted use for planning purposes. This should enable the buyer to decide if the current use is lawful.
- *Advertising*: because s55(5) of the Town and Country Planning Act 1990 stipulates that the use of an external part of a property for advertising will require planning consent, if there is any advertising on the subject property, questions should be asked about planning consents for the advertising hoarding.
- *Building regulations*: there may be an extensive history of building regulations matters affecting a subject property going back many years. Enquiries should therefore be made about all these building regulations matters, including about the existence of approvals or consents and confirmation of compliance.
- *Replacement windows*: as of 1 April 2002, building regulations have applied to the installation of replacement windows and doors under the Building (Amendment) Regulations 2002 (SI 2002/440). As a result, the conveyancer for a buyer must raise enquiries with the seller covering replacement windows. In essence, all replacement windows, roof lights, roof windows and glazed doors will have to comply with the building regulations. Confirmatory certificates will be available either from the local authority or from FENSA (Fenestration Self-Assessment through the Glass and Glazing Federation Self-Assessment Scheme).
- *Electrical works*: certain electrical works will require building regulations consent. As a result, the conveyancer for a buyer must raise enquiries with the seller covering electrical installations that may require such consent.
- *Assets of community value*: the Localism Act 2011 provides for a scheme called 'assets of community value'. It requires a local council to maintain a list of 'community assets'. Nominations for community assets can be made by parish councils or by groups with a connection with the community. Individuals cannot nominate community assets. If the nomination is accepted, the group will be given time to come up with a bid for the asset when it is sold. It would therefore seem prudent to make enquiries about whether this might apply to your subject property.

EXAMPLE

Maisie is buying a house in Carlisle and the seller has told her that all the windows in the house have recently been replaced with new double-glazed units. You should advise her that the Building (Amendment) Regulations 2002 apply to replacement windows and doors installed on or after 1 April 2002. The date of installation of the units should be confirmed by the seller on the Property Information Form (TA6). The seller should provide a FENSA certificate confirming the work was carried out by a FENSA-registered company. Alternatively, the local authority could issue a certificate to this effect.

6.8 Town and country planning decision tree

An example of a planning decision tree can be seen in **Figure 6.2**.

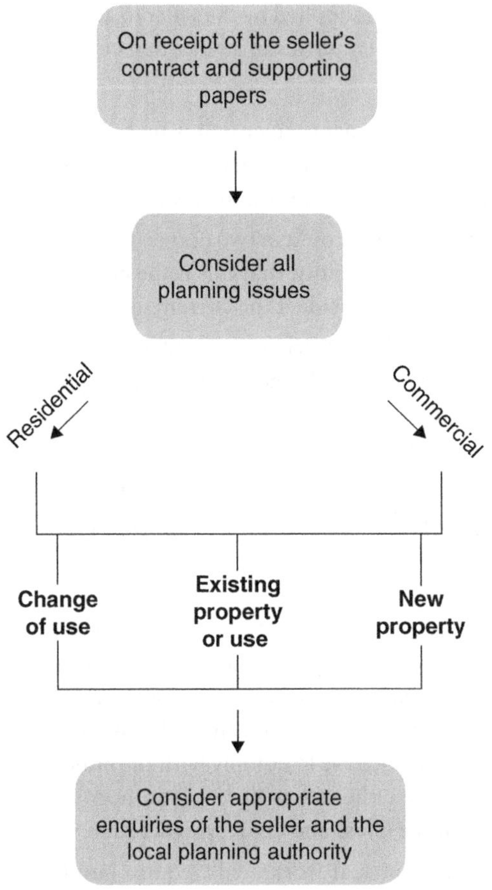

FIGURE 6.2 Planning decision tree

KEY POINT SUMMARY

- Does the client want to make any changes to the subject property that will amount to 'development' as defined by the Town and Country Planning Act 1990?
- If so, will the building works or change of use require express planning permission?
- If a change of use is proposed, will it require formal consent, or will it come within a use class, or will it be allowed by the blanket approval available under the General Permitted Development Order?
- If the property is newly built, obtain a copy of the building regulations approval as well as a copy of the planning permission and place these with the **deeds** on completion. Consider indemnity insurance if the detail is incomplete.
- Ensure that all the conditions attaching to a planning consent are seen and check that they have all been complied with.
- Obtain a copy of the building regulations consent for the past ten years. If the record is incomplete, consider indemnity insurance.
- Are there replacement windows in the subject property? If so, is there a FENSA certificate?

CHAPTER 7
Deducing and Investigating Title

FUNCTIONING LEGAL KNOWLEDGE

This chapter covers the following functioning legal knowledge required to pass the SQE 1 assessments:

Deducing and investigating title:

- key elements and structure of a registered and unregistered freehold **title**
- how to acquire and dispose of legal and equitable interests in land
- process of analysing **Land Registry** official copy entries
- process of analysing an **epitome of title** and deducing ownership
- issues that could arise from an **investigation of title** and further action required
- methods to protect and enforce third party interests
- purpose and process of reporting to the client

AUTHORITIES UNDERPINNING PRACTICE

The key authorities that underpin this area of practice are listed below. Note that for legislation you are linked to legislation.gov.uk.

Although much of the legislation on this government website is available in its amended form, the incorporation of new amendments into the text of legislation can be delayed. You should refer to legal databases to ensure you are referencing the most up-to-date legislation.

- Sections 44, 101, 103 and 104 of the Law of Property Act 1925
  https://www.legislation.gov.uk/ukpga/Geo5/15-16/20/contents
- Section 36 of the Administration of Estates Act 1925
  https://www.legislation.gov.uk/ukpga/Geo5/15-16/23/contents
- Law of Property (Joint Tenants) Act 1964
  https://www.legislation.gov.uk/ukpga/1964/63/contents
- Land Registration Act 2002
  https://www.legislation.gov.uk/ukpga/2002/9/contents
- Land Registration Rules 2003
  https://www.legislation.gov.uk/uksi/2003/1417/contents

Pre-exchange					Exchange & pre-completion				Completion & post-completion		
Stage 1 Taking instructions & advising client	**Stage 2** Draft contract	**Stage 3** Pre-contract searches, enquiries & planning	**Stage 4** Title	**Stage 5** Mortgage (applies throughout process)	**Stage 6** Exchange of contracts	**Stage 7** Purchase deed	**Stage 8** Pre-completion searches and requisitions	**Stage 9** Financial statements	**Stage 10** Completion	**Stage 11** SDLT & registration	**Stage 12** Delays and remedies

FIGURE 7.1 Conveyancing timeline

7.1 Introduction

In a modern conveyancing transaction, the parties will **deduce** and investigate title before contracts are exchanged. Put simply, deducing title is the process by which the seller demonstrates to the buyer that the seller owns the property and can convey it. Conversely, the process of investigating title is the means by which the buyer ensures that the seller owns the land and can convey it. This is done by examining the title that the seller has deduced.

If the Protocol is being used, the seller must deduce title at the same time as the draft contract and other pre-contract documents are forwarded to the buyer's solicitor; that is, the title documents will be part of the 'pre-contract package'. Indeed, this is the normal procedure, even if the Protocol is not being used.

7.2 Deducing title

7.2.1 Deducing title to registered land

After taking instructions, the seller's solicitor will simply apply to the Land Registry on Form OC1 for an up-to-date official copy of the registered title(s) being sold (and, if appropriate, on Form OC2 for official copies of documents referred to in the register). These will then be sent to the buyer's solicitor as part of the 'pre-contract package'. The Law Society's Conveyancing Protocol states that the official copies should be no more than six months old at the date of submission. For an example of a registered title, see **Appendix 2**.

7.2.2 Deducing title to unregistered land

The seller's solicitor will supply the buyer's solicitor with particulars of the **deeds**, tracing a chain of ownership through to the current seller (or someone whom the seller can compel to convey). This can be done either by a traditional abstract or, the preferred method today, an epitome of title. An epitome involves the preparation of a list or schedule, in chronological order, of all the material title deeds and events that form the chain of title, for example a **conveyance**, a **mortgage** or a death. Photocopies of all the relevant documents are then attached to the schedule. The photocopies must be legible, with copy plans correctly coloured.

The buyer should insist that the seller deduces title from at least 15 years before the date of the contract (this applies both at common law and under the Standard Conditions), and the chain of title must commence with a 'good root' (ie the starting point for the period of ownership) duly stipulated in the sale contract. A good root must satisfy the following criteria. It should:

- deal with or show ownership of the whole legal and equitable interest in the property (the buyer will normally be concerned only with the legal **estate**; if the proper conveyancing procedures are adopted, any equitable interests should be **overreached** and thus will not bind the buyer (see *City of London Building Society v Flegg* [1988] AC 54));
- contain an adequate, identifiable description of the property. A mortgage will fail this test if it lacks a full description of the property (mortgages often refer to a fuller description in the conveyance to the **mortgagor**). Similarly, an assent will fail if it simply vests the property 'for all the estate or interest of the deceased';
- do nothing to cast doubt on the title. A document will cast doubt if it depends for its effect on an earlier **instrument**, such as a power of attorney (see *Re Copelin's Contract* [1937] 4 All ER 447), but such doubt can be overcome if the seller can prove that the earlier document still subsisted at the time of its execution;
- at the date of the contract be at least 15 years old (s44 Law of Property Act 1925, as amended by s23 Law of Property Act 1969).

The best document for the root is a conveyance on sale. This is preferable to a gift of title, such as a voluntary conveyance or an assent, where it is unlikely that any prior title investigation was made before completion of the gift. As a general rule, a buyer should always insist on a conveyance on sale as the root of title (assuming one is available). If, unusually, a conveyance on sale is not available, the buyer must ensure that the alternative root document does in fact satisfy the good root criteria.

It is courteous, and indeed good practice, for the seller to supply the buyer with copies of old **land charges searches** that are present in the deeds. This saves the buyer from having to repeat the searches (provided they are valid). The seller should also supply an up-to-date search of the **index map** (SIM) at the Land Registry to confirm that no part of the title is registered and that there are no cautions against **first registration** (see **5.5** for more detail on these searches).

EXAMPLE

Yasmin is acting on the sale of Pembroke Lodge, a freehold house which has an unregistered title. To deduce title to the property, Yasmin will supply the following documents to the buyer's solicitors:

1. Epitome of title (list of relevant title deeds accompanied by photocopies of relevant deeds) or abstract of title (a summary of the relevant deeds) commencing with a good root of title which ideally would be a conveyance on sale at least 15 years old, dealing with the whole legal and beneficial interest, containing an adequate description of the property together with all subsequent documents leading to the current seller.
2. Search of the index map (SIM) showing if any part of the land has been registered and any cautions against first registration.
3. Land charges search against the seller and any other names revealed by the unregistered title.

7.3 Investigating title

The buyer's solicitor must ensure that the title is good and marketable and free from **encumbrances** that may adversely affect the use and enjoyment of the property. If you are acting for the buyer's **mortgagee** as well, it is important to appreciate your duty to your mortgagee client. You should check that the title is acceptable in conformity with the mortgagee's instructions, in particular regarding any special conditions in the mortgage offer. Also check the mortgagee's requirements in the *UK Finance Mortgage Lenders' Handbook*. The typical lender is seeking an assurance from you that no title deficiencies exist that may reduce the property's value or adversely affect the lender's ability to dispose of its security on the open market.

7.3.1 Breach of covenant

See **2.5** for a summary of the substantive law on freehold **covenants**. If an enforceable covenant on the title appears to have been breached, the seller should be asked to remedy the breach immediately. If this is not possible, the seller should be asked to consider the following possibilities to resolve the problem:

1. indemnity insurance;
2. obtaining the retrospective consent of the person with the benefit of the covenant; or
3. applying to the Upper Tribunal (Lands Chamber) for the covenant to be removed from the title.

As far as indemnity insurance is concerned, it should be noted that a common requirement of insurance companies is that no one (eg the person with the benefit of the covenant) should have been contacted in connection with the breach. Accordingly, it is generally wiser to try the indemnity route first.

7.3.1.1 Indemnity insurance

This involves arranging at the seller's cost an indemnity insurance policy from a reputable insurance company, in which the buyer, successors in title and any mortgagee are insured against loss that may arise as a result of the breach. The insurer will normally require a copy of the conveyance or Land Registry entry imposing the restriction, a statutory declaration from the owner of the property confirming that no enforcement action has been taken and counsel's opinion (if taken). Insurance is unlikely to be offered if the covenant was created recently (ie within the last 10–15 years). This is because of the increased risk of enforcement. (Title insurance is also available in respect of unknown covenants affecting property, for example where a registered title refers to a conveyance containing restrictive covenants but no copy has been filed at the Land Registry.)

7.3.1.2 Consent or release by person who now owns the land with the benefit

You may consider contacting the person who has the benefit of the covenant to obtain retrospective consent to the breach. Alternatively, you may seek agreement to a release or variation of the covenant. Should payment be required for the release or variation, this should be borne by the seller. The Land Registry will remove a restrictive covenant from the register only if clear evidence is shown that the person purporting to release the covenant has the right so to do. The Registry will thus need to inspect the title to the benefiting land to establish who currently has the benefit of the covenant. Obviously, this may not be easy in respect of covenants created many years ago. Indeed, it is often the case that the evidence produced of ownership is insufficient. If so, the Registry will add an entry to the register indicating that a deed is only 'expressed' to release the land from the covenant. Such an entry is not conclusive and should be approached with caution by intending buyers and lenders.

7.3.1.3 Application to the Upper Tribunal (Lands Chamber)

An application can be made to the Upper Tribunal (Lands Chamber) for an order that the covenant be removed from the title. This is unlikely to be successful unless the covenant is old and redundant. It is seen rather as an act of last resort and can be prohibitively expensive (do ensure that the application is made at the seller's cost—on the basis that it is the seller's problem).

If a breach of covenant problem cannot be resolved, the buyer (and any lender) should be advised very carefully about the various options available to remedy the situation and, if a proper solution cannot be found, withdrawal from the transaction may be the only alternative.

EXAMPLE

Julian acts for Emily who is buying a freehold house from Bill who built a small extension at the back of his property two years ago. Upon investigation of title, Julian notices a restrictive covenant which prevents any extensions to the property without the consent of the original developer. As part of the investigation of title, Julian would request evidence of such consent failing which he would advise Emily of her options in accordance with the previous commentary.

7.3.2 **Investigating title to registered land**

If your client is buying **registered land**, you must check carefully the official copies and other documents referred to on the register and compare them against the information given in the draft contract. You should consider in particular the following:

1 Confirm whether the estate is freehold or leasehold.

2 Does the title number correspond with the one given in the draft contract?

3 Consider the class of title; is it absolute, possessory, good leasehold or qualified? (See **2.8.6**.) Anything less than absolute title will generally be considered to be unsatisfactory.

4 Does the land described in the contract correspond with the title description?

5 Consider the title plan. Check that the land being bought is included within the title.

6 Are there any colourings or hatchings on the title plan that indicate rights of way or that land has been removed from the title?

7 Is the seller in the contract the same as the **registered proprietor**? If not, who has the ability to transfer the land?

8 Are there any encumbrances in the register, and how will these affect the buyer? Which of these will be discharged or removed on completion? (Always ensure that mortgages will be discharged on completion.)

9 Has the buyer in the draft contract agreed to buy the land subject to the encumbrances that will remain on the title after completion?

7.3.2.1 Adverse entries

If there are discrepancies, or if other adverse entries are present that protect third party interests, such as a notice, you should raise these as requisitions with the seller's practitioner. Other examples might be the presence of a restriction, a home rights notice, an apparent breach of covenant (see **7.3.1**) or possibly covenants referred to on the title but details of which were not given to the Land Registry on first registration. Your requisition should identify the defect or problem and require the seller to remedy it (if necessary, at the seller's cost).

7.3.2.2 Restrictions

A restriction (entered in the proprietorship register) makes it apparent either that the powers of the proprietor are limited or that a prior condition must be met before a disposition can be registered. The presence of a restriction does not necessarily mean there is a title defect because the seller may be in a position to satisfy the terms of the restriction. It is a matter of examining the precise terms of the restriction as the wording will indicate what procedure must be followed to conduct a valid disposition of the land. The buyer must either follow that procedure or require the seller to remove the restriction on or before completion. For example, if there is a **co-ownership** restriction indicating a **tenancy in common**, it may be the case that the purchase money will actually be paid to two trustees (or that a second trustee is being appointed), in which case the buyer can safely accept the position. However, if one of two trustees has died then a second trustee must be appointed to satisfy the restriction.

A restriction may cause problems where it has become inoperable. An example of this is where a restriction on a leasehold title requires the certificate of a management company (or its solicitor) before a transfer is registered but the management company has been struck off for failing to submit annual returns and so cannot give the certificate. In these circumstances, an application should be made to the Land Registry for the restriction to be cancelled on the basis that the management company named in it no longer exists and the transfer to the buyer can be registered.

7.3.2.3 Notices

A notice is an entry in the register in respect of the burden of an interest affecting the registered estate, for example a restrictive covenant. Apart from a bankruptcy notice (which is noted in the proprietorship register), notices will be entered in the **charges** register. The entry of a notice does not guarantee that the interest that it protects is valid, or even exists. A notice will simply ensure that the priority of the interest protected will not be automatically postponed on the registration of a subsequent registrable disposition for value. A notice may either be an agreed notice or a unilateral notice.

The buyer should insist on the removal of any unilateral notice on or before completion. An application to cancel a unilateral notice must be made on Form UN4. When the Registrar receives an application to cancel, they will serve notice on the beneficiary of the notice, who then has 15 business days in which to object to the application, failing which the notice is cancelled. Any dispute about whether the notice should be cancelled that cannot be resolved by agreement will be referred to the First-tier Tribunal (Property Chamber; Land Registration Division).

A buyer should take the same approach if a home rights notice has been registered by the seller's spouse or civil partner, who should also be asked to release all rights and vacate the property on completion.

In addition to this, before completion you must carry out a Land Registry search to update the information in the official copies (see **10.5** on pre-completion searches).

You must also check at the pre-contract stage for any **overriding interests** that are not entered on the register but that will bind the buyer irrespective of notice (eg rights of persons in actual occupation, **local land charges**, legal **easements** and **leases** for seven years or less). Overriding interests can be discovered through the buyer's inspection of the property, a local land charges search and pre-contract enquiries of the seller (in which the seller is asked to disclose details of occupier's rights and adverse interests).

EXAMPLE

James is selling his freehold house which he bought in his sole name before he married his wife Laura. James and Laura separated last year and he moved out but she continued to live in the property. The fact that Laura is in occupation will put the buyer on notice that she may have a beneficial interest in the property which, coupled with her occupation, would give her an overriding interest in the property binding on the buyer. As James's wife, Laura has a home right under the Family Law Act 1996, namely a right not to be evicted from the matrimonial home without a court order. The right must be protected by a home rights notice on the register and Laura may have already done this or could do so before completion. The buyer's solicitors must insist that Laura signs a release of any right or interest she may have and agrees to vacate the property on completion. Release is most likely to form part of the contract. If she then fails to vacate, the buyers have a direct remedy against her for damages/specific performance. Laura must be advised to seek independent advice on the implications of signing the release and should confirm in writing that she has taken such advice.

7.3.3 Investigating title to unregistered land

If your client is buying **unregistered land**, first check that the root of title offered by the seller is a good root and is at least 15 years old at the date of the contract (see **Figure 7.2**). You must then trace chronologically, from the root document, a chain of ownership all the way down to the current seller; a chain that is complete and without missing links.

EXAMPLE

1 If Jones and Clark bought the land previously, make sure it is they who later sell not Jones and Smith or even Jones and Clarke (spelling discrepancies should always be raised).

2 Ensure that you see evidence of any change of name. For example, if a previous owner purchased the property as an unmarried woman using her maiden name, and then after her marriage sold using her married name, you would want to see a certified copy of the marriage certificate.

3 Make sure that you see evidence of the death of any estate owner. For example, if a joint tenant has died and the survivor(s) has subsequently sold, you would want to see a certified copy of the death certificate.

Having traced the chain of ownership, you should now examine carefully each document in the abstract or epitome, checking for any deficiencies or omissions. Examples of defects might be a mortgage taken out by a previous estate owner that has not been discharged or an improperly executed or stamped document.

You need to ensure that the description of the property in the most recent conveyance or other document accords with that which the client is buying (this is a fundamental point that will always be thoroughly checked by the Land Registry on first registration). You need to ensure that the property benefits from all necessary easements. If there has been a sale of part, ensure that an acknowledgement for future production of retained original documents has been given, and that a sale-off memorandum has been endorsed on the previous conveyance. Check that all appropriate documents have been stamped. Finally, check whether the property should already have been registered—was it in a compulsory area on the date of a previous conveyance?

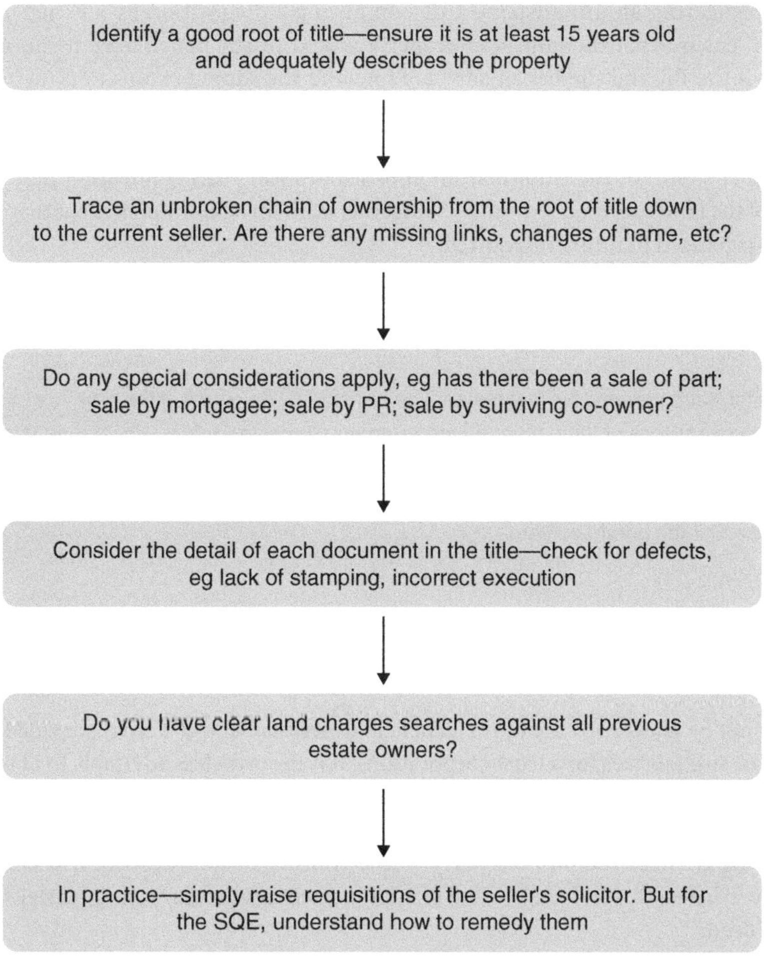

FIGURE 7.2 Investigating an unregistered title

Any defects should be raised with the seller's practitioner as **requisitions on title**. You should identify the defects and require the seller to remedy them, if necessary at the seller's cost. For further reading on the often complex area of investigating unregistered title, see Chapter 5 of *A Practical Approach to Conveyancing* by Mark Richards (Oxford University Press, 2022).

7.4 Some special title situations

There are special considerations where the person disposing of the property is not the sole legal and beneficial owner. In unregistered land, these considerations may also be of relevance so far as previous estate owners are concerned.

7.4.1 Personal representatives

A buyer should not complete a purchase from **personal representatives** (PRs) until the grant of representation has been issued by the court. It is the grant that confers authority on the PRs to deal with the assets of the deceased's estate. A certified copy of the grant must be given to the buyer's solicitor. You should ensure also that all PRs mentioned in the grant execute the **purchase deed**.

In most cases, the land will already be registered or the transaction will induce first registration (eg assent or conveyance). If, unusually, this is not the case, you should ensure that on completion a memorandum of the transaction is endorsed on the grant. Similarly, when investigating an unregistered title that contains an earlier disposition by PRs, ensure that a memorandum recording that disposition was endorsed on the grant. Also ensure there are no other endorsements on the grant recording earlier dispositions.

When investigating an unregistered title containing a disposition by a beneficiary as beneficial owner, ensure that the land was properly vested in the beneficiary by an **assent**. This applies even if the PR and the beneficiary are one and the same person (*Re King's Will Trusts* [1964] Ch 542).

When examining an earlier conveyance of unregistered land by PRs, check that it contains a statement under s36(6) of the Administration of Estates Act 1925 confirming that no previous disposition of the land was made by the PRs, together with an acknowledgement that the original grant will be produced in future if required.

EXAMPLE

Chloe acts for Sachin buying his first house. The registered title owner of the property has recently died and the **executors** of the deceased are arranging the sale. Before proceeding to **exchange of contracts**, she will insist that the executors obtain and produce a Grant of Probate, which authorises them to dispose of the deceased's assets. She should ensure that all executors referred to in the grant execute the purchase deed.

7.4.2 Dispositions by co-owners

A buyer will not be concerned about the beneficial interests behind a trust provided payment is made to at least two trustees (or a trust corporation). It is nevertheless advisable to obtain a release of any rights or interests that may be apparent in respect of the subject property, for example rights of an occupier who has a beneficial interest behind a trust.

All surviving trustees should be a party to the transfer or conveyance. If it is necessary to appoint a new trustee, this is done by deed of appointment and all surviving trustees should be a party to that deed.

7.4.2.1 Registered land

On a sale by a sole surviving co-owner, check whether there is a restriction entered in the proprietorship register protecting beneficial interests. If a restriction is present, the co-owners were tenants in common. To effect overreaching, insist on the appointment of a second trustee to join in selling the legal estate (unless devolution of the deceased's equitable share to the survivor can be proved). If there is no restriction, the co-owners were joint tenants. In this case, a transfer from the survivor alone can safely be accepted, accompanied by the death certificate.

EXAMPLE

Jon acts for Sunil who is buying a house from Carrie. Carrie originally bought the house with her partner Helen who has sadly died. The registered title reveals a restriction in the proprietorship register confirming that Carrie and Helen held the beneficial interest in the property as tenants in common. Jon should insist that a second trustee is appointed to join in selling the legal estate along with Carrie.

7.4.2.2 Unregistered land

On a sale by a sole surviving co-owner, establish whether the co-owners were joint tenants or tenants in common. This is done by consulting the conveyance to the co-owners when they purchased. This document should contain an appropriate statement to this effect.

As previously, if you are dealing with a surviving tenant in common, you should insist on the appointment of a second trustee to join in selling the legal estate (unless devolution of the deceased's equitable share to the survivor can be proved). If dealing with a surviving joint tenant, then, provided the three conditions in the Law of Property (Joint Tenants) Act 1964 are met, you can assume **severance** has not occurred and safely accept a conveyance/transfer from the survivor alone, together with the death certificate. The three conditions are:

1 No bankruptcy petition or order has been registered as a land charge against any of the joint tenants. Thus, you should conduct an appropriate land charges search against their full names or, if already made against previous estate owners, check the earlier search.
2 No memorandum of severance of the **joint tenancy** has been endorsed on the conveyance to the joint tenants. Thus, you should inspect the abstract or epitome and/or raise a requisition for confirmation of this.
3 The conveyance by the survivor states that the survivor is solely and beneficially entitled to the land (this is normally found in the recitals of the conveyance).

If the conditions listed in the Law of Property (Joint Tenants) Act 1964 are not met, insist on the appointment of a second trustee to join in selling the legal estate.

7.4.3 Sale by mortgagee

A mortgagee may exercise its power of sale and convey the mortgaged property in its own name provided a power of sale exists, has arisen and has become exercisable. These requirements and the explanations that follow apply equally to registered and unregistered land.

1 *Power of sale exists*. A power of sale is implied in every mortgage made by deed unless, unusually, the power is expressly excluded in the deed itself (s101(1)(i) Law of Property Act 1925). A legal mortgage must be made by deed (s85 Law of Property Act 1925), and so it follows that a legal mortgagee will always have a power of sale unless the power has been expressly excluded.
2 *Power of sale has arisen*. The power of sale arises on the legal date for redemption of the mortgage which is when the mortgage money, in theory, becomes due. This date is normally specified in the deed to be a date within the first six months of the mortgage.
3 *Power of sale has become exercisable*. Prima facie the power of sale becomes exercisable if one of the events in s103 of the Law of Property Act 1925 occurs, namely a formal demand for payment has not been complied with for three months, interest is unpaid for two months or the borrower is in breach of some other condition of the mortgage. In practice, however, the modern mortgage deed will generally exclude s103 and then expressly strengthen the mortgagee's position by enlarging the statutory grounds.

EXAMPLE

When acting for a buyer from a mortgagee, or when investigating an unregistered title that includes an earlier sale by a mortgagee, the buyer's practitioner will only need to be concerned with points 1 and 2 above. There is no need for the buyer to check whether the borrower is in default because even if the power is not exercisable, the buyer will still receive a good title (s104(2) Law of Property Act 1925). The question of whether the power can be properly exercised is a matter between the mortgagor and the mortgagee. Thus the buyer's practitioner, in determining whether a sale by a mortgagee was (or will be) valid, should simply inspect the mortgage deed to verify: (a) that the power of sale is not excluded (bear in mind that an exclusion would be exceptional); and (b) that the legal date for redemption has passed. If either of these has not occurred, the mortgagee cannot convey or transfer the legal estate.

7.4.3.1 Effect of sale by mortgagee

The mortgagee conveys the legal estate free from subsequent mortgages but subject to any mortgages having priority to the selling mortgagee. The buyer's practitioner should therefore ensure that the selling mortgagee discharges any subsisting prior mortgages from the proceeds of sale in the same way as a mortgagor who is selling would discharge a subsisting mortgage.

On completion of the sale, the mortgage under which the power of sale is exercised is not discharged (allowing the mortgagee to pursue the borrower for any arrears), but the buyer takes free from it.

If you are buying from a receiver appointed by the mortgagee, all mortgages must be cleared off on completion because the receiver acts as agent for the borrower.

7.4.3.2 Acting for selling mortgagee

The seller's practitioner must ensure that the power of sale has become exercisable otherwise the mortgagee may be liable in damages to the borrower. In addition, the seller's solicitor should ensure that the mortgagee is able to give vacant possession on completion. Accordingly, it may be necessary to obtain a court order for possession if the property is not already vacant.

The mortgagee should be made aware of its duty to obtain the best price for the property reasonably obtainable on the open market. However, this is not a matter of concern to the buyer. Once the mortgage debt is discharged, if there are any surplus monies these must be passed by the selling mortgagee to any subsequent mortgagee and, failing that, to the borrower personally. Again, this is of no concern to the buyer.

KEY POINT SUMMARY

- When buying from personal representatives (PRs), ensure that the grant has been issued and that all PRs execute the purchase deed.
- When buying from a sole surviving co-owner, establish whether they are a surviving joint tenant or tenant in common.
- If the survivor is a tenant in common, then a second trustee should normally be appointed.
- A mortgagee can sell under its power of sale provided the power exists, has arisen and has become exercisable.
- A buyer from a mortgagee is only concerned that the power of sale exists and has arisen.
- A buyer from a mortgagee must insist that any prior mortgages are discharged but takes free from any subsequent mortgages.
- Deducing title is the process by which the seller 'proves' title to the buyer.
- In registered land, the seller applies to the Land Registry for official copies of the title, including title plan and copy documents.
- In unregistered land, the seller prepares an epitome of title and attaches to it copies of the relevant title documents.
- An epitome is simply a list of all the material title deeds and events that form the chain of title, for example a conveyance and grant of probate.
- A good root of title (in unregistered land only) must be at least 15 years old.
- The best root is a conveyance on sale.
- Acting for the buyer, you must check that the title is good and marketable, free from adverse encumbrances. Bear in mind your duty to the buyer's mortgagee as well (assuming you are acting).
- If the land is unregistered, ask yourself, 'Will my client obtain absolute title on first registration?' Consider referring a difficult title problem to the Land Registry for guidance.
- For unregistered title, check that there is a good root and ensure there is an unbroken chain of ownership through to the seller. Check each document in the title for defects, such as improper stamping or execution.
- Acting for the buyer, you must raise requisitions regarding any problems. Make sure you obtain satisfactory replies to requisitions before exchanging contracts. If there is an unresolved problem, consider indemnity insurance from an insurance company at the seller's expense.

- If the title problem is complex, consult a specialist text such as Chapter 5 of *A Practical Approach to Conveyancing* by Mark Richards (Oxford University Press, 2022).
- Acting for the seller, initially investigate your own client's title, as you will have to disclose any incumbrances and defects in title in the draft contract. Anticipate any requisitions the buyer is likely to raise.
- Modern practice is to deduce title before exchange. This is obligatory if the Protocol is being used.
- In unregistered land, the seller should choose a good root of title at least 15 years old and show an unbroken chain of ownership down to the current seller. An epitome is easier to prepare than an abstract. Make sure all photocopies are accurate and plans properly coloured.
- In unregistered land, the seller may be retaining original documents on completion (eg on a sale of part). If the Protocol is being used, you should assist the buyer's practitioner by marking the epitome as examined against the originals. The buyer thus receives the epitome already marked up.
- In registered land, deduce title by supplying up-to-date official copies of title (including title plan and other relevant documents).
- Acting for the buyer, your primary duty is to check that the title is good and marketable, free from adverse incumbrances. Bear in mind your duty to the buyer's mortgagee as well (assuming you are acting).
- Acting for the buyer in unregistered land, first check that there is a good root and then ensure there is an unbroken chain of ownership through to the seller. Finally, check each document in the title for defects, for example improper execution or stamping.
- If in your title investigation you come across a disposition by someone acting in a special capacity, for example a mortgagee or personal representative, then have regard to the issues discussed in this chapter.

CHAPTER 8
Mortgages

FUNCTIONING LEGAL KNOWLEDGE

This chapter covers the following functioning legal knowledge required to pass the SQE 1 assessments:

Finance:

- sources of finance for a property transaction
- types of **mortgage**

Acting for a lender:

- lender's requirements
- purpose of a certificate of **title**

AUTHORITIES UNDERPINNING PRACTICE

The key authorities that underpin this area of practice are listed below. Note that for legislation you are linked to legislation.gov.uk.

Although much of the legislation on this government website is available in its amended form, the incorporation of new amendments into the text of legislation can be delayed. You should refer to legal databases to ensure you are referencing the most up-to-date legislation.

- Financial Services and Markets Act 2000
  https://www.legislation.gov.uk/ukpga/2000/8/contents
- Solicitors' Financial Services (Scope) Rules 2001
  https://www.sra.org.uk/solicitors/standards-regulations/financial-services-scope-rules/
- Money Laundering Regulations 2017
  https://www.legislation.gov.uk/uksi/2017/692/made
- Section 85 of the Law of Property Act 1925
  https://www.legislation.gov.uk/ukpga/Geo5/15-16/20/contents
- Land Registration Rules 2003
  https://www.legislation.gov.uk/uksi/2003/1417/contents
- Section 860 of the Companies Act 2006
  https://www.legislation.gov.uk/ukpga/2006/46/contents
- UK Finance Mortgage Lenders' Handbook
  https://lendershandbook.ukfinance.org.uk/lenders-handbook/
- SRA Code of Conduct
  https://www.sra.org.uk/solicitors/standards-regulations/code-conduct-solicitors/

Pre-exchange					Exchange & pre-completion				Completion & post-completion		
Stage 1 Taking instructions & advising client	**Stage 2** Draft contract	**Stage 3** Pre-contract searches, enquiries & planning	**Stage 4** Title	**Stage 5** Mortgage (applies throughout process)	**Stage 6** Exchange of contracts	**Stage 7** Purchase deed	**Stage 8** Pre-completion searches and requisitions	**Stage 9** Financial statements	**Stage 10** Completion	**Stage 11** SDLT & registration	**Stage 12** Delays and remedies

FIGURE 8.1 Conveyancing timeline

8.1 Introduction

This chapter examines the important issues arising in relation to a mortgage taken out by a client to assist in financing the purchase of a property. We will look at the most popular types of mortgage, the impact of the Financial Services and Markets Act 2000 and other matters including important professional conduct issues. We shall also consider briefly mortgages of leasehold property and mortgages of commercial property.

Your client buyer will often inform you that the mortgage has already been arranged, but it is your duty to ensure that the client's arrangements are satisfactory according to their needs and wishes. For example, someone without dependants who wishes to secure the lowest monthly outlay would generally be advised to take out an ordinary repayment mortgage, not a more complicated and expensive mortgage (see **8.2**). You should also warn clients about the dangers of attractive-looking fixed interest rate mortgages. Although they can be beneficial when interest rates are rising, they may not be as appealing when mortgage rates start to fall, and they often contain hidden penalties for early redemption. Always check the conditions of the mortgage offer carefully. (For a discussion of typical mortgage conditions, including retentions and indemnity guarantee policies, see **8.6**.)

CONDUCT POINT

You must ensure that the Money Laundering Regulations 2017 are complied with by verifying the client's identity. Your firm must have procedures in place for obtaining satisfactory evidence of your client borrower's identity. The most reliable evidence of identification is a passport, and safe practice is to inspect the borrower's full passport to confirm their identity and then keep a copy of it on file for future reference.

8.2 Common types of mortgage

8.2.1 Repayment mortgage

This is generally the cheapest mortgage in terms of monthly outlay. The loan is repaid over the mortgage term (normally 25 years) and each monthly repayment by the borrower to the **mortgagee** comprises part interest and part capital (in the early years of the mortgage the capital element is very small). The mortgagee will usually insist that a separate mortgage protection term assurance policy is arranged so that if (and only if) the borrower dies during the lifetime of the mortgage, the debt is repaid by the sum assured. The monthly premium on the mortgage protection policy is typically just a few pounds. A client without dependants who is looking for the lowest monthly mortgage cost would be well advised to consider this type of mortgage.

8.2.2 Endowment mortgage

An endowment mortgage is generally more expensive than an ordinary repayment mortgage. The mortgage is linked to a life assurance policy that matures at the end of the mortgage term. None of the capital loan is repaid during the life of the mortgage, the monthly payments to the mortgagee being interest only. In addition, the borrower pays monthly premiums on the life policy to a life company.

The maturity value of the policy should, in theory, be sufficient to repay the capital loan; there may even be surplus funds available if the investment has performed well. However, returns on endowment policies have suffered over recent years and there is no guarantee that the proceeds will repay the loan (especially for 'low-cost endowments' where initial premium contributions are even lower). Any shortfall on the mortgage debt will ultimately have to be funded by the client, who should be warned of this possibility. The risk of shortfall together with the abolition of tax relief on endowment policy premiums has reduced the attraction of this type of mortgage.

8.2.3 **Pension mortgage**

This is similar to an endowment mortgage but instead of the loan being linked to a life policy, it is linked to a personal pension policy. The proceeds of the policy on maturity are used to discharge the loan. This type of mortgage is likely to suit a self-employed person who has (or should be advised to have) a personal pension. Unlike an endowment policy, the contributions to the pension policy are tax deductible which is attractive, particularly for higher rate taxpayers.

8.2.4 **Interest-only mortgage**

This is the cheapest for the client in terms of monthly outlay because 'interest only' means exactly that—no capital is repaid and the mortgage is not linked to any life policy or pension or savings plan. Clients must be advised that they will need to find a method of paying off the loan eventually. Lenders should offer interest-only loans exclusively to borrowers who can demonstrate that they have other arrangements in place for repayment of the loan, for example out of an existing pension fund. However, this is not always the case, and you should make your client aware of the risks involved.

8.2.5 **Sharia-compliant mortgages**

Islamic law—known as Sharia—forbids Muslims from paying interest and this excludes many Muslims from the conventional mortgage products that are on offer. Specialist Muslim lenders, such as the Islamic Bank of Britain, offer Sharia-compliant alternatives. These usually involve the lender initially buying the subject property and then selling it on to the Muslim purchaser at a higher price. For further information on Islamic financing generally, see **Land Registry** Practice Guide 69.

8.3 **Mortgage Guarantee Scheme and Lifetime ISAs**

Since April 2021, under a new mortgage guarantee scheme, those looking to buy a property with a 5 per cent deposit are able to apply for a 95 per cent loan-to-value (LTV) mortgage deal with participating lenders. The scheme is available on properties costing a maximum of £600,000. To encourage lenders to offer 95 per cent LTV mortgages, the government will act as a guarantor, meaning that if the homeowner fails to keep up with repayments the government will cover the costs.

A first-time purchaser under 40 can utilise a Lifetime ISA (Individual Savings Account) to help fund their purchase and save up to £4,000 tax-free each year. The government will pay a 25 per cent bonus on the client's contributions, up to a maximum of £1,000 a year.

8.4 Financial Services and Markets Act 2000

When advising on mortgages you should have regard to the Financial Services and Markets Act 2000 (FSMA). Solicitors who conduct 'mainstream' investment business (eg advising on specific investments) must be authorised to do so by the Financial Conduct Authority (FCA). Only about 300 firms in England and Wales are currently authorised to conduct mainstream investment business. Solicitors who conduct 'non-mainstream' investment business that is incidental to their legal services (eg conveyancing) are regulated by the Solicitors Regulation Authority, which is a Designated Professional Body (DPB) under the Act. This will cover the overwhelming majority of firms.

8.4.1 The Scope Rules

The Law Society has issued 'Scope Rules' that limit and define the scope of what solicitors can and cannot do as members of the DPB. These are called the Solicitors' Financial Services (Scope) Rules 2001. The aim of the Rules is to ensure that in providing services to clients, solicitors carry on only regulated activities that *arise out of or are complementary to* the provision of services to their clients, such as conveyancing, corporate work and matrimonial, probate and trust work. Essentially, non-mainstream investment business falls within the Scope Rules, but mainstream investment business falls outside the Rules and requires authorisation from the FCA.

If firms consider that their activities will go beyond the Scope Rules, namely into mainstream investment business, they will need authorisation directly from the FCA; otherwise, they will be committing a criminal offence.

8.4.2 Generic advice only

If you offer the client generic mortgage advice about the different types of mortgage and their suitability for the client (eg 'in your circumstances I would recommend a repayment mortgage'), this will fall outside the FSMA as it is not a regulated activity. However, arranging or giving specific advice about different mortgage providers and mortgage products is a regulated activity and would require prior authorisation from the FCA. Unless a regulated mortgage is arranged by a person who is authorised under the FSMA or with a (properly authorised) financial institution, it will be unenforceable without the leave of the court. Similarly, offering specific advice on an investment product (eg a particular pension company in connection with a pension mortgage) would constitute a regulated activity, for which the firm would require prior authorisation. If your client is seeking non-generic (ie specific) advice, you should refer them to a reputable independent financial advisor who is authorised by the FCA.

8.4.3 Money laundering

As previously discussed, you should be on your guard against possible money laundering (see **3.8.2**). For example, do not accept large sums of cash from your borrower client.

8.5 Acting for borrower and lender

In a commercial property transaction, the lender will usually instruct its own solicitors (see **8.14**). However, in most residential transactions the lender will instruct you to act for it as well as the borrower. There are restrictions under the SRA Code of Conduct (the Code), which are now considered.

A solicitor must not act for both lender and borrower in a conveyancing transaction if there is a client conflict or a significant risk of a client conflict. However, clause 6.2(a) of the Code contains an exception where a solicitor may act for two clients, even where there is a client conflict, provided the clients have a substantially common interest. For example, where there is a clear common purpose in relation to a matter or a particular aspect of it between the clients and a strong consensus on how it is to be achieved and any client conflict is peripheral to that common purpose.

In the case of lender and borrower, the substantially common interest is that both parties will want to ensure that the subject property has a good and marketable title free from matters that would adversely affect the property's value. Accordingly, you could act for both lender and borrower in relation to a mortgage provided:

- the mortgage is a standard mortgage (see next) of property to be used as the borrower's private residence;
- you are satisfied that it is reasonable and in the client's best interests for you to act; and
- the certificate of title required by the lender is in the form approved by the Law Society and the Council of Mortgage Lenders.

A standard mortgage is a mortgage provided in the normal course of the lender's activities, where a significant part of the lender's activities consists of lending and the mortgage is on standard terms. In other words, the material terms of the mortgage documentation are not negotiated between the lender's and borrower's solicitors—they are standard terms.

It follows that a solicitor will normally be able to act for both lender and borrower in a straightforward mortgage of residential property where the lender is an institutional bank or building society lending on standard terms. However, if the mortgage is not on standard terms (eg in a commercial transaction), the lender and borrower will most likely need to be separately represented.

Where you are acting for both lender and borrower and a conflict occurs during the transaction, you must cease acting for both parties unless you can, with the consent of one party, continue to act for the other. The same would apply if the client conflict ceases to be peripheral to the common purpose. Examples of a conflict occurring would be where the borrower misrepresents to the lender that the purchase price is in fact higher than the price agreed with the seller, or where the terms of the mortgage offer are clearly unfair to the borrower, or where the solicitor becomes involved in negotiations regarding the loan agreement.

CONDUCT POINT

Only act for borrower and lender where the mortgage is a standard mortgage of property to be used as the borrower's private residence, you are satisfied that it is reasonable and in the client's best interests for you to act and the certificate of title required by the lender is in the form approved by the Law Society and the Council of Mortgage Lenders (see **8.9**).

8.5.1 *UK Finance Mortgage Lenders' Handbook*

You must acquaint yourself with the *UK Finance Mortgage Lenders' Handbook*, which contains standardised lenders' instructions for solicitors. You can access the Handbook via the Council of Mortgage Lenders' website. As a result of the mortgage market review in 2014, the lender's conveyancer is now required to inform the lender straight away if the seller has not owned the property for at least six months. Any sub-sale must also be reported. The Handbook is divided into three parts. Part 1 sets out the main instructions and guidance, which must be disclosed by the conveyancers. Part 2 details each lender's specific requirements that arise from those instructions. The instructions from individual lenders will indicate whether the conveyancer is being instructed in accordance with the Handbook, in which case the conveyancer should follow the instructions in the Handbook. Part 3 applies where the conveyancer is representing only the lender in a residential conveyancing transaction; that is, there is separate representation of the borrower and the lender. On 1 January 2010, the Building Societies Association (BSA) introduced a new set of standardised mortgage instructions, which are being used in some residential transactions involving BSA members. If a building society lender instructs you, check your instructions to see whether the BSA instructions or the *UK Finance Mortgage Lenders' Handbook* is applicable.

CONDUCT POINT

Ensure that no **conflict of interest** arises between borrower and lender. For example, if the solicitor becomes involved in negotiations regarding the conditions of the loan agreement, there will clearly be a conflict of interest. A conflict of interest will also arise if you discover that the borrower intends to breach a condition of the mortgage offer (eg to use the property for business purposes when such use is prohibited). In this situation, you must explain to the borrower that a conflict has arisen and you can no longer act for the borrower or lender unless the lender permits you to continue to act for the borrower alone. As you can no longer act for the lender, the lender's papers should be returned. However, due to your duty of **confidentiality** to the borrower (which continues even after termination of the borrower's retainer) you cannot disclose the reason why you can no longer act. You must simply inform the lender that a conflict of interest has arisen and leave it at that.

CONDUCT POINT

As a matter of conduct you will need to obtain the borrower's consent before passing on any confidential information to the lender. This is unless the lender can show to your satisfaction that there is a prima facie case of fraud. If the borrower refuses consent to disclose, you should send, if requested, only those parts of your file that relate to work done for the lender. Note that some lenders get borrowers to sign a waiver of confidentiality at the time of the mortgage application. In this case, you may need to disclose your whole file to the lender, but do check the client's waiver for details of what can be disclosed.

EXAMPLE

Hira acts for Peter buying his first flat with the aid of a mortgage from Halifax Building Society for whom she also acts. Peter tells Hira that he is glad that he has already received his mortgage offer as he was told last week that he would shortly be made redundant from his employment. In the light of this information, with Peter's consent, Hira must notify Halifax of his impending redundancy. If Peter refuses to give such consent, she must immediately cease acting for Halifax but cannot disclose the reasons for doing so because of her duty of confidentiality to Peter.

8.6 Mortgage offer

The typical buyer of a residential property will almost invariably require a mortgage, and it is for the solicitor to ensure before exchanging contracts that an acceptable written offer of mortgage is made and, if necessary, duly accepted. In this regard, you should make sure that you receive the written offer yourself. Do not rely merely on the client's word that it has been issued. Moreover, read the mortgage conditions carefully (both general and specific) and, after discussing the terms with your client, establish that the mortgage offer is acceptable.

8.6.1 Advising client on mortgage offer

You should advise the client about the precise terms of the mortgage offer. Be clear in your own mind that the client understands the terms and can comply with them. General conditions (found in the small print or separate booklets) will apply across the board to all mortgages by a particular lender. Common examples are not to make alterations to the property and not to let the property without first obtaining the lender's consent. Many people taking out a mortgage for the first time do not always appreciate that these restrictions exist, so it is important to draw them to their attention. There may also be special conditions relating to the particular mortgage, for example a requirement to carry out specified repairs to the property.

8.6.2 Special conditions in mortgage offer

You should ensure that any special conditions in the mortgage offer can be met by the client. The following special conditions occur quite often:

1. *Retention for repairs*. The lender's **survey** report may recommend that essential repairs are made, for instance to the roof. As a result, the lender may impose a mortgage condition that a specified sum is held back from the mortgage advance until the repairs have been carried out. If so, the client will, of course, have to fund the shortfall in order to complete; moreover, the client will also have to pay for the cost of the repairs after completion.
2. *Retention for making up roads and drains*. This may be made in respect of a new property to cover the risks associated with the developer defaulting in making up the roads and drains. The borrower/buyer may, in the circumstances of such retention, seek to persuade the developer/seller to agree a similar retention from the balance due on completion until the mortgage retention is eventually released. Developers are, however, notoriously reluctant to agree to this.
3. *Mortgage indemnity guarantee*. If the loan exceeds a certain percentage of the lender's valuation of the property, for example 75 per cent, the lender may require some additional security. This is to cover a situation in which the borrower defaults and the lender is subsequently forced to sell the property at a loss (ie for less than the outstanding debt). The additional security takes the form of a separate indemnity guarantee policy protecting the lender against this risk. The insurance company offering the guarantee charges a single premium (normally several hundred pounds), which the lender pays initially and then either deducts from the mortgage advance or adds to the loan account. Either way, the borrower ends up paying the premium and must be made aware of the position.

8.7 Lender's instructions to solicitor

The lender's instructions to the solicitor will usually be issued at the same time as the mortgage offer and could look like this:

EXAMPLE

CORNSHIRE BUILDING SOCIETY

Dear Sirs
Please act for the Society in the mortgage in accordance with the latest version of the UK Finance Mortgage Lenders' Handbook for England and Wales. We enclose a copy of the Offer of Advance, the Mortgage ***Deed*** *for execution by the borrower and a certificate of title for you to complete and return to us. We certify that these instructions comply with the SRA Code of Conduct.*
Yours faithfully

Cornshire Building Society
OFFER OF ADVANCE
Date: 3 September 2024
Lender: Cornshire Building Society 5 High Street Blakey Cornshire CL1 3EH
Borrowers' full names and addresses: Colin Smith of 20 Sun Street Blakey CL8 2TG
Solicitors: Brown & Co, West Chamber Blakey Cornshire CL1 2EG
Account number: 1234567
Property to be mortgaged: 5 Peppard Road Blakey Cornshire CL8 1LM
Tenure: Freehold
Purchase Price: £90,000
Amount of Loan: £40,000
Repayment Term: 25 years
Interest Rate (variable): 3.95%
Buildings Insurance Cover: £80,000

General Conditions:

1. *The General Conditions of the Lender apply, which are detailed in the enclosed booklet 'Information about your mortgage'.*
2. *This Offer of Advance may be varied or withdrawn if the mortgage is not completed within six months or if something occurs that in our view makes it undesirable for the loan or any part of it to be made. You must tell us of any changes in personal circumstances (e.g. loss or change of employment/pay) which occur before the mortgage is completed.*

Special Conditions:

3. *Lender's solicitors to obtain and place with the title deeds an* **undertaking** *signed by the Borrowers to carry out the following repair work to the Property within six months of completion:*
   - *Replace cracked tiles on roof.*
   - *Repair chimney flashings.*
4. *Lender's solicitors to confirm existence of legal right of way to the Property.*
5. *Colin Smith's existing mortgage with the Halifax secured on 20 Sun Street to be redeemed on or before completion.*
6. *Homeguard Insurance will be arranged as requested, details of which are as follows: Cornshire Homeguard—Buildings Option A reinstatement value £80,000.*

YOUR HOME IS AT RISK IF YOU DO NOT KEEP UP REPAYMENTS ON A MORTGAGE OR OTHER LOAN SECURED ON IT.

8.8 The mortgage deed

A legal mortgage must be made by deed (s85 Law of Property Act 1925). Apart from this requirement, it need take no other prescribed form, although where **registered land** is concerned, r103 of the Land Registration Rules 2003 provides that a legal **charge** may be in Form CH1. Although not compulsory at present, Form CH1 is seen as something of a 'stepping stone' towards a standard compulsory form of charge when e-conveyancing is introduced. Typically, the institutional lender will supply its own printed mortgage form, which is sent to the solicitor along with the 'instructions pack'. The solicitor will then simply complete the blanks (name of borrower, property address, etc) in readiness for execution by the borrower before completion.

8.8.1 Advising the client

Before your client executes the mortgage deed, it is important that you explain to the client its nature and effect. For example:

- Point out the initial rate of interest and amount of the first monthly repayment; explain that the lender may vary them at any time (unless the mortgage is fixed rate).
- Explain the borrower's **covenants**, such as the covenant to keep the property in good repair, the covenant not to make alterations without the lender's consent and any prohibition against letting or sharing possession without the lender's consent (lodgers often help to pay the mortgage).
- The borrower must understand that if there is any default on mortgage repayments or breach of covenant, the lender has the right to call in the loan and sell the property.
- Any penalty charges for early repayment should be explained (this is often the case in initially attractive-looking fixed-rate packages).
- If the mortgage secures 'all monies' owed to the lender, a breach of this mortgage would entitle the lender to call in other loans (if any) made to the borrower. Most mortgages are all

monies charges. Where there are joint borrowers, this would include sums advanced to them individually on sole mortgages on other properties.

- The lender's right to insure the property and recover the premiums from the borrower should be explained; the mortgage deed normally contains an express power for the lender to insure, extending the statutory power under s101(1)(ii) of the Law of Property Act 1925.

CONDUCT POINT

Any guarantor of the borrower who is executing the mortgage deed should be told to take independent legal advice before signing. This is because the guarantor may become liable instead of, or as well as, the borrower for all the money owing under the deed.

If the mortgage monies are being used to finance a contemporaneous purchase, the relevant parties must properly execute the mortgage deed before completion of the purchase. A good time for signing is when you see the client to explain the mortgage terms, and you can then act as the client's witness as well. There is no need for the lender to execute the deed unless, unusually, the lender is entering into new covenants.

Ensure that the client executes the mortgage before completion and leave it undated in your file. On completion, you will then date the mortgage deed at the same time as you date the **purchase deed**. You should check the lender's instructions at this stage as some lenders require to be advised as soon as completion takes place.

EXAMPLE

Erik acts for Nadia buying a house with the assistance of a mortgage from Barclays Bank. There is some work required to the roof of the property for which an estimate of £3,000 has been obtained. In general terms, Erik will advise Nadia on the following: the amount of the loan, repayment period and basis upon which repayment is to be made (eg capital and interest); the initial interest rate and for how long it is fixed; the borrower's covenants with the lender, including keeping the property in good repair and condition, not letting or sharing possession without the lender's consent, not making alterations without prior consent and keeping the property insured to its full reinstatement value; and the necessity for maintaining full monthly payments and observing the covenants in the mortgage, failing which the lender could repossess the property and sell it. It is also likely in the special conditions of the mortgage offer that the lender will make a retention of £3,000 pending completion of the roof repairs. In this case, Nadia will need to find the shortfall to enable her to complete the purchase.

8.9 Certificate of title to the lender

Before the lender is willing to release the mortgage advance, it will insist on a written certificate of title from the solicitor. The certificate should confirm that the title is good and marketable, free from adverse **encumbrances** and can be safely accepted by the lender as security. If the solicitor considers that the title is unacceptable, then this must be drawn specifically to the lender's attention. In conjunction with the *UK Finance Mortgage Lenders' Handbook*, a compulsory standard form certificate of title has been agreed between the Law Society and the Council of Mortgage Lenders. This should be used by conveyancers when reporting to their lender clients and requesting the mortgage advance. The certificate of title can be downloaded from the Law Society website. There is also a short-form version of the certificate which states that the conveyancer gives the certificate of title as if the same were set out in full, subject to the limitations contained in it. The use of this certificate of title is not obligatory for mortgage advances secured on commercial property or for so-called 'buy to let' mortgages of residential property where the owner does not occupy the property.

A solicitor who is in any doubt about whether a particular adverse matter will result in the mortgage offer being withdrawn, should refer the matter to the lender *before* contracts are exchanged.

Indeed, to avoid delay all queries should be referred to the lender as soon as they arise, which will normally be at the **investigation of title** stage; that is before exchange.

The certificate asks you to confirm that no breaches of planning condition or **building regulation** consent have occurred and, further, that you have complied with all the lender's instructions. Clearly, these are matters that must be checked before exchange but it is not always possible for the solicitor to be absolutely clear about certain matters, such as compliance with planning conditions. If in any doubt, you would be wise to qualify your certificate by adding the words, 'as far as we are aware from our usual searches, enquiries and investigation of title'.

The certificate of title will include a request to the lender for the mortgage advance. In most cases, the lender will agree to send the advance monies by telegraphic transfer, deducting the transfer fee from the advance. The advance monies are regarded as client's money and, as such, must be paid into your firm's client account.

Pending completion, the solicitor holds the mortgage advance on trust for the lender and must comply with the lender's instructions. Non-compliance will constitute a breach of trust (see *Target Holdings Ltd v Redferns* [1996] AC 421). In particular, do not release funds and complete until the borrower has properly executed and you have received the mortgage deed (and any other security documentation). If there is any delay in completion, the lender's instructions may require the advance to be returned, with interest.

In all cases, before the advance is drawn down the lender will require confirmation that the borrower is not bankrupt and that there are no insolvency proceedings. The solicitor for the lender should therefore conduct a bankruptcy search against each individual borrower's full name at the Land Charges Department (Form K16 is used for a 'bankruptcy only' search). If the borrower is a company, a company search should also be conducted to ensure that the company is not in liquidation and that there are no winding-up proceedings.

8.10 Postponing occupiers' rights

Lenders are naturally cautious about occupiers and will want to know whether any adult will be in occupation of the property after completion in addition to the buyer/borrower. The vigilant lender will require an occupier to sign a declaration postponing any interest behind that of the lender. It is important that the solicitor for the lender/borrower ensures that the occupier obtains independent advice before signing this declaration. This is because of the conflict between the interest of the occupier and that of the lender/borrower and also the possibility of the borrower exerting undue influence on the occupier to sign the declaration.

CONDUCT POINT

To avoid a conflict of interest and to counter any suggestion of undue influence, the lender must take reasonable steps to ensure that the signatory has an adequate understanding of the nature and effect of the transaction. Effectively, this means the solicitor must ensure that the signatory is separately advised (see *Barclays Bank plc v O'Brien* [1994] 1 AC 180). Your recommendation for separate advice and/or representation should be recorded in writing for future reference if necessary.

8.11 The *Etridge* case—guaranteeing another person's debts

In *Royal Bank of Scotland v Etridge (No 2)* [2001] 4 All ER 449, the House of Lords laid down guidelines for solicitors advising a spouse being asked to agree to a husband's or wife's business debts being secured on the matrimonial home. These guidelines also apply to cases where anyone in a non-commercial relationship has offered to guarantee the debts of another, such as a parent and child. Although a solicitor should exercise their own skill and judgement in advising on the merits of each transaction, the 'core minimum' guidelines when advising a spouse are as follows (using the example of advising a wife):

- Be satisfied that you have the necessary expertise and time to interpret or advise on what may be very detailed financial information.
- Be satisfied that you can properly act for the wife as well as the husband, namely that there is no conflict of interest.
- Obtain full financial information concerning the husband's account. This will normally include information on the purpose for the new facility, the indebtedness, the amount and terms of the borrowing and a copy of any application form.
- Meet the wife face to face in the absence of the husband (telephone calls and letters are not sufficient).
- Confirm the wife's understanding of the transaction, and correct any misapprehension she may have.
- Explain in non-technical language the nature of the documents and their practical consequences, for example if the husband's business fails, the risk of losing her home and being made bankrupt.
- Emphasise the seriousness of the risks involved.
- Explain the length of time the security will last.
- Explain that the wife has a choice and that the decision to proceed is hers and hers alone.
- If the wife wishes to proceed, there should be clear confirmation from her that this is the case, and she should authorise you to provide written confirmation of this to the lender.

You should also consider the following matters of good professional practice:

- Who will pay your fee for advising the wife? If the wife decides not to guarantee the proposed loan, will your fees get paid at all?
- Open a separate file and send the wife a retainer letter that clearly defines your relationship with her.
- Keep a clear record of your advice, especially if the transaction appears to be to the wife's disadvantage. Consider asking the wife to countersign a copy of that advice.
- The wife's authority for you to provide a 'certificate' to the lender should be given in writing.

8.12 Leasehold mortgages

For mortgages secured on residential leasehold properties, you should check the matters listed next. Refer to **Chapter 14** for more information generally on leasehold properties.

- Ensure you have a clear receipt for the last ground rent.
- Ensure there is no provision for **forfeiture** on bankruptcy of the tenant or any superior tenant.
- Ensure there is a mutual enforceability covenant allowing the tenant to enforce other tenants' covenants in the block.
- Check that the **lessor**'s covenants for repair and maintenance of the structure and common parts are adequate.
- Check that you have the current name and address of the lessor and any management company and that, if limited companies, neither have been struck off the register.
- Are you satisfied with the past three years' accounts of any management company? If not, send them to the lender for clearance.
- If the tenants control the management company, you must keep with the deeds an up-to-date copy of the company's memorandum and articles of association, the borrower's share certificate and a blank transfer signed by the borrower.
- Check that any management company has an interest in land and that the **lessees** are all members of it. If this is not the case, the lessor should be obliged to carry out the management company's obligations should it fail to do so.

- If required, check that the lessor's consent to the proposed lease **assignment** has been obtained.
- If required, check that the lessor's consent to the proposed mortgage on the leasehold property has been obtained.

8.13 Perfecting the mortgage after completion

Following completion, if the borrower is a company incorporated in, or with an established place of business in, England and Wales, the mortgage must be registered at the Companies Registry within 21 days of completion (s860 Companies Act 2006). If it is not registered, the charge will be void against the company's creditors or a liquidator or **administrator**. It is important not to delay in registering the charge as an extension of time cannot be given without a court order and such orders are rarely made. You should also note that the Land Registry's practice is not to raise a requisition requiring a charge to be so registered. The Registry will instead simply enter a note in the charges register referring to the relevant section of the Companies Act.

For registered land, you should lodge your application to register the mortgage at the Land Registry before the expiry of the priority protection period of your **official search** (see **12.5.1** for more details on this important pre-completion search). If the land acquired is unregistered, you must apply for first registration (and registration of the mortgage) within two months of completion.

If the mortgaged property is leasehold, you should check the notice requirements in the **lease**. It will usually be necessary to give notice to the lessor of any mortgage of the **leasehold estate** within a set time and to pay a fee. The notice should be given in duplicate with a request that one copy be returned receipted.

After registration at the Land Registry when the title information document is returned by the Land Registry, remember to check that the lender's mortgage appears properly in the charges register of the title and that the registered title is otherwise in order. Remember that legal mortgages rank in priority according to their order on the charges register; so, for example, do ensure that any intended first mortgage appears first in a list of mortgages on the register.

8.14 Commercial property mortgages

In relation to a mortgage of commercial property, the lender will normally instruct an independent firm to act for it. In these circumstances, the buyer's solicitor must ensure, before committing the buyer to **exchange of contracts**, that the lender's solicitor is satisfied with the title, the results of searches and all other matters.

8.14.1 Requesting information

The borrower's solicitor will be asked to supply copies of all relevant documentation relating to the transaction. Invariably this will include a full abstract or **epitome of title** or **official copies of the registered title**, all necessary searches, replies to pre-contract enquiries, **planning permissions**, details of all occupiers and, assuming the borrower is also buying, the dated and signed contract, replies to requisitions, pre-completion searches and the approved draft purchase deed.

8.14.2 Investigation of title

The lender's solicitor is essentially double-checking the work of the borrower's solicitor. Inevitably this results in duplication of work, but is unavoidable unless the lender is prepared to accept a certificate of title from the borrower's solicitor. If the lender's solicitor has any queries, these should be raised with the borrower's solicitor as formal requisitions. These in turn will be raised by the buyer's solicitor with the seller's solicitor. Although the lender's solicitor will attend to the post-completion work, the borrower's solicitor will normally be expected to supply a completed Land Registry application form.

CONDUCT POINT

The lender's solicitor will normally insist on an undertaking from the borrower's solicitor to be responsible for the lender's costs whether or not the matter proceeds to completion. This is primarily to cover abortive fees. Such an undertaking should be given up to a maximum specified sum, and only with the borrower's express authority. The borrower's solicitor should always consider the merit of obtaining monies in advance from the client before giving such an undertaking.

8.14.3 Procedure

The lender's solicitor will prepare the security documentation (eg mortgage deed) and stipulate that its contents must be properly explained to the borrower. It is normally a requirement that the documentation is executed in the presence of the borrower's solicitor, who will sign as witness. Unless completion occurs at a meeting attended by the lender's solicitor, the latter will normally appoint the borrower's solicitor to act as agent on completion. This is on the basis that the borrower's solicitor holds the mortgage advance to order pending completion and undertakes to supply immediately thereafter the following: all documents of title, the executed security documentation, a Land Registry application form and, if the borrower is buying as well, the executed purchase deed and Form DS1 (or in **unregistered land**, the seller's vacated charge). If the matter proceeds to completion, the lender's solicitor's costs and other payments, such as **stamp duty land tax** and Land Registry fees, will be deducted from the mortgage advance.

EXAMPLE

Ewan acts for Javed who intends to lend £50,000 to his nephew Younis to help him with his launderette business in Dover, which is running into financial difficulties. Younis and his wife live in a leasehold flat which they bought with the aid of a mortgage from Nationwide Building Society. Javed has told his solicitor that Younis is happy to give Javed a second charge on the flat to secure the loan. Younis does not wish to incur the expense of instructing his own solicitor and says he will gladly rely on Ewan's expertise to prepare the necessary paperwork. Ewan should consider the following issues:

- The SRA Code of Conduct effectively prohibits a solicitor from acting for both lender and borrower in a private mortgage. A conflict of interest would arise here if the borrower relied on Ewan's advice and expertise, so Younis must be advised to seek independent legal advice before signing the mortgage.
- As this is a proposed second charge, Ewan should inspect the first charge to establish whether the consent of the first mortgagee Nationwide is required to the creation of the second charge. If its consent is required, this should be obtained in writing before completion of the loan. Nationwide may require Javed to enter into a separate deed of postponement.
- Nationwide should be asked to confirm the current amount outstanding so that Ewan can check whether there is sufficient equity in the property to cover the proposed advance.
- The property is leasehold. The lease should be inspected to see if the landlord's consent is required to charge the property. If so, consent must be obtained before completion otherwise the charge will not bind the landlord. Following completion, it may be necessary to give notice of the charge to the landlord, and this should also be checked in the lease.
- Ewan should investigate title and conduct searches and enquiries in the same way as if his client were buying the property. Before he can advise his client to proceed, he must be satisfied that the title is good and marketable and free from unusual encumbrances. He must also obtain clear results to pre-completion searches, including a bankruptcy search against Younis's full name.

- As Younis lives in the flat with his wife, Ewan must establish if she is a joint owner, in which case she will also have to join in the mortgage as joint borrower. Even if Younis is the sole legal owner, his wife may have an equitable interest in the property and will have statutory rights of occupation under the Family Law Act 1996. She must give her written consent to the proposed charge and agree to postpone all rights behind Ewan's client's charge. Reasonable steps must be taken to ensure that she understands the nature of the transaction and the postponement of her rights (if any). She should therefore receive independent advice herself.
- Does Younis own the launderette premises? If so, have the parties considered the alternative possibility of Javed taking security on this commercial property? That route may prove less complicated.

8.15 Mortgage fraud

If you become aware that your client is engaging in fraudulent activities of any kind, you are obliged as a matter of professional conduct to discontinue acting for the client. Bear in mind that if you continue to act in these circumstances you risk:

- disciplinary proceedings from the Solicitors Regulation Authority for breach of the conduct rules;
- civil proceedings for negligence or breach of contract, for example by a lender who has suffered loss;
- criminal prosecution for aiding and abetting a fraud or conspiracy to defraud. A guilty verdict invariably means a custodial sentence and being struck off the roll.

The Law Society has issued a useful up-to-date practice note on mortgage fraud dated 13 January 2020.

KEY POINT SUMMARY

- Do not act for a buyer and a private lender.
- When acting for a buyer and institutional lender check compliance with the SRA Code of Conduct.
- Check the mortgage instructions contained in the *UK Finance Mortgage Lenders' Handbook*.
- Read the client's mortgage offer carefully, in particular the special conditions.
- Typical special conditions include retentions from advance in respect of repairs or making up roads and drains.
- Ensure that any special conditions can be satisfied.
- Check overall that the mortgage offer is satisfactory to the client.
- The mortgage deed will normally be in the lender's standard format and you will need to complete the blank parts.
- Advise the client of the nature and effect of the mortgage before they execute the deed.
- Advise the client in particular that their home is at risk if they do not meet the monthly repayments.
- Ensure that the client executes the mortgage deed before completion and leave it undated in your file.
- Date the mortgage deed on completion.
- Refer any queries to the lender before exchange of contracts.

- Always comply with the lender's instructions (refer to the *UK Finance Mortgage Lenders' Handbook*).
- Check for occupiers' rights (see **8.10**).
- Carry out a bankruptcy search against the borrower.
- Carry out a company search against a corporate borrower.
- In a standard mortgage of a private residence when reporting on title, use the standard form certificate of title agreed between the Law Society and the Council of Mortgage Lenders.
- If the borrower is a limited company, register the mortgage at the Companies Registry within 21 days of completion.
- For registered land, apply to register the mortgage at the Land Registry before the **priority period** of your pre-completion search expires.
- For unregistered land, within two months of completion apply to the Land Registry to register the mortgage at the same time as your application for first registration.
- When you receive the title information document from the Land Registry, check that the mortgage has been properly registered in the charges register.
- A commercial property lender normally instructs its own solicitors.
- They will 'double-check' that the security property is good and marketable and free from adverse matters.
- They will have a standard set of requirements for the borrower's solicitors.
- They will normally request an undertaking for costs from the borrower's solicitors.
- Inform your lender client of any price alteration or other information that may be relevant to the lending decision. However, you also have a duty of confidentiality to your borrower client, so the borrower must consent to any disclosure you make to the lender.
- If your instructions are unusual or the transaction is unusual, ask your client for a full explanation. If your client is attempting to commit a fraud or if you are in any doubt about your client's motives, discontinue acting.
- Ensure that all monies are paid through the solicitors' accounts, not between the parties direct.
- Be on your guard against false mortgage applications and inflated property valuations. If in doubt, make further investigations; do not accept the situation and just proceed with the transaction.
- When acting for more than one client (eg joint borrowers), take instructions from each client in person. To avoid possible forgery, best practice is for all borrowers to sign the mortgage deed in your presence.
- If you become suspicious about any transaction, you must take appropriate steps and, if necessary, stop acting for the client.
- For further guidance, see the practice note on mortgage fraud available on the Law Society's website.

PART D
Exchange and Pre-Completion

CHAPTER 9
Exchange of Contracts

FUNCTIONING LEGAL KNOWLEDGE

This chapter covers the following functioning legal knowledge required to pass the SQE 1 assessments:

Exchange of contracts:

- how to acquire and dispose of legal and equitable interests in land
- legal formalities required to create and transfer interests in land
- insurance and risk
- the practice, method and authority to exchange
- consequences of exchange

AUTHORITIES UNDERPINNING PRACTICE

The key authorities that underpin this area of practice are listed below. Note that for legislation you are linked to legislation.gov.uk.

Although much of the legislation on this government website is available in its amended form, the incorporation of new amendments into the text of legislation can be delayed. You should refer to legal databases to ensure you are referencing the most up-to-date legislation.

- Section 2 of the Law of Property (Miscellaneous Provisions) Act 1989
  https://www.legislation.gov.uk/ukpga/1989/34/contents
- Section 16 of the Law of Property (Miscellaneous Provisions) Act 1989
  https://www.legislation.gov.uk/ukpga/1989/34/contents
- Law Society formulae for exchanging contracts by telephone
  https://www.lawsociety.org.uk/topics/property/formulae-for-exchanging-contracts-by-telephone

Pre-exchange					Exchange & pre-completion				Completion & post-completion		
Stage 1 Taking instructions & advising client	**Stage 2** Draft contract	**Stage 3** Pre-contract searches, enquiries & planning	**Stage 4** Title	**Stage 5** Mortgage (applies throughout process)	**Stage 6** Exchange of contracts	**Stage 7** Purchase deed	**Stage 8** Pre-completion searches and requisitions	**Stage 9** Financial statements	**Stage 10** Completion	**Stage 11** SDLT & registration	**Stage 12** Delays and remedies

FIGURE 9.1 Conveyancing timeline

9.1 Introduction

Exchange of contracts is the most critical stage in the conveyancing process as it represents the point at which the parties become legally bound to proceed. In this chapter we shall examine pre-exchange matters, the process by which contracts are actually exchanged and matters that should be attended to immediately after exchange has taken place. We shall also consider the risk and responsibility for buildings insurance and the consequences of the buyer occupying the property before completion. There are also helpful decision trees in **Figures 9.2** and **9.3** at the end of the chapter.

9.1.1 **Synchronisation**

If your client is selling one property and buying another (assuming the two transactions are dependent upon each other), the importance of synchronising the two exchanges of contracts cannot be overstated. It is, of course, routinely the case that many clients selling a house or flat will also be buying another, and vice versa. In these cases, the conveyancer must ensure that exchange of contracts on both transactions is synchronised so that the client does not end up with two properties or none at all. Remember that either a seller or buyer in a conveyancing transaction can withdraw without liability at any time prior to exchange of contracts.

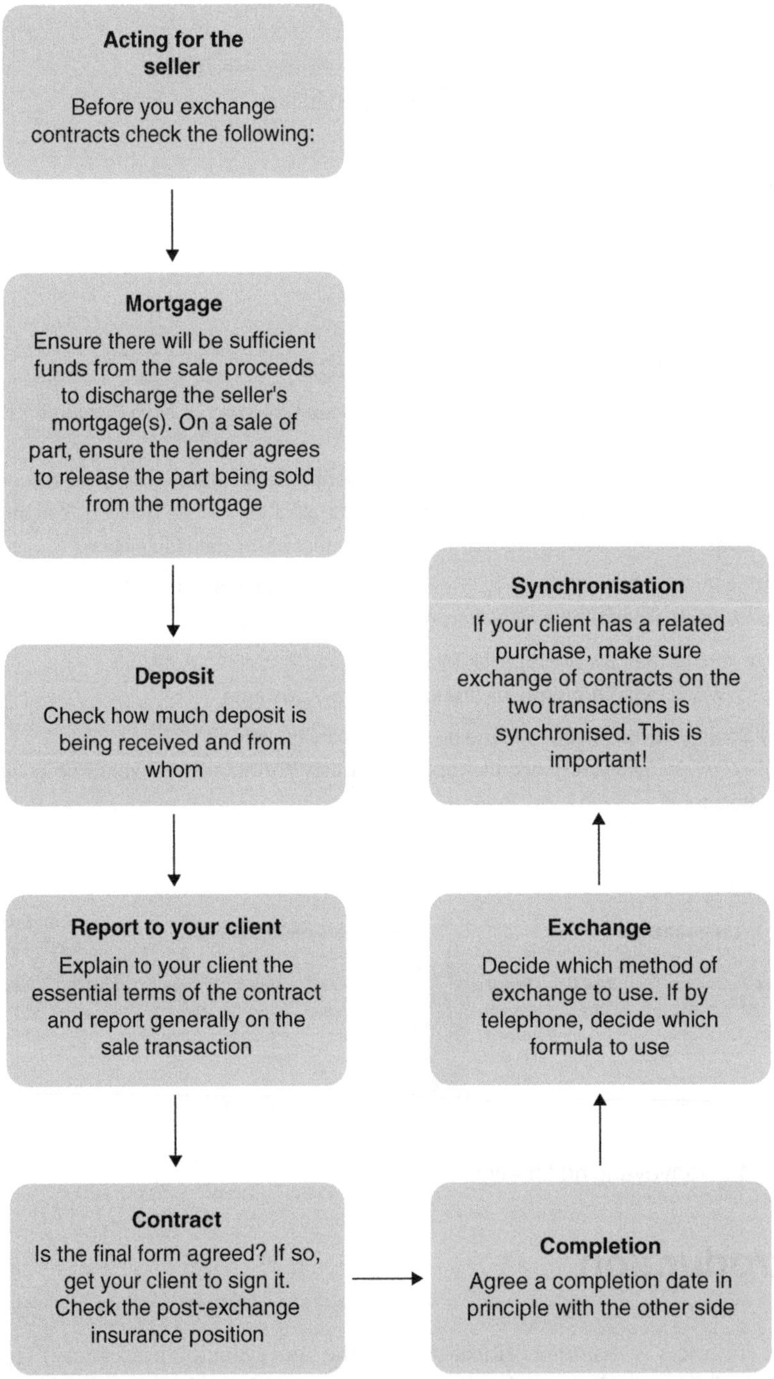

FIGURE 9.2 Exchange of contracts decision tree acting for the seller

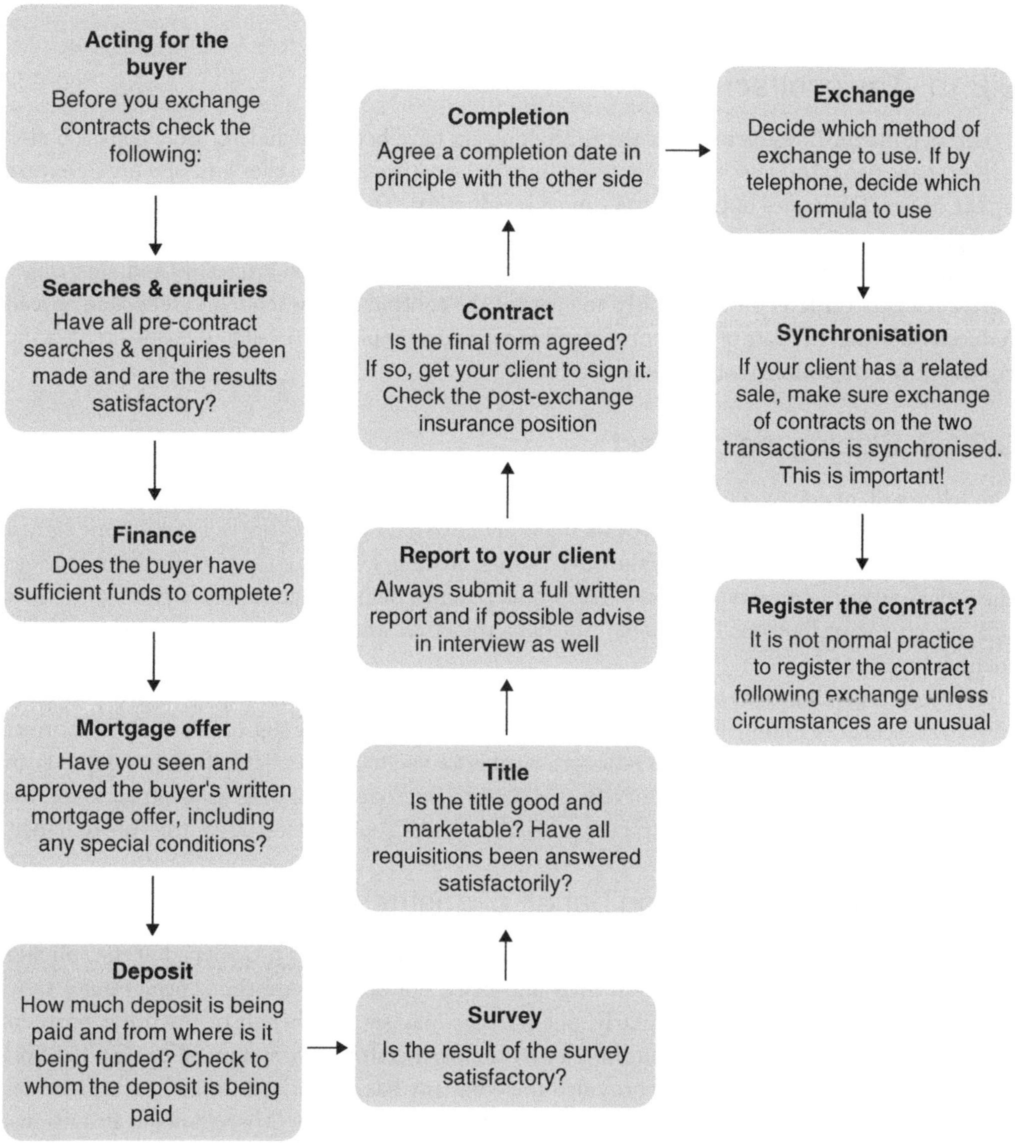

FIGURE 9.3 Exchange of contracts decision tree acting for the buyer

9.1.2 Commercial conveyancing

In a commercial transaction, such as the grant or **assignment** of a **business lease** or the transfer of a freehold property that is tenanted, synchronisation is likely to be of less significance. This is because there is usually no chain; only one property is involved and your client is dealing just with one other company or person, for example a commercial freehold with seller and buyer or a landlord granting a business lease to a commercial tenant. Indeed, in many commercial leasehold transactions, when the landlord and tenant are ready to proceed they may simply go straight to completion without exchanging contracts at all. Nevertheless, in each case it is always important to check whether your client has a related transaction in which synchronisation is required.

9.2 Pre-exchange matters

Before committing your client to an exchange of contracts, important checks must be made to ensure that your client is ready to proceed. Invariably the buyer's solicitor has more to do because of all the enquiries, searches and **title** investigation that have been carried out. We now examine the essential pre-exchange matters when acting for a seller and buyer, respectively.

9.2.1 Seller's pre-exchange checklist

9.2.1.1 The contract

When negotiations on the terms of the draft contract have been concluded, the seller's solicitor will prepare two fair copies of the contract: one for signature by the seller and one for signature by the buyer. The copies of the contract must be identical. The two parts should incorporate all the agreed amendments because otherwise, even if a purported exchange occurs, no contract will come into existence (see s2 Law of Property (Miscellaneous Provisions) Act 1989 and *Harrison v Battye* [1975] 1 WLR 58, in which only one part of the contract was amended to reflect an agreed reduced **deposit**). The date of the contract and the date of completion should not be inserted in the contract until the moment of exchange.

9.2.1.2 Signing the contract

The seller will, of course, need to sign the contract before exchange although the signature need not be witnessed. It is standard conveyancing practice to have two identical contracts, one signed by the seller and the other signed by the buyer, which are then exchanged so that the buyer receives the seller's signed contract, and vice versa. If this practice of exchange is to satisfy s2 of the Law of Property (Miscellaneous Provisions) Act 1989, the buyer and seller must each sign one of two identical copies.

If you are reporting to the seller in person, then this is a good time for the seller to sign the contract in your presence (assuming the terms are agreed). You can then hold the signed but undated contract on file in readiness for exchange. If it is not practicable for you to see the client, then the contract can be sent for signature with your written report. Ask the client to return the signed contract as soon as possible and emphasise that the contract should *not* be dated. You will date the contract on exchange.

9.2.1.3 Signing contract on behalf of another

One trustee or co-owner may sign on behalf of the other trustees or co-owners, but the solicitor should ensure that they have all given their authority, not only to sign the contract but also to proceed with the transaction. Similarly, one partner may sign on behalf of the other partners provided the transaction has been authorised by the partnership. A company officer (eg director) can sign on behalf of the company provided the company has authorised the transaction. As far as **personal representatives** are concerned, s16 of the Law of Property (Miscellaneous Provisions) Act 1994 provides that all proving personal representatives must be parties to the contract (and **purchase deed**). However, one personal representative can sign the contract on behalf of all, provided authorisation for signature has been given.

CONDUCT POINT

It is permitted for the conveyancing solicitor personally to sign the contract on behalf of the client, and in practice this is often done to save time. Strictly speaking, however, you should sign only if you have been formally appointed as the client's attorney (as attorney you can sign in your own name or the client's) or if the client has given you express authority to sign, preferably in writing. On a sale by auction, an auctioneer has implied authority to sign for both parties.

9.2.1.4 Non-owning occupiers

In addition, any non-owning occupiers will be expected to sign the contract to release any rights and agree to vacate the property on or before completion. See **4.2** for further information on this point and **2.3** for trusts and **co-ownership** generally.

9.2.1.5 Seller's mortgage

If the subject property being sold has an existing **mortgage** secured on it, the buyer will require the mortgage to be repaid and discharged on or before completion (repayment is normally made from the sale proceeds on completion). Accordingly, the seller's solicitor must ensure before exchange that there will be sufficient funds available from the proceeds of sale (and/or other sources) to discharge the mortgage. Failure to do so will amount to negligence if the client suffers loss. Request a **redemption statement** from the lender for confirmation of the outstanding mortgage debt.

9.2.1.6 Sale of part

If only part of the seller's property is being sold, it will not be necessary to discharge fully any mortgage on the property (although the seller may choose to do so if sufficient monies are available). The buyer will merely be concerned to ensure that the part of land being bought is released from the mortgage. The seller's solicitor must therefore enquire of the existing **mortgagee** how much is required for the release of the part being sold, and ensure that at least this sum will be available on completion to forward to the mortgagee.

9.2.1.7 Synchronisation of related purchase

If the seller is expecting to purchase another property at the same time as they are selling a property, then you must synchronise exchange of contracts on both sale and purchase transactions. The ways of achieving synchronisation by telephonic exchange are discussed in **9.3.3**. The dangers of not synchronising become apparent in the following disastrous chain of events:

- You exchange on the sale before the purchase.
- Your client's seller withdraws before you can exchange on the purchase.
- Your client is legally bound to complete the sale and does so.
- Your client has no property to move into and will have to find temporary accommodation and arrange furniture storage.

CONDUCT POINT

If you fail to synchronise exchange of contracts on a related sale and purchase and the client suffers loss, you will be negligent.

9.2.2 Buyer's pre-exchange checklist

9.2.2.1 Searches and enquiries

The buyer's solicitor must be satisfied with the results of all relevant pre-contract searches and enquiries, including the enquiries made of the seller's solicitor (see generally **Chapter** 7). Any outstanding matters must be resolved to the satisfaction of the client and the solicitor before contracts are exchanged. Increasingly, to check there are no problems, practitioners are carrying out the traditional pre-completion searches, for example an **official search** of the **Land Registry**, bankruptcy search before exchange as well as before completion (see **Chapter 10**).

9.2.2.2 Survey

As we have seen, ***caveat emptor*** ('let the buyer beware') applies to the purchase of land, and the buyer (and any lender) must be satisfied with the outcome of the **survey** before proceeding to exchange of contracts. Ensure that the survey carried out is more than a simple valuation. Surveys are examined in more detail at **3.3**.

9.2.2.3 Title

As we saw in **Chapter** 7, the purchaser's solicitor should **investigate title** before exchange. Many contracts expressly prohibit the raising of **requisitions on title** after exchange. Accordingly, the solicitor acting for the buyer and lender will have to be satisfied that the title is good and marketable, and free from **encumbrances** that might adversely affect the value of the property or its use and enjoyment. All outstanding requisitions on title should be resolved to your satisfaction before contracts are exchanged.

9.2.2.4 Buyer's financial arrangements

When taking instructions at the beginning of a transaction we have seen that you should check that the buyer's proposed financial arrangements are in order. See **Chapter 8** on mortgages.

9.2.2.5 Deposit

The deposit paid on exchange is normally 10 per cent of the purchase price, but check the contract to establish how much has been agreed.

9.2.2.6 Cleared funds

You must ensure that you have cleared funds for the deposit before exchange occurs. A bank transfer from the client is preferable but if the client is paying by cheque you must allow time for it to clear through your firm's account. The reason for this is that Standard Condition (SC) 2.2.4 requires the deposit to be paid either by electronic means from an account held in the name of a conveyancer at a clearing bank to an account in the name of a conveyancer, or by cheque drawn on a solicitor's or licensed conveyancer's client account.

9.2.2.7 Utilising deposit from related sale

If your client has a related sale, it may be possible to fund the deposit in other ways. Your client may be able to utilise the deposit receivable on a related sale; your client might consider offering a deposit guarantee instead of a money deposit; a **bridging loan** might also be a possibility. All of these methods (including the risks of bridging finance) were examined in some detail at **4.6**, but a further word should be mentioned here about **undertakings**.

9.2.2.8 Bridging finance and undertakings

If a bank has offered the client bridging finance, the bank will invariably require your firm's undertaking to repay the bridging loan from the proceeds of the client's related sale (note that a bridging loan will normally only be available where the client has a related sale). Indeed, the *whole* of the net proceeds are normally requested so that the balance received, after the bridging loan has been repaid, is credited to the client's bank account.

CONDUCT POINT

Before giving an undertaking to repay a bridging loan, you will need to consider its terms very carefully to ensure that you can comply with them. The bank is likely to have a standard form of undertaking but you should always consider whether this is satisfactory both to you and your client. Remember when undertaking to pay money that such payment should be conditional upon your firm actually receiving the funds in the first place. Furthermore, you should obtain from your client prior irrevocable written authority to give the undertaking. The undertaking should not be given until just before exchange, once you are satisfied that there are no outstanding matters to be resolved.

9.2.2.9 Buildings insurance

This is covered in **9.6**. If the buyer (or buyer's lender) is to insure the property after exchange, arrangements should be put in place before exchange so that all that is needed after exchange is, at most, a simple telephone call to put the policy on risk. Some lenders will automatically put insurance in place from exchange.

CONDUCT POINT

You have a duty to use reasonable care and skill in giving such advice as the particular transaction demands having regard to the level of knowledge and expertise of your client. So you would generally give fuller advice to a first-time buyer than you would to, say, an experienced property developer. Failure to give adequate advice may constitute breach of your duty, entitling the client to damages. Your advice to the client may be given orally or in writing, or by using both methods. For the avoidance of doubt it is best practice, at the very least, to report in writing.

9.2.2.10 Oral report

Ideally, you should try to report to your client in person as well as in writing. A sensible approach would be to start by sending your client copies of the relevant documentation, such as replies to pre-contract enquiries, local search, draft contract and, for **registered land**, **official copies of the title**. In your covering letter, you could invite the client to read the documents and to arrange an appointment with you to discuss the points arising from them. When subsequently you meet the client you can go through the papers, explaining their significance and highlighting any adverse matters that may be revealed.

EXAMPLE

Here are some examples of adverse matters upon which you should advise the buyer:

- The replies to enquiries may disclose a neighbour dispute.
- The title may contain **covenants** prohibiting business use or imposing fencing obligations.
- The local search may show that a flyover is being built within 200 metres of the property.

Your meeting with the client will also give you an opportunity to discuss the terms of your client's mortgage offer (if any) and the result of the survey. A full attendance note of your advice should be kept on file and your oral advice confirmed in a letter to the client. The letter is helpful for the client for future reference and the written record of your advice will also protect you against the forgetful client who later complains that certain matters were not brought to their attention. Dictate the attendance note and letter immediately after the interview when matters are still fresh in your mind.

9.2.2.11 Written report

Of course, it may not be practicable to report to the client face to face in which case you will make a full written report. Write the report in language that the client can understand. It should refer to all matters that may adversely affect the client's use and enjoyment of the property, particularly the following:

1. Advise that the property is being bought in its actual state and condition and that the client must be satisfied with the survey.
2. Explain the significance of the searches you have carried out (eg coal mining, commons, **local land charges**).
3. In respect of the local search:
   - advise whether the road fronting the property is publicly maintained;
   - advise whether there are any plans for new roads in the immediate vicinity of the property;
   - report that the search relates only to the subject property not neighbouring properties.
4. In respect of the water search:
   - advise whether foul and surface water drainage is connected to the public sewers;
   - advise whether the water supply is connected to the public water system.
5. In respect of the purchase contract:
   - confirm the property description (if appropriate, by reference to a plan);
   - confirm the price and deposit arrangements;
   - advise who will bear the risk of insurance between exchange and completion (see **10.6**);
   - explain any special conditions.

6 In respect of the seller's replies to enquiries (or Property Information Form):
- highlight any adverse matters;
- draw the client's attention to the fixtures, fittings and contents form so that the client knows which items the seller is taking and which are being left;
- advise which boundaries the seller has maintained.

7 Give the client information about outgoings. In particular:
- advise the client which band the property is in for council tax purposes;
- the current annual charge for water rates;
- if the property is leasehold, the rent and likely level of any **service charge** the client will have to pay.

8 In respect of the title:
- if registered, confirm the class of title (eg absolute);
- advise about any covenants that bind the property and any rights to which the property is subject;
- advise whether the property has the benefit of any rights or **easements** (eg a right of way along a private accessway).

9 If the client is obtaining a mortgage, explain the main terms of the mortgage offer and draw the client's attention to the general mortgage conditions and any special conditions. Advise that the property is at risk if repayments are not maintained or if the mortgage conditions are breached. Unless it is a fixed rate or capped mortgage, advise that the lender is entitled to raise the interest rate. Advise of any retention by the mortgagee.

10 If the property is leasehold, explain the main terms of the lease, in particular the tenant's covenants and the landlord's right to forfeit if the covenants are breached (see generally **Chapter 14** on leasehold properties).

11 Finally, invite the client to telephone you if any matters in the report are unclear or if the client has any questions or queries.

9.2.2.12 Approving the draft contract

The buyer's solicitor should consider the terms of the draft contract carefully in the light of the buyer's instructions, the replies to pre-contract enquiries, the results of searches and the title investigation. If amendments to the contract are necessary, these should be made in red and the contract then returned to the seller's solicitor for consideration. You should retain a copy of the amended contract on your purchase file.

When negotiations on the terms of the draft contract have been concluded, the seller's solicitor will prepare two fair copies of the contract; one for signature by the seller and one for signature by the buyer. The copies of the contract must be identical. The two parts should incorporate all the agreed amendments because otherwise, even if a purported exchange occurs, no contract will come into existence (see s2 Law of Property (Miscellaneous Provisions) Act 1989 and *Harrison v Battye* [1975] 1 WLR 58, in which only one part of the contract was amended to reflect an agreed reduced deposit).

9.2.2.13 Buyer to sign contract

The buyer will, of course, need to sign the contract before exchange although the signature need not be witnessed. See comments at **9.2.1** in relation to the seller's signature; the same principles apply when acting for the buyer. The date of the contract and the date of completion should not be inserted in the contract until the moment of exchange.

9.2.2.14 Synchronisation of related sale

If the buyer is relying on money from a related sale in order to assist the finance of the purchase (ie the purchase is dependent on the sale), then the solicitor must synchronise exchange of contracts on both sale and purchase transactions. The ways of achieving synchronisation by telephonic exchange are discussed at **9.3.3**. The dangers of not synchronising become apparent in the following disastrous chain of events:

- You exchange on the purchase before the sale.
- Your client's purchaser withdraws before you can exchange on the sale.
- Your client is legally bound to complete the purchase but is unable financially to do so. Your client is thus in breach of the purchase contract.
- Even if your client can secure alternative funds to complete (eg bridging loan), your client will end up with two properties.

As previously mentioned, if you fail to synchronise exchange of contracts on a related sale and purchase and the client suffers loss, you will be negligent.

9.3 Exchange of contracts

Once the seller and buyer are ready to proceed, the next step is to exchange contracts and thereby bring the contract into force. There are three principal methods by which exchange of contracts can be effected:

- in person; or
- by post (or document exchange); or
- by telephone (the most common method).

9.3.1 In person

In this method, the parties' solicitors meet, normally at the seller's solicitors' office. They physically exchange their respective clients' signed contracts and the buyer's solicitor hands over the client account deposit cheque. The **completion date** is written in and the contracts are then dated. A personal exchange is recognised as being the safest method because it is an instant exchange and the solicitors can personally check that the contracts are identical. However, exchange in person is very rarely used today unless the two offices are closely situated. Pressures of time and the need for synchronisation in chain transactions make personal exchanges largely incompatible with the requirements of modern conveyancing.

9.3.2 By post (or document exchange)

In this method, the buyer's solicitor posts the buyer's signed contract and the cheque for the deposit to the seller's solicitor. Upon receipt, the seller's solicitor posts the seller's signed contract to the buyer's solicitor. It may also happen the other way round by the seller sending their contract first. If the Standard Conditions are being used, SC 2.1 confirms the common law postal rule on acceptance laid down in *Adams v Lindsell* (1818) 1 B & Ald 681, namely that the contract comes into existence not when the second copy is received but when the second copy is posted (or deposited at the document exchange). Thus, even if the contract is lost in the post, a binding contract still exists.

We do not recommend postal exchange where either party has a linked transaction, namely a dependent sale or purchase. The reason for this is the time lag between the first contract being posted and the second contract being posted, and during this time either party is, of course, free to change their mind and withdraw.

9.3.3 By telephone

This is the most common method of exchange used by solicitors today. The moment of exchange occurs at the point in the telephone conversation when the solicitors agree that contracts are actually exchanged. The decision in *Domb v Isoz* [1980] Ch 548 formally endorsed the practice of telephonic exchange and, following a recommendation by Templeman LJ, the Law Society subsequently produced formulae for use by solicitors.

CONDUCT POINT

As the telephone formulae involve the use of professional undertakings, they should be used only between firms of solicitors and licensed conveyancers; that is, not where unqualified persons are involved. Any variations of the formulae should be recorded on the solicitors' files and confirmed in writing, in case of any later disputes.

9.3.3.1 Telephone formulae

Formula A

This formula should be used when one party's solicitor (usually the seller's) holds *both* signed parts of the contract together with the deposit cheque (the buyer's solicitor will have forwarded the buyer's contract and deposit cheque to the seller's solicitor to be held to order in readiness for exchange).

EXAMPLE

On the assumption that it is the seller's solicitor who holds both parts of the contract, formula A works as follows (S = seller's solicitor, B = buyer's solicitor):

- S confirms holding the seller's signed contract and the buyer's signed contract and deposit cheque.
- S and B agree that S will insert the agreed completion date in each contract.
- Exchange is formally agreed by B releasing the buyer's contract and S agreeing to hold the seller's contract to B's order.
- S undertakes to forward the seller's contract to B that day, either by first-class post, personal delivery or document exchange.

Following exchange, the solicitors must write file memos recording: their own names, the date and time of exchange, the formula used (and any variations to it), the completion date and the amount of the deposit being paid.

Formula B

This formula should be used when both solicitors hold their own clients' signed contracts (and the buyer's solicitor has cleared funds for the deposit).

EXAMPLE

The solicitors confirm that they hold the signed contracts, they insert the agreed completion date, each agrees to hold their client's contract to the other's order and they undertake to send the contracts out that day (plus, for the buyer, the deposit cheque). File memos should be made after exchange recording the details of the conversation (see formula A earlier).

Formula C

This formula should be used where there is a chain of transactions and the deposit monies are to be sent directly to another firm further up the chain.

EXAMPLE

The solicitor at one end of the chain (X) telephones the solicitor next in line (Y). Both solicitors confirm that they hold their clients' signed contracts. X undertakes that X will definitely exchange with Y if Y rings back X before a specified time later that day requesting X to exchange. The same undertakings are then given to the other solicitors in the chain until the penultimate one in the chain is reached. Now at the end of the chain, a formula B exchange can occur between the penultimate solicitor and the solicitor at the end (assuming they are both ready). Thereafter, the other contracts can be exchanged, one by one, back down the chain as the return calls are made. Thus the first call (eg by X to Y) activates formula C part 1; the return call (eg by Y to X)—when the exchange occurs—activates formula C part 2.

File memos should be made in respect of the conversations in parts 1 and 2, respectively. The part 1 memo will record the date and time of the conversation, the names of the solicitors speaking, any agreed variations to formula C, the final time later in the day for exchange, the completion date and the name of the solicitor to whom the deposit is to be paid (formula C assumes a 10 per cent deposit). The part 2 memo will record the request to exchange, the time of exchange and the identities of the speakers.

The following points should also be noted regarding formula C:

- Each caller activating part 1 (eg X in the earlier example) must give the name of two other persons in the office who could take the part 2 return call if X is unavailable. X is undertaking that X or one of the other persons will be available up to the final time for exchange.
- Formula C cannot be held over to the next day. If exchange does not take place during the day, the whole process must be restarted and part 1 will be reactivated on another day.
- The contract must allow the deposit to be passed on up the chain and it must ultimately be held as stakeholder (this is permitted by the Standard Conditions). Consequently, you may well find yourself undertaking that another solicitor will be sending deposit monies. Be aware that this is an undertaking to do something that is outside your direct control.
- You should obtain the client's express irrevocable authority (preferably in writing) to exchange using formula C. Unless the client's authority is irrevocable, there is the risk that the client will instruct you to withdraw from the transaction after you have given (in part 1) the undertaking that you will definitely exchange if requested to do so. This would leave you in 'no man's land' because if you now accept your client's instructions and refuse to exchange, you will be in breach of your undertaking. However, if you go ahead and exchange, you will be in breach of your duty to your client by acting contrary to your client's instructions.

9.3.3.2 Fax and email

An exchange of faxes or emails is not a valid method of exchanging contracts. The common law rule is reinforced by SC 1.3.3 which provides, in effect, that where the delivery of a document is essential (eg exchange of contracts), transmission by fax or email is not a valid means of delivery. Faxes or emails may be used, however, to activate the Law Society's formulae for telephonic exchange.

9.3.3.3 Reforming the exchange process

At the time of writing, the Law Society is consulting on a new code for signing and exchanging contracts for the sale of land. The draft code's intention is to allow the use of modern technology to conduct transactions, for example e-signatures such as PDF scans of wet-ink contracts and the use of secure e-signature platforms such as DocuSign (commonly used in letting agreements). As things stand, the so-called Immediate Exchange Protocol 2024 may replace formulae A and B, and the Release of Contracts Protocol 2024 may replace formula C of the Law Society's formulae for exchanging contracts. One key issue in these consultations, however, will be how to satisfy the requirements of s2 of the Law of Property (Miscellaneous Provisions) Act 1989 (see **4.4**). For more information on these proposed reforms to the exchange process, see their website: https://www.lawsociety.org.uk/topics/property/code-for-signing-and-exchanging-property-contracts.

TABLE 9.1

Formula A	Formula B	Formula C
Use where one party's solicitor holds both signed parts of the contract, together with the deposit.	Use where both solicitors hold their own clients' signed contracts (and the buyer's solicitor has cleared funds for the deposit).	Use where there is a chain of transactions and the deposit monies are to be sent directly to another firm further up the chain.

9.4 **Action to be taken immediately after exchange of contracts**

- If exchange has taken place by telephone, then appropriate memos and letters to the other side must be written in compliance with undertakings that have been given, if necessary accompanied by the signed contracts and deposit cheques.
- Remember to date the contract with the date of exchange and insert the agreed completion date.
- Enter the completion date in your diary so that it is not overlooked.
- Telephone the clients to inform them that you have exchanged and to confirm the completion date. Confirm your telephone conversation in writing (advise them not to open the champagne just yet, though—the other side still have to complete).
- The seller's solicitor should write to the seller's mortgagee, if any, requesting a redemption statement calculated to the date of completion with a daily rate of interest thereafter in case completion is delayed.
- If the buyer is to insure the property from exchange of contracts (see **9.6**), the buyer's solicitor must ensure that the insurance policy is activated immediately after exchange. In practice, the buyer's mortgagee will normally arrange the insurance and this will often occur automatically without any need for you to contact the mortgagee. However, the matter must be checked in each case.
- If necessary, the buyer's solicitor should protect the contract by registration (see **9.7**).
- The seller's solicitor can contact the estate agents (if any) who acted on the sale to advise them of the exchange and completion date. The agents will no doubt send their commission account for you to discharge out of the proceeds of sale on completion.

9.5 **The effect of a binding contract**

As soon as there is a valid contract, the beneficial ownership in the property passes to the buyer. Consequently, the buyer at common law bears the risk of any loss or damage to the property, subject to the seller's duty to look after the property (see next section). The buyer is, however, entitled to any increase in value of the property between exchange and completion. The seller has a lien over the property for the balance of the purchase money.

9.5.1 **Seller's duty as trustee**

The seller retains ownership of the legal **estate** as a qualified trustee for the buyer. The trusteeship confers on the seller a duty to exercise reasonable care to keep the property in the same condition as it was at the date of the contract (*Clarke v Ramuz* [1891] 2 QB 456, CA). Accordingly, in winter the seller should keep the heating on to ensure that the water in the pipes does not freeze. The seller should also replace any slates or windows that may become broken between exchange and completion and should probably also tend any garden of the property. The seller's duty continues even if the seller vacates before completion but the seller's duty will end if the buyer is allowed into occupation before completion (see **9.8**).

During the seller's trusteeship, the seller is entitled to remain in possession and to receive any rents and profits but must also discharge the outgoings of the property, such as council tax and water rates.

9.6 **Risk and responsibility for buildings insurance**

A solicitor will be negligent if proper advice is not given concerning risk and insurance and the client suffers loss as a result. It will be necessary for the solicitor to consider these matters at the draft contract stage because the question of who bears the risk of insurance of the property will depend upon the terms of the contract.

9.6.1 Standard Condition 5.1

If the Standard Conditions are being used, SC 5.1.1 reflects the open contract position by stating that the property is at the risk of the buyer from the date of the contract. It is therefore important for the buyer (or if the buyer requires mortgage finance, the buyer's mortgagee) to arrange adequate insurance of the property from the moment of exchange. This is because if the property is damaged (eg by fire), the buyer will still be contractually bound to complete the purchase.

SC 5.1.2 states that the seller is under no obligation to insure the property unless:

1 the contract provides that a policy effected by or for the seller and insuring the property or any part of it against liability for loss or damage is to continue in force; or

2 the property or any part of it is let on terms under which the seller (whether as landlord or as tenant) is obliged to insure against loss or damage.

SC 5.1.3 goes on to provide that if the seller is obliged to insure under SC 5.1.2, then the seller is to do everything necessary to maintain the policy and permit the buyer to inspect the policy or evidence of its terms. Moreover if, before completion, the property suffers loss or damage, the seller must pay to the buyer on completion the amount of the policy monies that the seller has received, so far as not applied in repairing or reinstating the property. If no final payment has been received, the seller must assign to the buyer, at the buyer's expense, all rights to claim under the policy in such form as the buyer reasonably requires. Pending execution of the assignment, the seller must hold any policy monies received in trust for the buyer. Finally, if the seller is obliged to insure under SC 5.1.2 they must cancel the policy on completion of the sale of the property.

9.6.2 Commercial property

The Standard Commercial Property Conditions (SCPCs) are discussed more fully in **Chapter 16**. Under the SCPCs, the buyer also assumes the risk from exchange of contracts.

9.6.3 Insurance and leases

SC 5.1.4 provides that where the property is leasehold and the property or any building containing it is insured by a reversioner or other third party, the seller must use reasonable efforts to ensure that the insurance is maintained until completion. If before completion the property or building suffers loss or damage, the seller must assign to the buyer on completion (at the buyer's expense) such rights as the seller may have in the policy monies, in such form as the buyer reasonably requires.

9.7 Protecting the contract by registration

A contract to purchase land is an **estate contract** and unless the buyer's solicitor protects the contract by registration, it will not bind a bona fide purchaser of the legal estate. If the property has an unregistered title, the appropriate protective registration is a C(iv) land **charge** against the name of the estate owner at the Central Land Charges Department in Plymouth. If the property has a registered title, the appropriate protective registration is a notice against the registered title using either Form AN1 (where the seller is in agreement, known as an agreed notice) or unilaterally by the buyer on Form UN1 (known as a unilateral notice).

If a solicitor fails to register a contract which subsequently becomes void resulting in loss to the buyer, the solicitor will be liable in professional negligence. Despite this, it has become standard practice amongst solicitors not to register the contract except in the following situations:

- where a dispute arises between the parties; or
- the buyer becomes suspicious of the seller possibly seeking to dispose of the property to someone else; or
- more commonly, where there is a long period of time between exchange and completion (eg in excess of six weeks).

Notwithstanding current practice, you should always bear in mind your professional duty to your client and, if in any doubt, you should register the contract. Note that an option to purchase or a right of pre-emption should always be protected by registration.

9.8 Occupation by the buyer before completion

Following exchange of contracts, the seller may receive a request from the buyer for access to the property before completion, perhaps to take measurements for carpets or curtains, or to take a final look around before moving in. A request of this nature should not cause any problems for the seller provided the keys are not handed over and the buyer's visit is supervised, perhaps by the estate agent who negotiated the sale.

Occasionally, however, the buyer will want to begin decorating or to carry out alterations or even actually to move in before completion. The seller should treat such requests with caution for the simple reason that the property does not properly belong to the buyer until the balance of the purchase price has been paid and the title to the legal estate has been transferred. Once in possession, a buyer might easily lose their motivation to complete. Moreover, a residential occupier cannot be compelled to vacate without an eviction order from the court (s2 Protection from Eviction Act 1977). An even worse scenario for the seller would be inadvertently to create a **tenancy** in which the buyer acquires security of tenure. In this case, the seller may be hard pressed to recover possession at all.

In the light of these dangers, if a buyer in a straightforward transaction requests anything more than a simple inspection, a prudent seller should refuse; after all, the buyer should not have long to wait until completion. Another possibility could be for the parties to agree an earlier completion, if this is convenient. However, you will need to consider the effect of this on any related sale or purchase because it may be that other parties in the chain do not wish to complete early.

9.8.1 Conditions of entry

Despite the earlier advice, there will be times when the seller will consider permitting the buyer into occupation before completion. For instance, there may be a very long period between exchange and completion or the property may be in need of urgent repairs that the buyer has undertaken to carry out. If this is the case, the seller will have to think carefully about the conditions under which the buyer will be allowed to occupy.

If the buyer goes into possession before completion, the position at common law is that the seller's liability to maintain the property ceases and the buyer is required to pay interest on the balance of the purchase monies. This alone is insufficient to protect the seller from the risks mentioned earlier but, if the Standard Conditions are used, help is at hand in SC 5.2. The principal protection afforded to the seller under SC 5.2 is that the buyer occupies as licensee not as tenant. The effect of this is that the buyer is conferred no security of tenure.

If occupation is agreed before completion, the solicitors for seller and buyer must each explain the conditions of the occupation agreement to their respective clients, and obtain their confirmatory instructions. The consent of any mortgagee should also be obtained if this is a requirement of the mortgage.

9.9 Variation of the contract between exchange and completion

A typical variation of the contract might occur where the parties decide after exchange to have a different date for completion. This occurred in *McCausland v Duncan Lawrie Ltd* [1997] 1 WLR 38, where the solicitors exchanged for completion on 26 March but subsequently realised that this was a Sunday, so they exchanged letters agreeing 24 March instead. The Court of Appeal held that the purported variation was unenforceable because any variation of the contract must comply strictly with the provisions of s2 of the Law of Property (Miscellaneous Provisions) Act 1989. This means that there has to be a further exchange of documents, signed by the parties, referring to the original contract and the subsequent variation.

9.10 Death of seller or buyer between exchange and completion

Where this unfortunate event occurs the obligations under the contract remain unaffected and the deceased's personal representatives are bound to complete, i.e. they 'step into the shoes' of the deceased. It is important to advise the other party to the contract as soon as possible, as it may be necessary to seek either a termination of the contract (unlikely) or a postponement of the completion date.

If the other side does not agree to this and completion is likely to be delayed, you can apply to the Probate Registry for an expedited or limited grant of representation. Ask the Probate Registry to deal with the application quickly so as to avoid the deceased's estate incurring liability for breach of contract.

If one of three or more co-sellers dies, the sale can proceed as normal. If one of two co-sellers dies, check whether they held as joint tenants or tenants in common. If tenants in common, it will be necessary to appoint a second trustee to act with the survivor. Unless the deceased's share passed by survivorship enabling a surviving co-seller(s) to sell the whole beneficial estate, do not complete until the grant of representation has been issued.

On the death of a sole buyer, any mortgage offer is likely to be withdrawn, so the personal representatives will have to find alternative funding. If you need to serve notice on a deceased estate owner, address it to the deceased and the deceased's personal representatives at the deceased's last known address; also send a copy to the Public Trustee.

9.11 Bankruptcy of seller or buyer between exchange and completion

In respect of a registered title, a notice on the title will alert the buyer that a petition in bankruptcy has been presented against the registered proprietor. A bankruptcy restriction will alert the buyer that a bankruptcy order has been made. The bankruptcy proceedings will also be registered at the Land Charges Department in Plymouth. The land charges registrations are relevant for buyers of *unregistered* land only—it is not necessary to conduct a land charges search against the seller when buying registered land.

A buyer who has relevant notice of bankruptcy proceedings should wait to take a transfer from the trustee in bankruptcy, not the seller. The buyer's solicitor should ask to see a copy of the bankruptcy order together with documentary proof of the trustee's appointment. Similarly, a buyer from a liquidator or administrative receiver of a company will require written evidence of the appointment.

Any disposition by a bankrupt (including payment of purchase money) after the presentation of the petition is void. The same rule applies on company insolvency. Anyone buying from, or selling to, a company being wound up should deal with the liquidator of the company. A person dealing with a liquidator must ensure that the formalities of the liquidator's appointment have been observed. The appointment of an administrative receiver will normally crystallize a floating charge so that it becomes a fixed charge on the company's property. A buyer must ensure that the property is released from the fixed charge.

A bankruptcy order will sever a beneficial joint tenancy. The bankrupt co-owner's beneficial interest vests in the trustee, who must execute the purchase deed with the surviving co-owner(s).

KEY POINT SUMMARY

- Are results of all searches and enquiries satisfactory? Check that all queries have been resolved.
- Is the result of the survey satisfactory?
- Is the title good and marketable? Check that all requisitions have been dealt with satisfactorily.

- Has the buyer received a mortgage offer (if needed) and are the conditions acceptable? Ensure that all conditions of the mortgage offer can be met.
- Acting for the buyer, are you in funds for the deposit payable on exchange?
- Is the buyer required to insure the property from exchange? If so, are arrangements in hand to do so?
- Have you reported in writing to the buyer?
- Have all the terms of the contract been agreed? Check that all agreed amendments are included in the final form of contract.
- Has your client signed the agreed form of contract?
- Agree the completion date to be inserted in the contract on exchange.
- Ensure that you synchronise exchange on any related sale or purchase.
- SC 5.1 reflects the open contract position by stating that the risk passes to the buyer on exchange of contracts. However, look carefully at 5.1.2 and 5.1.3 (or SCPC 8.2), which contain detailed provisions (the seller may already be obliged to insure, eg under a lease or pursuant to the contract).
- Under the Standard Commercial Property Conditions, the risk also passes to the buyer on exchange of contracts.
- Whoever assumes the risk, the seller should maintain their existing insurance until completion just in case damage occurs, the buyer defaults and completion does not occur.
- After exchange the seller is a qualified trustee of the legal estate and owes a duty to the buyer to exercise reasonable care to keep the property in the same condition as it was at the date of the contract.
- Is seller's mortgagee's consent required to sale, for example on sale of part?
- If occupation by buyer before completion is agreed (which is rare), the buyer should enter under **licence** only (eg under SC 5.2).
- Both seller and buyer should be advised of the conditions of any pre-completion occupation by the buyer and their instructions confirmed.
- Taking into account the net mortgage advance, the proceeds of any related sale and all costs and disbursements, does your buyer client have sufficient funds to proceed with the purchase?
- How much deposit is being paid and to whom? Obtain cleared funds before exchange. If bridging finance is required, you will need to give an undertaking to the lender.
- Report in writing to the client fully on all aspects of the transaction before obtaining the client's signature to the contract.
- It will be usual for the buyer to insure the property from exchange so, if appropriate, make all necessary arrangements so that the policy can be brought into force on exchange.
- If there is a related sale, ensure that you achieve synchronisation of the purchase and sale. Are all transactions in the chain ready to proceed?
- Decide on which method of exchange to use. Telephonic is the most common.
- If the seller has a mortgage, ensure that there will be sufficient sale proceeds to discharge it. On a sale of part, the lender must agree to release the part being sold from the mortgage.
- If there is a related purchase, ensure that you achieve synchronisation of the sale and purchase. Are all transactions in the chain ready to proceed?
- Make a diary entry of the completion date once exchange has occurred.
- If exchange was by telephone, prepare necessary memoranda for the file(s).
- Comply with any undertakings given on exchange, for example to dispatch the dated and signed contract and deposit monies.
- The seller's practitioner should request redemption statement from any mortgagee(s).
- The seller's practitioner should advise the estate agent (if any).
- If appropriate, the buyer's practitioner should protect the contract by registration.
- If the completion date is near, the buyer's practitioner should apply for pre-completion searches (see **Chapter 10**).

CHAPTER 10

The Purchase Deed and Pre-Completion Procedures

FUNCTIONING LEGAL KNOWLEDGE

This chapter covers the following functioning legal knowledge required to pass the SQE 1 assessments:

Pre-completion:

- form of **transfer** deed and formalities for execution
- pre-completion searches
- pre-completion steps

AUTHORITIES UNDERPINNING PRACTICE

The key authorities that underpin this area of practice are listed below. Note that for legislation you are linked to legislation.gov.uk.

Although much of the legislation on this government website is available in its amended form, the incorporation of new amendments into the text of legislation can be delayed. You should refer to legal databases to ensure you are referencing the most up-to-date legislation.

- Sections 52, 62, 67, 69, 79 and 198 of the Law of Property Act 1925
  https://www.legislation.gov.uk/ukpga/Geo5/15-16/20/contents
- Section 1 of the Law of Property (Miscellaneous Provisions) Act 1989
  https://www.legislation.gov.uk/ukpga/1989/34/contents
- Section 44 of the Companies Act 2006
  https://www.legislation.gov.uk/ukpga/2006/46/contents
- Sections 27 and 72 of the Land Registration Act 2002
  https://www.legislation.gov.uk/ukpga/2002/9/contents
- Land Registration Rules 2003
  https://www.legislation.gov.uk/uksi/2003/1417/contents
- Land Charges Act 1972
  https://www.legislation.gov.uk/ukpga/1972/61/contents
- Section 127 of the Insolvency Act 1986
  https://www.legislation.gov.uk/ukpga/1986/45/contents

Pre-exchange					Exchange & pre-completion				Completion & post-completion		
Stage 1 Taking instructions & advising client	**Stage 2** Draft contract	**Stage 3** Pre-contract searches, enquiries & planning	**Stage 4** Title	**Stage 5** Mortgage (applies throughout process)	**Stage 6** Exchange of contracts	**Stage 7** Purchase deed	**Stage 8** Pre-completion searches and requisitions	**Stage 9** Financial statements	**Stage 10** Completion	**Stage 11** SDLT & registration	**Stage 12** Delays and remedies

FIGURE 10.1 Conveyancing timeline

10.1 Introduction

This chapter deals with the **purchase deed** and key pre-completion procedures. The main purpose of the purchase deed is to transfer the legal **estate** in the property from the seller to the buyer. The contract sets out what the parties have agreed but it is the purchase deed that actually puts those agreed terms into effect. The transfer of a legal estate is void unless it is made by deed (s52(1) Law of Property Act 1925).

Pre-completion searches are a critical part of any property transaction. They may disclose major problems at a very late stage that need to be addressed swiftly if completion is not to be delayed. Indeed, the choice of searches and understanding the results of them can be fraught with all sorts of pitfalls for the unwary practitioner. In the first place, there is the obvious but well-repeated point that with two land law systems, registered and unregistered, there will always be confusion for the ill-prepared about which searches to make. Secondly, there is also the potential for confusion from the dual role of acting for the buyer and the lender at the same time. Thirdly, there is the variety of different but relevant searches that may confuse. The moral is to know your pre-completion searches and when to use them and, of course, to look closely at the results and deal with any adverse entries without delay.

10.2 Pre-completion procedures

The flowchart in **Figure 10.2** sets out the steps to be taken after exchange and before completion from the perspective of a practitioner acting for a buyer. These steps can apply to both commercial and residential transactions.

The flowchart in **Figure 10.3** sets out the steps to be taken after exchange and before completion from the perspective of a practitioner acting for a seller. Again, these steps can apply to both commercial and residential transactions.

These two flowcharts reflect the traditional way that these steps are taken in a conveyancing transaction. Recently, and in an effort to speed up the process, some solicitors acting for sellers have taken to issuing the draft purchase deed at the same time as they send out the draft contract, along with pre-answered standard pre-completion requisitions. (The Protocol Form is now called a 'Completion Information and Undertakings' (3rd edn).) This procedural change regarding the draft purchase deed is also promoted in the latest version of the Law Society's Conveyancing Protocol. As the change is not universally adopted, this chapter will continue to explain the process by way of the more traditional approach, but you need to be alive to the possibility of the new approach becoming more commonly adopted as time progresses.

10.3 Drafting and approving the purchase deed

The buyer's practitioner will draft the purchase deed once **exchange of contracts** has taken place. Its contents are governed by the terms of the contract. In some cases, the seller may prefer to draft the purchase deed, for example when selling new properties on an estate where uniformity of documentation is important.

The standard procedure is for the buyer's practitioner to submit two copies of the draft purchase deed to the seller's practitioner for approval, and to keep an extra copy on file for reference (in case minor points are raised over the telephone or by email). If the draft is approved as drawn, the top copy can be used as the engrossment. If the seller requires extensive amendments, these should be written clearly in red ink (or electronically via 'track changes') on one copy of the draft, which should be returned to the buyer's practitioner, while a copy of the amended draft is kept on the file for reference. A seller's amendment typically arises where the buyer has overlooked the inclusion of a clause required by the contract, such as an **indemnity covenant**.

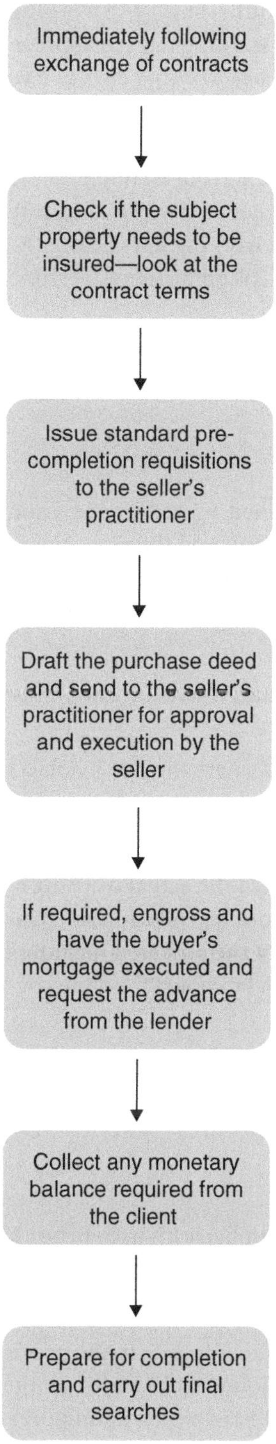

FIGURE 10.2 Buyer

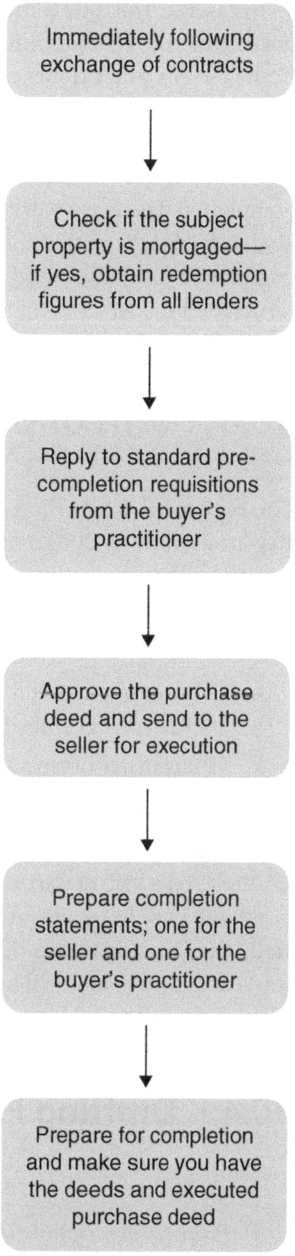

FIGURE 10.3 Seller

10.3.1 **Time limits**

Where the Law Society Standard Form of Contract is being used, practitioners should submit, approve and engross the draft purchase deed within the time limits laid down in SC 4.3.2. A breach of the time limits may be of importance if one of the contracting parties later claims compensation for delay in completion. Under SC 7.2.1, if there is default by the parties in performing their obligations under the contract (eg the buyer submits the draft purchase deed out of time), then the party whose total period of default is the greater must pay compensation to the other.

In essence, the time limits are as follows. The draft deed must be submitted at least 12 working days before the **completion date**; the seller's practitioner then has four working days to approve it; the buyer's practitioner must then send out the engrossment at least five working days before completion. SC 4.3.4 provides that if the period between the date of the contract and the completion date is less than 15 working days, the time limits are reduced pro rata. Fractions of a working day are rounded down (but cannot be less than one working day). For example, if the completion date is ten working days after exchange, the time limits are reduced by two-thirds (ie 10 divided by 15) so that the draft deed must be submitted at least eight working days before the completion date. The Standard Commercial Property Conditions (SCPCs) contain identical time limits (SCPC 7.3).

10.4 Form of purchase deed

For **registered land**, the purchase deed must be in the form prescribed by r58 of the Land Registration Rules 2003. For **unregistered land**, there is no prescribed form and the practitioner may use either the traditional form (a **conveyance** for freeholds; an **assignment** for leaseholds) or, alternatively, where the **title** is subject to first registration, a Land Registry transfer. The two main Land Registry transfer forms are:

- TR1: transfer of *whole* of registered land or *whole* of unregistered land where the title is subject to first registration (see the online resources);
- TP1: transfer of *part* of registered land or *part* of unregistered land where the title is subject to first registration.

Remember that the contents of the purchase deed are governed by the contents of the contract. For example, on a sale of part if new **easements** or **covenants** are to be created the actual wording of these will have been agreed in the contract and it will simply be a matter of reproducing substantially the same clauses in the purchase deed. Likewise, the description of the property, including reference to any plan, will have been settled at the contract stage and can be copied from the contract. A specimen TR1 is reproduced in **Appendix 3**.

10.4.1 Drafting Form TR1

Drafting Form TR1 is very easy and self-explanatory, but the following points should be noted.

- *Property description.* If the property is already registered, the title number is inserted in box 2. The property description then follows.
- *Date.* The date of the transfer is left blank until completion.
- *Consideration and receipt.* The statement of consideration is sufficient to satisfy the provisions of s5 of the Stamp Act 1891, which states that the consideration must be stated on the face of the deed. It is customary for the consideration to be written in words and figures. In commercial conveyancing where VAT is payable in addition to the purchase price, the amount stated should include the VAT. Any additional monies paid for chattels should not be included in the consideration on the transfer; a separate receipt should be given for chattels.
- In the consideration box, the transferor is stated as receiving the consideration. This statement of receipt of the purchase money is important to the buyer for three reasons:
  1. It acts as authority to the buyer to pay the purchase money to the seller's practitioner (s69 Law of Property Act 1925), so if the seller's practitioner absconds with the money it is the seller's loss not the buyer's.
  2. The receipt acts as sufficient discharge to the buyer (s67 Law of Property Act 1925).
  3. The receipt is evidence that the seller's lien over the property for the unpaid purchase price is at an end.
- *Title guarantee.* The seller's title guarantee implies covenants for title under the Law of Property (Miscellaneous Provisions) Act 1994. The form of title guarantee will have been agreed at the contract stage, so simply use the title guarantee as stated in the contract.

- *Declaration of trust.* Where the buyer is more than one person, the declaration of trust box should be completed stating whether the buyers are joint tenants or tenants in common (and their respective shares if unequal). Land Registry Form JO may be used instead. This form is useful if there is a short time between exchange and completion when it might not be possible to obtain the signatures of the buyers on the purchase deed. Conveyancers may also use Form JO where they do not wish the purchase deed signed by the seller to leave their possession.
- *Additional provisions.* Under SC 4.6.4 and SCPC 6.6.4, an indemnity covenant will be required where the sale is subject to any obligation on which the seller will remain liable after completion. If this is the case, the indemnity covenant should be inserted in the additional provisions box. A typical indemnity covenant would read:

  The Transferees jointly and severally covenant to observe and perform the covenants referred to in [Entry No. 1] of the ***charges*** register and to indemnify the Transferor against any future liability for their breach or non-observance.

EXAMPLE

Marsha acts for Mandeep and Kapil who are buying a registered leasehold flat. They exchanged contracts today for completion in two weeks time. Marsha's clients are making unequal contributions to the purchase price (60 per cent Mandeep, 40 per cent Kapil) and following your advice they have agreed to hold the property as tenants in common. To record this agreement when drafting Form TR1, in Panel 10 Marsha will place an 'X' in the third box and state they hold the property on trust for themselves as tenants in common and specifying the relevant shares: 60 per cent/40 per cent. Alternatively, she can lodge completed Form JO with the Land Registry application for registration specifying the relevant shares or referring to a separate Declaration of Trust.

CONDUCT POINT

Failure to accurately record your clients' instructions in relation to shared ownership may amount to a breach of the SRA Code of Conduct. You must act in the best interests of each client and you must provide a proper standard of service to your clients.

10.4.2 **Drafting Form TP1**

Form TP1 is very similar to Form TR1, but the following points should be noted.

On a transfer of part, a full description of the part being sold, including a plan showing the property edged red, will have been agreed in the contract. The description and a duplicate plan can now be incorporated in the TP1. The land being retained by the transferor should also be defined and marked on the plan edged blue. The plan should be to a stated scale and must not be merely for identification purposes. The description need not mention appurtenant rights and benefits shown on the register as these will pass as part of the title. Any other rights or benefits not shown on the register will also pass by virtue of s62 of the Law of Property Act 1925.

The additional provisions box will be used for such matters as definitions of terms not previously defined (eg 'the retained land'), new rights granted or reserved, new covenants, agreements, declarations and other provisions agreed between the parties in the contract. You should check the special conditions in the contract for any agreed additional clauses. If the contract provides for such matters as new easements, covenants or declarations, then they must be inserted expressly in the transfer, for it is the transfer that creates them (the contract is merely the agreement to create them). The precise form of wording will already have been agreed in the contract and can be taken directly from it. If more space is required, Form CS can be used as a continuation sheet, which should be securely fastened to the main form.

To counter any suggestion that the covenants on the part of the transferee may be unenforceable by the transferor's successors in title, the benefit of the covenants should be expressed to be annexed to each and every part of the transferor's retained land. The following wording could be used:

> For the benefit and protection of the Retained Land or any part or parts thereof and so as to bind so far as may be the Property into whosesoever hands the same may come the Transferee hereby covenants with the Transferor that the Transferee and the persons deriving title under him will at all times hereafter observe and perform the restrictions and stipulations set out in the schedule hereto.

Technically, the burden of the covenants need not be expressly annexed to the land being transferred, as this is implied by s79 of the Law of Property Act 1925 (see *Federated Homes Ltd v Mill Lodge Properties Ltd* [1980] 1 WLR 594). However, it is best practice to do so.

10.4.2.1 Negation of implied easements

On a sale of part, the seller should have included a special condition in the contract agreeing to negate any implied grants of easement in favour of the buyer over the seller's retained land. A declaration to this effect should now therefore be made in the TP1. A suitable form of wording, which would follow the wording of any special condition, might read as follows:

> It is hereby agreed and declared that the Transferee shall not by implication or otherwise become entitled to any rights of light or air that would restrict or interfere with the free use of the Retained Land for building or other purposes.

10.5 Plans

A plan in a purchase deed is generally only necessary where part of the seller's property is being sold. The plan must be accurate, with all colourings and markings correctly made, and it must be tightly bound into the engrossed deed. Metric measurements must be used on the plan (Unit of Measurement Regulations 1995 (SI 1995/1804)). The verbal description of the property in the main body of the document should naturally refer to any plan. The plan should be to a stated scale and must not be merely for identification purposes. For further information on plans generally, see Land Registry Practice Guide 40.

If any discrepancy arises between the plan and the verbal description in the deed, it is a matter of construction as to which should prevail. If the plan is described as being 'for identification purposes only', then the verbal description prevails. If the property is 'more particularly delineated or described' on the plan, then the plan will prevail (*Neilson v Poole* (1969) 20 P & CR 909).

10.6 Execution of purchase deed

In order to transfer the legal estate the seller must always execute the purchase deed (s52(1) Law of Property Act 1925). However, the buyer need only execute the deed if the buyer is either making a declaration (eg as to **co-ownership**), or entering into new obligations (eg giving the seller an indemnity covenant or agreeing new covenants on a sale of part).

If the buyer has to execute the deed as well, it is good practice for the buyer to do so first, before sending it across for the seller to execute. This saves time, but the prudent seller will also be disinclined to part with an executed deed before the money is actually received on completion. In these circumstances, the buyer's practitioner should make it clear that the buyer has executed the deed 'in escrow', which means that the deed has no legal effect until it has also been executed by the seller; namely, this is a condition of the buyer's execution.

As we have seen, the transfer of the legal estate must be by deed and, to be a valid deed, the document must state clearly on its face that it is a deed (s1 Law of Property (Miscellaneous Provisions) Act 1989). It is no longer necessary for a deed to be sealed (although a company may still use its seal), but it must be signed by the necessary parties in the presence of a witness, and delivered. Although the deed takes effect on delivery, the word 'delivered' is not necessary in the attestation clause.

EXAMPLE

A typical attestation clause for execution by an individual would read as follows:

Signed as a deed by [full name of seller]

in the presence of

[signature, name and address of witness]

Section 44(2) of the Companies Act 2006 provides that a document is validly executed by a company if it is signed on behalf of the company by either two authorised signatories (the company's directors and the company secretary) or by a director of the company in the presence of a witness who attests the signature.

EXAMPLE

A typical attestation clause for execution by a limited company would read as follows:

Executed as a deed by ABC Ltd

[Signature] . . . Director of the above-named company

[Signature] . . . Secretary of the above-named company

All parties who execute the deed should also sign any plan. This is an acknowledgement that the plan is an integral part of the document.

10.6.1 Electronic signatures

In July 2020, the Land Registry announced its intention to start accepting electronic signatures of purchase deeds. To sign the deeds electronically, a conveyancer will need to upload the deed to an online platform which sends a link to the signatories. Once they have completed the necessary authentication checks, they 'sign' the document electronically in the physical presence of the witness, who also signs. The conveyancer is then notified that the signing process has been done and can submit the completed deed to the Land Registry with their registration application. The online platform will require a two-factor authentication process for the signatories and witness. A link to the document is emailed and an authentication code is then sent to the individual's mobile phone. At the time of writing, a few electronically signed property deals have already taken place under a Land Registry pilot scheme.

For more information on the execution of deeds generally, see Land Registry Practice Guide 8 (Execution of Deeds).

10.7 Advising the client

If you send the purchase deed to the client for signature and return, your covering letter should explain the purpose and contents of the document and contain clear instructions as to its execution. Ideally, the letter should also specify a date by which the signed document should be returned to you and request that the client leaves the document undated (it is dated on actual completion). Many practitioners write in pencil at the top, 'Do not date'.

Inform the client that the witness to the client's signature should be over 18 and independent from the client (eg not the signatory's spouse, relative or another party to the deed). The witness should sign and then write their address and occupation below. If the witness's signature is illegible, the full name should also be written in block capitals. If seeing the client in person, it is quite in order for the solicitor to witness the client's signature after explaining the purpose and contents of the deed.

10.8 Pre-completion procedures when acting for the buyer

Once exchange has taken place, an immediate check is required to see if the contractual terms pass an insurance obligation on to the buyer at the time of the formation of a binding agreement. If they do, then insurance arrangements must be made without delay. Requisitions (usually questions of just a procedural nature rather than in relation to the title) must be issued to the sellers along with a draft transfer. If the buyer is utilising **mortgage** finance, the mortgage deed must be prepared and executed in readiness for completion. The balance of the purchase price after taking into account the **deposit** must be calculated and collected from the client in good time for completion. If the buyer is relying on mortgage finance, then a clear report on title will be required by the lending institution before it will release the mortgage advance. Finally, all relevant pre-completion searches must be made and checked to ensure that the buyer is ready to complete by the contractual completion date.

10.8.1 Standard requisitions

A requisition, in the context of conveyancing, is a formal written question that requires a formal written answer. In the past, **requisitions on title** were raised after exchange because in conveyancing transactions following very traditional pathways, title was not **deduced** until after exchange. Only **encumbrances** were disclosed with the draft contract not the full title. However, modern conveyancing practice has ensured the early disclosure of the full title prior to exchange, and certainly this has been the case with registered land for some time. As a consequence, the nature of requisitions has changed and those that are raised after exchange in residential transactions are now standard form pre-completion requisitions or questions. This format has been adopted in the Law Society's Conveyancing Protocol with the use of the Completion Information and **Undertakings** form. Most practitioners have adopted a pre-printed form for requisitions using either forms pre-printed by themselves or those issued by law stationers and they are stored electronically and issued in the main by email. Alternatively, the Protocol Form is used. Whichever form is used, the purpose of it is to sort out completion arrangements rather than raise detailed questions about the title. The Completion Information and Undertakings form used in Protocol cases is a core element of the Law Society's Conveyancing Protocol. In commercial transactions, the standard forms may still be encountered but you are more likely to encounter bespoke requisitions on title, especially in the larger transactions.

Apart from producing a standard pre-completion requisitions form, the document was also drawn up to ensure that practitioners remain aware of the danger of giving thoughtless undertakings to discharge mortgages. This kind of trap will arise when an answer is given to a question that is written in such a way as to place on the person giving the answer a duty beyond that contemplated. Because of this, there are many warnings on the form. Indeed, the heading to the form includes a clear warning that replies to three questions (3.2, 5.2 and 5.3) on the form are treated as a solicitor's undertaking.

Question 1 on the Completion Information and Undertakings form asks whether or not vacant possession is to be given on completion and what is to happen to the keys. Question 2 is concerned with deeds in unregistered land and asks about their location and requests a list of what deeds are to be handed over at completion. Question 3 asks where completion will take place and, if completion is to take place by post, that the Code for Completion is to be adopted. It also asks for confirmation that the mortgages mentioned in answer to question 5 will be covered by the terms of the Protocol. Question 4 asks how much will be payable on completion and asks for bank details to facilitate the electronic transmission of the completion money. Question 5 is very important as it covers mortgages and charges. Sellers are required to list all mortgages to be covered by any redemption undertakings at completion. The question then asks for confirmation of the seller's solicitors, whether they undertake to redeem or discharge the mortgages and charges listed on completion and to send to the buyer Form DS1, DS3 (charge release forms), the receipted charge(s) or confirmation that notice of re-lease or discharge in electronic form has been given to the Land Registry.

CONDUCT POINT

Be careful how you reply to the Protocol Requisitions form as some answers may amount to enforceable solicitor's undertakings. Failure to comply with your answer, for example to pay off mortgages, will amount to a breach of the Solicitors' Code of Conduct. Paragraph 1.3 states that you must perform all undertakings given by you and do so within an agreed timescale or if no timescale has been agreed then within a reasonable amount of time.

10.9 Pre-completion procedures when acting for the seller

When the seller has a mortgage on the title, then there is one particularly important pre-completion step, namely the necessity to obtain redemption figures for all outstanding mortgages on the title to ensure that the property can be sold free of mortgage. (It is also sensible at the same time to ask for a daily rate of interest charged by the lender so that if there is any delay in redeeming the mortgage, fresh figures will not be required for a short delay as the additional interest due can be calculated by reference to the daily rate.)

Furthermore, if the seller is selling through an estate agency, once contracts have been exchanged there is the question of who is to deal with the estate agents' commission account. In many cases, the agents will submit their commission account to you on exchange. When you receive it, it is best simply to advise the agents that you will take your client's instructions on the account. In this way, the agents will not be in a position to assert that anything you have written should be interpreted as an undertaking to pay their account.

The seller's practitioner must ensure that the purchase deed, which is usually prepared by the buyer, is acceptable and complies with the terms of the contract. They must also ensure that it is signed by the seller (and witnessed) in readiness for completion. It is also prudent to prepare Form DS1 (charge release form) in readiness for completion or keep a record of the charge details if another system of discharge is to be used, such as an e-DS1. (An e-DS1 is an electronic form of discharge submitted by lenders through the Land Registry Portal.)

10.10 Pre-completion searches

Pre-completion searches are made to ensure that the information with regard to the title supplied prior to exchange remains the same up to completion. So in the case of registered land, the search will refer to the date of the copy registers supplied by the seller, namely the issue date of the **official copies from the Registry**, and will disclose any changes since that time. As for unregistered land, the search may disclose many different types of entry, such as any mortgages not detailed in the abstract of title and that have been created as a second or subsequent charge since the seller purchased the property. There is another purpose to these searches and that is to obtain a protective period during which completion and registration can take place and during which the buyer will have priority over anyone else seeking to register an entry against the subject property.

The buyer's practitioner will be the person to carry out pre-completion searches. This is because the buyer (and the buyer's lender) will want to ensure that the title is in order and is free from undisclosed encumbrances and is therefore available to be a security for a loan without restraint. (Of course, if the lender is separately represented, then the lender's practitioner will carry out all searches on behalf of the lender. Sometimes a lender's practitioner will pass on this obligation to the borrower's practitioner.)

The choice of appropriate pre-completion searches can be resolved by reference to **Figure 10.4**.

If your client/buyer is a company and it is taking out a loan for a lender for whom you also have instructions, you may well need to complete a company search against your client to make sure, on behalf of the lender, that the company remains viable (not in liquidation etc) and can borrow money.

Q.1 Is the seller a company?	
Yes Complete a search against the company name at Companies House	No Go to Q.2
Q.2 Is the property registered?	
Yes Complete the appropriate Land Registry search—Go to Q.3	No Complete a Land Charges K15 search against all estate owners from at least the root of title and go to Q.4
Q.3 Is this a sale of the whole of the registered title?	
Yes Complete a Land Registry OS1 search	No It is a sale of part, so complete a Land Registry OS2 search

Q.4 Is this a residential purchase with a mortgage from a bank or building society?	
Yes Complete a K16 bankruptcy search against the borrowers	No Go to Q.5
Q.5 Have you advised your client to inspect the property prior to completion?	
Yes Go and do something else!	No. This should be done to check the state of the property, whether there are any unlawful occupiers, etc

FIGURE 10.4 Pre-completion searches decision tree

10.10.1 Registered land

A buyer will be supplied with official copies of the registers of the title of the subject property prior to exchange. A binding agreement will have been put in place for the sale and purchase of the property on the basis of the title disclosed in those official copies. These are dated and timed by the Land Registry, and the title is therefore accurate only as at the date and time of the official copy entries. It is imperative that a search is carried out from the date of those official copy title details to see if there have been any entries made after the date of the official copies. Because third party protective entries can be made, there may be entries made since the date of the official copy entries that even the seller may not know about.

A Land Registry pre-completion search is important not only for the purpose of revealing the state of the title at the time of the search, but also because it will confirm the state of the title at the point of registration. This will be done as a consequence of priority having been given to the search applicant. The effect of this is that any entry due to be made in the registers of the subject property during the **priority period** will be postponed in favour of the application to register on behalf of the person making the search. The priority period is 30 working days from the search certificate date. The effect of the priority period is actually to freeze the title and the entries in the registers to those disclosed in the official copies as varied, if at all, in the search result, but only until the expiry of the priority period (see s72 Land Registration Act 2002). Thus, the search prevents registration of an adverse interest for 30 business days (the priority period) to allow the purchaser, **lessee** or lender to lodge their protected application.

The person named on the search application is the person entitled to priority. The position is complicated because most buyers proceed on the basis of a mortgage so that the **mortgagee** will also require priority protection. To avoid the necessity of making two searches, one for the buyer and the other for the lender, a search is made in the name of the lender and the buyer takes advantage of the lender's priority period. Accordingly, where a practitioner acts for the buyer and lender, the Land Registry search should always be in the name of the lender (r151 Land Registration Rules 2003 (SI 2003/1417)).

There are several types of Land Registry search forms, including those described shortly. Searches can be submitted to the Registry either by post, online via the Land Registry Portal or the NLIS.

10.10.1.1 Form OS1, search of the whole of a title

This search is the standard pre-completion search affording the searcher priority when the whole of the registered title is being purchased, mortgaged or leased. A 'search from date' must be stated, being the date of the official copies supplied by the seller. There is also the option to insert 'FR' instead of a date, and this option will arise for a pending first registration search.

10.10.1.2 Form OS2, search of part of a title

This search is used when the subject property forms part of a larger title from which it is being sold. In many respects it is the same as an OS1 search save that it does not relate to the whole of the title. Because of this difference, practitioners must remember not only to describe the subject property carefully in the search, but also to describe it in one of two alternative ways. The search of part must describe the subject property either by reference to a plan attached to the search request or by a plot number shown on an estate plan that has been given prior approval by the Land Registry (an estate plan will normally be used on the sale of new properties within a large estate). If the search is to be accompanied by a plan, it must be submitted in duplicate and best practice dictates that the plan should be to scale and should clearly mark the subject property. It should also make clear on what floor level the property is located when it is a flat in a block. The search plan should not be marked 'for identification purposes only'.

10.10.1.3 Form OS3, non-priority searches

Forms OS1 and OS2 exist for the benefit of a person or company that (for valuable consideration and at arm's length) is buying, leasing, mortgaging or converting to commonhold all or some of a registered title. The forms cannot be used in other circumstances. Accordingly, an OS3 search should be used in cases other than these. For example, a lender, pursuant to its power of sale, which is selling the mortgaged property, should make an OS3 Land Registry search to ascertain the existence, or not, of any subsequent mortgages on the title. Similarly, a buyer of an equitable interest in the subject property will also wish to make a final search and because of the nature of the interest being purchased, Form OS3 must be used as the other searches relate to legal estates (see r155 Land Registration Rules 2003). In cases where this search is used, the search result will disclose entries subsequent to the official copies in the possession of the searcher but it will not give any priority to that searcher.

10.10.1.4 Form HR3, mortgagee search

Where, as a consequence of the default of the borrower, a lender wishes to enforce its rights as a mortgagee of a home, it must first serve notice of the action on any non-owning spouse or a party to a civil partnership union who has registered a protective entry on the title in respect of rights of occupation. The search discloses whether any notice or caution is registered to protect a spouse's or civil partner's right of occupation under the Family Law Act 1996, the Matrimonial Homes Act 1967 or 1983 or the Civil Partnership Act 2004. It is possible for entries to have been made of which the lender is unaware (eg a notice), and in these circumstances the mortgagee can make a search to update the title utilising Form HR3, which will disclose home rights registrations. (A caution would exist to protect entries made before 13 October 2003 under legislation prior to the Land Registration Act 2002.)

Land Registry Practice Guide 12 covering **official searches** and outline applications can be found on the UK government website (see the link in **Appendix 1**).

It should be stressed that the Land Registry priority period of 30 working days for official searches cannot be extended. Accordingly, the buyer's application for transfer of ownership must be submitted to the Land Registry within this time frame, otherwise there is a risk of a new adverse entry taking priority on the register which will, of course, bind the buyer and thereby result in a negligence action against the buyer's solicitor.

10.10.2 Unregistered land

When dealing with unregistered land, the most critical pre-completion search is made in the Central Land Charges Register (CLCR). Full searches in this register are only necessary when dealing with unregistered land and are completely irrelevant so far as registered land is concerned. The correct search form is Form K15 (not to be confused with a mere bankruptcy search, also sent to this Registry, which is K16). Searches can be submitted to the Registry by post, online via the Land Registry Portal or the NLIS. The search result confers a priority period of 15 working days on the searcher/applicant. Accordingly, if completion takes place during this period, the searcher/applicant will take free of any entries placed on the register between the date of the search and the completion date, on the proviso that completion did indeed take place within the priority period. (You should note that it is not necessary to apply for first registration of title within the search priority period; the time limit is two months from the completion date: see s6(4) Land Registration Act 2002.) Applicants can now ask for search results to be issued electronically. No paper certificate is issued. A result in PDF (electronic form) format is issued instead.

The Central Land Charges Register is a computer database of the names of estate owners and any charges registered against particular estate owner's names, that is actually maintained by the Land Registry. Applicants must therefore list the names of estate owners disclosed in the abstract or **epitome of title** for land charge search purposes. If the abstract or epitome includes search results against listed names, then a fresh search will not normally be required. Land charges are classified into six categories, each of which is labelled by a letter. Some of these categories have sub-categories. For example, *Class C* comprises four subdivisions and contains many of the most important land charges encountered in practice, of which the following two appear regularly:

- *Class C(i) (s2(4)(i) Land Charges Act 1972).* This is the first of the more commonly encountered entries and relates to the registration of a *puisne* mortgage. This is a legal charge that does not have protection by the deposit of the title deeds. This situation will arise in unregistered land where this mortgage is a second legal charge.
- *Class C(iv) (s2(4)(iv) Land Charges Act 1972).* This is an **estate contract**. It is commonly encountered in practice as it affords protection in relation to contracts made by estate owners (sellers), or others entitled to take a conveyance (buyers), where the contract relates to the conveying or creation of a legal estate. Accordingly, if a binding contract is made, either party can register this protective entry although in practice it is usually the buyer who will seek protection. This will be the case particularly if completion is delayed or is contractually a long time off, or if the buyer does not trust the seller. Equally, if the seller has cause to mistrust the buyer, a protective registration is possible. A conditional contract is registrable even though the condition remains outstanding and unfulfilled at the date of registration of the estate contract.

Other classes commonly encountered include:

- *Class D(ii) (s2(5)(ii) Land Charges Act 1972).* This registration covers restrictive covenants created after 1925 other than restrictive covenants in a **lease** or pre-1926 restrictive covenants. Lease covenants are not registrable because their enforceability will depend on the law relating to covenants in landlord and tenant terms. Freehold, pre-1926 restrictive covenants cannot be protected by this registration as the traditional doctrine of notice will apply.
- *Class F (s2(7) Land Charges Act 1972).* This class arose from the provisions of the Family Law Act 1996 relating to a spouse's right of occupation, namely matrimonial home rights. Civil partnership unions are now covered by similar legislation with comparable rights of occupation. Where there is a non-owning spouse or partner in occupation, that spouse or partner can register a Class F charge to protect a right of occupation, to protect their home rights. Failure to register will mean that the occupying spouse or partner loses all protection against a buyer for value of the home in question.

10.10.3 Names and searches

A **land charges search** should be made against the seller and all estate owners disclosed in the abstract or epitome of title, and diligent practice dictates that the search is made against all estate owners since 1925. The search will also need to mention the period of years of ownership for each estate owner, together with an indication of the county in which the property is located. County names required by the search should be correctly entered and former county details should be stated; for example, if a property was formerly in the county of Middlesex, this should be mentioned as well as the 'new' county location. This applies to several 'new' counties, such as Cumbria. With regard to London, parts of Greater London were previously in outlying counties—that is, not actually part of an administrative area of London such as the London County Council—and became part of the (now defunct) Greater London Council in 1965. These former details should always be mentioned in the search request.

It is possible that there may be an entry on the register against a previous owner not known to the buyer as the period of ownership was before the root of title. If the root of title in the contract is a conveyance to the seller 16 years ago, the buyer will see just one deed, namely that conveyance, and can only search against one name, that of the seller.

The unsatisfactory point here is that the buyer will be bound by prior entries against previous owners but will be unable to call for pre-root title details (under s198 Law of Property Act 1925 the buyer is deemed to have notice of all such registrations, even though they are undiscoverable). It is possible that compensation may be available for an undiscoverable and adverse land charge under s25 of the Law of Property Act 1969. If the buyer had no knowledge of the charge, the charge was registered against an owner not disclosed in the abstract or epitome of title (and the root of title was at least 15 years old), the buyer may seek compensation from public funds. (The buyer may be able to take action against the seller if the seller knew about the encumbrances but did not disclose them; see the seller's duty of disclosure in **4.3**.)

To avoid this problem, you should ask for:

1 copies of the title deeds and documents from 1925; or
2 names of title owners from 1925; or
3 all previous land charge search results that are with the deeds.

Searches carried out on behalf of previous buyers may be relied on and it may be possible to construct the preceding chain of ownership for reassurance in this way.

Best practice is to quote the name (or names if more than one version) that appears in the title deed by which the estate owner took the title. Accordingly, great care must be taken as to the accuracy of names, and practitioners should ensure that all former names, if known, are searched against. This will apply to companies and to individuals.

10.10.4 **Effect of non-registration**

The effect of non-registration varies with the different registers as follows:

A, B, C(i), C(ii), C (iii) and F	Void as against a purchaser/lessee/mortgagee for valuable consideration of the subject property or an interest in it unless registered (s4 Land Charges Act 1925)
C(iv) and D	Void as against a purchaser *of a legal estate* in the land for money or money's worth unless registered (ibid)
Pending action	Void as against a buyer for valuable consideration if not registered (ibid, s5)
Writ or order	Void as against a buyer for valuable consideration if not registered (ibid, s6)
Arrangement deed	Void as against a buyer for valuable consideration if not registered (ibid, s7)

EXAMPLE

Anders acts for Lionel who is buying an unregistered freehold farmhouse from Mr Edward Barnes and Mrs Lucille Barnes who bought the farmhouse in 1987. As the property has an unregistered title, Anders will ensure that he has clear land charges searches against the full names of Edward Barnes and Lucille Barnes for the period 1987 to the present year as well as against the names of previous estate owners revealed by the deeds. Bear in mind that there may be entries on the searches that you might expect, for example if the property is being sold to Lionel subject to restrictive covenants that Mr and Mrs Barnes entered into when they bought in 1987, you would expect to see Dii entries against their names to protect those covenants.

10.11 Acting for the lender

Title searches for mortgagees are the same as those for a buyer: OSl and OS2 searches for registered land, K15 searches for unregistered land and company searches if appropriate. Lenders will also require a bankruptcy-only search against all proposed borrowers. This is, of course, because a bankrupt does not have capacity to enter into a mortgage agreement or deed. (Lenders may also require a company search against proposed corporate borrowers.) These bankruptcy searches are made on Form K16. All registered bankruptcy petitions and orders will be disclosed. Clearly, if an entry is disclosed the lender must be informed without delay and the mortgage will almost certainly not proceed. It is critical that the full names of the borrowers be stated precisely and all former names and aliases must also be given. Results can be awkward in that sometimes entries will be disclosed against a surname only. If this happens, consideration must be given to supporting information such as the address and, if necessary, an office copy (an official copy) should be sought on Form K19. It is appropriate when you are completely satisfied that the entry does not apply, to certify for the lender on the search result that the entry does not relate to the borrower. In the majority of commercial loans the lender is usually separately represented and, as such, the lender's solicitors will make their own final searches.

EXAMPLE

Omar acts for Danielle White who is buying a registered leasehold flat in Cardiff with the aid of a mortgage from NatWest Bank for whom he also acts. The searches he must make before completion specifically to protect NatWest's interest are:

- A bankruptcy search on Form K16 against the full name of Danielle White. If entries are revealed, he should certify the search certificate himself to the effect that they do not relate to his client. If he is unable to do so, he must cease to act for the lender.
- A Land Registry search submitted on Form OS1 naming NatWest Bank as the applicant. This effectively updates the official copies he received at the beginning of the transaction and confers a priority period during which no changes can be made to the register. Following completion, it is essential that his application for registration is submitted to the Land Registry before the priority period of the search expires.

10.12 Buying from a company

If the seller is a limited company there will be an additional search that will apply to both registered and unregistered land. Where a company is selling, a search of the companies register at Companies House should be carried out. Company information is available online at http://www.companies-house.gov.uk/. In large-scale commercial conveyancing transactions, two company searches will be made; one immediately after exchange and the second on the morning of completion.

The Land Registration Act 2002 is quite clear in that it states that the grant of a legal charge is a registrable disposition (s27(2)(f)). It also states that the effect of non-registration at the Registry of a mortgage means that it is void and takes effect as a mere contract made for valuable consideration to create the mortgage (s7(2)(b)). It is therefore clear that no company charge whatever, be it fixed or floating, will affect a buyer unless it is protected by some form of registration at the Land Registry. A company search will still be necessary because a buyer may wish to be sure that the company still subsists and has not been struck off the register, such as for failing to file returns. If it has been struck off the companies register, then the company ceases to exist in law and cannot therefore enter into a deed, transfer or conveyance. If the company is subject to winding-up proceedings, these will be shown by a company search.

In the case of unregistered land, the company search is very important. The search will reveal subsisting floating charges, specific (or fixed) charges created before 1 January 1970 and the commencement of any winding-up proceedings. All three are of material importance to a buyer and, if disclosed in the search result, would clearly be adverse. No purchaser should proceed until the seller has in the appropriate way shown how and when the adverse entry is to be dealt with. Bearing in mind that any disposition by a company subject to winding-up proceedings is void (s127 Insolvency Act 1986), it will be appreciated just how important a company search can be.

10.13 Physical inspection of the subject property

Lastly, the subject property should be inspected prior to completion. The reason for this is primarily to check on exactly who is in occupation. The existence of a third party occupant might amount to an **overriding interest** to which the purchase would be subject. The contract for sale may include a list of items included in the sale or there could be items listed in replies to enquiries. In either case, the buyer will want to be sure that the listed items actually exist and are within the subject property.

Finally, when the subject property is a new property, just prior to completion it must be examined to list any problems that need to be dealt with by the developer. A 'snagging list' should be compiled by the buyer as soon as the developer asserts that the property is ready for completion. This will be done by revisiting the property with or without a surveyor and listing all the outstanding defects that need to be remedied by the seller.

CONDUCT POINT

Failure to carry out the appropriate pre-completion searches in a property purchase may amount to a breach of the SRA Code of Conduct. You must act in the best interests of each client and you must provide a proper standard of service to your clients.

10.14 Completion and financial statements

Completion or financial statements are prepared to show a client how much is required to complete or how much will be available on completion or how much is needed on completion. Statements sent to the seller are usually called financial statements and those sent to the buyer are called **completion statements**.

In detail they are as follows:

1 A financial statement prepared by the seller's practitioner for the seller. The purpose of this statement is to show the seller how much will be left over on completion by way of the net proceeds of sale, either to be applied towards an allied purchase or as the simple net proceeds of sale. It will therefore detail all monies coming in, less all monies paid out and then normally showing the net balance payable to the seller client.

EXAMPLE

Theo acts for Roy on the sale of his freehold house which is subject to a mortgage with Halifax Building Society. Following exchange of contracts, to enable Theo to prepare a completion statement for Roy he will obtain a redemption figure from Halifax Building Society for all monies due to the lender on completion (with a daily interest rate) and check this with Roy. He will also obtain his confirmation that the estate agents' account and his own firm's account are to be paid from the proceeds of sale before accounting to him.

2 A completion statement prepared by the seller's practitioner for the buyer's practitioner. The purpose of this statement is to show to the buyer how much is required to be paid over at completion. Clearly, if this is only the balance of the purchase price after taking into account the deposit, then a full-scale statement is unnecessary. These statements can be quite complex and lengthy when the subject property is leasehold. In these circumstances, the statement will have to include apportionments of monies paid in advance or still outstanding and due to be paid. This will include ground rent, insurance payments and **service charges**.

EXAMPLE

A solicitor acts for Steven buying a freehold house for £500,000. A 10 per cent deposit was paid on exchange of contracts. The balance due on completion to be shown on the seller's completion statement will be £450,000.

3 A financial statement prepared by the buyer's practitioner for the buyer. The purpose of this statement is to show the buyer how much will be needed to complete the purchase of the subject property. This will normally be prepared and issued shortly after exchange so that the buyer can put their practitioner in funds in good time for completion. If the figures are to be fully comprehensive, a bill of costs should accompany this statement. Failure to use cleared funds at completion is a breach of the Solicitors Accounts Rules. The statement will therefore show monies coming in, such as from the lender and the client, less monies to be paid away, such as the balance of the purchase price along with costs and disbursements. Consequently, the statement will show how much is needed from the client to complete. The largest disbursement is **stamp duty land tax** (SDLT). When calculating the amount, we suggest you refer to the HMRC online calculator to verify the amount payable. You can then include a verified amount in the financial statement so that the funds are in place for completion and for the speedy payment of SDLT after completion and thereafter a timely application to the Land Registry for registration.

EXAMPLE

Ciara acts for Seema buying a flat in South Shields for £129,000 with the aid of a mortgage. For illustrative purposes, Ciara's financial statement to Seema prior to completion may look like this:

Purchase price		£129,000.00
DEDUCT deposit paid on exchange		£1,290.00
		£127,710.00
DEDUCT net mortgage advance		
Gross advance	£52,750.00	
less retention for repairs	£1,000.00	
less telegraphic transfer fee	£23.00	
NET advance		£51,727.00
		£75,983.00
No Stamp Duty Land Tax chargeable		£0.00
		£75,983.00
ADD costs and other payments		
Legal fees	£295.00	
VAT thereon @ 20 per cent	£59.00	
Local search fee	£75.00	

Coal search fee	£23.50	
Commons search fee	£10.00	
Land charges fee	£1.00	
Land Registry fee	£180.00	
Land Registry search fee	£5.00	£648.50
REQUIRED from you to complete		£76,631.50

KEY POINT SUMMARY

- If the land being purchased is the whole of a registered title (freehold or leasehold), use Land Registry Form TR1.
- If the land being purchased is part of a registered title (freehold or leasehold), use Land Registry Form TP1.
- If the land being purchased is unregistered, use TR1 (whole) or TP1 (part) (freehold or leasehold).
- If the land being purchased is unregistered and the transaction is complex (eg sale of part), it may be easier to use a precedent conveyance (for freehold) or assignment (for leasehold).
- If **personal representatives** are transferring land to a beneficiary under a will or **intestacy**, use an **assent** (there is a prescribed Form AS1 for registered land (AS3 for part)).
- If personal representatives are selling land to a third party, use the appropriate Land Registry form (see earlier point).
- Approve the draft purchase deed.
- The seller always executes the purchase deed.
- The buyer need only execute the purchase deed if it contains new obligations or declarations.
- If so, the buyer often executes the purchase deed first 'in escrow'.
- The parties who execute the purchase deed should also sign any plan attached to the deed.
- Electronic execution of deeds is likely to become standard practice in the future.
- When acting for buyer and lender together and if purchasing registered land, apply for a Land Registry search in the name of the lender only; in this way the buyer will also obtain the benefit of the search priority protection.
- When buying from a company, consider the necessity of a company search to check on the continuing ability of the seller company to sell.
- Do not get confused about which search is required, and this applies to both commercial and residential transactions:

For registered land:

- OS1 (buying the whole title), OS2 (buying part of the title);
- K16 land charges bankruptcy search against the buyer, if you are also acting for a lender (or a company search against the buyer if not an individual);
- company search against the seller if buying from a company.

For unregistered land:

- K15 full land charges search against past and present estate owners, post-1925;
- K16 land charges bankruptcy search against the buyer if you are also acting for a lender;
- company search against the seller if buying from a company.

- If buying unregistered land, try to get pre-root title details for your land charges search or all old land charge search results.

- Where the title is subject to a mortgage, obtain redemption figures immediately after exchange.
- If the title is registered, ensure Form DS1 (or, if applicable, e-DS1) is prepared before completion, or take a copy of the charges register, to ensure the necessary details of the registered charge can be entered on the form to be sealed by the lender after completion.
- If the title is leasehold, make sure you get all up-to-date receipts and demands relating to ground rent and service charge payments (including buildings insurance premiums) for apportionment, and check that the last receipt for ground rent is clear, namely that there are no alleged outstanding breaches of covenant.
- Make sure the purchase deed is signed and witnessed in readiness for completion.
- Comply with any time limits in the contract regarding submission of the draft, approval and engrossment (eg SC 4.3).
- The contents of the purchase deed are governed by the contents of the contract; ensure that all agreed clauses are included in the draft but no more.
- Explain the contents of the deed to the client and arrange for valid execution prior to completion; advise the client to leave the deed undated until completion has occurred.
- Reply to any standard-form pre-completion requisitions raised on behalf of the buyer.
- Arrange for the seller to execute the engrossed purchase deed.
- If the property is leasehold, obtain from your client receipted accounts or recent demands to enable apportionment as at the completion date.
- If the property is leasehold, obtain all necessary consents to the sale from **lessors**, management company, etc.
- Prepare a completion statement and seek instructions on the estate agents' commission account when received, and where the net proceeds of sale should be sent.
- Finalise completion arrangements and prepare Form DS1, e-DS1, DS3 or the mortgage vacating receipt, with any undertaking in respect thereof drawn up in accordance with Law Society recommendations.
- If the property being sold is tenanted, prepare an authority to the tenant to pay all future rent from the completion date to the purchaser.
- Check you are in possession of all the deeds if any are required by the buyer at completion.
- Check where the keys will be and how they are to be handed over on the day of completion. They are normally released by the estate agents to the buyer direct.
- Following exchange of contracts, check on the insurance and ensure that it is in place if the burden passed from the seller to the buyer on exchange of contracts.
- Raise standard-form pre-completion requisitions and approve the answers.
- Engross the approved purchase deed and if required arrange for the buyer to execute it and send it to the sellers for signature to be held in escrow pending completion.
- Arrange for the buyer to execute the mortgage deed.
- Prepare and dispatch all necessary final searches and approve or action search results.
- Obtain and approve the seller's completion statement with all supporting receipts or recent demands.
- Prepare and dispatch to the lender its report on title and request the mortgage advance.
- Draft your bill of costs and ensure it includes all disbursements.
- Calculate and request the balance required to complete (including all costs and disbursements) from your buyer client.
- Finalise completion arrangements and, if completing by post, ensure that the seller's practitioner will act as your agent without charge on completion.
- Ask the seller's practitioner to confirm that they act as agent for the seller's lender in relation to redemption at the time of completion.
- Ensure that there is a final pre-completion inspection of the property to check on vacant possession, fixtures and fittings to be left, etc.

PART E
Completion and Post-Completion

CHAPTER 11

Completion and Post-Completion Procedures

FUNCTIONING LEGAL KNOWLEDGE

This chapter covers the following functioning legal knowledge required to pass the SQE 1 assessments:

Completion and post-completion:

- methods and effect of completion
- post-completion steps

Stamp duty land tax and land transaction tax (Wales): basis of charge in both England and Wales for:

- residential property
- non-residential freehold property

Law Society Conveyancing Protocol

AUTHORITIES UNDERPINNING PRACTICE

The key authorities that underpin this area of practice are listed below. Note that for legislation you are linked to legislation.gov.uk.

Although much of the legislation on this government website is available in its amended form, the incorporation of new amendments into the text of legislation can be delayed. You should refer to legal databases to ensure you are referencing the most up-to-date legislation.

- The Law Society's Code for Completion by Post **https://www.lawsociety.org.uk/en/topics/property/code-for-completion-by-post**
- Sections 43 and 79 of the Finance Act 2003 **https://www.legislation.gov.uk/ukpga/2003/14/contents**
- Land Registration Act 2002 **https://www.legislation.gov.uk/ukpga/2002/9/contents**
- Land Registration Rules 2003 **https://www.legislation.gov.uk/uksi/2003/1417/contents**

Pre-exchange					Exchange & pre-completion				Completion & post-completion		
Stage 1 Taking instructions & advising client	**Stage 2** Draft contract	**Stage 3** Pre-contract searches, enquiries & planning	**Stage 4** Title	**Stage 5** Mortgage (applies throughout process)	**Stage 6** Exchange of contracts	**Stage 7** Purchase deed	**Stage 8** Pre-completion searches and requisitions	**Stage 9** Financial statements	**Stage 10** Completion	**Stage 11** SDLT & registration	**Stage 12** Delays and remedies

FIGURE 11.1 Conveyancing timeline

11.1 Introduction

Completion is the moment in time when the buyer pays over the balance of the purchase price to the seller in exchange for the **deeds** (if any), executed **purchase deed** (normally Form TR1), keys and, if the contract so provides, vacant possession. In **unregistered land**, the **conveyance** or **assignment** constitutes the passing of **title** of a legal **estate** and, as such, this is effectively completion of the transaction in all respects (subject, of course, to the requirement to submit the title to the **Land Registry** for first registration).

This is not the exact position in **registered land**, where the passing of title of a legal estate is only properly completed with the registration of the buyer as the **registered proprietor** at the Land Registry. On a practical basis, as the buyer has the obligation to register, completion is, to all intents and purposes, at the time the money is handed over in exchange for the **transfer** (and any supporting deeds such as the original **lease** in registered leasehold titles). However, practitioners must always remember to proceed with registration without delay, and to do so within their search **priority period**. Failure to do so might mean your client failing to be registered or finding an undisclosed third party interest affecting the title.

11.2 The how, where and when for completion

When contracts are exchanged, it is usual to insert the **completion date** in the agreement, there having been prior negotiations between the parties to reach the agreed completion date. It is not unusual to see a completion period of just 14 days or less. The period can be of any reasonable length but, if the Standard Conditions are used and no period is stipulated in the contract, or if the date is overlooked at the time of exchange, Standard Condition (SC) 6.1.1 provides that completion is due on the 20th working day after exchange.

11.2.1 When: the time for completion

The latest time for completion on the completion date must also be negotiated and will figure in almost all conveyancing contracts. Certainly SC 6.1.2 now, in effect, sets a final time of 2 pm on the day of completion. It does so by providing that if completion does not take place by that time, completion is deemed to be overdue and interest will be payable. Normally completion will take place at the offices of the practitioner acting for the seller. SC 6.2 provides that completion is to be effected somewhere in England and Wales, being either the offices of the seller's solicitor or at some other place that the seller reasonably specifies. SC 6.2.1 states that both parties to the contract are to cooperate in agreeing arrangements for completing the contract. Rarely will the deeds remain with solicitors acting solely for a lender. This will happen if the lender is separately represented or possibly if the lender has commenced repossession proceedings. In these circumstances, completion may have to take place at the lender's solicitors' offices, although efforts should be made to persuade such solicitors to allow the seller's solicitors to deal with completion and redemption together.

11.2.2 How: when your client is selling as well as buying—synchronisation

It is fundamental to a client who is selling and buying, in the absence of any express instructions to the contrary, that the completion of the two transactions be on the same day. In effect, the sale must be synchronised with the purchase to enable the net sale proceeds to be applied towards the purchase price. If there is a whole chain of transactions, of which the client's sale and purchase form part, then, for much the same reason, all of the transactions in the chain must fall for completion on the same date with purchase following sale right along the chain.

11.2.3 How: the mechanics of completion

Completion can be dealt with in various ways: in person, by appointing an agent to complete on your behalf, or through the post. Until the early 1980s, most completions were in person. Now postal completions will normally prevail in domestic conveyancing cases. Only complete by post if you believe it safe to do so (see **11.4**). In all forms of completion, the practitioner for the buyer should pay close attention to the acquisition/purchase deed. It should be checked to make sure that it has been properly executed and can be dated with the date of completion. An individual who is selling should have an independent witness to their signature. The witness must also sign and put in their name and address. If a company is executing, then care should be taken to ensure that one of the two ways of executing a deed by a company is properly effected. A company can either seal a deed with the company seal or the deed can be signed by two directors, a director and the secretary, without the seal (see s36A Companies Act 1985 introduced by the Companies Act 1989). Additionally, s44(2) of the Companies Act 2006 provides that a document is validly executed by a company if it is signed on behalf of the company by either two authorised signatories (the company's directors and the company secretary) or by a director of the company in the presence of a witness who attests the signature. The company officers will sign using wording that shows the purchase deed was 'Executed as a deed by' the signing parties in their capacities as officers of the company. If an attorney has signed, a check should be made to ensure that the deed has been executed in one of the two permissible ways for an attorney (ie AB by his attorney CD or CD as attorney for AB).

11.3 Deeds and unregistered land

Where there is a sale of part of a title the seller will, if the property is unregistered, retain the deeds. The buyer will want to examine their copy deeds against the originals and mark them up at completion as so examined. The wording is 'Examined at the offices of [insert the name and address of the seller's solicitors]', and this is then followed by a signature of the examining practitioner for the buyer together with a note of their firm's name and address and the date. In this way, the buyer will acquire an examined abstract or **epitome of title** which will, with the purchase deed, constitute the title deeds for the part sold off. If completion is to take place in person, the buyer will be able to examine the abstract. If there is an agency completion, the agent can examine the abstract. This will be so in Protocol cases, as the seller agrees to act as the buyer's agent in these circumstances.

Completion in person will normally be at the offices of the seller's practitioner. As has been noted, SC 6.2 provides that completion is to be effected somewhere in England and Wales, being either at the offices of the seller's solicitor or at some other place that the seller reasonably specifies. SC 6.7 states that 'the buyer is to pay the money due on completion by a direct transfer of cleared funds from an account held in the name of a conveyance at a clearing bank and, if appropriate, an unconditional release of a **deposit** held by a stakeholder'. This means that the only method of payment at completion and authorised by the Standard Conditions is by direct electronic bank transfer. As a result, unless SC 6.7 is amended no other method of payment, such as by a banker's draft, can be made. (Direct payments are to be preferred as banker's drafts are drawn directly on the issuing bank (or building society if it is a building society cheque) rather than on the account of a customer, and signed by a bank or building society official. A banker's draft is not a cheque but, like a cheque, it is subject to the Bills of Exchange Act 1882 and is cleared in the same way as a cheque over several business days.)

Finally, when buying a leasehold property, remember to inspect the last receipt for ground rent to make sure it is an unqualified clear receipt. If there is a clear ground rent receipt, you can assume that in the absence of any other information to the contrary, of which you have had notice, there are no subsisting breaches of **covenant** affecting the subject property, to which the **lessor** may refer.

11.4 Postal completions: completion and the Protocol

Since 1990, the Law Society has tried to urge practitioners, and in particular solicitors, to adopt all the elements of the Law Society's Conveyancing Protocol. One such element is the inclusion of the Law Society's Code for Completion. This inclusion underpins the use of postal completions in residential and commercial conveyancing transactions.

11.4.1 The Law Society's Code for Completion by Post

This is available to download on the Law Society website. The current edition was issued in May 2019. The 2019 amendments to the Code were made in response to the Court of Appeal decision in *P&P Property Ltd v Owen White & Catlin LLP and Crownvent Ltd* [2018] EWCA Civ 1082 and *Dreamvar (UK) Ltd v Mishcon De Reya and Mary Monson Solicitors* [2018] EWCA Civ 1082 as a consequence of which both buyers' and sellers' conveyancers may potentially be liable in the event of identity fraud by an imposter seller. The 2019 changes offer buyers increased protection from fraudsters. Essentially, the Code is a set of guidance notes and principles that solicitors can adopt in order to arrange completion by post in an orderly and uniform manner across the profession. If the Code is to be used in non-Protocol conveyances, it must be expressly adopted by both sides (preferably in writing), but for Protocol cases the Code will apply unless otherwise agreed. In all cases, if a practitioner considers that to adopt the Code would create a conflict between the interests of the client and the requirements of the Code, then the Code must not be adopted.

The main Code provisions are as follows:

- The crucial element of the Code is that the buyer's solicitor appoints the seller's solicitor as their unpaid agent for completion. The buyer's solicitor is now required to use reasonable endeavours to ensure that sufficient funds are collected from the buyer and any **mortgage** lender in good time to transmit to the seller's solicitor on or before completion. The seller's solicitor is to provide to the buyer's solicitor replies to completion information and **undertakings** in the Law Society's standard form at least five working days before completion.
- The buyer's solicitor should provide full instructions for the 'agent' relating to the buyer's requirements. These instructions must clearly set out for the seller's solicitor what the buyer's solicitor requires them to do and what is to be sent on from the seller to the buyer, after completion has been effected.
- The seller's solicitor must confirm that they have been appointed the authorised agent of any **mortgagee** authorising the receipt of monies required to redeem. This section was introduced to the Code as a consequence of the decision in *Edward Wong Finance Co Ltd v Johnson, Stokes and Master* [1984] AC 296, PC. This was a Hong Kong case where monies were handed over against an undertaking regarding the forwarding of the deeds and the discharge of the existing **charge**. Sadly, this was a case where the seller's solicitor unlawfully absconded with the completion monies without having paid anything to the lenders. Even though the buyer's solicitors had acted in accordance with the general practice of the legal community within the colony, it was held that they were negligent in the way they arranged completion. To get around the problem, the seller must be appointed the mortgagee's agent. In this way, if the same circumstances arose the mortgagee could not refuse to complete because of the default of its agent. If there is any doubt, then we suggest you ascertain the amount required to redeem and on the day of completion send the redemption amount direct to the mortgagee and the balance to the seller's solicitor.
- The buyer's solicitor will send the completion monies by bank telegraphic transfer (a CHAPS payment) and on receipt the completion takes place. Until completion has taken place, the seller's solicitor will effectively hold the purchase monies to the order of the buyer's solicitor. At the point of completion, the deeds and documents are held by the seller's solicitor as agent for the buyer's solicitor and no lien can be claimed.
- That day (ie the day of completion), the deeds and documents must be sent to the buyer's solicitor and once posted properly they are at the buyer's risk.
- Adopting the Code involves the giving of a professional undertaking that will be enforced through the Law Society.
- The Code can be used only if there is no obvious conflict but, if such conflict exists, the appointment of an agent would be inappropriate.
- The undertaking to redeem charges within the Code includes confirmation that a satisfactory **redemption statement** has been obtained from the lender(s). In essence, this means

that the amount for redemption is known and ascertained and as a consequence that the undertaking can and will be fulfilled.

- All references to the 'Seller' in the Code are references to the person or persons who will be at the point of completion entitled to convey the legal and/or equitable title to the property. In addition, all references to the 'Seller's Solicitor' in the Code are to the solicitor purporting to act for the party named as the seller in respect of the contract or purported contract that the buyer has entered into in order to acquire the property.
- Paragraph 4(ii) of the Code makes explicit the effect of the decisions in *Twinsectra Ltd v Yardley* [2002] UKHL 12, *Lloyds TSB Bank plc v Markandan & Uddin (a firm)* [2012] EWCA Civ 65 and *P&P Property Ltd v Owen White & Catlin LLP and Dreamvar (UK) Ltd v Mishcon de Reya (a firm)* [2018] EWCA Civ 1082, that the seller's solicitor holds any purchase money received on trust for the buyer and is under a fiduciary duty not to deal with that money other than in accordance with the terms of the Code. This states that the money is either: (a) paid away only in respect of a completion in which the seller executes and delivers a valid conveyance or transfer; or (b) repaid to the person who remitted it, if completion does not take place.
- In the light of the decision in *P&P Property Ltd v Owen White & Catlin LLP and Dreamvar (UK) Ltd v Mishcon de Reya (a firm)* [2018] EWCA Civ 1082 referred to earlier, para 8(i) of the Code constitutes an undertaking that the seller's solicitor has authority from the true owner of the title to the property named in the contract to receive the purchase money, and that such person is at the point of completion entitled to convey such title as the contract states will be conferred.
- Finally, it should be noted that nothing in the Code shall override any rights and obligations of either the seller or the buyer under the terms of the sale contract or otherwise.

These steps are summarised, where a buyer must arrange completion, in **Figure 11.2**.

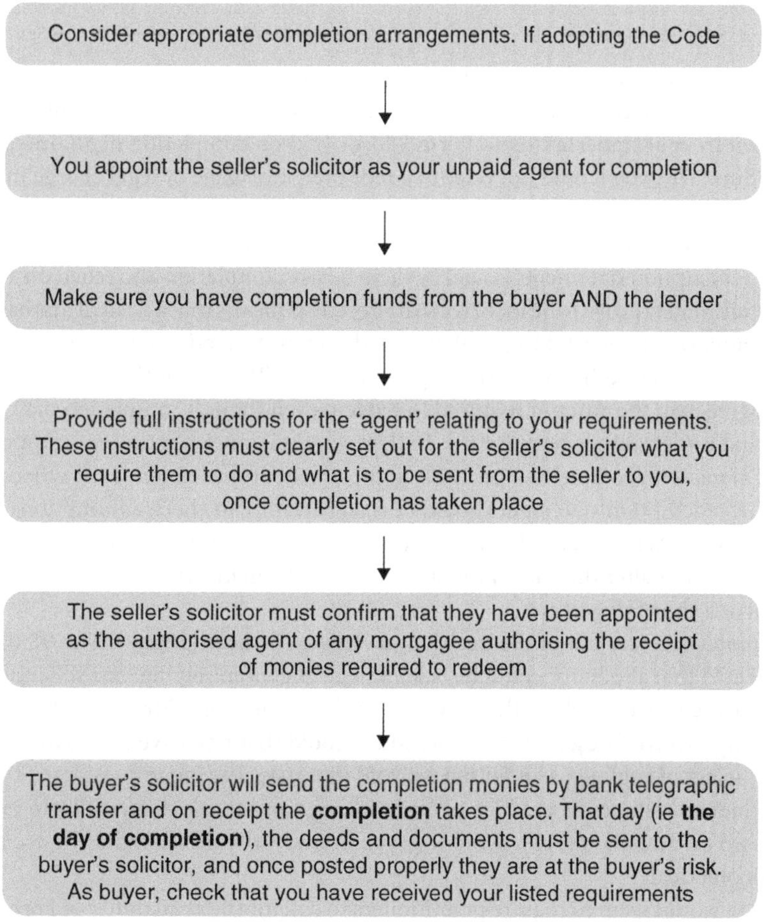

FIGURE 11.2 Completion action plan: using the Law Society Code for Completion

11.5 **Dealing with the discharge of the seller's mortgage**

Conveyancers for both parties to the contract will normally agree the arrangement to apply at completion for the discharge of the seller's mortgage and will do so after exchange (and thus well before completion), when dealing with post-exchange standard form requisitions. Indeed, most pre-printed forms of requisitions include a standard question on the mortgage discharge arrangements. Whatever is agreed, these arrangements should cover all the subsisting mortgages on the title and not just the first and most obvious mortgage. Inevitably, where there is a first mortgage and the seller has received instructions to deal with redemption for the lender, sale proceeds will be applied immediately after completion for the purposes of redemption. This being so, the vacating receipt for unregistered mortgages, or Form DS1/DS3 for a registered charge, will not be available on completion. In these circumstances, practitioners must rely on professional (and enforceable) undertakings. Such undertakings must only be taken from solicitors or licensed conveyancers and not from an unqualified person whose 'undertaking' will, of course, be unenforceable. A professional body, such as the Law Society, will ensure that the undertaking is complied with.

EXAMPLE

The Law Society has issued a recommended form of wording for the undertaking:

> *In consideration of you today completing the purchase of [insert subject property postal address or description] we hereby undertake to pay over to [insert identity of the lender] the money required to discharge the mortgage/legal charge dated [insert date of mortgage/legal charge] and to forward the receipted mortgage/legal charge/Form DS1/DS3 to you as soon as it is received by us from [insert identity of lender].*

Remember that a receipted mortgage or legal charge is appropriate for unregistered land, and Form DS1 (or e-DS1: see **11.6**) is appropriate for registered land (DS3 for release of part). Thus, you would not refer in your undertaking to Form DS1 or DS3 on completion of an unregistered land transaction. Similarly, you would not refer to a receipted mortgage or legal charge in a registered land transaction.

A problem arises when the lender is not a member of the Council of Mortgage Lenders. Members will stand by redemption statements issued by them before completion and relied on at completion and that may ultimately prove to be incorrect. In effect, this means that a deed of discharge, forming the subject matter of an undertaking, will be issued even if the lender has issued incorrect figures (and therefore has received incorrect redemption monies). This is not the case for non-members who can disagree over the amount required to redeem even though completion may have already taken place and undertakings been issued. In these circumstances, actual redemption may need to take place along with completion, probably at the offices of the lender or the offices of the lender's solicitor. A redemption statement should be read carefully to check assumptions made by the lender about payments to be made by the borrower. It might assume that the next instalment due before completion but after the date of the statement will be made. If it does, the seller must make that payment or a shortfall will arise.

Another problem arises out of the decision in *Patel v Daybells* [2000] EGCS 98 (QBD, 19 July 2000). Gray J held that a solicitor could be held to be negligent in relying on a solicitor's undertaking in the style mentioned earlier. The judge posed three questions. First, does the acceptance of the undertaking involve foreseeable risk? Secondly, could that risk have been avoided? Thirdly, if so, was there an act of negligence in failing to avoid that risk? The judge considered that there was a risk in the industry-standard practice of undertakings and that a different form of completion (probably based on attendance) can avoid the risk. Frankly, the decision may be accurate but it is definitely not practical.

The decision would seem to require practitioners to call for the availability of Form DS1 or DS3 at completion. However, lenders will not provide the form at that time as they have not yet been paid.

One way to address the difficulty is to ensure that the seller's practitioner is also the agent of the seller's lender. If then the agent fails to redeem by paying over an incorrect amount, the dispute will be between the agent (the seller's practitioner) and principal (the seller's lender), because with this procedure the lender will be bound to redeem. Express appointment as agent by the lender is required, and the buyer's practitioner should ask for a copy of the letter of appointment as confirmation. In practice, this is unlikely to be forthcoming and the risks attendant on industry-standard completion undertakings for domestic property particularly will remain.

Finally, a buyer's practitioner needs to exercise special care where the seller has a high-value mortgage. In the *Patel* case, it was stated that there could be 'exceptional circumstances' where accepting an undertaking at completion was negligent. This could be where the value of the seller's mortgage exceeds the minimum level required for indemnity insurance for solicitors. This is currently £1 million so if a buyer's practitioner is aware of this situation prevailing, either the cover must be increased or the seller's solicitors must warrant that the insurance cover exceeds the amount required to redeem (or Form DS1/DS3 must be available at completion).

CONDUCT POINT

Be very careful about how you reply to the Protocol Requisitions Form as some answers amount to enforceable solicitor's undertakings. Failure to comply with your answer, such as to pay off mortgages, will amount to a breach of the SRA Code of Conduct. Paragraph 1.3 states that you must perform all undertakings given by you and do so within an agreed timescale or if no timescale has been agreed then within a reasonable amount of time.

11.6 The electronic discharge (e-DS1)

The Land Registry has developed a scheme with banks and building societies that will make DS1 forms a rarity. It has developed an electronic discharge (e-DS1) to replace the DS1.

e-DS1s are a form of electronic discharge of registered mortgages. An e-DS1 is an electronic form of discharge submitted by corporate lenders or their agents through the Land Registry Portal or website. An e-DS1 cannot be lodged for a discharge of part of the land charged. Practitioners will need to agree a revised form of undertaking to take account of the new method of electronic discharge.

The revised form of undertaking could take the following form:

> In consideration of your today completing the purchase of [subject property] we hereby undertake forthwith to pay over to [the lender] the money required to discharge the mortgage/legal charge dated [insert date] and to forward to you a copy of the lender's letter confirming successful redemption of their charge and lodgement of an e-DS1 at HM Land Registry as soon as we receive it from the Lender.

EXAMPLE

Luke is completing today on the sale of his client Harriet's freehold house which has a registered title and is mortgaged to Barclays Bank. He has agreed with the buyer's solicitors to use the Law Society's Code for Completion by Post. In the morning, he receives a call from the buyer's solicitor that the completion monies are on their way via a CHAPS transfer and shortly thereafter he receives confirmation from his firm's accounts department that the funds have arrived. Luke calls the buyer's solicitors to confirm completion and then calls the estate agents to release the keys to the buyer. In the post that night he will send to the buyer's solicitors the transfer deed (TR1) duly executed by his client and dated today's date. In accordance with his undertaking to discharge the seller's mortgage, he will remit sufficient redemption monies to Barclays Bank and request the bank to lodge an E-DS1 at the Land Registry to remove its legal charge. In accordance with his client's instructions, after discharging his fees and the estate agent's commission account, he will remit the balance of the sale proceeds to Harriet.

11.7 The outcome of completion

The necessary outcome of completion for the seller is to receive the full purchase monies, including (especially if leasehold) all apportionments. Never accept cash payments at completion. If the buyer offers to pay in legal tender (here meaning banknotes), you should immediately be concerned about the dangers of money laundering. Where you act for that buyer you need to be sure that the client is not committing a money laundering offence. A practitioner is in danger of committing an offence by not reporting such circumstances. Efforts should therefore be made to investigate the source of these cash funds and the identity of the client. SC 6.7 (5th edn) provides that 'the buyer is to pay the money due on completion by direct transfer of cleared funds and, if appropriate, an unconditional release of a deposit held by a stakeholder'. The effect of this is that the only method of payment at completion permitted by the Standard Contractual Conditions is by direct electronic bank transfer.

CONDUCT POINT

Always be alive to the dangers of money laundering. If a client offers to pay you large amounts in cash or if a buyer makes a similar offer, question whether in accepting this money you might be involving yourself in money laundering.

11.8 Post-completion procedures

Whether they are acting for the seller or the buyer, once completion has taken place, conveyancing practitioners still have much to do. However, the buyer's solicitor will have more work to do as in most transactions acting on behalf of the buyer means after completion dealing with the possible payment of stamp duty land tax and then registration of the title and/or transfer. So far as the seller is concerned, if there is a mortgage, paying off any lender is required as well as accounting to the client for the net proceeds of sale. All these post-completion procedures will now be considered.

The flowchart in **Figure 11.3** sets out the steps to be taken after completion from the perspective of a practitioner acting for a buyer.

The flowchart in **Figure 11.4** sets out the steps to be taken after completion from the perspective of a practitioner acting for a seller.

11.9 Acting for the seller

If the seller has a mortgage, then this must be redeemed (ie all monies due to the lender must be repaid as to both capital and interest), unless there was a sale of part of the mortgaged property when it is possible for a part-redemption to occur.

11.9.1 Redemption arrangements

Once completion has taken place, and preferably on the day of completion, the redemption monies must be sent to the lenders in full settlement of the debt due to them. (Redemption is the removal of a financial obligation, eg the repayment of a loan; in property law a mortgage or charge.) The method of transmission of these monies is dictated by the calculation of the redemption statement. Some lenders issue a statement calculated to a month end. In these circumstances, and on the assumption that completion has not taken place at the end of the month, a payment by a client account cheque sent by post will be acceptable. If, however, the statement is calculated to the day and has a daily rate, the redemption monies can be sent by post but extra days of interest must

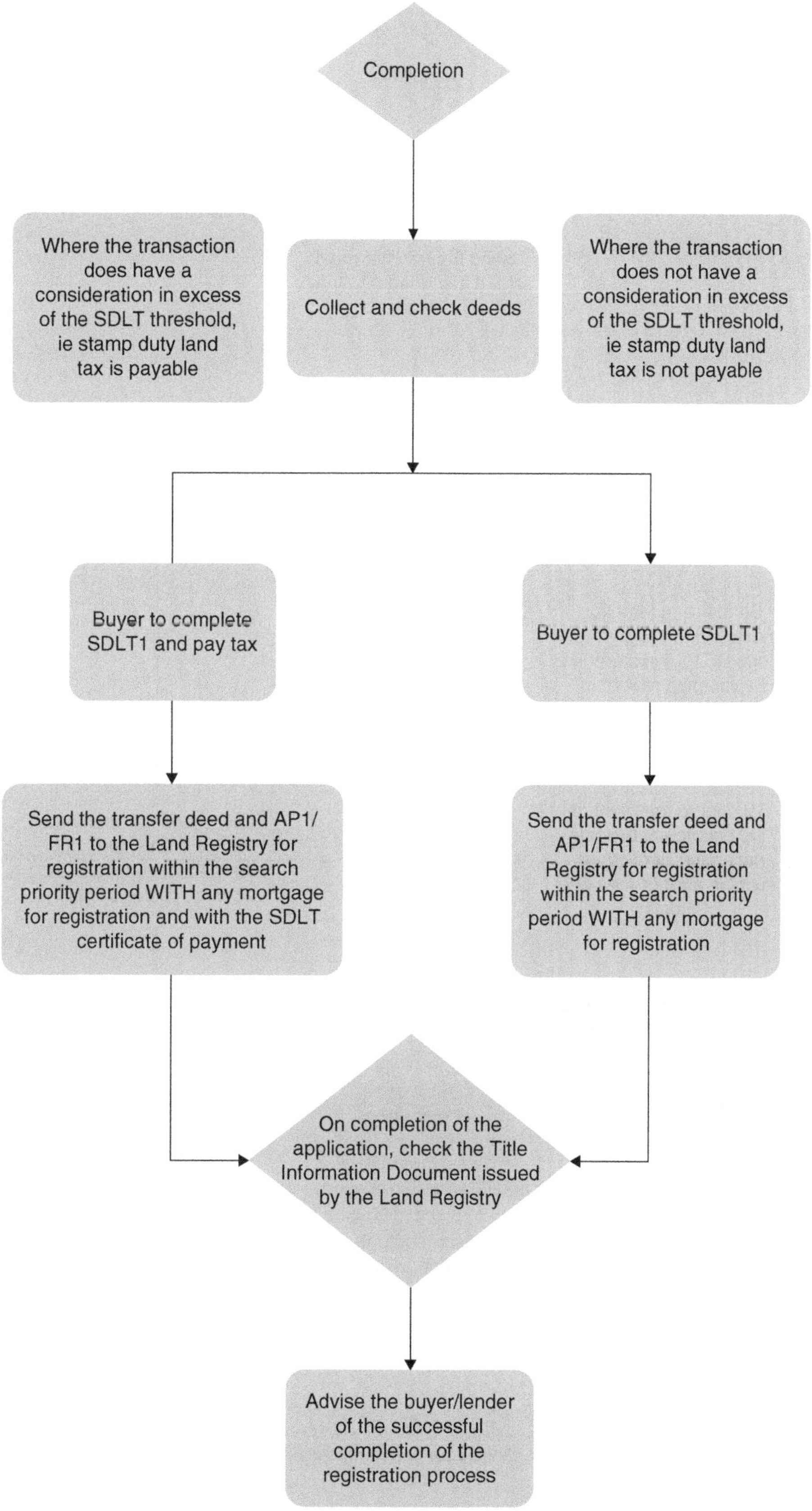

FIGURE 11.3 Buyer: post-completion steps

be added until the cheque is received and cleared. This would normally add an extra seven days to the total interest. It will probably be more economic for the client if the monies were sent by bank transfer and with the client paying the fee for this, usually in the region of £25. This can normally be accomplished on the day of completion. The Protocol states that the seller must provide

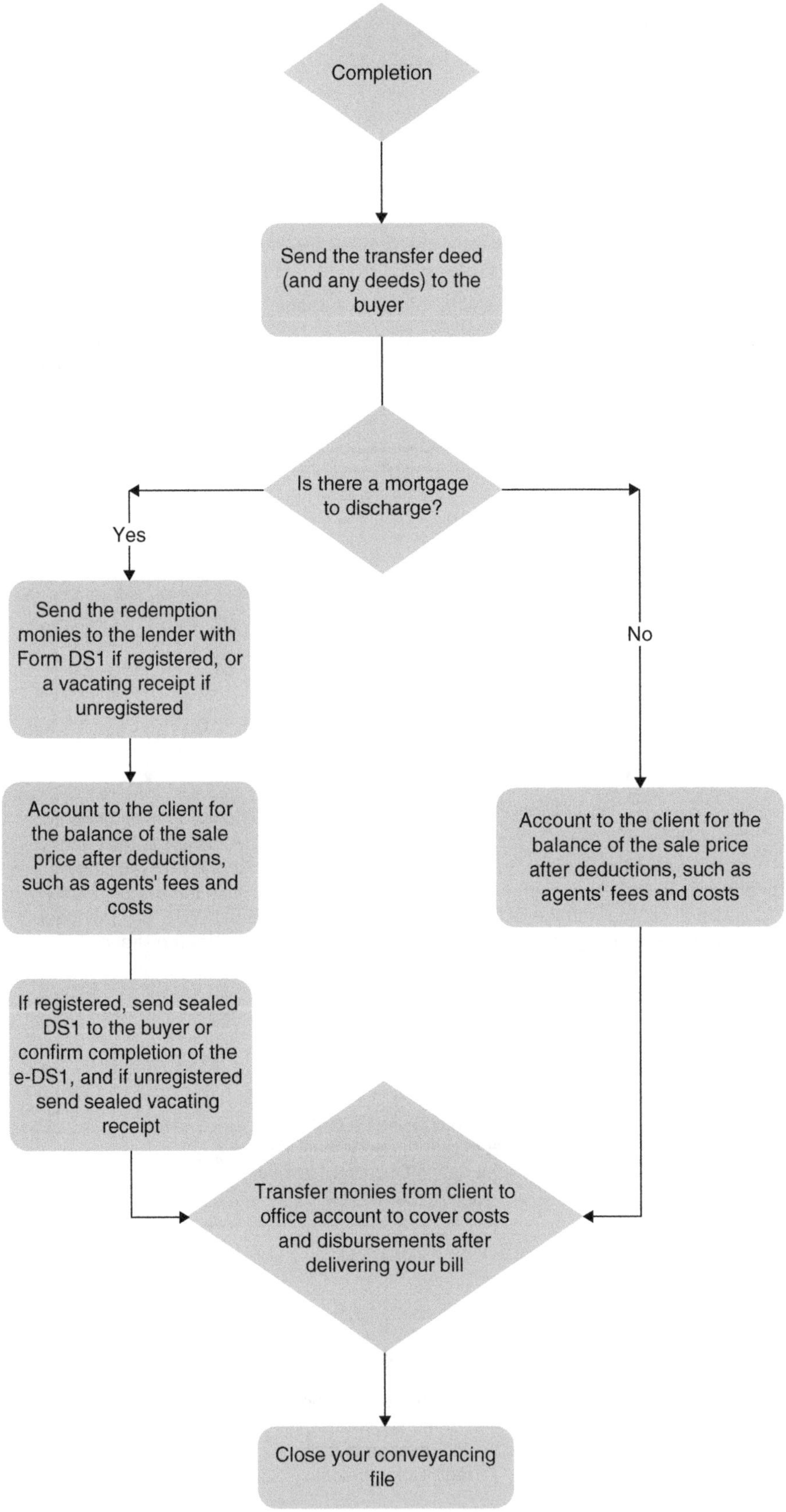

FIGURE 11.4 Seller: post-completion steps

the buyer with sealed Form DS1 as soon as it is received. If the lender has discharged any registered charge by electronic means, the seller must notify the buyer's solicitor when confirmation is received from the lender. If none is received, the seller must contact the lender to obtain such confirmation.

11.9.2 Methods for proving redemption

The methods for confirming payment of the redemption monies are:

- *Form DS1—used in registered land.* This is a very simple form that repeats the title details (county, location, title number and description of property), and in which you must insert the name and address of the registered lender and the dates of the mortgage. In the form, the lender acknowledges that the property identified in panel 2 of Form DS1 is no longer charged as security for the payment of sums due under the redeemed charge. The deed must be executed by the lender and dated with the date of completion. You will need to refer to **official copies of the registers** to complete Form DS1 as you will need to insert the date of the mortgage.
- *Mortgage vacating receipt—used for unregistered land only.* The position is a little more complicated and applies to unregistered land only. Mortgages will be released by way of a receipt usually endorsed on the back of the original deed. The receipt, also known as a vacating receipt, must be executed by the lender and dated with the date of completion. The receipt confirms payment of the redemption monies. An undertaking will have been given at completion and the sealed document should therefore be sent to the buyer's practitioner as soon as it is received back from the lender. When sending it on to the buyer, a request should be made for the undertaking to be fully discharged; that is, released.
- *Electronic discharge (e-DS1)—used in registered land.* These are a form of electronic discharge of registered mortgages. An e-DS1 is an electronic form of discharge submitted by corporate lenders or their authorised agents through the Land Registry Portal or website. When an e-DS1 is to be used, the lender will inform the Land Registry of the discharge of their mortgage over whole titles to land by an electronic submission of the form, sent through the Land Registry's Portal. It is intended that the e-DS1 will replace Form DS1. Receiving an electronic (rather than paper) submission direct from the lender helps to reduce delays. Although the charge will not be cancelled immediately, in many cases the application will be processed automatically by the Land Registry computer system so the charges register will be updated quickly, possibly in a matter of seconds. The Land Registry will issue an electronic acknowledgement to the user.

EXAMPLE

The form of undertaking required when an e-DS1 is being used would be as follows:

In consideration of your today completing the purchase of [subject property] we hereby undertake forthwith to pay over to [the lender] the money required to discharge the mortgage/legal charge dated [insert date] and to forward to you a copy of the lender's letter confirming successful redemption of their charge and lodgement of an electronic discharge at HM Land Registry as soon as we receive it from the lender.

An e-DS1 cannot be used to release part of a registered property from a registered charge; see below for releases of part.

- *Release of part, Form DS3—used in registered land.* In registered land, Form DS3 is required when releasing part of a title from a registered charge. The lender will still require and retain the redundant charge certificate because even though it is not proof of title it will contain the original charge over the retained land. Form DS3 should show the extent of the released land by reference to a scale plan.
- *Electronic discharges—used in registered land.* The Land Registry has also introduced a system with selected lenders regarding the electronic discharge of registered mortgages. An electronic discharge (ED) is a discharge of a registered charge sent electronically by a lender direct to the Land Registry. The Land Registry's computer system makes a number of checks and, if everything is in order, it cancels the charge entries. In most cases, the charge entries will be cancelled immediately and automatically on receipt of the discharge. An ED cancels the charge entries automatically and, in most cases, immediately. It does not require

a separate formal paper application to discharge the charge. It is a computer-to-computer-system-driven process. The Nationwide Building Society uses this method of mortgage discharge. An electronic discharge can only be sent for a discharge of the whole of a charge, not part.

CONDUCT POINT

Be very careful about how you handle enforceable solicitor's undertakings. Failure to comply with an undertaking, such as to pay off mortgages, will amount to a breach of the SRA Code of Conduct. In particular, note para 1.3, 'You perform all undertakings given by you, and do so within an agreed timescale or if no timescale has been agreed then within a reasonable amount of time.'

11.9.3 Estate agents' fees

If you are instructed to pay the selling agents' fees, then you must do so within a reasonable time of completion and obtain a written form of receipt for the payment. The receipt may be required by the seller if the cost may be a permitted deduction for **capital gains tax** purposes (as is the case for legal fees in connection with the disposal).

11.10 Acting for the buyer

The buyer has much to finalise after the completion of the transaction and in particular must deal with stamp duty land tax and registration matters both at the Land Registry and at Companies House if a company client is involved with a mortgage.

11.10.1 Registration at Companies House

In the case of a new mortgage by a company borrower, a certified copy of the mortgage *must* be lodged and accepted for registration by the Registrar of Companies within 21 days of completion. (This must be accompanied by Form MR01, particulars of mortgage or charge, as required by Part 25 of the Companies Act 2006. The certified copy will be retained at Companies House and made available for the public register. You should not submit the original written mortgage or charge. Form MR01 should only be used to register charges created on or after 6 April 2013 by companies registered in England and Wales.) If you fail to comply with this very strict time limit, you cannot register the mortgage without an order of the court and such orders are given only in exceptional circumstances. Failure to register is an unanswerable case of professional negligence that would have to be referred to your indemnity insurers. There is a fee payable for the registration of a charge at Companies House. The papers and fee should be sent to Companies House, Crown Way, Cardiff, CF14 3UZ (or by document exchange at DX 33050); the office is open 24 hours a day for delivery of documents. Part 25 of the Companies Act 2006 sets out this requirement in ss 860–877. Applications to register charges can also be submitted electronically. You can file online using the 'WebFiling' facility at Companies House. (The email address for Companies House is enquiries@companies-house.gov.uk.)

11.10.2 Stamp duty land tax

The stamp duty land tax (SDLT) regime came into force on 1 December 2003. Section 43 of the Finance Act 2003 defines land transactions as being the focus for land tax, and is an extremely wide definition covering dealings in estates and interests including those that are equitable. The starting threshold for the payment of land tax is £250,000 for residential property and £150,000 for non-residential or commercial property.

11.10.2.1 First-time buyers' relief

There are different rules if your client is buying their first home. A first-time buyer gets a discount (relief) that means your client pays less or no tax if:

- your client completes their purchase on or after 22 November 2017;
- the purchase price is £625,000 or less; and
- your client, and anyone else your client is buying with, are first-time buyers.

First-time buyers will pay no SDLT on the first £425,000 of the purchase price with the remainder being charged at 5 per cent. No relief can be claimed where the total price exceeds £625,000. A first-time buyer is defined as someone who has never owned a freehold or leasehold interest in a dwelling before and who is purchasing their own or main residence. In the case of joint purchasers, all of them must be first-time buyers to be eligible for the relief.

Before 4 December 2014, SDLT was charged at a single rate for the entire price of the property. Since 4 December 2014, SDLT is charged at increasing rates for each part of the price. For residential properties (assuming the purchaser is not a first-time buyer), the purchaser will pay:

- nothing on the first £250,000;
- 2 per cent on the next £125,000;
- 5 per cent on the next £675,000;
- 10 per cent on the next £575,000;
- 12 per cent on the rest (above £1.5 million).

EXAMPLE

If the purchaser who is not a first-time buyer buys a residential property for £325,000, they will pay SDLT of £3,750. This is calculated as follows:

Purchase price bands (£)	Percentage rate (%)	SDLT due (£)
Up to £250,000	0	0
Above £250,000 and up to £925,000	5	3,750
Total SDLT due		3,750

The HM Revenue and Customs calculator for SDLT is a useful resource to help work out how much your client will pay.

For non-residential and mixed-use properties the purchaser pays the following rates of SDLT:

- property price, premium or value up to £150,000 (annual rent no greater than £1,000) = 0%
- properties between £150,001 and £250,000 = 2%
- properties over £250,000 = 5%

The following is an example calculation of commercial property SDLT.

EXAMPLE

If you buy a freehold commercial property for £275,000, the SDLT you owe is calculated as follows:

- 0% on the first £150,000 = £0
- 2% on the next £100,000 = £2,000
- 5% on the final £25,000 = £1,250
- Total SDLT = £3,250

11.10.2.2 Higher rates of SDLT on purchases of additional residential properties

Higher rates of SDLT are now charged on purchases of additional residential properties, such as buy-to-let properties and second homes, with effect from 1 April 2016. The higher rate is 3 per cent above the current SDLT rates. HMRC has issued the guide in **Figure 11.5** to check if a party is liable to pay this additional charge.

EXAMPLE 1

If an additional residential property is purchased for £300,000, the SDLT is calculated as follows:

- 3% on the first £250,000 = £7,500
- 8% on the remaining £50,000 (the portion between £250,000 and £300,000) = £4,000
- The total SDLT due is therefore: £7,500 + £4,000 = £11,500

EXAMPLE 2

If an additional residential property is purchased for £100,000, the SDLT is calculated as follows:

- 3% on £100,000 = £3,000

11.10.2.3 Foreign buyers

From 1 April 2021, all non-UK residents buying residential property pay a 2 per cent surcharge on top of any stamp duty already chargeable on their purchase.

11.10.2.4 When should a land transaction return be completed?

The Revenue will require the completion and submission of a land transaction return to their data-capture centre in Merseyside and payment of the tax due within 14 days of completion of the conveyancing transaction. Payment is required either on completion or when there is substantial performance of the contract. This will be if the buyer goes into possession or pays a substantial amount, probably 90 per cent of the price. The centre address is HMRC Stamp Taxes, BT Stamp Duty Land Tax, HM Revenue and Customs BX9 1LT or more usually it is filed online. If a return is filed late the buyer will be liable to a fixed penalty of £100 or, if more than three months late, £200.

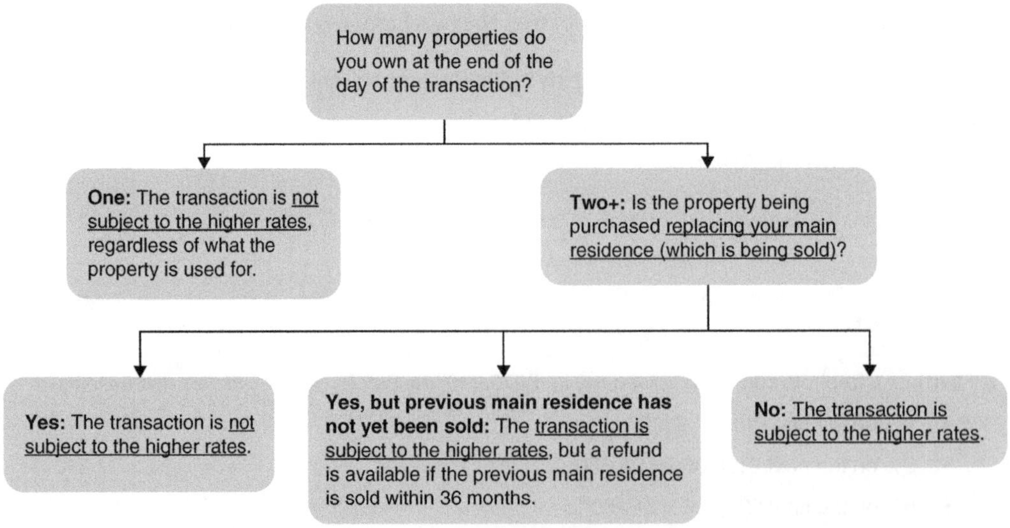

FIGURE 11.5 SDLT flowchart

The buyer may also be liable to a tax-related penalty not to exceed the tax payable. Online submissions are also possible and details of the service can be found on the HMRC website.

The land transaction return should be submitted to notify:

- any transfer of a freehold or assignment of a lease for consideration, whether or not giving rise to a charge;
- any transaction for which relief is being claimed;
- the grant of a lease for a contractual term of seven years or more or that gives rise to a charge; and
- any other transaction giving rise to a charge.

The following transactions are not notifiable and as such no land tax return is required:

- the acquisition of a freehold or leasehold interest in land for no chargeable consideration (note that there will normally be chargeable consideration where there is a gift of property subject to an existing debt such as a mortgage);
- transactions made in connection with the ending of a marriage;
- transactions varying the dispositions made, whether effected by will or laws of **intestacy**, within two years after the person's death not involving any consideration in money or money's worth;
- a transaction that effects something other than a major interest in land chargeable with tax at 0 per cent. An example of such a transaction would be an interest which is not a major interest in land, such as the grant of an **easement** where the consideration does not exceed £125,000. This would attract land tax at 0 per cent, provided it is not linked to any other transaction that would bring the total consideration to more than £125,000. Notification would not be required.

Furthermore, the following transactions do not require an SDLT return to be lodged either:

- freehold transactions of £40,000 or less;
- leasehold purchases of leases of seven years or more where the value is £40,000 or less; and
- leasehold purchases of leases of less than seven years where the total value of the transaction is not more than the residential or non-residential SDLT threshold.

11.10.2.5 Stamp duty land tax and leases

When you buy a leasehold property, the amount of SDLT you have to pay depends on whether it is an existing lease or the grant of a new one. If it is an existing lease, you only have to pay SDLT on the consideration paid to buy the new lease at the same rates for freeholds. How you calculate SDLT on a new lease depends on the consideration, the rent payable under the lease and whether it is a residential or non-residential lease. SDLT is payable in relation to the rental element of **commercial leases**. The charge is at a rate of 1 per cent on the net present value (NPV) of the total rent payable over the term of the lease. Future rents will be discounted at 3.5 per cent per annum in order to arrive at the NPV. Leases where the NPV of the rent over the term of the lease does not exceed £250,000 on residential property and £150,000 for commercial property will be exempt. The Revenue has suggested that some 60 per cent of all commercial leases could avoid any SDLT on the rental element. There is an online calculator for SDLT payable in leasehold transactions that can be accessed here at https://www.gov.uk/business-tax/stamp-taxes.

11.10.2.6 The SDLT5 or certificate of payment

Once the Revenue has received and processed a proper land tax return and payment, it will issue a certificate of payment. This is called a Land Transaction Return Certificate or SDLT5. The certificate is issued under s79 of the Finance Act 2003 and evidences that land tax has been accounted on the particular transaction notified to the Revenue. This must be sent to the Land Registry to enable an application to register to proceed. The Land Registry will not proceed with a registration application without an SDLT5 certificate being provided.

11.10.2.7 Land transaction tax (in Wales)

Since April 2018, land transaction tax (LTT) has replaced UK SDLT in Wales. Like SDLT, LTT is payable when a party buys or leases a building or land over a certain price. The legislation is broadly consistent with SDLT, preserving the underlying structure and mirroring key elements. Higher rates of SDLT on purchases of additional residential properties (including second homes) came into effect on 1 April 2016, and the higher rates also apply in Wales as part of the LTT legislation. Note, however, that the higher residential rates of LTT increased by 1 per cent across all bands on 22 December 2020. This applies to sales of second homes and buy-to-let properties as opposed to the main residential home.

Tables 11.1 and **11.2** show the main Welsh non-residential (commercial) and residential tax rates and bands.

11.10.3 **Registration of title**

After completion, title will not pass to the buyer without registration taking place at the Land Registry. It is therefore vital to ensure that completion is swiftly followed by an application for registration to the Land Registry.

11.10.3.1 The documents that should be sent to the Land Registry

Until recently, all original deeds and documents were sent to the Land Registry to ensure that registration of each transaction was properly completed. Now if you are applying for first registration, you must send to the Land Registry original supporting documents. For all other applications, the Land Registry recommends sending certified copies as they destroy original documents once they have made a scanned copy. For applications submitted through e-DRS (an electronic application system explained at **11.10.3.7**), the Land Registry only accept certified copies.

The original deeds and documents and or certified copies are lodged together with a Land Registry application form, the details of which are set out under the heading 'Form AP1'. Practitioners who use the Land Registry Portal can now lodge applications to change the register electronically. Initially, this covers only simple applications but the Land Registry plans to develop the process to allow more complicated applications. The service is called 'e-lodgement' to differentiate it from 'e-conveyancing'. There is also e-DRS (see **11.10.3.7**).

TABLE 11.1 Land transaction tax (LTT): main non-residential rates

Price threshold	LTT rate
£0–£225,000	0%
£225,001–£250,000	1%
£250,001–£1 million	5%
Above £1 million	6%

TABLE 11.2 Land transaction tax (LTT): main residential rates

Price threshold	LTT rate
£0–£225,000	0%
£225,001–£400,000	6%
£400,001–£750,000	7.5%
£750,001–£1.5 million	10%
Above £1.5 million	12%

11.10.3.2 Existing registered titles; dealings with whole or part

These applications must be lodged at the Land Registry within the priority period given on the pre-completion Land Registry search result. Where the land is registered and the dealing is with the whole of the title, any existing land or charge certificate should not be sent to the Land Registry with the dealing application cover AP1 (application to change the register). The application should be accompanied by the transfer deed and all new mortgages. The Land Registry will require a certified copy of each mortgage sent for registration with a clear indication of priority. The certification can be in the following form:

> I/We hereby certify this to be a true copy of the original [signed, here signed in the firm name or by the practitioner applying].

In cases where e-DS1 is not being used, all discharges of previous mortgages on Form DS1 must be lodged with the application. On a dealing making a transfer of part, the appropriate application cover is also the AP1, which now covers both whole-of-title and part-of-title dealings. Otherwise, the documents will be the same as for a dealing with the whole of the title. However, it is possible that a mortgage discharge will be of part with the charge remaining on the residue of the seller's title. In this case, Form DS3 will be required but it should have with it a scale plan showing the area to be released from the charge. This will be required from the seller's lender and must accompany the AP1 application form. Where SDLT has been paid, SDLT5 must be lodged with the application for registration. (SDLT5 will be required even if no tax was payable. Transactions taxed at 0 per cent will still require an SDLT1 to be submitted if the value was over £40,000.)

The appropriate Land Registry fee must accompany the application. Fees are set out in the current Land Registration Fees Order and are listed in scales according to the consideration paid for the property. There is a provision that makes a 50 per cent reduction for customers who submit transfers of whole, charges of whole, transfers of charges and other dealings of whole applications electronically. Fees can only be paid by cheque or direct debit.

11.10.3.3 Form AP1

This form is used when an applicant wishes to apply for a change in the register such as a change of ownership. It is an easy form to complete as it has been designed to be completed by filling out a series of self-explanatory boxes. When listing the applications being made, if there are mortgages being released (ie fully paid off), these should be listed before the transfer and new mortgage, if any, so that the applications are listed chronologically. A list of documents lodged with the form should also be set out and should include all certified copies. A box for this purpose is included within the form. There are extensive details required about identity towards the end of the form: see later regarding identity checks.

EXAMPLE

Roza has just completed the purchase of a house with a registered title in London on behalf of her client Sonya, which she bought with the aid of a mortgage. Roza is also acting for Sonya's mortgagee, Nationwide Building Society. The seller had no mortgage on the property. Roza must now arrange payment of SDLT within 14 days of completion and lodge the SDLT return. Thereafter she will apply to the Land Registry to register the transfer to Sonya and the mortgage in favour of Nationwide Building Society. This must be done within the priority period of her **official search** made prior to completion. The documents she will send to Land Registry are Form AP1, executed TR1, the client's mortgage deed (and certified copy), SDLT5 certificate and the relevant Land Registry fee. She will keep dated copies for her file.

11.10.3.4 First registration

Section 6(4) of the Land Registration Act 2002 requires applications for first registration to be made within two months of completion. The application cover required is normally Form FR1 for both freehold and leasehold properties. In both cases, the Registry requires a list in triplicate of all documents lodged within the cover form, and Form DL is required for this purpose. The Registrar will want to see all the documents of title to enable a decision to be taken as to the class of title to be granted. Consequently, practitioners should include and list:

- all the documents of title as abstracted, including all old **land charges search** results;
- all searches and pre-contract enquiries with replies;
- the original contract;
- **requisitions on title** with replies;
- the original executed conveyance, or transfer, or deed of assignment with certified copy;
- the buyer's mortgage deed, if any, with a certified copy;
- all receipted discharged mortgages, including any paid off by the seller; and
- if the property is leasehold, the lease (and a certified copy where a new lease is being granted).

EXAMPLE

Rob has just completed the purchase of an unregistered freehold house in Lincolnshire on behalf of his client Caroline. It was a sale by **executors**, the owner of the house, Matthew Brown, having died several months ago. After arranging payment of SDLT within 14 days of completion, Rob must now consider his application for first registration at the Land Registry to be made within two months of completion. Accordingly, he will apply for first registration by submitting Forms FR1 and DL (documents list) to the Land Registry together with executed TR1, clients' mortgage deed, all deeds and documents relating to the title, land charges search certificates, SDLT certificate (SDLT5) and the relevant Land Registry fee. As the sale was by executors, he must also lodge with his application to the Land Registry a certified copy of the Grant of Probate which gives authority for the executors to dispose of Matthew Brown's assets. He will keep dated copies for his file.

11.10.3.5 Identity checks

The Land Registry, in an attempt to reduce fraudulent registration applications, have added identity panels to application forms AP1 and FR1. Evidence of identity will always be required for transfers, leases, charges and applications for first registration. Evidence is not required where the value of the land is worth less than £5,000. Conveyancers making a registration application must list all parties to the transaction and, where a party is not represented by a conveyancer, a separate section on the form (section 2) must also be completed.

11.10.3.6 Where to send your application

Members of the public should send applications and correspondence to: Land Registry Citizen Centre, PO Box 74, Gloucester, GL14 9BB. Business customers (ie legal professionals) send paper applications and correspondence by Royal Mail or DX to the relevant Land Registry office. However, preferably firms are encouraged to submit applications online by signing up to business e-services. Benefits include a 50 per cent fee reduction for some application types, no postage costs, an electronic audit trail and reduced processing times.

11.10.3.7 e-DRS (Electronic Document Registration Service)

With e-DRS, firms can send and receive applications to change the register electronically, for example using AP1s. To use this service, your firm will need a Land Registry Portal access account. There are no additional fees for using e-DRS. The fees payable for submitting applications via e-DRS are based on the current Land Registration Fee Order. The current Order gives a 50 per cent reduction for electronic applications.

The following application types may be submitted by e-DRS:

- Dealings of whole of registered land for up to 50 registered titles.
- Most types of dealing transaction that are currently received by post.
- Transfers of part.
- First registrations of leases and lease extensions.

Since 14 March 2016, Land Registry Portal users are able to view information about their applications using a search facility called 'Application Enquiry'. The application allows customers to search using the title number or the Land Registry reference number to find more details about their application. The Land Registry has also introduced e-Despatch for users of its online portal. If you send your registration applications in the post, you will receive the application results online in your PDF download area in the portal. The only exception to the new system is for first registrations which will continue to be returned by post.

Be aware that since November 2022, the Land Registry no longer accepts scanned or PDF copy documents through its online channels for changes to existing titles. Applications to change the register must go through its online digital registration service. So rather than a scan of a paper form, or a PDF, the details of the application are entered directly into the service, capturing the data digitally. Digital data is more structured, more accurate (due to the pre-submission checks) and will enable the Land Registry to automate more applications. For more information on submitting forms online, see https://www.gov.uk/guidance/hm-land-registry-digital-applications#how-to-submit-digitally.

11.10.3.8 Land Registry early completion policy

In cases where e-DS1 is not being used, all discharges of previous mortgages on Form DS1 must be lodged with the application. In this regard, early completion is a policy governing applications to discharge mortgages that the Land Registry has applied from 3 August 2009. The policy will apply to all situations where an application for a discharge of whole has been made with another application but proof of redemption (evidence of the discharge of the charge) has not been provided.

In essence, if there is no DS1 or other satisfactory proof of the mortgage discharge, the Land Registry will reject the application for discharge but complete any other accompanying applications where it is possible to do so, such as a transfer of title. The entries relating to the existing charge will be left in the register until proof of redemption is received by the Land Registry. If the discharge of a charge is the sole application, regardless of the method of discharge, the Land Registry will reject it if proof of redemption has not been supplied.

Accordingly, if a property has been sold and the buyer submits the registration application without adequate proof of redemption, the Land Registry will vest the property in the new owner but will leave the old owner's mortgage in the charges register. To avoid this, proper evidence of redemption, for example a DS1 or evidence of the electronic equivalent, should always be included with the registration application.

11.10.4 **Registration with the lessor**

Almost all leases include a covenant on the **lessee**'s part requiring the lessee to give notice to the lessor of all transfers, assignments, mortgages or other dealings affecting the legal title. The purpose of the clause is to ensure that the lessor is aware of who is the lessee and therefore responsible for the performance of all the covenants in the lease and, in particular, the payment of rent. The covenant normally stipulates a time limit for giving notice, usually 28 days from the date of the deed or completion, and calls for copies of the relevant documents (the transfer, mortgage, etc) to be lodged with the lessor's solicitor. A fee may be required by the terms of the covenant, payable to the lessor's solicitor. (If the fee is stated, then that is all that must be paid, as the VAT is deemed to be included in that figure. However, many covenants state the fee and go on to provide that VAT will also be payable on the fee by the lessee.) Notice should be given in duplicate so that a receipted copy can be placed with the deeds. It is quite permissible to give notice by letter.

EXAMPLE

The following would serve as the basis for a notice of assignment:

> *To [lessor] of [address] [insert the date] With regard to the Lease made the [here insert the date of the lease] between (1) [insert the name of the original lessor] and (2) [insert the name of the original lessee] relating to [here insert the postal address or description of premises] ('the Lease') TAKE NOTICE that by a transfer or an assignment dated the [insert the date of*

the assignment or transfer] the Lease was transferred or assigned by [insert the name and address of the outgoing lessee] to [insert the purchaser, transferee or ***assignee****] of [the incoming lessee's address] ('the Purchaser') for the residue of the term granted by the lease.*

Some leases do not state a fee but refer to a 'reasonable fee'. In these circumstances, you will need to agree what is reasonable before the lessor's solicitor will receipt the notice.

11.10.5 Share transfer registration

Particularly when dealing with leasehold properties, it may be that each owner in the block or development is entitled to own a share or shares in a management company. If there is such an arrangement, the share certificate should be obtained on completion along with a stock transfer form completed and signed by the seller. These two documents should then be submitted to the secretary of the company with a request that a new share certificate be issued in the name of the buyer. The new certificate should be kept with the deeds. In many cases, these companies are limited by guarantee and therefore do not have or issue share certificates. Where this is the case, the change of ownership (and hence guarantee) should be confirmed in writing to the company secretary. A membership certificate may be issued.

KEY POINT SUMMARY

- Acting for seller, check you have all the necessary deeds, that you have prepared Form DS1 or, if appropriate, are ready to deal with an e-DS1, or a vacating receipt for a mortgage of unregistered land, and that you have the executed purchase deed.
- To minimise personal risk and liability, wherever possible only give undertakings about redemption in the form approved by the Law Society.
- Be aware that in Protocol cases (and in non-Protocol cases but where the Code for Completion is being adopted) the Code incorporates professional undertakings.
- Acting for buyer, check all searches to ensure they exist and remain in force and ensure the buyer carries out a final inspection immediately before completion.
- Can you accept an undertaking from the seller regarding the mortgage? Preferably not if the lender is not a member of the Council of Mortgage Lenders.
- Seek written confirmation that the seller's practitioner is the agent of the lender at completion.
- Is it cost-effective to complete in person? Do you trust the seller's practitioner? If not, complete in person or appoint an agent.
- Acting for seller, prepare a schedule of deeds and documents to be handed over at completion and obtain the buyer's practitioner's signature thereon to confirm the transmission of these documents.
- Agree the time and place for completion and the style of completion—postal, agency or in person.
- Make sure the seller is moving out and (if the contract so provides) ascertain the time that full vacant possession will be available, namely when the property will be empty.
- When seeking payment of the sale price along with apportionments ensure that the buyer's practitioner has a **completion statement** and copy receipts or current demands.
- Ensure the keys are released and the selling agents duly informed of completion.
- If the land is unregistered, remember to attach all necessary endorsements on the most recent title deed (normally only on a sale of part) and a memorandum on any relevant grant of representation.

- When completion is by post make sure all the proper safeguards (undertakings, etc), are in place and evidenced in writing.
- Acting for buyer, if completing in person, on receipt of the deeds and documents of title always check that all the expected documents have indeed been passed over to you. Tick off each one using a checklist.
- In registered land, ask for the executed transfer (and original lease if the title is an existing registered leasehold).
- If the seller has a mortgage, ensure that you obtain the seller's practitioner's undertaking to redeem in the form suggested by the Law Society together with their confirmation of appointment as agent on completion for the seller's lender.
- Check the execution of the purchase deed and inspect any relevant powers of attorney in support and obtain certified copies of the powers.
- If relevant, inspect original grants of representation and compare with your previously supplied office copy grants.
- Inspect and approve all original receipts or current demands relevant to the details in the completion statement.
- If the subject property is subject to a **tenancy**, obtain a rental authority issued by the seller or the seller's practitioner authorising the tenant to pay all future rent to the buyer or as the buyer directs.
- If completion is by post, inform all parties by phone of completion, namely the seller, the practitioner acting for the buyer and, if any, the selling agents, so that the keys for the subject property can be released.
- Acting for seller, immediately following completion post the deeds and documents of title with the executed and dated purchase deed, and keep a dated file copy of the purchase deed.
- Acting for seller, if the subject property is subject to a mortgage, send on the day of completion sufficient redemption monies to the lender along with Form DS1 for registered land and the mortgage deed for receipting in unregistered land.
- Acting for seller, if the mortgage is an endowment one, send to the lender all the mortgages of life policies for release and also give notice of reassignment to the life companies.
- When the receipted documents are returned to you from the lenders, remember to check the details; and if all is well send Form DS1/DS3 or vacated mortgage to the buyer's practitioner with a request that you be released from your undertaking given at completion.
- On receipt of the released mortgage of life policy and receipted notice or reassignment from the life office, send to the client seller the original policy and all released mortgages of life policies and notices as these will be required by the client should a policy claim arise.
- Pay to the client the net proceeds of sale and supply full accounts, including a note of your own charges, if you have not already done so; or alternatively apply the net proceeds towards a related purchase if these are your instructions.
- If you have instructions to do so from the seller, pay the estate agents their commission charges and request a receipted account from them.
- Remind the client seller to cancel all standing orders to the lender, any buildings insurance and payments to the local authority in the nature of council tax.
- If there is a sale of part and the deeds are in your possession, ensure that you have instructions about their custody and, if they are to remain with you, place them all within a fireproof safe.
- Advise the buyer, and the buyer's lender, that you have effected completion in accordance with the contract terms.
- Acting for buyer, ensure that the seller's practitioner has sent, or will have sent later on the day of completion, all the deeds and documents to you in the post.
- On receipt of the purchase deed, ensure that the correct SDLT is paid within 14 days of completion to avoid any penalty fee for late payment.

- Since 1 April 2016, there has been a 3 per cent SDLT surcharge (4 per cent in Wales) when an additional residential property is bought by someone who already owns a home, namely second homes and buy-to-let properties.
- Consider if your client is entitled to claim the SDLT first-time buyer relief. If the price of the subject property exceeds £625,000 then no relief is available.
- If the title is unregistered, submit the deeds for first registration within two months of completion; and, if the title is registered, submit the dealing for registration within your search priority period.
- Make sure you use the correct form for your Land Registry application and include certified copy mortgages. Also include a certified copy transfer where it is a transfer of part imposing new restrictive covenants and remember to include the appropriate Land Registry fee. Include SDLT5.
- Be prepared to comply with Land Registry identity verification requirements.
- Consider using the e-DRS online application service.
- If there is a mortgage created by a limited company, make sure the mortgage is registered at Companies House within 21 days of the completion date, and remember this is an unequivocal deadline incapable of extension without recourse to the court.
- Give notice of assignment to life offices of any life policies forming part of the security for the lender.
- If the subject property is leasehold and if the lease terms require it, give notice of assignment or transfer to the lessor's practitioner, pay any requisite fee and request a receipted copy of the notice to be placed with the deeds.
- If the subject property is subject to a tenancy, give notice to the tenant of the change of ownership and indicate to whom all future rent should be paid.
- Send all relevant deeds and documents (eg a registered lease) to the lender, if the lender requires them.
- Make sure you have transferred monies to your office account for all costs and prepaid disbursements.
- If the deeds are in your possession (ie there is no mortgage on the title), ensure you have instructions about their custody and, if they are to remain with you, place them all in a fireproof safe.
- Always check the contents of the Title Information Document on its issue from the Land Registry and, where there is a mortgage, send to the lender a deeds schedule in duplicate for receipting. Alternatively, retain the deeds where the lender's instructions state they are not required.
- Send a photocopy of the title to the client for information and retention.
- Make a final check of your file to make sure there are no forgotten points or items still outstanding.

CHAPTER 12
Delays and Remedies

FUNCTIONING LEGAL KNOWLEDGE

This chapter covers the following functioning legal knowledge required to pass the SQE 1 assessments:

Remedies for delayed completion:

- common law damages
- contractual compensation
- notice to complete
- rescission

AUTHORITIES UNDERPINNING PRACTICE

The key authorities that underpin this area of practice are listed below. Note that for legislation you are linked to legislation.gov.uk.

Although much of the legislation on this government website is available in its amended form, the incorporation of new amendments into the text of legislation can be delayed. You should refer to legal databases to ensure you are referencing the most up-to-date legislation.

- Section 50 of the Senior Courts Act 1981
  https://www.legislation.gov.uk/ukpga/1981/54/contents
- Section 49 of the Law of Property Act 1925
  https://www.legislation.gov.uk/ukpga/Geo5/15-16/20/contents
- Section 2 of the Misrepresentation Act 1967
  https://www.legislation.gov.uk/ukpga/1967/7/section/2

Pre-exchange					Exchange & pre-completion				Completion & post-completion		
Stage 1 Taking instructions & advising client	**Stage 2** Draft contract	**Stage 3** Pre-contract searches, enquiries & planning	**Stage 4** Title	**Stage 5** Mortgage (applies throughout process)	**Stage 6** Exchange of contracts	**Stage 7** Purchase deed	**Stage 8** Pre-completion searches and requisitions	**Stage 9** Financial statements	**Stage 10** Completion	**Stage 11** SDLT & registration	**Stage 12** Delays and remedies

FIGURE 12.1 Conveyancing timeline

12.1 **Introduction**

This chapter considers what can be done if a conveyancing contract is delayed, disputed or denied. A conveyancer must be able to advise a client when a transaction goes wrong and remedies are sought to correct that wrong. The remedies that may be available to a potential claimant will therefore also be considered throughout the rest of this chapter.

In an agreement for the sale and purchase of a legal **estate** in land that is regulated by the Standard Conditions (SC) or the Standard Commercial Property Conditions (SCPC) the **completion date** will either be specified on the front page of the contract within the particulars or, more rarely, by SC 6.1 or SCPC 8.1. This states that completion will be 20 working days after the date of the contract. In this way, the normal arrangements for completion are straightforward. However, practitioners need to be aware of the position should completion be delayed.

12.2 Late completion

What can be done if one of the parties delays completion, namely fails to complete on the contractual completion date? Such a delay will be a breach of contract. It was held in the House of Lords in *Raineri v Miles* [1981] AC 1050 that failure to complete was a breach entitling the innocent party to a claim for damages arising from the delay. When **time is of the essence**, there is no leeway for delay; completion must be on the date specified, failing which all remedies will be available to the aggrieved party. It now seems to be that if a contract states a completion date without qualification, that date is not a strict and binding date that would allow the innocent party to withdraw from the contract on the occasion of the breach. On the other hand, if it is expressly stated that time is of the essence, then a strict interpretation arises and, if there is a failure to complete on the stipulated date, there will be a breach of contract of such magnitude that the innocent party will be free to pursue all remedies, which can include immediate termination or rescission of the contract.

12.3 Time of the essence

'Time of the essence' means that any date fixed in the contract cannot be extended and is firmly fixed. Delays will not be allowed. Time will be of the essence for a conveyancing contract:

- if the parties agree to it being written into the contract; or
- where a **notice to complete** has been correctly served; or
- where time is of the essence by necessary implication from the surrounding circumstances of the case.

In a contract regulated by the Standard Conditions, SC 6.1 and SCPC 9.1.1 specifically state that time is not of the essence unless a notice to complete is served. The parties to the contract can vary this term to make time of the essence but this cannot be achieved unilaterally.

In the absence of an SC 6.1 (or an SCPC 9.1.1) provision declaring that time is not of the essence, it may become of the essence where the time of completion is clearly expressed to be an essential, almost paramount, term.

EXAMPLE

Examples of where time is of the essence:

- In *Harold Wood Brick Co Ltd v Ferris* [1935] 1 KB 613, where completion was required 'not later than . . .'.
- In *Barclay v Messenger* (1874) 43 LJ Ch 449, where if the purchase monies were not paid by a certain date the contract would be null and void.

What, then, are the implications where time is not of the essence and yet one party has delayed completion? One element of this predicament is clear; the injured party cannot refuse to complete the contract. If the injured party seeks to establish grounds for terminating the agreement, then the appropriate course of action is to make time of the essence and a notice to complete (see **12.5**) should be served on the recalcitrant party without further delay.

12.4 Consequences of delay: compensation

Where there is delay in completing a transaction that delay, however short, will amount to a breach of contract. If there is delay, even of a matter of hours (or even minutes), the innocent party is entitled to seek damages for any loss occasioned as a result of the delay. In the circumstances of a brief delay of a few hours, any loss sustained is unlikely to be such as to justify making a claim in the courts for breach of contract. As a result, it has become the norm to include compensation provisions within the express contract terms. These compensatory terms do not preclude a claim in the courts but, where such steps are taken, any compensation paid under the contractual terms must be taken into account when computing damages.

The common law has made provision for compensation but, if certainty is required, compensation terms should always be included in a conveyancing contract. The common law position is that where completion is delayed in an open contract, the buyer will be entitled to any income from the property but must bear all outgoings. Furthermore, if the seller remains in the subject property, they will be required to pay a fee for occupation unless the delay has arisen as a consequence of any default by the buyer. The seller will be entitled to interest on the unpaid purchase monies. If the seller causes the delay, then they must pay the outgoings. Accordingly, the position at common law seems to be that the intention is to deal with the parties as if completion had actually taken place, even though in reality no such step has been taken. Notwithstanding that the innocent party will be entitled to seek damages, it is clear that to allow open contract provisions to prevail in these circumstances would be unwise.

12.4.1 Compensation and (1) the standard and (2) commercial property conditions

The Standard Conditions contain clear and precise provisions for compensation for a breach of contract that arises from delayed completion. SC 7.2 states that if a party to the contract defaults and delays completion, the defaulting party must pay compensation to the innocent party. (Reference can also be made to SC 4.3 entitled 'timetable' in working out who may be at fault under the terms of the contract.) Compensation is quantified as interest at the rate specified in the agreement as the 'contract rate' to the intent that the interest is on the unpaid purchase price. If a **deposit** has been paid and the buyer is in default, interest is calculated on the unpaid balance of the purchase price or the total purchase price if the seller is in default. Interest is payable for each day that there is delay. SC 7.2.4 states that if the subject property is tenanted, then the seller can elect to take the rent rather than interest. Accordingly, if the rent is likely to exceed the value of the interest, notice should be served on the defaulting buyer to confirm that the rent is to be taken by the seller rather than interest. Of course, SC 7.2.4 can be varied in the special conditions to allow the seller to take the interest and the rent should the buyer default and delay completion. SC 7.2 also contemplates the possibility of both parties being in default. In these circumstances, the party at greater fault must pay compensation. There are corresponding provisions in SCPC 10.3.

The interest rate defined by the Standard Conditions as being the 'contract rate' is 'the Law Society's interest rate from time to time in force'. This is declared each week in the *Law Society's Gazette*. There is space on the front of the contract for an alternative rate to be declared and this could be, for example, 'four per cent above the base rate of Lloyds TSB Bank plc or such other lending rate as the bank shall declare in place thereof'.

Where interest is allowed by the contract, it will be payable on completion being delayed even if this is only by a matter of minutes. The Standard Conditions stipulate a time and day for completion: see SC 6.1.1 and 6.1.2 and SCPC 9.1.1 and 9.1.2. If the time limit is breached but completion takes place on the contractual date, completion is deemed to take place the next working day and interest will accrue. The worst time for this to occur is on a Friday, when three days' interest will arise for the period over the weekend to the next working day, being the following Monday. All this will be allowed by the contract, even though completion actually took place late on the previous Friday.

The compensatory provisions in the SCPC are at 10.3, which provides that only the buyer can be required to pay compensation for delayed completion. If the seller is in default, then the buyer must rely upon remedies in common law, such as an action in the courts for damages.

EXAMPLE

Sarah has exchanged contracts to complete a purchase of a house on Monday 5 April, having paid 10 per cent of the purchase price on exchange. The 'contract rate' defined in the contract is 4 per cent above the base rate of Barclays Bank plc. Unfortunately, Sarah's **mortgage** advance was delayed and she was unable to complete until Wednesday 7 April. As she has completed two days late, she will have to pay to the seller interest at the 'contract rate' on the 90 per cent balance of the purchase price that was due on completion.

12.5 Notices to complete

In a conveyancing contract time is not of the essence if regulated by the SC or SCPC unless the Special Conditions provide otherwise. As a result, an innocent party suffering from a delayed completion cannot consider the agreement as repudiated following the defaulting party's delay. This is an unsatisfactory position because the defaulting party may have no intention whatsoever of completing and yet the contract would in theory subsist. To bring the matter to a head and to terminate the agreement, the innocent party must take steps to precipitate a change, and this will be by way of a notice to complete. The notice will in all cases give a final date for completion, failing which there will be no further time for the defaulting party. Time is now of the essence of the contract. The notice can inform the defaulting party that unless completion takes place by the date stated in the notice, the party serving the notice will be entitled to all remedies, including a repudiation of the agreement. Because notices to complete deal with timing, practitioners need to reflect on two elements: first, when can the notice be served; and, secondly, how long must the notice be before it expires?

SC 6.8.1 states that at any time on or after the date fixed for completion, either party who is ready, able and willing to complete may give the other a notice to complete. SC 1.1.3 goes on to define when a party is ready, able and willing; namely, they would have been in a position and ready to complete but for the default of the other party and, in the case of the seller, even though the property remains subject to a mortgage, if the amount to be paid at completion will be enough to pay off the mortgage.

SC 6.8.2 states that the parties are to complete the agreement within ten working days of giving the notice to complete. The ten-day period excludes the day on which the notice is given. The condition goes on to state the essential wording, namely, 'for this purpose, time is of the essence of the contract'.

SC 6.8.3 states that a buyer who delays completion and has paid less than a 10 per cent deposit at exchange must pay the remaining monies required to make up a full 10 per cent deposit, and must pay these monies immediately on receipt of the notice. In practice, this is unlikely to happen if the reason for not completing is a lack of finance. However, the seller can claim the full 10 per cent deposit.

If there is still no completion after the service and expiry of a notice to complete, the Standard Conditions that set out what is to be done are SC 7.4, where the buyer is in default and SC 7.5 where the seller defaults. If SC 7.4 comes into operation, the seller may rescind; and if there is rescission, the seller may forfeit and keep the deposit, resell the property and claim damages. These provisions are not exclusive and the seller therefore retains all other rights and remedies that may also be available. If SC 7.5 is operative, the buyer may rescind; and, if there is rescission, the buyer can demand repayment of the deposit with any interest thereon. Again, these provisions are not exclusive and the buyer therefore retains all other rights and remedies that may otherwise be available (see also s49 Law of Property Act 1925). In both cases, the conveyancing papers must be returned and any protective registrations cancelled. The notice is binding on both parties and not just the party originally in default. Thus time is of the essence for both the seller and the buyer. There are corresponding provisions in the SCPC (see SCPC 9.8, 10.5 and 10.6).

12.5.1 The form of notice to complete

If you need to serve a notice to complete in connection with a contract incorporating the SC, the following is a suitable precedent. It will be addressed to the defaulting party:

> On behalf of [insert your client seller/buyer and address] we hereby give you NOTICE that with reference to the contract dated [insert the date of the agreement] and made between

[insert the seller's full names and the buyer's full names] for the sale and purchase of [insert the property address or description in the contract] we place on record the fact that the sale/purchase of the property has not been completed on the date fixed in the contract for completion. We further give you NOTICE that the seller/buyer [delete the party not ready] is ready able and willing to complete. We therefore give you NOTICE pursuant to condition 6.8 of the ***Standard Conditions of Sale*** (5th edition) and require you to complete the contract in compliance with that condition.

EXAMPLE

William is a first time buyer who has exchanged contracts to complete on the purchase of a house on 7 May. The seller is Abigail. Unfortunately, William's completion monies are not available and he fails to complete on 7 May. Time is not of the essence of the contract. As William has failed to complete on the date specified in the contract, Abigail (if ready, able and willing to complete herself) may serve a notice to complete on William (SC 6.8.1). The notice makes time of the essence and completion must take place within ten working days, not including the date of service. If a reduced deposit was paid on exchange, William must immediately make that up to a full 10 per cent deposit (SC 6.8.3). If William fails to comply with the notice, Abigail may rescind the contract, keep the deposit and claim damages (SC 7.4).

CONDUCT POINT

Failure to draft a notice to complete correctly may amount to a breach of the SRA Code of Conduct. You must act in the best interests of each client and you must provide a proper standard of service to your clients. Use the precedent in **12.5.1**.

12.5.2 **Tactics**

Whether or not to serve a notice to complete depends upon what your client wants to do based upon your advice about what happens when a notice is served. For example, if the likelihood of completing is slim then a notice should be served to bring the contract to an end as soon as possible with a view to selling to someone else at the earliest opportunity. On the other hand, if the delay is not likely to last very long, then there may be no need to serve a notice bearing in mind that interest accrues whether or not a notice has been served; see **12.4.1** regarding this form of compensation. Moreover, if there is a chain of transactions and the delay is not caused by your immediate seller or buyer, then there may be little or no point in serving a notice to complete in these circumstances. Of course, if in the chain notice is served elsewhere it may be necessary to replicate the process to ensure timings remain as coherent as possible. Whatever the situation, you should always keep the client fully informed of developments and give the client the choices when considering a decision about what to do when a party is in breach of the terms of a contract.

In most cases, what needs to be done will be to serve a notice and then put pressure on the defaulting party. Normally, the defaulting party is the buyer who cannot raise their finances. If this occurs, then the best course of action is to bring the contract to an end by serving a notice and then forfeiting the deposit. The seller can then sell elsewhere.

12.6 **Remedies**

There will always be cases where completion does not occur or, though it does occur, a dispute over the subject property arises after completion. The following sections cover, first, what remedies are available if completion has not taken place and, secondly, what remedies are available if a dispute and potential consequential claim arise after completion. In all cases where a claim is necessary, specialist litigation assistance should be suggested to the client as the best way of advancing it.

12.6.1 Where the contract has not been completed

Where a contract has not been completed, and where a cause of action has arisen, an innocent party to that contract can consider four available and different remedies. These remedies are:

1 specific performance;
2 a claim for compensation by way of damages;
3 rescission; and
4 a vendor and purchaser summons.

12.6.2 Specific performance

Specific performance is an equitable remedy in the form of a discretionary order of the court that is intended to compel the defaulting party to perform and complete the contract for the sale and purchase of land. The remedy is available to both buyer and seller where the other party has committed a breach of contract and where an award of damages would be insufficient compensation for the party suffering loss (this would be the case in most conveyancing matters, bearing in mind the unique nature of the subject matter of most conveyancing contracts). If a judgment for that one remedy is granted, it will thereby preclude recourse to the other remedies. SC 7.4 and SC 7.5 make it clear that an innocent party's right to apply for an order for specific performance is not precluded by the fact that a notice to complete has been served and not complied with. There are corresponding provisions in SCPC 10.5.3.

Specific performance is an equitable remedy, and the principles of equity will prohibit an award where it would breach equitable principles. So, for example, where there is an element of fraud or illegality, or the award would cause one party exceptional hardship, the court will refrain from granting an order for specific performance. If damages would properly compensate the innocent party for the loss sustained, then the court will order damages and not specific performance. Even where an order for specific performance is obtained, damages can still subsequently be ordered if the innocent party cannot enforce the order. An award for damages can be made pursuant to s50 of the Senior Courts Act 1981. However, it should be remembered that specific performance can be awarded before the contractual date for completion of the transaction; that is, where a serious breach is likely to occur steps can be taken to seek an order for specific performance even though a breach of contract has yet to arise.

EXAMPLE

Tania is selling her property to Liam but Liam has failed to complete on the contractual completion date. Tania has served notice to complete on Liam making time of the essence but Liam has still failed to complete. As an alternative to rescinding the contract, Tania could seek a decree of specific performance from the court which would compel Liam to complete the purchase. However, Tania should be aware that specific performance is an equitable remedy which is at the discretion of the court and damages may be awarded in lieu.

12.6.3 Damages, including forfeiting or returning the deposit

Where a claim for damages is to be advanced, credit must be given for any deposit forfeited by the seller. (This is also true for any compensation payments made pursuant to SC 7.2.) Section 49(2) of the Law of Property Act 1925 empowers the court, if it thinks it appropriate, to order the repayment of any deposit where it has refused to make an order for specific performance. It has been held that the court has an unfettered discretion to order the return of the deposit if this is the fairest way of dealing with the dispute. The parties cannot agree to exclude s49(2) (see *Aribisala v St James* [2007] EWHC 1694 (Ch)).

12.6.4 Rescission

Rescission has over time gathered two meanings. First, it can mean an order of the court whereby the parties are put back into such a state as would have prevailed had the contract never existed. In effect, the court will order the 'undoing' of the conveyancing contract. This may be ordered where there has been a claim arising out of some vitiating factor such as fraud, mistake or misrepresentation. Secondly, rescission can mean the result of the innocent party accepting the repudiation of the agreement as a consequence of the defaulting party's breach of a major term in the agreement. Rescission can arise by a term in the conveyancing contract, or by agreement, or by an order of the court.

The Special Conditions refer to rescission in two different circumstances:

1 *SC 7.1.* This condition allows rescission for misrepresentation. SC 7 allows rescission where any statement or plan in the contract or the negotiations leading to it is or was misleading or inaccurate as a consequence of an error or omission. However, SC 7.1.1 limits this provision by allowing rescission only where there is an element of fraud or recklessness or where, if the innocent party took the property, it would, prejudicially, be substantially different from that which the innocent party expected as a result of the error or omission. This is the one area of conveyancing contracts where an exclusion clause is subject to the reasonableness test in s11 of the Unfair Contract Terms Act 1977.

2 *SC 8.3.* Where the subject property is leasehold and where the **lease** terms require the landlord's consent or **licence** to a change of tenant, if that **licence to assign** is not forthcoming, either party can seek rescission.

There are corresponding provisions in the SCPC at 10.1 and 10.2.

To summarise, if there is misrepresentation or mistake, rescission can arise on the fundamental basis of the undoing of the contract. If there is a defective **title**, failure to complete or misdescription, rescission can arise for the breach of contract. Finally, rescission can also arise under the terms of the contract. If this is the case, then the contract terms govern when it is exercisable and the ramifications thereof.

12.6.5 Vendor and purchaser summons

Section 49(1) of the Law of Property Act 1925 provides that 'A vendor or purchaser of any interest in land . . . may apply in a summary way to the court, in respect of any requisitions or objections, or any claim for compensation, or any other question arising out of or connected with the contract', and if such an application is made, the court can 'make such order upon the application as to the court may appear just'. This procedure allows either party to a conveyancing contract to apply to court for its deliberation on a point of dispute without having to apply for specific performance. An example of what could give rise to a summons of this kind is a reference to the court to ascertain if the seller has shown good title and thus complied with the terms in the contract to that effect. If the court did decide that good title had not been shown, the court could order the return of the deposit with interest and costs.

12.7 After completion

Completion of a conveyancing contract narrows down the available remedies. In the main, it is the buyer who will commence proceedings, as the seller will have the sale proceeds.

At common law, the contract is considered to be at an end as it is deemed to have merged with the **purchase deed**. The result of this is that the buyer can only sue the seller under **covenants** for title through title guarantee, contained or referred to in the purchase deed; there is no right to sue under the contractual terms. (Merger takes effect only where the contract and purchase deed cover the same subject matter. If the contract contains ancillary matters, then these will not be affected by merger.) However, SC 7.3 (and SCPC 10.4) provide that completion does not cancel liability to perform any outstanding obligation under the contract. This has the effect of negating the doctrine of merger.

If, unusually, the doctrine of merger effectively puts paid to the terms of the contract, the aggrieved buyer can only sue for damages on the covenants for title through title guarantee, implied in the purchase deed.

12.7.1 Covenants for title: title guarantee

You will recall that there is provision in the Law Society's form of contract for the seller to give the buyer a title guarantee (see **4.8**). After completion, the primary remedy is a claim for breach of title guarantee. Title guarantee is governed by the Law of Property (Miscellaneous Provisions) Act 1994. The title guarantee regime contemplates three possibilities: full title guarantee, limited title guarantee or no guarantee at all. In the last situation, the contract will offer no form of guarantee whatsoever, to the extent that there will be no post-completion remedy arising out of the guarantee available to an innocent party in the event of a dispute arising after completion. The other two possibilities are full and limited guarantee and are in effect statutory guarantees that will be implied in a purchase deed by the use of the phrases 'with full guarantee' or 'with limited guarantee'. SC 4.6.2 stipulate that the seller is to **transfer** the property with full title guarantee, but subject to SC 4.6.3 (this refers to SC 3.1.2 and the matters affecting the property, ie **encumbrances**). There are corresponding provisions in the SCPC.

12.7.1.1 Full title guarantee

If the seller sells with full title guarantee, the seller covenants that:

- the seller has the right to sell the property;
- the seller will at the seller's cost do all things that can be reasonably done to give to the buyer the title the seller purports to give;
- if the nature of the title to the subject property is not clear, it is freehold;
- if the property is registered, the buyer will receive at least the class of title that prevailed before the transfer;
- the seller will provide reasonable assistance to enable the recipient to be registered as proprietor of the **registered land**;
- if the interest is registered, the disposition is of the whole interest;
- where the interest passing is leasehold, the disposition is of the whole of the unexpired portion of the term of years created by the lease, the lease still subsists, and there is no subsisting breach that could give rise to **forfeiture**;
- the person making the disposition disposes of it free from all **charges** and encumbrances and from all other rights exercisable by third parties other than those that the person does not and could not reasonably be expected to know about. (Remember that the contract will include specific reference to encumbrances to which the sale is expressly subject.)

12.7.1.2 Limited title guarantee

If the seller sells with limited title guarantee, the seller covenants that all the covenants set out earlier will be complied with save the last covenant, which is replaced by the following:

- the person making the disposition has not since the last disposition for value subjected the property to charges or incumbrances that still exist, or granted third party rights that still exist.

12.7.2 Other post-completion remedies

12.7.2.1 Misrepresentation

A misrepresentation is an untrue factual statement made by one party and relied on by the other, which induces the other party to enter into the contract and, as a consequence, suffer loss. A misrepresentation can be deliberately dishonest and is then termed a fraudulent misrepresentation.

Of a lesser degree, the misrepresentation can be simply careless and is then termed a negligent misrepresentation. Alternatively, and of a lesser degree again, the misrepresentation may be made innocently and be a genuine mistake, whereupon it will be termed an innocent misrepresentation. If there is a suggested fraud, the aggrieved party may sue for damages (by way of the tort of deceit) and rescind the contract. The problem here is that the party alleging fraud must prove it. This is likely to be difficult and costly. Consequently, claims are more usual at the lesser degree of negligent misrepresentation. In this case, the innocent party may take action pursuant to s2 of the Misrepresentation Act 1967 for either damages or rescission of the contract. If the misrepresentation was innocent, the only remedy available is rescission.

EXAMPLE

Dee is selling her flat to Anita. In the Property Information Form which Dee filled in before **exchange of contracts**, Dee failed to disclose a serious neighbour dispute that has been ongoing for many years. If Anita suffers loss as a result of Dee's non-disclosure Anita may sue Dee for damages pursuant to s2 of the Misrepresentation Act 1967.

12.7.2.2 Misdescription

A misdescription is an error in the property particulars of the contract. A patent example would be to state incorrectly the tenure as freehold when it is in fact leasehold, or vice versa. If the misdescription is sufficiently significant it will entitle the innocent party to seek rescission and damages. A significant misdescription is one that would lead to the innocent party being deprived of what they thought they were going to receive under the terms of the contract. Most such cases give rise to a claim under the Misrepresentation Act 1967.

12.7.2.3 Non-disclosure

This can arise where the seller has not complied with an obligation to disclose matters in the contract or in documents referred to in the contract. Again, if the non-disclosure is sufficiently significant to lead to the innocent party being deprived of what they thought they were going to receive under the terms of the contract, then that party may seek to rescind the contract.

12.7.2.4 Rectification

This can arise in different ways. Both the contract and purchase deed can be the subject of rectification. If the contract is involved, then an application to the court can be made. If rectification is ordered to correct either an omission or an incorrectly recorded contract term, then the court has the discretion to set the date on which the contract is effective. If the purchase deed is involved, again an application to the court can be made to ensure that all the terms in the contract, and that should be in the purchase deed, are incorporated in it. Section 65 of and Sch 4 to the Land Registration Act 2002 set out the grounds on which an application to correct an entry within a registered title can be made. Rather than rectification, the 2002 Act refers to 'alteration' of the registers. Under the Act, rectification is just one kind of alteration (it is an alteration involving the correction of a mistake that prejudicially affects the title of a registered owner (Sch 4, para 1)). A right of indemnity will flow from rectification. The order for rectification is discretionary and the court will not make an order if it would be unjust to the **registered proprietor** to do so. Section 103 and Sch 8 permit an indemnity to be claimed from the Chief Land Registrar, inter alia, by a person who has suffered loss as a result of any rectification of the register. This indemnity is not available to a claimant who is deemed to have caused or contributed to the loss by fraud or a lack of proper care. Since changes to the **Land Registry** indemnity rules made with effect from 27 April 1997, indemnity payments will be made whether or not there has been actual rectification. The First-tier Tribunal (Property Chamber; Land Registration Division) (formerly the Adjudicator to HM Land Registry) has power (on direct application to the tribunal) to rectify or set aside a conveyancing document (s108(2) Land Registration Act 2002). This is an important function as previously the Land Registrar could only refer such matters to the High Court, which inevitably resulted in delay and further costs. This power applies only in relation to a document that does any one of the following:

- effects a qualifying disposition of a registered estate or charge where that disposition is either a registrable disposition or one that creates an interest that may be protected by a notice, such as a transfer, grant of a lease or a deed creating a restrictive covenant; or
- is a contract to do so; or
- effects a transfer of an interest that is the subject of a notice in the register, for example a **conveyance** of a **profit à prendre** that was noted on the register but not registered with its own title, and there was an error in that conveyance.

The general law about the effect of a High Court order for rectification or setting aside a document applies to an order made under this power (s108(4)). See the link in **Appendix 1** for further information.

12.7.3 **Liens**

A seller will be entitled to claim a lien (ie a right to retain possession of another's property pending discharge of a debt) over the subject property in relation to any unpaid element of the purchase price. The lien is in effect an equitable charge enforceable by the court by way of an order for the sale of the property or for the setting aside of the contract. The lien should always be protected by a notice on the title in registered land and as a C(iii) land charge registration for **unregistered land**.

A buyer is entitled to claim a lien if the deposit is returnable and was paid over originally to the seller's practitioner as agent for the seller. The lien claimed will be in respect of the deposit monies. The lien should be protected by registration.

KEY POINT SUMMARY

- Has the time for completion set out in the contract elapsed?
- If it has, does the client want you to serve a notice to complete, namely have you taken instructions approving this step?
- If you have instructions, have you served a notice using the appropriate wording and in such a way as to enable you to prove service of the notice?
- Has the period set out in the notice expired and, if so, does the client want to rescind the agreement, sell the property elsewhere and sue for damages?
- Is there some other form of breach of contract? If so, have you obtained a full history of the conveyancing transaction with all supporting papers; and what remedy does the innocent party want?
- Are you able to quantify the client's loss arising from the breach? If so, how much is that loss?
- Is it economic sense to commence proceedings bearing in mind the costs that will be incurred?
- Apart from the other party to the contract, might there be a claim elsewhere, for example against a conveyancing practitioner or surveyor in negligence?
- If the other party is late for completion, remember that under the SCs either party is entitled to claim compensation for delay at the contract rate of interest on a daily basis, until completion takes place.
- Specific performance can be claimed along with damages and rescission, but the claimant must at the eventual hearing select one remedy in respect of which judgment is to be sought.

CHAPTER 13
New Properties

FUNCTIONING LEGAL KNOWLEDGE

This chapter covers the following functioning legal knowledge required to pass the SQE 1 assessments:

New properties:

- how to acquire and dispose of legal and equitable interests in land
- legal formalities required to create and transfer interests and **estates** in land
- the core knowledge areas of real estate law and practice as they relate to the conveyancing of new properties

AUTHORITIES UNDERPINNING PRACTICE

The key authorities that underpin this area of practice are listed below. Note that for legislation you are linked to legislation.gov.uk.

Although much of the legislation on this government website is available in its amended form, the incorporation of new amendments into the text of legislation can be delayed. You should refer to legal databases to ensure you are referencing the most up-to-date legislation.

- Section 2 of the Law of Property (Miscellaneous Provisions) Act 1989
  https://www.legislation.gov.uk/ukpga/1989/34/contents
- Section 62 of the Law of Property Act 1925
  https://www.legislation.gov.uk/ukpga/Geo5/15-16/20/contents
- Section 38 of the Highways Act 1980
  https://www.legislation.gov.uk/ukpga/1980/66/contents
- Section 104 of the Water Industry Act 1991
  https://www.legislation.gov.uk/ukpga/1991/56/contents
- The Consumer Code for Home Builders 2024
  https://consumercode.co.uk/downloads/second-edition-2010/
- NHBC Buildmark Scheme
  https://www.nhbc.co.uk/

13.1 Introduction

The sale of a new property is a more complicated transaction than the sale of an existing one for several reasons. First, a new property on an estate will comprise part of the developer's **title** to the whole estate, and a property lawyer must therefore think about 'sale of part' considerations, such as the grant and **reservation** of new **easements** and the imposition of new **covenants**. There is a clear overlap here with the general topic of the draft contract, which we considered in **Chapter 4**. There is also some overlap with the topics of leasehold and commonhold, as the new property could, of course, be the grant of a **lease** or a new commonhold unit. You are therefore referred to **Chapter 14** on leasehold.

A developer's solicitor does not normally use the Law Society's Conveyancing Protocol, but the spirit of it is usually invoked as the solicitor will invariably be required to send out a comprehensive package of documents at the beginning of the transaction to assist the buyer's solicitor. You will need to appreciate the items that are relevant for the pre-contract package. For properties being sold 'off plan', namely before being built, the buyer must be supplied with a Predicted Energy Assessment and then a full Energy Performance Certificate once the property has been completed.

Where the property is in the course of construction, there will be a complication over the timing of completion because the builder/developer will not know precisely the date when the building will be physically completed. Accordingly, the builder cannot agree a fixed **completion date** and this can have a knock-on effect where the buyer of the new property has a related sale.

There are obvious planning considerations where a property is newly constructed and it must be remembered that as well as the dwelling itself, you must consider estate roads, drains and sewers, and their future maintenance and adoption by the local authorities. In this respect, you will appreciate the overlap with the material you covered earlier in the course when you considered town and country planning, searches and enquiries. Remember that enquiries over and above the standard pre-contract enquiries will be appropriate where your client is buying a new property.

Some important aspects relating to new properties are now examined, including acting for a developer or buyer, road and sewer agreements, structural defects insurance and synchronising completion of a related sale when acting for the buyer of new property.

13.2 Acting for the developer

Acting for the developer, the trainee solicitor is likely to become involved in the day-to-day running of the conveyancing files for the individual plots. Typically, a partner or senior assistant will first prepare the initial documentation, for example a standard form contract, replies to standard enquiries, relevant search results, copies of the relevant planning consents and evidence of title. Once the legal paperwork has been set up, the trainee solicitor may handle the plot sale files. This will involve sending out to the individual buyers' solicitors the standard documentation with a covering letter or information pack, responding to any additional enquires and dealing with any suggested amendments to the contract and **purchase deed**. This will, of course, be followed by exchange and completion.

Assuming title is registered, **deduction of title** on the plot sales is achieved by supplying **official copies** and a title plan. However, very often the title plan of an estate is large and unwieldy, and in this case the seller's practitioner may apply to the **Land Registry** on Form OC1 for a certificate of official inspection of the title plan. This certificate on Form CI will certify that the subject property (ie the individual plot) to which it relates is within the seller's title. It will also indicate the entries on the title that affect the plot in question. Form CI will also assist the buyer's practitioner when carrying out the pre-completion **official search**; instead of having to attach a plan to Form OS2, the practitioner will simply quote the plot number specified on the Form CI.

Since 1 September 2008, the *UK Finance Mortgage Lenders' Handbook* (formerly the *CML Lenders' Handbook*) has required builders and developers of newly built, converted or renovated properties to complete a 'disclosure of incentives' form. This informs the lender what discounts and other incentives have been offered to the borrower/purchaser, thereby helping the lender to see the true value of the new property. The disclosure of incentives form was replaced in February 2018 by a more general disclosure form which includes information on tenure type, method of construction and information on ground rents. The completed form must be supplied to the conveyancer acting on behalf of the lender providing the mortgage finance for the property. The form must be supplied to the valuer acting on behalf of the lender upon request. The form is designed to ensure full disclosure of the financial aspects of the transaction and key information about the property. It is not meant to be used to provide a valuation. It should be completed by reference to the UK Finance frequently asked questions (FAQ).

Acting for the developer, the sale of a plot in a new development of properties will constitute a sale of part of the developer's title. It is important therefore to bear in mind the key issues relating to sale of part contracts which were considered in **Chapter 4** (see **4.10**). Some of the essential components of the draft contract are as follows:

- Include a full and accurate description of the property being sold by reference to a scaled plan.
- Negate any implied grant of easements in favour of the buyer under s62 of the Law of Property Act 1925 and the rule in *Wheeldon v Burrows* (1879) 12 Ch D 31, whilst making provision for the grant and reservation of new easements and the imposition of new covenants.
- Annex to the contract the standard form of purchase deed for the plots. The purchase deed will include all relevant terms such as new restrictive covenants and easements.
- Provide for legal completion to take place within a certain specified period after the seller's practitioner has notified the buyer's practitioner that the property has been completed and is fit for occupation.
- Specify that the builder will provide NHBC (or similar) protection and that the NHBC documentation will be supplied to the buyer before completion.
- If the buyer is paying an additional price for 'extras' (eg specially designed kitchen or bathroom fittings), the contract should itemise the extras and state the additional sums being paid.
- A full 10 per cent deposit paid on exchange to be held as agent (so that it can be released to the developer client).
- The developer may wish to reserve the right to vary the method of construction or the materials used in the construction of the new properties.

In addition, do not forget other important issues of a more general nature, such as the following:

- If, unusually, the developer's title is unregistered, consider applying for voluntary first registration. It is easier to dispose of registered plots.
- Contact the developer's lender, if any, to make arrangements for the release of the individual plots from the lender's **charge** as and when they are sold.
- In conjunction with the developer client, arrange for a site inspection by a qualified surveyor and preparation of an estate layout plan for approval by the Land Registry.
- Draft the standard form of purchase deed and arrange for it to be approved by the Land Registry at the same time as the estate layout plan.
- Ensure that road and sewer agreements with supporting bonds are, or will be, in place (see later for further commentary on this).
- Check that the developer is registered with NHBC, or an alternative provider, and that all appropriate documentation is available.
- Carry out all necessary searches, copies of which are to be made available to the buyer's practitioner.
- Prepare information pack and/or covering letter.

13.3 Acting for the buyer

It is common for the seller to refuse to negotiate any amendments on the standardised documentation. However, the buyer's practitioner should as a matter of course always consider the draft documentation carefully and seek to make amendments that properly protect the buyer's (and any lender client's) interests. Here is a reminder of the principal concerns for the buyer when approving the draft contract for the sale of a new property:

- Ensure that the buyer has all necessary easements, such as for access, services and rights of entry onto adjoining plots.
- Ensure that the proposed covenants will not adversely affect the buyer's use and enjoyment of the property or the future sale or marketability of it; consider your **mortgagee**'s instructions.
- Allow for the buyer/mortgagee's surveyor to inspect the property both before and after physical completion.
- Insist on a long-stop date for completion, after which your client can rescind the contract.

- The seller should be obliged to build in a good and workmanlike manner with good and substantial materials.
- Provide for the seller to rectify any snagging items, to remove all builder's rubbish before completion, to erect boundary fences and to landscape the garden and adjoining areas.
- If the seller reserves the right to vary the methods of construction or building materials, this should be qualified by a proviso that neither the value of the property nor the accommodation shall be materially diminished.
- If the property is still in the course of construction on **exchange of contracts**, the risk of insurance should remain with the seller until physical and legal completion has occurred (so SC 5.1.1 is not appropriate).
- Deposit to be held as stakeholder.
- Provide for NHBC protection; all relevant documentation to be supplied to the buyer on or before completion.

13.4 Road and sewer agreements

One problem area for students is the requirement for road and sewer agreements. As for estate roads, remember that the roads and street lighting on a new estate will only become adopted by the local authority (and thus maintainable at the public expense) after the estate has been physically completed. The local authority is empowered to make up the roads and charge the house buyers for the cost of doing so, and it is for this reason that buyers require the developer to enter into an agreement with the local authority under s38 of the Highways Act 1980. In this agreement, the developer agrees to make up the roads and street lighting to an adoptable standard (ie to a standard acceptable to the authority) and the authority agrees to adopt them subsequently. As additional protection for the buyers in the case of the developer's insolvency, the s38 agreement should be supported by a bond or guarantee from the developer's bank or insurer, which provides for the buyers to be indemnified for any costs paid to the local authority should the developer default. The developer should complete a similar agreement and supporting bond in respect of the making-up and adoption of the drains and sewers on the estate. This agreement is made with the local water authority under s104 of the Water Industry Act 1991.

Importantly, it is a standard requirement of mortgagees of properties on new, large estates that s38 and s104 agreements with supporting bonds are in place before completion of the mortgage. This is confirmed in the *UK Finance Mortgage Lenders' Handbook*. If they are not in place, the lender will usually wish to make a retention from the advance which will be released to the borrower only as and when the agreements come into force.

EXAMPLE

Damian acts for first time buyer Wanda who is buying a house in the course of construction with the aid of a mortgage. Damian's local search reveals that no road or sewer agreements are yet in place in relation to the new development. He will follow this up with the developer's solicitor urgently, as without these agreements Wanda's lender is likely to make a retention from the mortgage advance.

13.5 Structural defects insurance

All new dwellings and conversions should be insured against structural defects, and it is a standard requirement of lending institutions that new residential properties are protected in this way. Without such insurance, the property will become unmortgageable and its future marketability will be adversely affected. The most popular current scheme, which is now in use almost universally, is the NHBC Buildmark scheme. In some cases, a lender may be willing to accept an architect's certificate of completion of the building instead of an NHBC scheme. This may apply, for instance, where the architect has supervised the construction of the building under a JCT contract (ie an agreement incorporating a standard set of conditions for a building contract). The insurance cover is effectively provided by the architect's professional indemnity insurers in the event of professional negligence on the part of the architect. There are, however, potential dangers in accepting an architect's certificate. In *Hunt v Optima* [2014] EWCA Civ 714, original buyers (and subsequent buyers) who received and relied upon an architect's certificate after exchange of contracts or completion were unsuccessful in a negligence action against the architect. The Court of Appeal ruled that the architect owed a duty of care only to those buyers who received the certificate before exchange of contracts. So if you are acting for a buyer (or subsequent buyer) or lender who is relying on an architect's certificate, you should heed the warnings of this case and ensure that the client is properly advised of the potential risks. The lender may be willing to accept the monitoring of the development by a professional consultant employed by the borrower alone or by the borrower and the builder jointly. If so, and the *Lenders' Handbook* is being used, the professional consultant must complete a Professional Consultant's Certificate in the required form set out in the *Lenders' Handbook*.

The NHBC Buildmark scheme is in two parts, comprising separate agreements in the form of warranties given by the builder and the NHBC, respectively. In the first part, the builder agrees that the new dwelling will be constructed in a good and workmanlike manner and in line with the requirements of the NHBC. The builder also agrees to put right any defects in the property, notified to the builder in writing, that occur during the first two years (known as the initial guarantee period) and that occur as a result of the builder's failure to comply with the NHBC requirements. In the second part, the NHBC gives separate warranties (ie the insurance) that will compensate the buyer against loss suffered as a result of:

- the builder becoming insolvent before the dwelling is finished (limited to 10 per cent of the contract sum or £10,000, whichever is the greater);
- the builder failing to fulfil its own warranty to correct defects arising in the initial guarantee period; and
- any repair works to the property the cost of which exceeds £500 that occur during the eight years following the initial guarantee period. This eight-year period is known as the structural guarantee period. Cover includes double or multiple glazing and the costs of clearing up contamination as a result of action taken by a local authority or the Environment Agency.

NHBC has an online system for the acceptance of Buildmark cover. Conveyancers can access a secure online account to obtain all relevant documentation and utilise the system to notify NHBC when exchange of contracts and completion have taken place. NHBC validates the completion information and makes the insurance certificate available to download. For further information, visit the NHBC website.

The Consumer Code for Home Builders came into force on 1 April 2010. The Consumer Code was formed by agreement between NHBC and MD Insurance Services Ltd (trading as Premier Guarantee and LABC New Home Warranty). These organisations have agreed that builders and developers registered with them will adopt the Consumer Code. The Consumer Code applies to home buyers who, on or after 1 April 2010, reserve to buy a new or newly converted home built by a home builder under the insurance protection of one of the supporting home warranty bodies. The purpose of the Code is to ensure that home buyers are treated fairly, know what service levels to expect, are given reliable information upon which to make their decisions and know how to access speedy, low-cost dispute-resolution arrangements if they are dissatisfied.

The New Homes Ombudsman Service (NHOS) was introduced in 2022 as part of changes brought in by the Building Safety Act 2022. Under this Act, there is a requirement for an independent scheme to resolve complaints made by buyers of new-build homes against developers where the developer has failed to resolve the complaint. Under the new system, if new-build home owners are not happy with the quality of their homes or the service provided, they will be able to approach the Ombudsman for all complaints. This will be available for two years after the completion of the purchase of a new home. The intention is to implement a single agreed code of practice for all developers and build on current protections as well as placing more stringent requirements on developers.

EXAMPLE

Alex acts for first time buyer Nasreen who is buying a flat in the course of construction from Taylor Wimpey. As part of his conveyancing duties, Alex will ensure that NHBC cover is provided in relation to the new flat and that all relevant documentation is provided to Nasreen on completion.

CONDUCT POINT

Failure to ensure that your client has NHBC protection when purchasing a new property may amount to a breach of the SRA Code of Conduct. You must act in the best interests of each client and you must provide a proper standard of service to your clients.

13.6 Synchronising completion of a related sale

Another problem area is the situation where a client is buying a new property and also selling an existing property at the same time. How do you synchronise completion dates when the developer/seller will not agree a fixed completion date on the new property? One way round this is to seek a condition in the sale contract regarding completion similar to that in the purchase contract, namely that completion shall occur a specified number of days after the seller's practitioner notifies the buyer's practitioner that the client is ready to complete. However, if your client's buyer insists on a fixed completion date (eg because there is a chain behind), you would have to advise the client that it will not be possible to synchronise the two completions. If the client still wished to proceed, you would canvass two options. The client could either seek bridging finance to complete the purchase first (the consent of the existing lender may be required) or, more usually, complete the sale first and move into temporary accommodation until completion of the new property occurs. Whichever option the client decides upon, you must as a matter of great importance still ensure that the *act of exchange of contracts* is synchronised, so as to prevent the client ending up with two properties or none at all (see **Chapter 9** generally regarding synchronisation of exchange on related sale and purchase transactions).

EXAMPLE

Harry's clients Jasmin and Ella are buying a new house and have a related sale. They want him to ensure that their sale and purchase are completed on the same day. The developer does not know precisely when the new house will be finished and so cannot agree a fixed completion date. Ideally, a fixed completion date should not be agreed in the sale contract. A condition regarding completion similar to the one in the purchase contract should be agreed in the sale contract, namely completion shall occur a specified number of days after notification in writing by the sellers' solicitor to the purchaser's solicitor that the sellers are ready to complete. If, for example, the purchase contract provides for 14 days' notice suggest not less than 13 days' notice in the sale contract to give one day's leeway. Both contracts should also provide for the same 'long-stop' date after which either party may rescind.

KEY POINT SUMMARY

- The developer's solicitor should supply a full package of pre-contract documentation including replies to enquiries, standard form contract and **transfer** deed.
- Check the documentation for sale of part considerations, such as an adequate description with scaled plan and grant of easements.
- Check that planning consent for the development has been obtained and that there are no outstanding planning issues.
- Ensure that road and sewer agreements are in place with supporting bonds.
- If the property is in the course of construction, a fixed completion date cannot normally be agreed on exchange of contracts.
- The developer will instead serve notice to complete following physical completion. Advise the client of the implications of not synchronising completion on any related sale.
- Carry out your pre-completion Land Registry search on Form OS2, quoting the plot number on Form OC1.
- Ensure that NHBC protection for structural defects insurance is in place.

PART F
Leaseholds and Commercial Property

CHAPTER 14
Leaseholds

FUNCTIONING LEGAL KNOWLEDGE

This chapter covers the following functioning legal knowledge required to pass the SQE 1 assessments:

Structure and content of a lease
Procedural steps for the grant of a lease or underlease
Procedural steps for the assignment of a lease
Licence to assign and licence to underlet
Leasehold covenants—liability on covenants in leases:

- Leases granted before 1 January 1996
- Leases granted on or after 1 January 1996

Remedies for breach of a leasehold covenant
Termination of a lease

AUTHORITIES UNDERPINNING PRACTICE

The key authorities that underpin this area of practice are listed below. Note that for legislation you are linked to legislation.gov.uk.

Although much of the legislation on this government website is available in its amended form, the incorporation of new amendments into the text of legislation can be delayed. You should refer to legal databases to ensure you are referencing the most up-to-date legislation.

- The Fire Safety (England) Regulations 2022
https://www.legislation.gov.uk/uksi/2022/547/contents
- Section 6 of the Land Registration Act 2002
https://www.legislation.gov.uk/ukpga/2002/9/contents
- Land Registration (Amendment) (No 2) Rules 2005
https://www.legislation.gov.uk/uksi/2005/1982/contents/made
- Section 146 of the Law of Property Act 1925
https://www.legislation.gov.uk/ukpga/Geo5/15-16/20/contents
- Section 19 of the Landlord and Tenant Act 1927
https://www.legislation.gov.uk/ukpga/Geo5/17-18/36/contents
- Leasehold Reform Act 1967
https://www.legislation.gov.uk/ukpga/1967/88/contents
- Leasehold Reform (Ground Rent) Act 2022
https://www.legislation.gov.uk/ukpga/2022/1/contents
- Landlord and Tenant Act 1985
https://www.legislation.gov.uk/ukpga/1985/70/contents
- Landlord and Tenant Act 1988
https://www.legislation.gov.uk/ukpga/1988/26/contents
- Landlord and Tenant (Covenants) Act 1995
https://www.legislation.gov.uk/ukpga/1995/30/contents

- Commonhold and Leasehold Reform Act 2002
  https://www.legislation.gov.uk/ukpga/2002/15/contents
- Fire Safety (England) Regulations 2022
  https://www.legislation.gov.uk/uksi/2022/547/contents
- Building Safety Act 2022
  https://www.legislation.gov.uk/ukpga/2022/30/contents/enacted
- UK Finance Mortgage Lenders' Handbook
  https://lendershandbook.ukfinance.org.uk/lenders-handbook/

14.1 Introduction

A lease is a contractual relationship that offers a party, called a tenant (or **lessee**), a legal **estate** in land that is granted by a superior **title** holder, commonly called the landlord (or **lessor**). They have been used in land law for many years, but the use of leaseholds has really taken off in urban environments with the conversion of large houses into several flats and the development of **business leases** for commercial properties. However, the relationship between the lessor and lessee (otherwise landlord and tenant) can be a troublesome one and the interface between the parties can be riddled with litigation. In recent years, there has been an increase in demand for the reform of this relationship. This has recently given rise to several statutory attempts at reform.

Substantial changes have been made to leasehold property law and conveyancing by the Commonhold and Leasehold Reform Act 2002. There is now an alternative new form of holding a **freehold estate**. It is called commonhold land. It is actually a freehold but held by commonhold across several estate owners in combination. The purpose of the alternative form of holding is to address the current deficiencies in relation to the enforceability between lessees of covenants and other lease provisions (for the same reason, it also addresses the related problems with freehold flats, ie **flying freeholds**). Commonhold has not proved popular with developers and the number granted across the country could be less than a hundred. This chapter will focus upon purely leasehold considerations.

A lease is an agreement whereby an estate in land or property is created but only for a finite term. So a lease term can be for 99 years or six months or whatever length of time is agreed between the parties to the lease agreement. The term needs to be clear and definite and with an agreed start date. Different types of leases with differing contents are required to deal with different types of property. No one lease is exactly the same as another. A lessor will require the lease to include clauses and/or covenants (obligations) that adequately protect the reversionary interest (the interest of the superior title holder). To that end, the lessor will include a long list of obligations, of covenants requiring the lessee to do and not to do various things. However, above all else the lease must contain the most important protection for the lessor, which is an express right of re-entry or **forfeiture** for a tenant's breach of covenant as the law does not imply this. A lessee will also require essential clauses or covenants but these are in many cases entirely opposite to those favoured by the lessor. A lessee will seek to limit the number and extent of the lease covenants. Moreover, a prudent lessee will also seek covenants from the lessor to perform the obligations resting with the lessor, for example to keep the main structure of the property, of which the subject property forms part, insured and in good repair.

Leases form an important part of a conveyancer's workload. Flats now make up a quarter of all housing in the UK. Research by the Royal Mail has shown that London alone has 1.9 million flats.

One contemporary problem relates to the normally small ground rent paid on long residential leases. Some recently granted leases have included rent increase provisions that meant in some cases rents doubled every ten years. (So, for example, a commencing rent would be at £250 per annum but after just 50 years could be £4,000.) This kind of high rent and the resultant high cost of buying in the freehold (**enfranchisement**: see later in this chapter) led the government to announce in December 2017 its intention to stop houses being newly sold on long leases. The Law Commission was asked to propose reforms that would promote transparency and fairness in the residential leasehold sector and provide a better deal for leaseholders as consumers. It published its detailed report and recommendations on leasehold houses and flats in 2019.

The Leasehold Reform (Ground Rent) Act 2022 restricts ground rents on newly created, long residential leases (with some exceptions) to a token one peppercorn per year. This effectively restricts ground rents to zero financial value, making leasehold ownership fairer and more affordable for leaseholders. The Act gives power to local authorities to impose fines of up to £30,000 if a landlord demands ground rent. However, the Act only applies to *new* leases so does not assist existing leaseholders faced with high and escalating ground rents.

14.2 Lease contents

This section contains an examination of some of the more commonly encountered elements or clauses in most leases. Essentially, it sets out what you might expect to see in a lease of either residential or commercial property.

14.2.1 Land Registry prescribed clauses in leases

The **Land Registry** has issued rules requiring certain lease contents to be in a particular position in registrable leases (new leases with a term of more than seven years). As a result, they are called prescribed clauses leases. These provisions were contained in the Land Registration (Amendment) (No 2) Rules 2005 (SI 2005/1982). The compulsory requirements have been limited to a set number of 'prescribed clauses' with a requirement that these particular clauses must appear at the start of the lease. New r58A states that 'a prescribed clauses lease must begin with the required wording or that wording must appear immediately after any front sheet'. A prescribed clauses lease will cover any lease the term of which triggers compulsory registration and which is granted on or after 19 June 2006. The information that must appear at the lease commencement includes:

- lessor's title number;
- the parties to the lease;
- a full description of the property being leased;
- prescribed statements (those required by statute, eg involving a charity or pursuant to the Leasehold Reform, Housing and Urban Development Act 1993);
- the term for which the property is leased;
- any premium;
- prohibitions or restrictions on disposing of the lease;
- rights of acquisition such as a contractual right for the tenant to renew the lease (an option to renew); and
- **easements.**

There is a helpful Land Registry Practice Guide (No 64) that offers guidance on the requirements for prescribed clauses leases and this is available on the Land Registry website.

EXAMPLE

Daniel is buying a registered lease of a flat in Manchester. The lease was granted in 2004. As the lease predates 19 June 2006, the lease is not required to contain the prescribed clauses required under the Land Registration (Amendment) (No 2) Rules 2005.

14.2.2 Typical lease covenants and other provisions

The following are typical covenants found in most residential leases and that will form the subject of negotiations between both parties to the intended lease.

14.2.2.1 To pay rent and other outgoings, including service charges

A covenant to pay rent is fundamental and should appear in all leases that include a rental obligation. The lessee will want to introduce another clause that suspends the payment of rent if the property is destroyed or damaged by an insured risk. The lessor should agree this, provided the lessor can control the insurance of the whole property and thus include loss of rent as an insurable risk. This leads on to consideration of the payment of other outgoings such as insurance. This can be by way of an additional rent and the lease can be drafted to give effect to this. Similarly, any **service charge** payable can be made a rent in the same way. (This benefits the lessor because if there are arrears, these can be recovered as a rent rather than as a result of a breach of covenant. As a consequence, a notice pursuant to s146 of the Law of Property Act 1925 can be avoided. However, statute may limit this power, depending on the nature of the property.) The lease should stipulate that the rents are payable in advance, failing which they will be payable in arrears. If the lease includes a rent review provision allowing the rent to be increased (and/or decreased) at regular intervals, there should also be a specific covenant requiring the lessee to enter into review procedures and to pay the rent at the reviewed level. Rent reviews are rare in residential leases which tend to include fixed increases at regular intervals. The lease will also require the lessee to pay all outgoings applicable to the subject property, such as council tax and water rates.

14.2.2.2 Insurance covenants

Insurance can be dealt with in one of two ways. First, the lessee can be made to covenant to insure or, secondly, the lessor can agree to insure. Where the lease is of a whole house or of one of two maisonettes, then it would be sensible to expect the lessee to insure. However, where there is a building in multiple occupation, the converse should apply so as to ensure that there is an appropriate level of cover rather than the patchwork of different policies that would occur if all the lessees insured separately. In this situation, the lessor should arrange insurance so that the whole of the building can be covered by one policy, with all the lessees obliged by way of a lease covenant to pay, perhaps as a rent, a proportion of the annual premium. Where the lessor insures, a prudent lessee will want to see the lease include a covenant requiring the lessor to expend any monies claimed and received from the insurance company on reinstating the damaged or destroyed property. This is particularly so where reinstatement will be necessary to all parts of the building to give support to the subject property itself. Some lessees might at this point require the lessor to make up any deficiency in the insurance proceeds from the lessor's own resources. Clearly, the lessor will resist such an onerous obligation. The point will have to be negotiated. If the lessor does accept the point, it is an incentive to over-insure the premises rather than under-insure.

EXAMPLE

A typical lease insurance provision might read:

> *to insure and keep insured the building of which the demised premises forms part against loss or damage by the Insured Risks [with the Insured Risks defined elsewhere in the lease, i.e. fire, storm, tempest, flood, etc.] and such other risks as the lessor's surveyor for the time being considers necessary in the full cost of reinstatement, together with architects' surveyors' and other fees payable, together with the costs of site clearance and the securing of the damaged property and making good any shortfall out of the lessor's own monies.*

The lessee will also want a covenant requiring the lessor to supply a copy of the policy on request, as well as details of the existing cover by way of a copy of the current policy cover schedule and the current premium receipt.

An insurance provision should require either the lessor or the lessee, depending on who is covenanting to insure, to arrange insurance cover in the full reinstatement value. The cover should also include all architects' and surveyors' fees incurred in connection with the rebuilding or reinstatement of the property. This will ensure that the property is not under-insured. Damage caused by the action of terrorists is no longer covered in normal buildings policies and separate cover for damage occasioned in this way must be arranged, in particular for property located near potential targets, such as in the main cities or near major stations. This needs to be covered in the insurance covenant.

14.2.2.3 To keep the property in good repair

Where there is a property in multiple occupation, the usual repairing arrangement is for the lessee to be required to keep in good repair the inner skin of the demised property. This would require the lessee to keep properly maintained the plaster, the ceiling and flooring materials, but not much else. All structural elements of the property, including the floor and ceiling joists, the load-bearing walls, the roof and foundations should be repairable by the lessor, with all the lessees paying a service charge to reimburse the lessor for this expense. The rationale for this arrangement is that there is a need for a single consistent approach to the whole question of structural repairs and maintenance.

A defined standard of repair required for leases was set out in *Proudfoot v Hart* (1890) 25 QBD 42. In that case, it was held that the standard of repair was to be determined according to several factors, including the subject property's age and character and the environment in which the property was located. In effect, this has meant that there is a clear difference in the expected standard of repair between a Victorian property and one that was built in the 1990s. As to the meaning of 'repair', the courts have made it clear this includes renewal (see *Lurcott v Wakeley and Wheeler* [1911] 1 KB 905). A covenant requiring the lessee 'to put and keep the property in good and substantial repair' is particularly onerous. This is way above mere repair and will be interpreted as requiring the lessee to carry out all repairs and renewals, substantial or not, from the start of the lease (see *Elite Investments Ltd v TI Bainbridge Silencers Ltd* [1986] 2 EGLR 43). This kind of covenant is, however, encountered frequently in practice. In addition, a covenant to keep in repair implies a covenant to put and keep in repair.

To ensure compliance with repairing obligations, modern leases will always include a covenant allowing the lessor to enter the demised premises, on prior written notice, to view the state of repair. If the repairing covenant is in breach, the lessor will then be able to serve a notice on the lessee calling for work to be carried out to ensure the proper repair of the subject property. Moreover, the lessor, in the case of default by the lessee, will have the benefit of a further covenant enabling the lessor to enter the subject property to carry out the necessary repairs and to charge the lessee for the cost of the work required (*Jervis v Harris* [1996] 1 All ER 303, CA).

14.2.2.4 User

It is possible for the lease to include a covenant imposing an absolute restriction on the lessee against changing the use from any user precisely stated in the lease. In the case of a residential lease, it is desirable that the user clause be such that there can be only one permitted use that cannot be changed. The reason for this is that this form of extremely restrictive covenant will guarantee conformity of use amongst all the lessees and ensure that there is no breach of planning law.

EXAMPLE

A typical user clause might read:

> *not to use the demised property other than a residential house/flat/maisonette and for no other purpose whatsoever.*

Because the covenant is absolute, the lessor cannot be compelled to allow a change of use.

The covenant can be qualified, requiring the lessor's consent before the use can be changed, and this is more commonly seen in **commercial leases**. (In such commercial leases, an absolute user covenant will mean that the rental on review could be subject to a reduction in valuation. This is because a restriction on user makes the lease less attractive to lessees and will therefore command less as a rental. However, a qualified covenant may avoid this limitation on the rent review.) There is no statutory provision that implies that the lessor's consent cannot be unreasonably withheld, as is the case with **alienation** covenants. Section 19(3) of the Landlord and Tenant Act 1927 provides that if a consent for a change of use is required, then the lessor is not allowed to demand a premium or extra rent for giving that consent. The lessor can require costs to be paid by the applicant, including all legal fees. A premium or extra rent can be demanded if alterations to the structure of the property are also proposed.

14.2.2.5 Alienation

In this context, the term 'alienation' covers covenants against assignments, underlettings, **mortgages** and other material dealings with the legal estate. There is no such restriction against alienation unless there is express provision to that effect in the lease. Many leases include a covenant whereby the lessee cannot assign the lease without the prior written consent of the lessor, such consent not to be unreasonably withheld. Some leases extend this provision to include sub-lettings as well as assignments. If the lease states that the lessor's consent is required but does not refer to reasonableness, then statute adds this qualification (s19(1)(a) Landlord and Tenant Act 1927). The Landlord and Tenant Act 1988 requires the lessor to deal with applications for consent to an assignment within a reasonable time of the making of the application. Should the lessor fail to do so, the lessee can, if the lessee has suffered loss as a consequence of the lessor's delay, sue the lessor for damages for breach of statutory duty.

In modern conveyancing, it is now considered inappropriate to fetter a lessee's right to deal freely with a long leasehold legal estate. The lessee of such an estate should be able to deal with it unchecked, just as any absolute owner would in relation to a fee simple. Therefore, the question for a practitioner should be: is there any restriction against alienation; and, if so, should there be such a provision in the lease of the subject property? Frankly, the answer is in the negative where the lease is a long lease of residential property. However, there can be exceptions. For example, the lease may require an incoming lessee, before being registered with the lessor as the new leaseholder, to enter into a direct covenant with the lessor to observe all the terms and especially the covenants in the lease (the lessor will require this because there is no privity of estate after the **assignee** sells on). The same arrangement could be predicated upon the incoming lessee applying for licence to assign. The licence would then incorporate an observance covenant in the same format.

EXAMPLE

A typical alienation clause of this kind might read:

> *not to assign **transfer** underlet or part with or share possession of the demised premises or any part thereof without the written consent of the Lessor PROVIDED ALWAYS that it shall be lawful for the Lessor to withhold such consent unless before the assignment transfer or underlease is completed the lessee procures the execution of and delivers to the lessor a **deed** to be prepared by the Lessor's legal practitioner at the full cost of the lessee and which contains a covenant by the proposed assignee transferee or sub-lessee to perform and observe during the term assigned transferred or granted the covenants by the lessee and the conditions contained in this lease in the same manner as if such covenants and conditions were repeated in full in that deed.*

14.2.2.6 Alterations, additions and/or improvements

The reversioner will want to ensure that unauthorised alterations do not take place. Additionally, the reversioner will want to be sure that the alterations that do take place are such that the integrity of the structure will not be adversely affected. This will also be the case for additions and improvements. Lessees of long residential leases will argue that they should be free to do what they like with their property. Certainly, this would seem to be a tenable argument where the lease is of a house. However, it is less tenable where the lease is of a flat or maisonette. Clearly, in these circumstances alterations, additions and improvements could very well affect adjacent or adjoining property, and the lessor may therefore feel that there should be controls over what may be done by the lessee in the way of alterations.

A covenant dealing with alterations can include an absolute bar such as 'not to make or allow to be made any alterations additions or improvements to the demised premises'. If this is the prevailing covenant, the lessee cannot carry out any work whatsoever. This could be seen to be unfair to a long leaseholder, and consequently such clauses are sometimes qualified to allow the lessee to carry out non-structural alterations within the demised premises that do not cut or maim any load-bearing walls or timbers. An absolute bar on alterations or additions must be considered unacceptable in a long lease. If one appears in a draft, the lease should be amended to allow alterations with the lessor's written consent. To the extent that proposed alterations amount to improvements, s19(2) of the Landlord and Tenant Act 1927 will then apply so that consent cannot be unreasonably withheld, and the lessor cannot demand any payment beyond their reasonable legal and other expenses incurred in granting consent (see *Woolworth & Co Ltd v Lambert* [1937] Ch 37). However, to avoid any argument about whether an alteration is or is not an improvement, the clause should be amended to allow alterations or additions with the lessor's consent, such consent not to be unreasonably withheld (this is known as a fully qualified covenant). In this way, the lessor will be required to justify any refusal of permission, ultimately in court, and would therefore not be an avenue the landlord would explore without real justification. The statute does not stop the lessor from seeking a reasonable sum should the proposed amendments diminish the value of the premises, or any adjacent premises in the ownership of the same lessor. Similarly, if the alteration or addition does not add to the letting value of the premises, the statute does not prevent the lessor from obtaining from the tenant a covenant to reinstate the premises to their former condition at the end (or sooner determination) of the lease.

14.2.2.7 Quiet enjoyment

A covenant for quiet enjoyment is given by the lessor for the benefit of the lessee and should appear in all leases. If an express covenant is absent, an implied covenant will apply. An express covenant will override an implied one.

EXAMPLE

A typical express covenant for quiet enjoyment might read:

> *that the lessee paying all the rents reserved by this lease and performing and observing all the covenants contained in this lease shall peaceably hold and enjoy the demised premises without any interruption by the lessor or any other company or person rightfully claiming under or in trust for the lessor.*

The purpose of the covenant is to confirm that the lessee can physically enjoy the complete benefit of the property without the lessor adversely disturbing that enjoyment. The courts have held that this covenant could apply to scaffolding outside the property (see *Owen v Gadd* [1956] 2 QB 99, although that case related to a shop where the scaffolding was outside the shop door and window and consequently affected the lessee's business). In contrast, in *Kenny v Preen* [1963] 1 QB 499 the court held that the lessor's conduct where he banged on the door, sent threatening letters and shouted abuse at the lessee amounted to a breach of covenant for quiet enjoyment.

14.2.2.8 Service charge provisions

Where the lessor is under an obligation to keep in good repair a building of which the subject property forms part, the cost of those repairs will usually be recoverable from the lessee. That cost along with other expenses incurred by the lessor in providing services (eg lighting and heating of common parts) on behalf of all the lessees, will form a service charge.

The following should apply to a lease of part of a residential block, namely a flat in a conglomeration of flats all paying a service charge to the one lessor:

- The lease may provide for a service charge payable as a rent with payments on account made quarterly at a rate to be decided by the lessor's surveyor (whose decision shall be final, save for manifest error) at the start of each year but having regard to expenditure in the previous year. At the end of the year, accounts should be prepared without undue delay to reconcile payments made and received. Excess monies held should go to a sinking fund (see next), while any underpayment should be paid by the lessees within 21 days of the supply of the year-end accounts.
- There should also be a sinking fund created for the express purposes of ensuring that there are sufficient monies available to cover major expenses such as lift replacements or external redecoration schemes.

- The lessor should be obliged by a covenant to carry out clearly identified obligations listed in a schedule to the lease, including repairs and renovations to the main structure and common parts, and lighting and heating the common parts.
- The lessor should be obliged to provide at least two estimates where expenditure other than those of a moderate nature is required.
- Different lessees in the block may pay different charges. Consideration should be given to a fair distribution of the burden of payment, for example should occupants on the ground floor be required to pay towards the cost of the repair of a lift?

Many of these items are now required by statute (see ss18–30 Landlord and Tenant Act 1985). Section 19 of this Act imposes a requirement of reasonableness as to service charges. Section 20 requires, where the cost of work exceeds £250, two estimates to be obtained, with notice being given to lessees who must be consulted about the proposed works (provisions within the Commonhold and Leasehold Reform Act 2002 have extended these rights to cover improvements as well as service charges). The best method of avoiding the potential problems in this area is to draft the lease so that the maintenance of the property is carried out by a management or maintenance company with each lessee owning a share in that company. If this arrangement is created, then the maintenance of the whole block will be in the control of the lessees who can control the expenditure in whatever way they wish. Lessors should ensure that the service charge provisions allow them to recover expenditure arising out of the need to comply with fire safety regulations where this is legally possible (see **14.2.2.9**).

The Commonhold and Leasehold Reform Act 2002 introduces a requirement that ground rent will not be payable unless it has been demanded. The demand is to be made by giving the tenant a prescribed notice. The reforms in the Act prevent the application of any provisions of a lease relating to late or non-payment (eg additional charges such as interest) if the rent is paid within 30 days of the demand being issued. It also introduces additional restrictions on the commencement of forfeiture proceedings for breaches of covenants or conditions of a lease. It modifies s81 of the Housing Act 1996 to prohibit the commencement of forfeiture proceedings, including the issue of a notice under s146 of the Law of Property Act 1925, in respect of non-payment of service charges or administration charges. This is not the case if the charge has been agreed or admitted by the tenant, or a court or the First-tier Tribunal—Property Chamber; Residential Property (formerly the Leasehold Valuation Tribunal)—has determined that it is reasonable and due. It also prohibits the commencement of forfeiture proceedings for other breaches unless a court or the First-tier Tribunal has determined that a breach has occurred.

14.2.2.9 Mutual rights

In residential blocks in multiple occupation and where maisonettes are concerned, easements, both granted and reserved, will almost certainly have to be detailed in the lease. There will need to be mutual rights by way of easements and exceptions for matters such as the paths of conducting media (ie gas pipes, electricity cables, sewers, etc) serving the property that have to pass across other parts of the block. Similarly, rights of access to and from the subject property will need to be detailed, showing the common areas to which the lessee may have access. The reverse will also be true. There will be other lessees who may require rights over the subject property by way of express **reservations** detailed in the lease.

EXAMPLE

The best example would be the mutual right of lessees in a multi-occupied block to access to other parts for the purposes of emergency repairs or general upkeep. Another common element required will be a mutual proviso for support and protection between flats in a block or maisonettes. This protects the core of any multi-occupation arrangement.

In respect of fire safety, lessors should reserve the rights needed to comply with their new responsibilities under the fire and safety regulations imposed as a result of the Grenfell Tower Inquiry. The Fire Safety (England) Regulations 2022 place a responsibility on building managers to carry out an annual inspection of fire doors at the front of flats which lead onto communal areas. Lessors must therefore reserve the right to carry out an annual inspection of fire doors at the entrance of individual flats and to carry out any operational repairs to those doors. Ideally, lessors should retain ownership of sprinklers and other fire safety equipment situated within individual flats, together with the right to install and upgrade equipment as necessary. They should also have the right to impose new fire safety requirements on lessees to meet any changing circumstances. It should be added that if you are acting for a lessee, you should ensure that the terms of any new lease are sufficiently up to date with modern fire regulations. In 2024, the Law Society issued a useful guide to assist solicitors involved in flat sales and purchases to understand the Building Safety Act 2022. The guide includes information on who pays to remediate tall buildings affected by fire safety issues. See https://www.lawsociety.org.uk/topics/property/building-safety-act-2022-guide-for-conveyancers.

14.3 *UK Finance Mortgage Lenders' Handbook* and leases

UK Finance, formerly the Council of Mortgage Lenders (CML), issued the *CML Lenders' Handbook for Solicitors and Licensed Conveyancers England and Wales* in 1999. It is regularly updated to cover changes in the law and/or conveyancing practice. It provides conveyancing practitioners with comprehensive instructions on what lenders expect practitioners to do when acting for them. The Handbook was issued after close consideration between the Law Society and seven of the leading UK lenders. It is now known as the *UK Finance Mortgage Lenders' Handbook*.

A lender will not, under any circumstances, accept as security for a loan a lease that contains forfeiture on bankruptcy of the lessee. In other words, if the lease allows a right of re-entry on the bankruptcy of the lessee, the lease will not be mortgageable. The reasoning is that if the lessee did become bankrupt and the lessor forfeited, the lender's security would evaporate. Additionally, where there is a property that contains several units, all on separate leases, a lender (and indeed a lessee) would not want each lessee to be responsible for the repair of their own section of the structure. Clearly, this would lead to an inconsistent and patchy approach to repair that can be avoided if this responsibility rests with the lessor. The same argument will apply to insurance arrangements for multi-occupied property. Moreover, any absolute prohibition against an assignment or mortgage of the whole of the subject property would be unacceptable in a long residential lease. Finally, although strictly speaking nothing to do with leases, it is worth emphasising that flying freeholds (ie freehold flats or maisonettes not attached to the ground) are unlikely to be acceptable to a lender or a buyer. In particular, a flying freehold will involve positive covenants that cannot be enforced. The pivotal problem arises from the current inability to enforce positive repairing covenants against a freehold **covenantor**'s successors in title. It is this deficiency that makes a freehold flat a poor choice in the property marketplace. (There is no reason why a leaseholder should not also own a share of the freehold with other leaseholders in the same block.) In future, the position may be changed by the Contracts (Rights of Third Parties) Act 1999. It is possible that the Act will provide a method of enforceability but this has yet to be properly tested in the courts. Many lessors expressly exclude this Act from their leases. Commonhold will also assist.

EXAMPLE

Arlo acts for Conrad who is buying a leasehold flat which has an unusual but attractive balcony extending over his next-door neighbour's garden. As the balcony overhangs the neighbour's land it would appear to constitute a flying freehold. Arlo should therefore check the lease to ascertain whether it contains provisions for this. If not, provided the lender is in agreement, the seller should be asked to put in place (at the seller's expense) a defective title indemnity policy.

CONDUCT POINT

Always check the requirements of your lender in the *UK Finance Mortgage Lenders' Handbook*. Failure to carry out instructions on behalf of a client may amount to a breach of the SRA Code of Conduct. You must act in the best interests of each client and you must provide a proper standard of service to your clients.

14.4 Defective leases

A residential lease will be considered defective if any of the following occurs in the lease you are considering for your client buyer:

- the lease contains a forfeiture on bankruptcy provision;
- the lease fails to include proper repairing covenants that ensure the ongoing maintenance and renewal of the main structure, roof, foundations and common parts. This will require the involvement of the lessor or management company;
- the property is in a newly constructed block of flats where the developer is not offering an NHBC guarantee or similar guarantee scheme. Although not strictly a lease defect, many **mortgagees** will not lend in the absence of this protection;
- the lease does not include a covenant by the lessor to take action against another lessee for breach of covenant at the request of a lessee who agrees to indemnify the lessor for that action;
- the lease has inadequate insurance provisions, or the lessor is under no obligation to look after unlet or unsold property in a large block.

Where there are two maisonettes on lease, it has been the occasional practice also to transfer the freehold of the flats to the lessees at the time of the granting of the lease. However, in doing so the transfer is in two parts. This means that each lessee is the freeholder for the other maisonette. This sounds a simple solution that, in theory, sets up a commonality of responsibility for repairs and maintenance. However, there is one major flaw: one of the two freehold titles will be a 'flying freehold'. This is unsatisfactory conveyancing practice. In place of this arrangement the single freehold title could be vested in the joint names of the two lessees, or in a limited company jointly owned by the lessees.

14.5 Liability on covenants in leases: enforcement

For many years, it was the case that the original lessor and lessee were liable to each other under the covenants in their lease for the full term granted by the lease. As a consequence of the effects of privity of contract, this liability remained enforceable in the courts even if the lessee had subsequently assigned the residue of the term of the lease. The practical effect of this was that a lessee could be sued for arrears of rent even though that lessee had not been the tenant in occupation for many years and where there had been various subsequent lessees liable to pay rent under the terms of the original lease.

This outdated element of landlord and tenant law led to some very unfair situations where an original tenant had been called on to pay rent many years after assigning their interest in the subject property. A measure of reform was made by the provisions of the Landlord and Tenant (Covenants) Act 1995. Most of these provisions apply only to new leases created on or after 1 January 1996. In essence, a lessee who assigns such a lease automatically enjoys a release through statute of any continuing liability under the lease covenants. However, a lessor can require the outgoing lessee to enter into a form of guarantee stipulated by the statute and known as an **authorised guarantee agreement** (AGA) under which the outgoing lessee becomes liable for future breaches of covenant by the incoming assignee (but not subsequent assignees). This is clarified in **Figure 14.1**.

T may be asked to give a guarantee to L (or L2) for the liabilities of A under the lease. This guarantee is also an AGA.

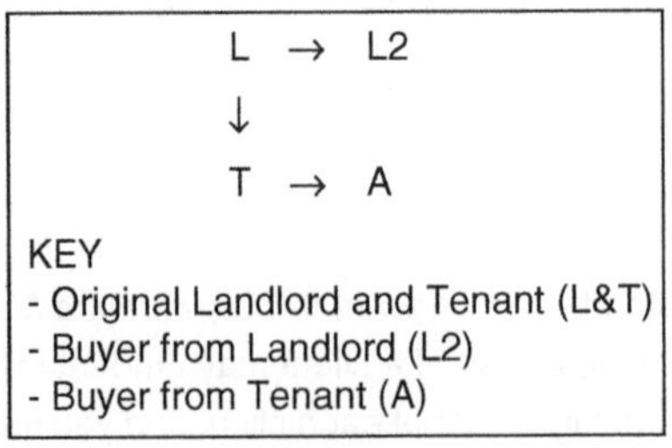

FIGURE 14.1 Liability on covenants in leases

The statute made a major change to the law—the benefit and burden of lease covenants pass automatically on assignment without any question of whether or not they touch and concern the land. The successor in title, the assignee, will take the benefit and burden of the lease covenants by reason of statute and the **assignor**, the original lessee, will be released from liability.

Where a buyer is purchasing a flat in a block containing many other similar flats and where all are on long leases, the doctrine of privity of contract can cause major problems where one lessee is involved in a dispute with another about the enforcement of lease covenants. To enable enforcement to take place, and for all lessees in the block to know the extent of the lease terms for all occupants of the block, the lease should state that all the leases granted for the block will or do contain the same terms as that for the subject property. Coupled with this, there should be a covenant by the lessor on request by one lessee (and with that lessee agreeing to indemnify the lessor's costs) to enforce lease covenants against another lessee. Without this provision, one lessee has no legal right to enforce covenants against another lessee, as the covenant is not with the other lessee but with the lessor. However, the lease can be drawn up to include a covenant between the lessor, lessee and all the other lessees in the block. If this appears, each lessee can take action against any other lessee.

EXAMPLE

Harry owns a leasehold flat in Waltham Towers, Bristol. Despite diplomatic efforts on his part, noisy tenants living upstairs continue to disturb him at night and he wants action taken against them. You will advise him that he has no direct contractual relationship with the neighbouring tenant but you will check the lease to ensure that it contains a clause requiring the landlord to take action against other tenants who breach the covenants in their leases (known as a mutual enforceability clause).

14.6 Granting new leases

A new lease is granted by a lessor or landlord and is taken by a lessee or tenant. The lease will almost always be in two parts, the original part executed by the lessor and the counterpart executed by the lessee. Both parts will be identical; and when exchanged and dated the lease will, at the moment of exchange, come into formal and legal existence and thereby create a brand new legal estate. The lessor will be able to receive not only any premium to be paid on the grant of the new lease but thereafter any periodically recurring rent provided for in the lease.

14.6.1 Lease-specific changes in the conveyancing process

Before the draft contract can be prepared, a draft lease must be drawn up that will form the subject of the agreement. It is perfectly possible to adopt the same contract forms, incorporating the Standard Conditions, used on a freehold sale for a leasehold disposal, whether this is to be the grant of a new lease or an assignment or transfer of an existing lease. (SC 8 deals with leasehold property, SC 8.1 covers existing leases and SC 8.2 new leases. If the lessor's consent is required, this is covered by SC 8.3.) When the contract is drafted it should be sent to the buyer's practitioner, together with the proposed form of draft lease in duplicate. The draft contract and lease will then be approved with or without amendments. After exchange, the agreed form of lease must be engrossed and executed in duplicate by the contractual parties, in readiness for completion. Where necessary, the seller will have to obtain all necessary consents for the grant of the new lease from either or both the seller's mortgagee and superior title holder. At completion, the buyer may be required to pay lease-specific outgoings in advance, such as rent and service charges. There will possibly be **stamp duty land tax** (SDLT) on the lease rental as well as the consideration, and Land Registry forms are required for any application to the Registry for first registration of a registrable lease. Section 6 of the Land Registration Act 2002 stipulates that first registration must take place within two months of the completion of a grant of a new lease for a term of more than seven years, or the assignment on sale of an existing lease where the term left to run exceeds seven years at completion.

14.6.2 **Acting for the lessor**

The draft lease must reflect the precise wishes of the lessor and the particular nature of the property to be sold. If the lessor wishes to sell a flat within a block but retain control of that block, the lease terms must reflect these instructions. There will be times when the lessor will instruct you to proceed in a way that is unsatisfactory, for example the lessor may want to grant a new lease for a flat in a block, getting rid of all responsibility for the lessor, who only wants to receive the rents. This may mean you will be required to draw up a lease that is unsaleable, being unacceptable to a lender as a consequence of the absence of proper repairing arrangements for the whole block. To draft such a lease would be bad conveyancing practice. If this situation does occur, you should write to your client expressing as clearly as possible your reservations about the nature of your instructions and inviting your client to reconsider. If the instructions remain the same, our advice is to stand firm and not proceed: it could amount to professional negligence to do so.

CONDUCT POINT

Failure to carry out appropriate proper drafting of a lease may amount to a breach of the SRA Code of Conduct. You must act in the best interests of each client and you must provide a proper standard of service to your clients.

You could suggest to the lessor that there is an alternative to simply giving each lessee their own individual repairing and insuring responsibilities, and that is to pass these responsibilities to a management company. Each lessee would be given a share in the management company and the lessor would receive the rents without any further liability for future maintenance and insurance arrangements. Furthermore, if there are freehold covenants, the lease should include a covenant on the part of the lessee to observe and perform those covenants with an indemnity against any future breach.

When drafting the contract, you will need to insert in the particulars the estate and term to be offered to the buyer. You can do this by express reference or by attaching the draft lease to the contract as an annexure (SC 8.2.3 states 'The lease is to be in the form of the draft attached to the agreement'). With a new long lease, nothing more about **deducing title** needs be said as SC 8.2.4 stipulates that 'If the term of the new lease will exceed seven years the seller is to deduce a title that will enable the buyer to register the lease at Land Registry with an absolute title.' This should therefore require the seller to deduce the superior title.

14.6.3 **Acting for the lessee**

On receipt of the draft lease and contract, you should check both very carefully to make sure that they describe and demise the subject property accurately. You must also be sure that your client understands the relevance of all the lease terms. To ensure that this is so, you should write to your client with a detailed report on all the terms in the lease. In this way, the buyer cannot in the future allege that you did not advise them of any particular provision that may cause future problems.

As the Land Registry has issued rules requiring certain lease contents to be in a particular position in registrable leases, namely new leases with a term of more than seven years, make sure the draft lease incorporates these prescribed clauses.

14.6.3.1 The draft lease and contract: lessee concerns

Points of concern about the draft lease and contract terms that should be carefully considered include the following:

- The description of the subject property in the lease: are all the walls, floors and ceilings included or excluded?
- Is there a garden at the front and/or rear and if so do either or both form part of the property to be purchased?

- Are there adequate rights of access to and from the subject property over the parts leading to the premises?
- Are there mutual rights of support, protection and entry for repairs?
- Is the buyer aware of rental at the levels shown in the draft? What are the provisions, if any, for the increase of rent and are they onerous?
- Are the lessee's covenants reasonable and in particular is there any restriction on alienation; and, if so, is that restriction fair to a long leaseholder?
- Does the lease allow forfeiture on bankruptcy? If so, take steps immediately to remove this provision.
- Is there a covenant requiring the lessor to enforce covenants against other lessees in the block? This must be included.
- Does the contract make proper and exact reference to the estate and term to be sold to your client?
- Are there any lease-specific special conditions and, if so, are they acceptable in the context of your instructions for the buyer?

14.6.4 Giving notice

There is one further lease-specific task to be performed after completion where the new lessee has purchased with a mortgage. Most modern leases require notice of assignment and charge (or mortgage) to be given to the seller's solicitor. Where there is the grant of a new lease, clearly only notice of charge must be given along with the payment of any fee for the registration. There is a double obligation where you also act for the lender, as it is important that the lessor is aware of the lender's interest in the property should the lessee, in the future, breach any of the terms of the lease.

14.7 Assigning existing leases

Practitioners need to be aware that in the standard contract there is just one specific Standard Condition relating to leaseholds: SC 8.1.2 states 'The seller having provided the buyer with copies of the documents embodying the lease terms, the buyer is treated as entering into the contract knowing and fully accepting those terms.' This covers a sale where the lease terms are not all in one document, namely where there has been a subsequent deed of variation of the original lease terms. It also states that there is a clear assumption that all the necessary copies have been supplied and the buyer therefore takes the property in full knowledge of the lease terms and is deemed to have accepted the transaction on that basis.

14.7.1 Lease-specific changes in the conveyancing process

We set out next the common changes to the conveyancing process arising in leasehold transactions.

14.7.2 Acting for the seller: good leasehold issues

If the property being sold is registered at the Land Registry with good leasehold title, the same provisions as to the deduction of title apply, and SC 4.1.2 stipulations also apply. The buyer must also receive a copy of the lease registered at the Land Registry along with any deeds varying it or affecting it and that have been registered. However, the problem for the buyer of a good leasehold title is that the registration is such that there is no guarantee of the validity of the lease; that is, that the lease has been validly granted. The Registry will issue this class of title when the superior title, the reversionary title, has not been seen and approved by the Registrar. As a consequence, a buyer faced with a good leasehold title should demand that the superior title be deduced; and because the Standard Conditions are silent on the point, an extra special condition should be inserted in the contract to that effect. (In practical terms, this should be unnecessary if title is to be **investigated** before contracts are exchanged.) The buyer cannot persist, as the law does not support this insistence. If the superior title is not available, the buyer should be advised not to proceed as a good leasehold title may not be acceptable to a lender. The seller could be asked to upgrade the title as a good leasehold title can be upgraded to absolute so long as an applicant is able to produce to the Registrar the freehold reversionary title together with any superior leasehold titles.

CONDUCT POINT

Always check the requirements of your lender in the *CML Handbook*. Failure to carry out instructions on behalf of a client may amount to a breach of the SRA Code of Conduct. You must act in the best interests of each client and you must provide a proper standard of service to your clients.

14.7.3 Information required on a sale

Obtain details of any rents, service charge and insurance payments made by the client seller, as you will require these to prepare answers to **preliminary enquiries** or Property Information Forms. You will also need to see copies of the last three years' service charge accounts, as the buyer will inevitably ask for these prior to exchange. (In Protocol cases, the seller's practitioner is required to ask the client to produce service or maintenance charge accounts for the last three years, where appropriate, and evidence of payment.) Check the lease to see what assignment preconditions there are and take steps to comply with them, such as making provision in the contract for the buyer to enter into a deed of covenant at the time of completion directly with the lessor. If necessary, apply for a licence to assign supported by references from the buyer prior to **exchange of contracts**. SC 8.3 applies if a consent to assign or sub-let is required to enable completion to take place. SC 8.3.2(a) states that 'The seller is to apply for the consent at his expense, and to use all reasonable efforts to obtain it.' In support of this application, SC 8.3.2(b) requires the buyer to 'provide all information and references reasonably required'. Either party may rescind the contract if three working days before the day for completion the lessor's consent has not been issued, or if issued it has attaching to it 'a condition to which the buyer reasonably objects'. Rescission is effected by giving written notice to the other party to the agreement; and on rescission arising in this manner, neither party is 'to be treated as in breach of contract and condition 7.2 applies'. This condition provides that the **deposit** is to be repaid with interest and the buyer is to return any documents and to cancel any registration of the contract; that is to say, the parties are to return to the position they were in as if the contract had not existed.

If there is a management company owned by the lessees, before exchange the seller must supply copies of the memorandum and articles of association of that management company together with, where appropriate, a copy of the seller's share certificate (remember, if the company is limited by guarantee there will be no share certificate).

EXAMPLE

Ceri acts for Suki who is selling her registered leasehold flat in Queens Wharf, Liverpool, a city-centre block of flats. Suki has a share certificate in the Queens Wharf Management Company. When considering what documents to send to her buyer's solicitors, as well as the usual documents to be included in the pre-contract package (eg draft contract in duplicate and official copy entries of the leasehold title), Ceri will need to obtain and send the following additional documents:

- Official copy of the registered lease and any deed of variation of the lease.
- Completed Leasehold Information Form (TA7) and replies to enquiries made of the landlord/managing agents (LPE1).
- Service charge accounts and receipts for the last three years and an up-to-date ground rent receipt.

- Block insurance policy and schedule for the building.
- As there is a management company, a copy of the seller's share certificate, memorandum/articles of any management company and any regulations made by the landlord or management company.
- **Official copies** of the freehold and any intermediary titles.

Queens Wharf Management Company will have been set up to carry out the maintenance and repair of the common parts of the building, paid for through the tenants' service charges. Suki's share certificate shows that the tenants are shareholders in the company. As well as obtaining the share certificate from Suki, Ceri will arrange for her to sign a stock transfer form to assign the share certificate to the buyer. She will send the certificate and signed stock transfer form to the buyer's conveyancer on completion.

14.7.4 Acting for the buyer

If you are acting for a buyer, you should always check the amount of time left to run on the lease, namely the residue of the term granted, especially if the buyer is purchasing with the assistance of a mortgage. This is particularly so for two reasons. First, if the residue of the term is fairly limited it will be unacceptable to many lenders which will generally decline to lend if the lease term has less than 60 years left to run. However, some lenders are insisting on at least 85 years left to run so you should check this in each case. Secondly, the lender may have based the loan on a term of years stated to it by the buyer. If that figure turns out to be inaccurate, the lender must be told the correct details by you and you need to obtain its written approval to the amended details prior to an exchange of contracts. The same is true for any rental details.

14.7.5 Lease-specific enquiries and the contract

Where a leasehold is being purchased, lease-specific enquiries should be made covering insurance and maintenance details and should include a request for the last three years' service charge accounts, along with a copy of the current insurance policy and up-to-date schedule of cover. This can be done by way of the Protocol forms, the seller's leasehold information form parts I and II.

The Law Society has issued a conveyancing form called LPE1. It is intended to be used for collecting information about a subject property where that information is held by landlords, management companies and managing agents. The information that the form intends to gather will normally be about ground rent, insurance and service charges. This form should be used when a lessor or management company must be contacted to obtain information from them about a leasehold property that is in the process of being sold.

Carefully check the contract to make sure it properly describes all the leasehold title to be purchased. Reference should be made in the contract to the property description in the lease. Look through the lease terms to make sure it contains all the necessary terms and that it does not include any that should be avoided. Check to see if the lease plan remains accurate. Check the lease to see what obligations there are, if any, on any incoming lessee before the transfer can take place. If the lessor's consent is required for the transfer of the residue of the lease to your client, consider the need for references. Add together the amount of the current annual rent and service charges and obtain references for that amount. The references should be provided by the buyer's bankers and their accountants, if any, and perhaps with one further reference as to the buyer's character. If the client is not known to you as an established client, you should decline to supply a reference for someone you do not know. If there is a management company, call for a copy of the memorandum and articles of association and a copy of the seller's share certificate. If the company is limited by guarantee, there will be no share certificate. Provide the buyer with a full and detailed written report of the terms of the lease and ask the client to confirm in writing that the terms of the lease are understood and accepted. Does the lease contain all the terms considered appropriate to the type of property to be purchased? If not, you may need to approach the seller with a request that a deed of variation be obtained from the lessor to correct the position. The deed of variation can include a necessary lease term or exclude an undesirable one. Leases that are more than 20–5 years old may not include a lessor's covenant to enforce covenants by other lessees. A variation is one way in which this kind of lease can be modernised so as to include such a clause.

EXAMPLE

You act for Wan Li who is buying a registered leasehold flat in London with the aid of a mortgage. The lease was granted in May 1980. You will consider in particular the following:

- As the lease was granted back in 1980, check if the remaining term is long enough (most lenders insist on a least 60 years left so check with your client's mortgagee).
- Is the property description accurate and complete, for example as to the inclusion or exclusion of walls, ceilings and floor?
- Are the easements benefiting the property adequate, such as rights of access, support and entry for repairs?
- Ensure the tenant's covenants are not excessively onerous and are mutually enforceable (given the age of the lease, the latter may not be the case in which case a deed of variation will be required).
- Alienation provisions must be reasonable and not excessively restrictive.
- There should be no provision for forfeiture upon the tenant's bankruptcy. This will be unacceptable to the mortgagee.
- The landlord's repairing and insuring obligations must be adequate.

14.8 Enfranchisement

Enfranchisement in the context of leasehold properties is the statutory right for leaseholders to call for the superior title, the freehold or an extension to their lease term. The law exists to give protection to leaseholders who might otherwise see their estate disappear by reason of the passing of time.

Leasehold houses: the Leasehold Reform Act 1967 applies to long leases of houses, namely those for a term exceeding 21 years. In *Day v Hosebay Ltd; Howard de Walden Estates Ltd v Lexgorge Ltd* [2012] UKSC 41, the Supreme Court considered the meaning of a house for the purposes of this Act. A 'house' was defined in s2(1) of the 1967 Act and the two tests in the Act are commonly referred to as:

1 Is the building designed/adapted for living in?

2 Is it a house, reasonably so called?

The 2012 decision was a short one based almost entirely on the current use of the premises in question. In *Hosebay*, the buildings that were being used as self-catering hotels were not 'houses' even if they were adapted for living in (and Carnwath LJ questioned this as there is a difference between 'living' and 'staying' somewhere). The buildings in *Hosebay* were not houses 'reasonably so called'. The fact that they might look like houses and might be referred to as houses for some purposes was not sufficient to displace the fact that their use was entirely commercial. So a building is a house if it is at least primarily a building for living in as a residence. It does not apply to a flat. To qualify for enfranchisement rights under this Act, there is a requirement that the lessee/claimant must have held the lease for at least two years. On paying the lease value calculated in accordance with formulae stipulated by the 1967 Act as subsequently amended by the Commonhold and Leasehold Reform Act 2002, the lessee may thereby enfranchise, namely buy in the freehold. As an alternative to buying the freehold, the lessee can call for an extended lease of a further 50 years. Where this form of extension is required, the rent will be fixed at a modern ground rent and will be open to review after 25 years.

Leasehold flats: from 1 November 1993, the Leasehold Reform, Housing and Urban Development Act 1993 introduced a mechanism for the collective enfranchisement of lessees of flats within a block. This mechanism has been amended and greatly improved by the Commonhold and Leasehold Reform Act 2002. To qualify, a leaseholder must hold a lease for a term exceeding 21 years. There is a requirement that those participating in the enfranchisement must occupy half of the flats in the block (s119 2002 Act). The purchase of the freehold and subsequent management of the building are to be carried out by a 'Right to Enfranchise Company', of which the participating leaseholders are members. All relevant leaseholders will have the right to participate in the purchase by joining the company. As well as the purchase price, on enfranchisement lessees may also have to pay the lessor's reasonable costs. In the alternative, a lessee can call for a new lease that will extend the existing term by another 90 years (see s39). There is a requirement that the lessee must have held the lease for at least two years. The rent to be paid will be a mere peppercorn, but a premium valued under specific terms of the statute will be payable. If the lease has fewer than five years to run, the lessor can seek to oppose the lessee's application where the lessor can show an intention to demolish and/or reconstruct the property and needs vacant possession to carry out these plans. If granted, the lease will have immediate effect but will not stop subsequent collective enfranchisement action.

KEY POINT SUMMARY

- In the light of the type of lease to be given or taken by your client, are the terms contained within it suitable to a lease of that kind? Try to step back and take an overview to ensure the contents are suitable.
- When instructed by buyer and lender, always remember your dual obligation to ensure that the lease to be purchased suits both your clients and their individual requirements and instructions.
- In particular, are the insurance arrangements suitable for the type of subject property? In brief, if the property is a house, the lessee should insure; if a flat, the lessor should insure; if a maisonette, either will do. The same is true for repairs.
- If your client is taking a long residential lease, reject clauses restricting alienation except if the restriction is there to ensure a direct covenant between the lessor and your client, the assignee.
- When acting for a proposed lessee intending to buy a leasehold residential property with a mortgage, never agree a lease that allows forfeiture on bankruptcy as this will not be acceptable to a lender.
- Always ensure the lease to be purchased contains a lessor's covenant allowing one lessee to enforce lease covenants against another lessee through the assistance of the lessor.
- Does the new lease contain all the terms considered appropriate to the type of property to be sold or purchased?
- Does the new lease contain any terms that are unacceptable to the buyer's lender or to the buyer?
- Has the contract been drafted properly in the context of the proposed terms of the new lease, and what lease-specific special conditions are there and are they acceptable?
- On the assumption that the lease requires it, have you remembered to give notice of the buyer's charge to the lessor and have you paid the registration fee?
- If the seller is seeking to sell a good leasehold title, always insist that either the title be upgraded to absolute or the superior title be deduced and amend the draft contract to include a special condition to that effect.
- If you are acting for a seller of an existing lease, make sure you have details of all specific outgoings, as well as copies of the last three years' service charge accounts.
- If there is a management company, ensure you have the details of the constitution of the management company such as the company memorandum and articles of association.
- If you are acting for a buyer, make sure the lease terms are acceptable to your client and the client's lender and supply references if needed in support of an application for licence to assign if required by the terms of the lease. The financial references should be for the total of the annual rent and the current annual service charge.
- Be aware of the new fire safety regulations as they affect leasehold flats.

CHAPTER 15
Commercial Leases

FUNCTIONING LEGAL KNOWLEDGE

This chapter covers the following functioning legal knowledge required to pass the SQE 1 assessments:

Commercial leases:

- structure and content of a **commercial lease**
- procedural steps for the grant of a **lease** or **underlease**
- procedural steps for the **assignment** of a lease
- **licence to assign** and **licence** to underlet
- liability on leasehold **covenants**
- remedies for breach of a leasehold covenant
- Code for Leasing Business Premises

AUTHORITIES UNDERPINNING PRACTICE

The key authorities that underpin this area of practice are listed below. Note that for legislation you are linked to legislation.gov.uk.

Although much of the legislation on this government website is available in its amended form, the incorporation of new amendments into the text of legislation can be delayed. You should refer to legal databases to ensure you are referencing the most up-to-date legislation.

- Land Registration Rules 2003
  https://www.legislation.gov.uk/uksi/2003/1417/contents
- Law of Property Act 1925
  https://www.legislation.gov.uk/ukpga/Geo5/15-16/20/contents
- Landlord and Tenant Act 1927
  https://www.legislation.gov.uk/ukpga/Geo5/17-18/36/contents
- Leasehold Property (Repairs) Act 1938
  https://www.legislation.gov.uk/ukpga/Geo6/1-2/34/contents
- Part II of the Landlord and Tenant Act 1954, Part II
  https://www.legislation.gov.uk/uksi/1983/133/contents/made
- Landlord and Tenant Act 1988
  https://www.legislation.gov.uk/ukpga/1988/26/contents
- Landlord and Tenant (Covenants) Act 1995
  https://www.legislation.gov.uk/ukpga/1995/30/contents
- Commonhold and Leasehold Reform Act 2002
  https://www.legislation.gov.uk/ukpga/2002/15/contents
- Code for Leasing Business Premises
  https://www.rics.org/uk/upholding-professional-standards/sector-standards/real-estate/code-for-leasing-business-premises-1st-edition/

15.1 Introduction

Property practice covers both commercial and residential property transactions. This means that a suitably prepared property lawyer will need to be aware of the requirements for both areas of practice, although a specialist will, of course, concentrate on one or other. While many areas of commercial conveyancing can resemble similar practices and procedures utilised in residential conveyancing, the nature of the subject matter has in many aspects of the process dictated a different approach. For most property lawyers concerned with commercial conveyancing, the subject will be seen to be synonymous with commercial leases. As SQE students (or students on other professional property law courses), you can expect to be examined on all aspects of a commercial lease.

In commercial property, an individual or company will own the freehold as an investment, and that freeholder will grant a commercial lease to an occupying **lessee**. The lease terms regulate the basis on which the lessee will be allowed to occupy the premises for the purposes of carrying on a business. Inevitably, this has meant that there is no one common form of commercial or **business lease**. Practitioners will encounter a multitude of lease formats.

For commentary on leaseholds generally, refer to **Chapter 14**.

15.2 Exempt information documents

Commercial **lessors** may be concerned that registered leases will be available to the public as a result of the register being open to review by anyone. The effect of this could be that lessees might find out the lease terms for adjacent or adjoining property, and this could be material to lease renewal negotiations in a large estate or could reveal concessions granted to another lessee. However, the Land Registration Rules 2003 allow for applications to remove from public view sensitive material. If the Registry approves an application, it will be an exempt information document (EID). An application will be approved if the Registry is satisfied that the document contains 'prejudicial information'. Rule 131 defines prejudicial information as:

- information that relates to an individual who has applied for the document to be designated an EID and if disclosed to other persons (whether to the public generally or specific persons) would, or would be likely to, cause substantial unwarranted damage or substantial unwarranted distress to the applicant or another; or
- information that if disclosed to other persons (whether to the public generally or specific persons) would, or would be likely to, prejudice the commercial interests of the applicant, namely the person who applied for the document to be designated an EID.

EXAMPLE

Sandeep Developments Ltd (Sandeep) has just completed the grant of a 15-year lease of retail unit 1 in a brand new shopping centre. A generous rent-free period was given to the lessee and Sandeep does not wish this information to be available to prospective lessees of other units in the shopping centre as it may prejudice Sandeep's future negotiations with them. Sandeep therefore applies to the **Land Registry** for the lease of retail unit 1 to be an 'exempt information document'.

CONDUCT POINT

Be very careful about how you agree a lease and subsequently apply for registration of the lease for your client. Is there sensitive information that needs to be exempt? Failure to consider this point could amount to a breach of the SRA Code of Conduct. You must act in the best interests of each client and you must provide a proper standard of service to your clients.

15.3 Commercial lease contents

A commercial (or business) lease should contain specific elements, and these are listed next. However, how and where they appear in any one lease will vary greatly. Some leases will use schedules, some will not. Consequently, practitioners must have in mind a basic list of necessary contents for a commercial lease as follows:

- heading, date and parties;
- a clear parcels clause setting out a full description of the property (if necessary by reference to a lease plan), with all attaching rights;
- exceptions and **reservations**, namely a detailed list of all the rights retained by the lessor;
- the length of the lease term and the commencement date for that term (not always the date of the lease), known as the habendum;
- the rental details (known as the reddendum) including rent review clauses, frequency of payment and payment dates, and whether the rent is paid in arrears or in advance;
- lessee's covenants;
- lessor's covenants;
- provisos, including a **forfeiture** clause and other clauses regulating the mechanics of the operation of the lease terms, such as a provision for arbitration in case of dispute between the parties or a clause setting out how covenant notices are to be served (**service charge** details could also appear at this point);
- an attestation clause.

The Land Registry has issued rules requiring certain lease contents to be in a particular position in registrable leases (new leases with a term of more than seven years). As a result, they are called prescribed clauses leases, and details of these requirements can be found at **14.2.1**. These registration requirements will apply to commercial and residential leases that are for a term exceeding seven years.

15.4 Payment of rent

So far as the lessor is concerned, this is the rationale for the very existence of the lease. The lessee is allowed the use and enjoyment of the subject premises in consideration of the rental expressed in the lease. The amount to be paid must be stated in clear and definite terms. However, a lease can be granted without including a rental element or with a period of non-payment, namely a rent-free period. Whether there is a rent-free period or not, the lease should state a commencement date for the payment of rent and the frequency of payment. Most modern leases provide for rent to be paid quarterly in advance. Traditional quarter days are commonly used, but the more precise modern quarter days are becoming increasingly evident, such as the first day of January, April, July and October. Modern leases will also include a provision referring to other payments, such as service charges, as rent. Including these payments as rent enables the lessor to use the remedies of Commercial Rent Arrears Recovery and forfeit for non-payment. The remedy of Commercial Rent Arrears Recovery is not available for a breach of covenant other than non-payment of rent. Modern business leases will also include a further provision allowing the lessor to collect interest on late rent.

15.5 Rent reviews

Perhaps of greatest concern to the lessor is the nature and extent of the rent review provision. Rent review clauses allow the lessor to vary the rent stated in the lease so as to increase the income from the subject property. This has been especially important in times of inflation as the lessor of a long lease at a fixed rental was at a severe disadvantage when inflation was running at high levels. Each passing year meant that the lessor in such an unfortunate position was losing even more in real terms as inflation ate into the value of the fixed rental. To combat this potential increasing loss, lessors have included in leases a provision allowing the rent to be reviewed at fixed intervals, usually only in an upward direction. (If the review mechanism permits downward reviews, as well as upward, the rent could actually be reduced on review.) Some leases simply link the annual rent to inflation, for example the retail price index. Others state the amount to be paid in the future by way of fixed increases. However, most do not state the amount of the increase but try to define in the lease how the lease rental should be revalued on review.

It therefore follows that in a rent review the critical element is on what basis the rent should be reviewed. The intention of the lessor is to move the rent to the current market value for the subject premises. However, this gives rise to the all-important question of what that market value is and how it will be ascertained. Furthermore, the procedure for triggering and handling the review is critical. These valuation and procedural elements will be considered next.

15.5.1 Valuation

The new lease should contain a definition of a formula by which the new reviewed rent should be ascertained. If the lease terms say the intention is to fix a 'rack rent', then this is the full rent for the property. Thus, such a rental would reflect the changes in the property market as assessed by a valuer or surveyor. Alternatively, if the lease required the rent to be reviewed as a 'market rent', then this will be the same as for a new lease granted under the terms of the Landlord and Tenant Act 1954, but including the factors that the Act contemplates being ignored.

There is nothing to stop the lease incorporating detailed assumptions on which the review is to be based. If the lease stipulates assumptions to be made on a rent review, then they will be central to the valuation process for the subject property. Typical assumptions are that the rent is to be reviewed at the renewal date, assuming the property is vacant for a term equal to that either originally granted or the residue of the term and for the permitted user stated in the lease. (As to the term, it can be argued that a higher rental will arise if the term is longer than the unexpired residue at the time of review. In the absence of any express lease term to the contrary, courts will generally assume the lease term on review to be the period of the unexpired term (see *Lynnthorpe Enterprises Ltd v Sidney Smith (Chelsea) Ltd* [1990] 2 EGLR 148, CA)).

Modern rent review clauses will also allow the valuer to ignore any diminution in the value of the rental as a result of the lessee having failed properly to repair the subject property. Some review clauses also import assumptions with regard to improvements made by the lessee. If the lease is silent on the point, the rent review will be based on the nature of the premises at the time of review, including any improvements made by the lessee, even though they were made at the lessee's cost (see *Ponsford v HMS Aerosols Ltd* [1979] AC 63). Assumptions can also cover sub-lettings to take into account any profit rental the lessee may be receiving from sub-lessees. Courts will also generally accept that the hypothetical lease will include a rent review (see *British Gas v Universities Superannuation Scheme* [1986] 1 All ER 978).

15.5.2 Procedure

Modern rent review clauses trigger the process by requiring the lessor to serve a notice on the lessee calling for a review of the rent at the rent review date. Some trigger notices will be required by the review procedure to state what the lessor requires as a new rental. Others may simply call for the review process to be commenced. If an amount is specified, some clauses require the lessee to agree or disagree with the stated amount within a specified period. A trap exists here for the unwary. If **time is of the essence** for the lessee's response then, should that time limit not be complied with, the rental stated by the lessor, no matter how exaggerated it may be, will prevail as the rent for review. In *Starmark Enterprises Ltd v CPL Enterprises Ltd* [2001] EWCA Civ 1252, there was no mention of time being of the essence for service of the tenant's counter-notice. Nevertheless, an out-of-time counter-notice was deemed invalid because the parties to the lease had clearly stipulated the consequences of a party's failure to serve a notice within the time agreed by them.

Lessors can also be late calling for review by not complying with a timescale stated in the lease rent review provisions. In *United Scientific Holdings Ltd v Burnley Borough Council* [1978] AC 904, it was held that unless the clause makes it so, time is *not* of the essence for a rent review clause. If the clause makes time of the essence of part or all of the procedure, then the time limits are absolute and incapable of extension. In the absence of express provision, though, delay will not defeat a lessor's claim for a rent review. Time can be of the essence even if the rent review provision does not include that actual wording. If the words of the rent review clause are such that it is possible to show that there was an intention to make time limits absolute, then the courts will infer time to be of the essence. Time of the essence can also arise if other wording in the lease supports that possibility. Accordingly, if the lessee can, by notice, terminate the **tenancy** at the review date, it has been held that this means that time is of the essence for the review (see *Al Saloom v Shirley James Travel Services Ltd* (1981) 42 P & CR 181).

15.5.3 Arbitration and disputes

Sensible rent review clauses will also have two further provisions. First, there will be the possibility of referring the rent to an arbitrator for a final decision should the lessor and lessee be unable to agree the level of the new rent. Secondly, there should be a clause covering what must be done in the event of a dispute between the parties. This will again sensibly entail arbitration. In both clauses, if arbitration is contemplated it will involve provisions in the Arbitration Act 1996. Should the appointment of the arbitrator be in dispute, the lease can provide that, for the time being, the appointment be by the President of the Royal Institute of Chartered Surveyors.

EXAMPLE

Four years ago Bill granted a 15-year factory lease in Bristol to Chris with rent reviews every three years. The lease is silent as to whether time is of the essence of the rent review date. Market rents in Bristol have risen but Bill overlooked last year's first rent review date until now. Even though Bill is a year late calling for a review, Chris cannot refuse it because the lease does not provide that time is of the essence of the rent review date.

15.6 Covenants by the lessee

15.6.1 Repairing obligations

This is a subject area of great difficulty in two principal ways. First, deciding what part of the subject property must be repaired by the lessee does rather depend on the extent of the definition of the lessee's property in the lease. Secondly, when the extent of the property is known, the measure of the burden of the repairing liability must be clearly defined; from simple repairs necessary to deal with ordinary wear and tear, right up to the lessee being under a strict obligation virtually to replace the whole property.

Where there is a property in multiple occupation, say an office block containing several office suites all let to different lessees, the usual repairing arrangement is for the lessee to be required to keep in good repair the inner skin of the demised property. This would therefore require the lessee to keep properly maintained the plaster, the ceiling and the flooring materials, but not much else. All structural elements of the property, including the floor and ceiling joists, the main or load-bearing walls, the roof and foundations should all be repairable by the lessor, with all the lessees paying a service charge to reimburse the lessor for this expense (the further need for clear and appropriate service charge covenants flows from this form of repairing arrangement). The rationale for this arrangement is that there is a need for a consistent approach to the whole question of structural repairs and maintenance. On the other hand, if the lease is of the whole building, such as a lease of a shop and upper part, or indeed one office building let to one lessee, then it is common for the sole lessee to be responsible for all the repairs to the building.

15.6.2 The standard of repair

The required standard of repair was famously set out in *Proudfoot v Hart* (1890) 25 QBD 42, where it was held that the standard of repair is to be determined according to several factors, including the subject property's age and character and the environment in which the property is located. In effect, this has meant that there is a clear difference in the expected standard of repair between a Victorian property and one that was built in the 2020s. As to the meaning of 'repair', the courts have made it clear this includes renewal. It should be remembered that a covenant requiring the lessee 'to put and keep the property in good and substantial repair' is particularly onerous. This is way above mere repair and will be interpreted as requiring the lessee to carry out all repairs and renewals, substantial or not, right from the start of the lease. This kind of covenant is, however, encountered frequently in practice. In addition, a covenant to keep in repair implies a covenant to put and keep in repair. As a result, each lease-repairing covenant, seen in the light of the subject property, will dictate the nature and extent of the repairs required.

Most commercial leases will also include clauses calling on the lessee to decorate internally (and externally if the lessee has the total repairing liability) at regular intervals during the term of the lease. Common repainting and redecorating intervals are every five years internally, and every three years externally. Many such covenants also call on the lessee to decorate and repaint in the final year of the term whether or not this coincides with the fixed intervals. Overall, the purpose of clauses such as these is to ensure that the nature and extent of the lessee's decorating liability is clearly defined so as to ensure the proper upkeep of the subject property.

EXAMPLE

Amir acts for Wilco Investments Ltd which is granting a 16-year commercial lease of detached factory premises in Leicester to Sadiq. When drafting the lease, Amir will ensure that it contains a covenant by the lessee to decorate the exterior of the premises every three years and the interior of the premises every five years, as well as both the exterior and interior during the last year of the term.

15.6.3 Repair and service charges

Where the lessor is under an obligation to keep in good repair a building of which the subject property forms part, the cost of those repairs will usually be recoverable from the lessee. That cost, along with other expenses incurred by the lessor in providing services (eg lighting and heating of common parts) on behalf of all lessees, will form a service charge. If in the lease it is described as a rent, then in the event of its non-payment the procedure for forfeiture for non-payment of rent can be used (see **14.12**). Normally, there will be a service charge payable as a rent, with payments on account made quarterly at a level to be decided by the lessor's surveyor (whose decision shall be final, save for manifest error) at the start of each year, but having regard to the expenditure during the previous year. At the end of the year, accounts are prepared to reconcile the payments made and received. The lessor will usually be obliged by a covenant to carry out clearly identified obligations listed in a schedule to the lease, including repairs and renovations to the main structure and common parts, and lighting and heating the common parts. This obligation is usually made conditional on the lessees paying the service charge rental. The Commonhold and Leasehold Reform Act 2002 introduces additional restrictions on the commencement of forfeiture proceedings for breaches of covenants or conditions of a lease. It modifies s81 of the Housing Act 1996 to prohibit the commencement of forfeiture proceedings, including the issue of a notice under s146 of the Law of Property Act 1925, in respect of non-payment of service or administration charges.

15.7 User obligations

It is possible for the lease to include a covenant imposing an absolute restriction on the lessee against changing the use from any stated user precisely defined by the lease. More usually, the covenant can be qualified, requiring the lessor's consent before the use can be changed, and this is more commonly seen in commercial leases. In such business leases, an absolute user covenant will mean that the rental on review could be subject to a reduction in valuation. This is because a restriction on user makes the lease less attractive to tenants and it will therefore command less as a rental. However, this limitation on the rental income can be avoided by a fully qualified covenant, namely including wording such as 'such consent not to be unreasonably withheld'. This is because there is no statutory provision that the lessor's consent cannot be unreasonably withheld, as is the case with **alienation** covenants (see **14.9**). However, s19(3) of the Landlord and Tenant Act 1927 provides that if consent for a change of use is required, then the lessor is not allowed to demand a premium or extra rent for giving that consent. The lessor can require costs to be paid by the applicant, including all legal fees. A premium or extra rent can be demanded if alterations to the structure of the property are also proposed.

EXAMPLE

Eleanor acts for Tiger Investments Ltd which is granting a 15-year commercial lease of office premises in Liverpool to Samantha with rent reviews every three years. The draft lease will contain a covenant by the lessee not to change the use of the premises without the consent of the lessor. When drafting the lease, Eleanor will ensure that such lessor's consent cannot be unreasonably withheld. Unless the covenant is fully qualified in this way, it may have an adverse impact on the lessor as it would otherwise make the lease less attractive to a lessee and thus depress the rent on review.

15.8 Alteration restrictions

The reversioner will want to ensure that unauthorised alterations do not take place, especially where the lease term is short in duration. Furthermore, the reversioner will want to be sure that the alterations that do take place are such that the integrity of the structure will not be adversely affected. This will also be the case for additions and improvements to the subject property that are carried out by the lessee.

A covenant dealing with alterations can include an absolute bar such as: 'Not to make or allow to be made any alterations additions or improvements to the demised premises.' If this is the lease covenant, the lessee cannot carry out any work whatsoever.

The lease could allow alterations to the property with the lessor's written consent. To the extent that proposed alterations amount to improvements, s19(2) of the Landlord and Tenant Act 1927 will then apply so that consent cannot be unreasonably withheld, and the lessor cannot demand any payment beyond reasonable legal and other expenses incurred in the granting of consent for the relevant works. The statute does not stop the lessor from seeking a reasonable sum should the proposed amendments diminish the value of the premises or indeed any adjacent premises in the ownership of the same lessor. Similarly, if the alteration or addition does not add to the letting value of the premises, the statute does not prevent the lessor from obtaining from the lessee a covenant to reinstate the premises to their former condition at the end or sooner determination of the lease.

What amounts to an improvement was considered in *Lambert v FW Woolworth and Co Ltd* [1938] Ch 883. In that case, it was decided that an improvement will be considered as such from the lessee's viewpoint and whether it made the subject premises more useful or more valuable to the lessee.

15.9 Alienation restrictions

Alienation covers covenants against assignments, underletting, **mortgages** and other material dealings with the legal **estate**. This covenant is of great concern for business lessors. The reason for this is that a business lessor will want to know who is in occupation of the property, and in particular that the financial strength of the person or company in occupation is such that the rents required by the lease will be paid. As a consequence, the lessor will seek to validate intending lessees to try to be sure that they will be able to pay the rents. Once the lessor has approved the status of the incoming lessee, the lessor will normally require the proposed **assignee** to enter into a **deed** of licence. This will incorporate direct covenants between the lessor and assignee requiring the assignee to comply with the lease terms for the residue of the term of the lease. This is now subject to the terms of the Landlord and Tenant (Covenants) Act 1995.

There is no restriction against alienation unless there is express provision to that effect in the lease. Many commercial leases include a covenant whereby the lessee cannot assign the lease without the prior written consent of the lessor, such consent usually not to be unreasonably withheld. This is known as a fully qualified covenant. Some leases extend this provision to include sub-lettings and assignments. If the lease states that the lessor's consent is required but does not refer to reasonableness, then statute adds this qualification (s19(1)(a) Landlord and Tenant Act 1927) (the Court of Appeal issued guidelines on what amounts to reasonableness in the context of s19 in *International Drilling Fluids Ltd v Louisville Investments (Uxbridge) Ltd* [1986] Ch 513, and see later). However, if the lease includes an absolute prohibition, then the lessee simply cannot assign the lease and must remain in the premises for the residue of the term. Section 19(1A) of the Landlord and Tenant Act 1927 (introduced by s22 Landlord and Tenant (Covenants) Act 1995) allows the parties to a lease to agree conditions or circumstances that must be satisfied before the lessor will give consent. Section 19(1)(a) only relates to qualified covenants against assigning, namely not sub-letting or charging. If the lease requires the lessee to offer a surrender of the lease back to the lessor prior to seeking an assignment, that provision is unenforceable (see *Allnatt London Properties Ltd v Newton* [1984] 1 All ER 423) unless the provision is covered under s38 of the Landlord and Tenant Act 1954.

15.10 Alienation of part

Many modern business leases will include an absolute covenant against dealing with part of the subject premises. There are two good reasons for including such a provision. First, good estate management practice dictates that the fewer lessees there are in a block, the easier it is to manage the building as a whole. However, the second reason is far more compelling. Under the Landlord and Tenant Act 1954, business lessees in occupation at the end of a commercial lease are entitled by statute to renew their lease (see **Chapter 17**). If there have been sub-lettings of parts, the lessor is required by statute to issue new leases to all the sub-lessees in occupation and not to the original lessee who became the sub-lessor but did not remain in occupation. In this way, the superior lessor could accidentally end up with several lessees where originally there was one.

EXAMPLE

Corina acts for Ullah Investments Ltd which is granting a five-year commercial lease of first-floor office premises in Hull to Zaheer. When drafting the lease, she will ensure that it includes a covenant by the lessee not to assign or underlet the whole of the office premises without the lessor's consent and also an absolute prohibition against the lessee assigning or underletting part of the demised premises.

CONDUCT POINT

Failure to include comprehensive lessee covenants when drafting a commercial lease on behalf of a commercial lessor may amount to a breach of the SRA Code of Conduct. You must act in the best interests of each client and you must provide a proper standard of service to your clients.

15.11 Covenants by the lessor

15.11.1 Quiet enjoyment

A typical express covenant could read:

> That the lessee paying all the rents reserved by this lease and performing and observing all the covenants contained herein shall peaceably hold and enjoy the demised premises without

any interruption by the lessor or any other company or person rightfully claiming under or in trust for the lessor.

The nature of the covenant is to confirm that the lessee can physically enjoy the complete benefit of the property without the lessor adversely affecting that enjoyment. It is the extent of the impact of the covenant that is open to interpretation. In *Owen v Gadd* [1956] 2 QB 99, where scaffolding was erected by the lessor outside a shop door and window and consequently affected the lessee's business, it was held that there had been a breach of covenant by the lessor.

15.11.2 **Insurance by lessor**

In modern commercial leases, it is common practice for the lessor to insure but for the lessee to covenant to reimburse the lessor for the insurance premium. This is almost always the arrangement that prevails where there are several commercial lettings in one building. This is a desirable arrangement as it will be cost-effective to have one policy covering the whole building and will avoid inconsistencies of insurance cover that might arise if there were to be a separate policy for each letting. Where the lessee reimburses the lessor, it would seem that the lessor is under no obligation to consider various insurers to find the cheapest premium (see *Havenridge Ltd v Boston Dyers Ltd* [1994] 2 EGLR 73). The insured risks should be carefully defined and should clearly include damage caused by fire, storm, flooding, subsidence, burst pipes, riot and other usual risks covered by standard buildings insurance policies. However, the risk of damage from acts of terrorism may need separate specific cover, and this should be precisely stated in the lease insurance provisions.

15.12 **Forfeiture**

All commercial leases should include a clause enabling the lessor to re-enter the subject property and terminate the lease term as a consequence of a breach of covenant by the lessee, or of the happening of a specified occurrence. The usual reasons stipulated in such a clause, giving rise to the right to forfeiture, include non-payment of rent, breach of another lease covenant and the lessee's liquidation or bankruptcy. Each of these is considered shortly.

If the lessor wishes to forfeit, this can be achieved in two different ways. First, the lessor may commence court proceedings for forfeiture and seek an order for possession of the subject premises. Secondly, the lessor can simply peaceably re-enter the premises and thereby physically retake possession. This second, apparently simple, alternative is not without its problems. Statute imposes some quite substantial restrictions on this remedy. When proceeding to forfeit a commercial lease, the lessor should be careful not to demand or accept rent from the lessee as in law this may constitute a waiver of the lessor's right to forfeit on the grounds that the lessor is thereby acknowledging the continued existence of the lease.

15.12.1 **For non-payment of rent**

In the absence of an express provision to the contrary, the lessor must make a formal demand for the rent. Most leases will include such an express provision requiring the lessee to pay the rent usually within 14 or 21 days of the payment date (one of the quarter days), whether the rent is formally demanded or not. In the absence of payment, the lessor may either commence proceedings or peaceably re-enter. The lessee may be entitled to relief from forfeiture. The lessee can apply to court for this form of relief and, if the rent arrears and costs are discharged before the court hearing for forfeiture, the lessee will be so entitled. In certain circumstances, the lessee can seek relief at any time during a period of up to six months from the making of the order for forfeiture or from when the lessor peaceably re-entered. See s210 of the Common Law Procedure Act 1852 for High Court actions and s138 of the County Courts Act 1984 for county court proceedings and for peaceable re-entry cases.

15.12.2 For breach of another lease covenant

This area is regulated by the provisions of s146 of the Law of Property Act 1925. Usually, no enforcement steps can be taken without a notice being prepared based on these statutory requirements and served upon the lessee. The notice must:

- specify the particular breach complained of;
- if the breach is capable of remedy, require the lessee to remedy the breach; and
- require the lessee to make compensation in money for the breach.

If there is non-compliance with the notice, the lessor can peaceably re-enter or obtain possession by way of a court order. The lessee can nevertheless still seek relief from forfeiture. If there has been peaceable re-entry, the relief is available even after re-entry (see *Billson v Residential Apartments Ltd* [1992] 1 AC 494). If there is a court order and the lessor has re-entered, the right to relief is no longer available to the lessee. Relief is granted on such terms as the court thinks fit (s146(2) Law of Property Act 1925). If the breach complained of involves a repairing covenant, the s146 notice may also involve the terms of the Leasehold Property (Repairs) Act 1938. If the covenant is contained in a lease for a term of at least seven years and at the date of the service of the notice there are at least three years of that term left to run, the 1938 Act will apply. In these circumstances, the s146 notice must include explicit reference to the lessee's additional right to serve a counter-notice in writing within 28 days of the receipt of the s146 notice, claiming the benefit of the Act (s1(2) Leasehold Property Repairs Act 1938). If a valid counter-notice is served, the lessor cannot take proceedings to enforce any right of re-entry or forfeiture for the continuing breach without leave of the court. Indeed, the courts have proved to be reluctant to grant such an order except in cases of substantial breach by the lessee. The Commonhold and Leasehold Reform Act 2002 also prohibits the commencement of forfeiture proceedings for breaches other than for rent unless a court or the First-tier Tribunal (Property Chamber; Residential Property) has determined that a breach has occurred.

15.12.3 Liquidation or bankruptcy

Common sense dictates that an insolvent lessee is unlikely to be able to comply with lease covenants and it is probable that the covenant to pay rent is going to be breached sooner rather than later. This being so, most modern commercial leases will include the right to re-enter on the lessee being declared bankrupt or, if a company, being put into liquidation. The right is usually expressed to arise on the appointment of a receiver, a liquidator or company **administrator**. The right to forfeit must be express as none is implied and without such a clause the fact of the lessee's bankruptcy will not automatically put an end to the lease term. The lessor must serve a s146 notice in most cases but not where the lessee was a publican or the lease is of agricultural land (s146(9) Law of Property Act 1925). The bankrupt lessee, if seeking relief, must take steps to do so within the first year following the bankruptcy, failing which the right to relief is lost.

15.12.4 Forfeiture and the Commonhold and Leasehold Reform Act 2002

This Act introduced a new requirement that ground rent will not be payable unless it has been demanded. The demand is to be made by giving the tenant a prescribed notice. The reforms in the Act prevent the application of any provisions of a lease relating to late payment or non-payment (eg additional **charges** such as interest) if the rent is paid within 30 days of the demand being issued. The Act also introduces additional restrictions on the commencement of forfeiture proceedings for breaches of covenants or conditions of a lease. It prohibits the commencement of forfeiture proceedings, including the issue of a notice under s146 of the Law of Property Act 1925, in respect of non-payment of service or administration charges. This is not the case if the charge has been agreed or admitted by the tenant or a court or the First-tier Tribunal (Property Chamber), formerly the Leasehold Valuation Tribunal, has determined that it is reasonable and due. The Act also prohibits the commencement of forfeiture proceedings for other breaches unless a court or the First-tier Tribunal (Property Chamber) has determined that a breach has occurred.

As well as forfeiture, you should, of course, be aware of other remedies available for breach of covenant, such as Commercial Rent Arrears Recovery, specific performance and damages. There may also be the possibility of pursuing a guarantor who has guaranteed the liabilities of the lessee or forfeiting a rent deposit given by the lessee. Self-help by the lessor may be another option for breach of a lessee's repairing obligation under the principle in *Jervis v Harris* [1996] 1All ER 303, CA (see **14.2.2**).

EXAMPLE

Hassan, a business lessee in occupation of a factory building in Swansea, is in breach of his repairing covenant and the lessor wishes to forfeit the lease. Rent has been paid up to date. As this is a covenant other than non-payment of rent, the lessor must first serve a s146 notice on Hassan specifying the particular failure to repair, requiring the lessee to remedy the breach and requiring Hassan to make compensation in money for the breach. If there is non-compliance with the notice, the lessor may then proceed to obtain possession of the premises by way of a court order. The lessor should immediately stop demanding or accepting rent to avoid inadvertently waiving its right to forfeit.

15.13 Commercial leases: Code of Practice

The Code for Leasing Business Premises in England and Wales 2019 (the Code) is the result of collaboration between commercial property professionals and industry bodies representing both lessors and lessees. The objective of the Code is to improve the quality and fairness of initial negotiations on lease terms and to promote the issue of comprehensive heads of terms that should make the legal drafting process more efficient. The government-supported Code and the accompanying template heads of terms should be used as a checklist for negotiations before the grant of a new lease and at the time of any lease renewal. The full text of the Code can be accessed from the website of the Royal Institution of Chartered Surveyors.

KEY POINT SUMMARY

- If the commercial lease is to be registered, do you need to consider applying for an EID to protect sensitive detail?
- If you are drafting a new commercial lease incorporating a rent review mechanism, make sure that on review the rent cannot be reduced below the rental level that prevailed prior to the date of review. Furthermore, avoid strict time limits that make time of the essence for the review procedure.
- If you are involved with an application for licence to assign, remember that the terms of the Landlord and Tenant Act 1988 require the application to be dealt with within a reasonable time, failing which the lessee could be entitled to a claim for damages arising from any undue delay.
- In relation to user clauses, there is no statutory provision that implies that the lessor's consent cannot be unreasonably withheld, as is the case with alienation covenants. However, if there is an absolute or simple qualified covenant against changes of user it can have a deflating effect on any rental value on review. The covenant should be fully qualified, namely 'Not without the lessor's consent such consent not to be unreasonably withheld.'
- If you are acting for a lessor seeking to forfeit, you should advise the client about the potential dangers of waiver. If the lessor is seeking to forfeit and then demands and/or accepts rent, the courts will infer a waiver of the right to forfeit.
- As well as forfeiture, consider other lessor's remedies.

CHAPTER 16
Commercial Freeholds and Key Elements of Tax Law

FUNCTIONING LEGAL KNOWLEDGE

This chapter covers the following functioning legal knowledge required to pass the SQE 1 assessments:

Key conditions contained in the Standard Commercial Property Conditions
Commercial freehold pre-contract enquiries

Value added tax:

- Basis of charge
- What constitutes a taxable supply
- Differences between standard, exempt and zero-rated supplies
- Reasons why a client would make an option to tax and the effect that has.

Stamp duty land tax and land transaction tax:

- Basis of charge in both England and Wales for non-residential freehold property

AUTHORITIES UNDERPINNING PRACTICE

The key authorities that underpin this area of practice are listed below. Note that for legislation you are linked to legislation.gov.uk.

Although much of the legislation on this government website is available in its amended form, the incorporation of new amendments into the text of legislation can be delayed. You should refer to legal databases to ensure you are referencing the most up-to-date legislation.

- Part II of the Landlord and Tenant Act 1954
  https://www.legislation.gov.uk/uksi/1983/133/contents/made
- Section 4 of the Law of Property (Miscellaneous Provisions) Act 1994
  https://www.legislation.gov.uk/ukpga/1994/36/contents
- Landlord and Tenant (Covenants) Act 1995
  https://www.legislation.gov.uk/ukpga/1995/30/contents
- Section 3 of the Landlord and Tenant Act 1985
  https://www.legislation.gov.uk/ukpga/1985/70/contents
- Section 48 of the Landlord and Tenant Act 1987
  https://www.legislation.gov.uk/ukpga/1987/31/contents
- Value Added Tax Act 1994
  https://www.legislation.gov.uk/ukpga/1994/23/contents
- Finance Act 2003
  https://www.legislation.gov.uk/ukpga/2003/14/contents
- Stamp Duty Land Tax Act 2015
  https://www.legislation.gov.uk/ukpga/2015/1/contents

- Land Transaction Tax and Anti-avoidance of Devolved Taxes (Wales) Act 2017
  https://www.legislation.gov.uk/anaw/2017/1/contents
- The Economic Crime (Transparency and Enforcement) Act 2022
  https://www.legislation.gov.uk/ukpga/2022/10/contents/enacted

16.1 Introduction

There is a considerable commercial market in the sale and purchase of freehold properties that are subject to the occupation of **lessees** with statutory security of tenure. This is particularly so in relation to property occupied by business tenants, but many of the special factors required in transactions involving commercial property will apply also to properties sold with residential tenants. Commercial conveyancing services support the market in and for commercial property. Buying and selling tenanted properties will feature strongly in the work of a commercial conveyancer and, as such, a basic understanding of some key elements of tax law will also be required. These topics are all covered in this chapter.

16.2 The Standard Commercial Property Conditions

The Standard Commercial Property Conditions (SCPCs) were issued on 17 May 1999 for use in commercial transactions. A second edition was issued in June 2004 and a third edition in May 2017. A 2018 revision has also been issued. As we have seen, in simple residential transactions the pre-printed contractual Standard Conditions of Sale (5th edn) are almost universally used by conveyancing practitioners. However, if a commercial element in a proposed agreement is more complicated, and in particular if there is a lessee in occupation as a commercial tenant, then the SCPCs are likely to be more appropriate.

The SCPCs are divided into two parts. Part 1 contains general conditions building on those in the first and second editions, while Part 2 contains new clauses, in particular detailed provisions covering VAT, transfers of a going concern, capital allowances and reversionary interests in flats. As such, the emphasis is clearly on more complex commercial transactions. In general Part 1 applies, unless expressly excluded, while Part 2 will only apply if expressly incorporated. Completing tick boxes on the back page of the agreement effects express incorporation: see SCPC 1.1.4(a) and (b).

Both sets of conditions have a front page that allows practitioners to insert basic yet vital details for the agreement such as details of the seller, the buyer, the property, **title** information and specified encumbrances (by SCPC 4.1.2(a) the seller sells subject to **encumbrances** specified in the contract, ie on the front page). The front page on the second edition of the SCPCs allowed for the sale of chattels to be included in the purchase price. This is no longer the case in the third edition so chattels must be dealt with under the special conditions if they are to form part of the contract. On the penultimate page there are special conditions that can be included in the contract by utilising selections from tick boxes. So, there is a special condition (4), that will provide for vacant possession or for a sale subject to listed tenancies. Another special condition (5), provides for contents or chattels to be included in the sale or to be sold separately. There are also conditions varying methods of payment and times for completion (6 and 7). Special condition 8 can be used in sales of part to stipulate a form of transfer that includes express terms such as **covenants** or rights and **reservations**. Finally, there is a special condition on the back page that has tick boxes enabling the specific incorporation of Part 2 conditions, for example conditions covering VAT, capital allowances and reversionary interests in flats.

CONDUCT POINT

Be very careful about how you draft a commercial sale contract for your client. Failure to do so properly and in the light of your client's instructions could amount to a breach of the SRA Code of Conduct. You must act in the best interests of each client and you must provide a proper standard of service to your clients.

16.2.1 Part 1: conditions

Part 1 contains general conditions building on those in the first and second editions. It is of interest that there is no mention on the front page of the SCPCs of title guarantee. There is such a provision in SCPC 7.6.2, but this is subject to any encumbrances affecting the subject property and covered by SCPC 4.1.2. Most, if not all, conveyancing practitioners will be familiar with the Standard Conditions as they are used in the vast majority of domestic conveyancing transactions. The SCPCs may not be so familiar. Consequently, the following section is an examination of some of the more important features of the SCPCs.

16.2.2 Condition 1: general

In this section in the second edition there was a definition for 'direct credit'. The effect of this was that payments at exchange and completion could not be made by banker's draft and could only be made by bank telegraphic CHAPS payment transfers. The purpose of this inclusion was to take account of the general commercial practice of requiring completely cleared funds at exchange or completion. In the third edition there is no such definition but at SCPC 9.7 it states that 'The buyer is to pay the money on completion by electronic means in same-day cleared funds from an account held in the name of a conveyancer . . .'. The SCPCs define when a party is ready, able and willing to complete, namely when they might be able to serve on the other party who is not so ready a **notice to complete** (such a notice is also defined as a notice requiring completion of the contract in accordance with SCPC 9). A party is so ready if it would complete but for the default of the other party: see SCPC 1.1.3.

Following the Bank of England's takeover of the Clearing House Automated Payment System (CHAPS), and its impact on the definition of 'clearing bank' in the Standard Conditions of Sale and Standard Commercial Property Conditions, revisions to these conditions have been settled. The new wording is:

> 'clearing bank' means a bank admitted by the Bank of England as a direct participant in its CHAPS system.

Since this is the only change being made to the current editions, the forms will now be known as:

- the Standard Conditions of Sale (5th edn, 2018 revision)
- Standard Commercial Property Conditions (3rd edn, 2018 revision).

SCPC 1.4.1 prohibits the transfer of the benefit of the contract. Practitioners should also be aware that SCPC 1.4.2 is a total prohibition against sub-sales in whole or in part. The buyer must be named as the transferee in the **purchase deed**, and no other party can be mentioned unless they are a named party in the agreement. This section is therefore close to the terms of the Standard Conditions and is there to ensure that the named buyer and only the named buyer completes with the seller.

SCPC 1.3 recognises the use of email to deliver and serve a notice (as well as by fax). If the recipient's email is stated in the contract (on the back page within the section for details of the seller's and buyer's conveyancers), then adding the email address authorises service by email (see SCPC 1.3.3(b)). An email is treated as being received one hour after despatch (see SCPC 1.3.7(e)).

16.2.3 Condition 2: VAT standard-rated supply

Under this condition the seller warrants that the sale will constitute a supply chargeable to VAT at the standard rate. So if the sale is not a taxable supply, then Condition A1 in Part 2 should be expressly incorporated into the agreement to confirm this VAT status.

16.2.4 Condition 3: formation

As to the date of the formation of the agreement, the terms cover the moment of exchange, namely it will be at the time of posting or at the time of deposit in the DX or by some other procedure agreed between the parties. SCPC 3.2 regarding the **deposit** states that the deposit (at 10 per cent) except by auction sale is to be paid by the buyer by electronic means in same-day cleared funds from an account held in the name of a conveyancer. In contrast to domestic **conveyances**, most transactions where the parties are selling and/or buying tenanted properties are unlikely to be part of a chain of transactions. Consequently, the deposit is paid to the seller's solicitor as stakeholder and is to be released to the seller on completion with accrued interest. However, where there is an auction sale, the deposit is to be held by the auctioneer as agent for the seller thus enabling the seller to get hold of the deposit prior to completion. Furthermore, if there is a deposit paid at an auction sale by cheque and all or any part of the payment is dishonoured on first presentation, then the seller has an option to terminate on dishonour. The seller does not need to represent the cheque as the provision talks of first presentation and can simply give notice to the buyer that the contract has been discharged by the buyer's breach.

16.2.5 Condition 4: matters affecting the property

SCPC 4.1.2(d) has been written to put the burden on the buyer to carry out all searches and enquiries that a prudent buyer would make before entering into a contract of this type. In essence, the property is sold subject to all matters that would be disclosed, such as a **local authority search** save for monetary **charges**. The SCPCs now also state that the encumbrances affecting the subject property are either specified in the contract, discoverable on inspection or disclosable in searches or enquiries. The SCPCs also state that a leasehold property is sold subject to any subsisting breach of covenant regarding the condition of the property.

16.2.6 Condition 5: occupational leases

Condition 5 covers **leases** and applies if any part of the property is sold subject to a lease (and a lease is defined as including a **sub-lease**, **tenancy** and agreement for a lease or sub-lease). SCPCs 5.1.3 and 5.1.4 state that the seller is not to serve a notice to end the lease or accept surrender, and is to inform the buyer without delay if the lease ends. These elements are included in the SCPCs to prevent the seller from taking unilateral action that might adversely affect the value of the premises by ensuring that after exchange and before completion the seller cannot force the tenant out of the subject property or take steps towards ejecting the tenant. SCPC 5.2 is a major leasehold condition by seeking to cover property management for the period between exchange and completion. It sets out extensive provisions for the conduct of litigation proceedings affecting leasehold premises in court or by arbitration. (However, you should note that this does not cover rent review matters that are covered by Condition 6: see next.) Furthermore, the seller is not to grant or formally withhold any **licence** consent or approval required by the terms of the occupational lease. This means that once contracts are exchanged the seller must always seek the buyer's permission in relation to any matters that arise from the lease terms and that need the consent or involvement of the **lessor**. However, SCPC 5.2.7 provides that the buyer is not to withhold consent so as to place the seller in breach of a statutory duty or of an obligation to the lessee. Therefore, if the circumstances are such that the lessor should grant a **licence to assign** and by refusing would be in breach of a statutory duty, the buyer cannot dictate that the seller adopt this stance. SCPC 5.2.9 requires the seller to manage the property in accordance with the principles of good estate management until completion. Quite whether parties to a contract in dispute can agree as to what might amount to good estate management is open to debate.

16.2.7 Condition 6: rent reviews

This was a wholly new condition included in the second edition and continues in the third edition. The purpose of the condition is to explicitly cover rent review matters that will arise between exchange and completion. SCPC 6.1.4.4 imposes on both seller and buyer an obligation to cooperate promptly and effectively regarding the process of the rent review and the documentation required to facilitate the review process. Most importantly, neither can approve a rent without the written approval of the other (SCPC 6.1.5). The condition also covers how the cost of the rent review should be paid as between the seller and the buyer, for example SCPC 6.1.6 states that the seller and the buyer are to bear their own costs of the rent review process. More detailed time-related provisions follow relating to the payment of costs (see SCPCs 6.1.7 and 6.1.8).

SCPC 6.2 is a new condition that applies where the seller is the lessor of a tenancy where it is continuing under Part II of the Landlord and Tenant Act 1954 but no agreement has been reached on an **interim rent** or on the termination of the tenancy or the terms of the new tenancy. In this situation, the seller remains responsible for negotiations but the parties to the contract must consult and cooperate between exchange and completion.

16.2.8 **Condition 7: title and transfer**

Conditions 7.1–7.4 are the same in both sets of conditions (requirements for both registered and unregistered titles are set out in 7.1.2). However, SCPC 7.6.5 has been drafted so that where the seller will, after completion, be bound by an obligation affecting the property, then, provided the obligation is disclosed to the buyer before exchange, the seller is entitled to an indemnity from the buyer. There must be disclosure, failing which there is no binding obligation to afford any such indemnity.

If the property is registered, there may be exempt information documents (EIDs) such that they may not be disclosed on or with the **official copies of the registers**. Accordingly, where there are any such EIDs, the buyer should make sure that the seller is obliged by a contractual term to provide the buyer with full copies. As a precautionary measure, it may be appropriate to include this in all contracts (EIDs are discussed in detail at **15.2.1** regarding **commercial leases**).

SCPC 7.6.4 is a new condition. It comes into operation when the subject property is leasehold and requires the leasehold property transfer **deed** to state that the covenants implied by s4 of the Law of Property (Miscellaneous Provisions) Act 1994 will not extend to a breach of the lessee's covenants in the lease that relate to the physical state of the subject property.

16.2.9 **Condition 8: risk and insurance**

This clause expressly states that the subject property is at the buyer's risk from the date of the agreement. SCPC 8.2.2 describes the seller's obligations about insurance in the situation where the seller is required by SCPC 8.2.1 to keep the subject property insured between exchange and completion. SCPC 8.2.5 is new and covers the situation where the leasehold property insurance is maintained by the reversioner. In this situation, the seller must use reasonable efforts to ensure that the insurance is maintained from exchange to completion. If after exchange and before completion the property is damaged by an insured risk, the seller is obliged to pay to the buyer on completion the amount of the policy monies received by the seller. If no final insurance payment has been made, then the seller is to assign to the buyer all rights to monies under the insurance policy and to hold any monies received in trust for the buyer.

16.2.10 **Condition 9: completion**

In this section, being the condition regulating all matters at completion, the buyer instead of the seller is assumed to own the property from the start of the **completion date**. The completion date will be the actual date of completion where the whole property is sold with vacant possession, otherwise it is the date specified in the agreement. This clearly affects apportionments (see SCPC 9.3.3). These are further regulated at SCPC 9.3.4 where the detailed arrangements required for completion date apportionments are set out. Sums are to be treated as accruing from day to day throughout the period for which payment is or has to be made and at the rate applicable for that period. The SCPCs also cover unquantified sums such as final year-end **service charges** (see SCPC 9.3.5). These are to be payable with interest on late payment, but because of the larger amounts involved in commercial property it would be safer to set up an agreed retention with the buyer's solicitor by way of the special conditions. Alternatively, the seller's solicitor could retain the monies in a designated client deposit account pending settlement, with the interest accruing to the seller in any event. This provision should also be covered by way of a special condition in the agreement.

SCPC 9.3.6 applies where a lease affects the property being sold and there is a service charge. On completion, the buyer is to pay to the seller any element of the service charge incurred by the seller but not yet due from the tenant. In the light of this provision, it is vital that practitioners acting for a buyer in these circumstances raise detailed enquiries about any such expenditure. It is therefore important that proof of payment be produced along with proof that it was necessarily incurred and repayable under the terms and conditions of the lease. This is required to avoid subsequent problems with the lessee in obtaining reimbursement, and is covered by SCPC 9.3.6(a).

SCPCs 9.3.7 and 9.3.8 both seek to cover the position where there are arrears. The terms of these clauses are complicated and should be considered in detail for each subject property and amended as necessary. SCPC 9.3.7 states that SCPC 9.3.8 applies if there are arrears, there is no contractual **assignment** to the seller of the right to collect those arrears and the seller is not entitled to recover any arrears from the tenant. In these circumstances, SCPC 9.3.8 requires the buyer to seek to collect all the arrears in the ordinary course of management but is not obliged to commence court proceedings for their recovery or exercise the commercial rent arrears recovery (CRAR) procedure. Any monies received are to be apportioned between the parties in the ratio of the sums owed to each. Leases granted post-1995 are covered by s3 and s23 of the Landlord and Tenant (Covenants) Act 1995 to the extent that unless specifically assigned to the buyer, the right to collect arrears remains with the seller. This is relevant in the context of these SCPCs, and the conditions required activate SCPC 9.3.8. It also means that pre-1996 leases are such that the seller will not be able to recover arrears by commencing proceedings or instructing bailiffs after completion (see s141 Law of Property Act 1925).

Finally in this section, SCPC 9.5 says that as soon as the buyer has performed all its obligations on completion the seller must part with the title documents. SCPC 9.7 requires payment to be by electronic means in same-day cleared funds from an account held in the name of a conveyancer. SCPC 9.8 states that at any time on or after the completion date a party who is ready, able and willing to complete may give to the other a notice to complete. Ten working days is the notice period excluding the day on which the notice is given. For this purpose, **time is of the essence**: see SCPC 9.8.2.

16.2.11 Condition 10: remedies

Little of this particular condition is changed from the Standard Conditions to the SCPCs, although there is one alteration of consequence for buyers. It should be noted that SCPC 10.3.1 provides that liability for interest arises only on the default of the buyer. If the seller defaults and delays completion in the absence of a special condition, all that a buyer can do is sue the defaulting seller for damages. Moreover, SCPC 10.3.4 states that if completion is delayed the seller may give notice to the buyer that it will take the net income from the subject property until completion takes place together with any interest due pursuant to SCPC 10.3.1.

16.2.12 Condition 11: leasehold property

As one might expect for a set of conditions designed to cover commercial transactions and especially those dealing with the selling and buying of tenanted properties, this section contains substantial provisions. There are detailed alterations from the terms of the Standard Conditions where leases are concerned and particularly in relation to the normal requirement to obtain the consent of the lessor in a commercial lease assignment or transfer.

Dealing first with new leases (ie a contract for the grant of a new lease), SCPC 11.2 reiterates the provisions of the Standard Conditions as to definitions and under the SCPCs the lease is to be in the form of a draft attached to the agreement itself. Accordingly, it is contemplated that new leases will be part of the actual agreement by attachment. If the lease term exceeds seven years, the seller is to **deduce title** to enable the buyer to register with absolute title. This means that a lessor will have to show the lessee its superior title. To avoid this disclosure, lessors should only grant seven-year leases or shorter.

SCPC 11.3 deals with the landlord's consent and has been substantially retained in the same format as that which appeared in the previous edition of the conditions. For example, SCPC 11.3.3(b) states that the seller is to enter into an **authorised guarantee agreement** (AGA). An

AGA is where the seller (the outgoing tenant) guarantees the liabilities of the buyer (the incoming tenant) under the lease. Similarly, the buyer is to use reasonable endeavours to provide guarantees of the performance and observance of the tenant's covenants and the conditions in the seller's lease. SCPC 11.3.1(b) defines consent as 'consent in a form that satisfies the requirement to obtain it'. Completion can now be postponed if there is a delay in obtaining the consent of the lessor (SCPCs 11.3.4 and 11.3.5). Completion can be postponed until five working days after either the seller notifies the buyer that consent has been given or a court has declared that consent has been unreasonably withheld. (The previous edition set a time limit of four months from completion but this is no longer the case in the third edition.)

16.2.13 **Commonhold**

In previous editions there were conditions covering commonhold. These have been removed because commonhold is rarely, if ever, used.

16.2.14 **Condition 12: contents**

Previously this was entitled 'chattels' but now has the modern title of contents. It should be noted that in SCPC 12.4, it now provides that ownership of any contents covered by the agreement passes to the buyer at completion, but that the contents are at the buyer's risk from exchange. This reflects the provision in the SCPCs relating to the insurance risk for the subject property, where the risk also passes at the contract date. The reverse is the case for both the subject property and the contents in the Standard Conditions (SC 10.4 states that ownership of the contents passes to the buyer on actual completion).

16.2.15 **Part 2: conditions**

Part 2 contains clauses and detailed provisions covering VAT, a transfer of a going concern, capital allowances and reversionary interests in flats. There is nothing in the Standard Conditions that matches them. The main details of these four provisions are:

- *VAT.* Under SCPC2, the seller warrants that the sale will constitute a supply chargeable to VAT at the standard rate. So if the sale is not a taxable supply, then Condition A1 in Part 2 should be expressly incorporated into the agreement to confirm this VAT status. A1 states that the sale does constitute a supply that is taxable for VAT purposes.
- *A transfer of a going concern.* Condition A2 covers a transfer of a going concern. In this case, the seller warrants that it is using the property for the business of letting to produce a rental income.
- *Capital allowances.* Condition B supports a buyer in any claims it may make pursuant to the terms of the Capital Allowances Act 2001. In doing so, it requires the seller to provide copies of relevant information and cooperation and assistance, as the buyer may reasonably require. You should be aware that in the 2007 budget the (then) Chancellor announced that on plant and machinery from 2008/9 the capital allowance would be reduced from 25 to 20 per cent. Furthermore, on industrial and agricultural buildings the Chancellor announced the abolition of the buildings allowance but phased over a four-year period. It is clear that capital allowances are to be reduced or abolished altogether. Accordingly, capital allowances until April 2011 were available for certain sorts of capital expenditure on agricultural and industrial buildings, but after that date they were withdrawn. The conditions have also been changed to take into account changes that came into force in April 2014 regarding claims for capital allowances for expenditure on plant and machinery that are fixtures.
- *Reversionary interests in flats.* C1 covers the provisions of the Landlord and Tenant Act 1987 and the tenants' rights of pre-emption on a sale. The condition requires the seller to warrant that on the facts the tenants do not have any rights arising from this statute, namely the relevant notice has been served but no response was forthcoming. Condition C2 covers the position where the tenants are entitled to a right of first refusal in auction sales.

EXAMPLE

Lionel and his family have run a successful wholesale clothing business for many years. Lionel has decided to sell the business and invest in commercial property. He has formed a company called Ezra Holdings Ltd in which he, his wife and their three sons are all shareholders. Subject to contract, Ezra Holdings Ltd has agreed to buy the freehold of 18 Minchin Street, London W2 for £700,000 subject to and with the benefit of two occupational **business leases**. The premises were built in the 1950s. A **mortgage** offer has been received by the client to assist in the acquisition.

Some key issues to consider when taking instructions and giving advice to the client:

- The draft contract should incorporate the Standard Commercial Conditions of Sale.
- Consider carefully the terms of the mortgage offer. Will the directors of the company be asked to stand as guarantors? If so, they will need to be separately advised (professional conduct point). Is any other collateral security required for the loan, such as assignment of life policies?
- As it is a commercial mortgage, the lender is likely to be separately represented by another firm of solicitors. If so, additional costs will be incurred.
- Consider the client's financial circumstances generally and be satisfied that the client can adequately fund the purchase and all associated costs including stamp duty land tax. How will the deposit payable on **exchange of contracts** be financed?
- Occupational leases of the property. Ask for copies of the leases at an early stage and consider and advise the client on their terms. In particular, are the leases in a form that would be satisfactory to an institutional investor? Two important considerations that could affect the value of the freehold **reversion** are:
- Is the lessor entitled to a clear rent with upward only rent reviews?
- Do the leases impose full repairing and insuring obligations on the lessee?
- Examine replies to the Commercial Property Standard Enquiries (see **16.3**) and consider how the two commercial leases are affected or regulated by legislation, for example possible renewals under Part II of the Landlord and Tenant Act 1954.
- **Survey**. Given the high value of the property and its age, your client should be advised to take out a full structural survey.
- Advise generally on client care, costs and your firm's complaints procedure.
- Money Laundering Regulations. As Ezra Holdings Ltd is a newly formed company you will need to verify the beneficial ownership of the company and the identity of the shareholders.
- Include in the initial letter to the client your firm's terms and conditions of business together with an estimate of your conveyancing charges and stamp duty land tax.

16.3 Commercial freehold properties that are tenanted: the buyer's perspective

16.3.1 Additional commercial enquiries

In addition to the standard enquiries that are always raised, and the additional enquiries already mentioned, it is appropriate to make further enquiries in relation to commercial lettings insofar as they may be affected or regulated by legislation. In essence, a buyer will want to know how far, if at all, the lease is influenced by Part II of the Landlord and Tenant Act 1954. A buyer will want to know if there has been a court application (as if there is no clause to that effect in the lease, the contracting out will be to no effect) and, if so, will want to see what order the court made. If the lease has been recently renewed under the terms of the Act, a prudent buyer will want details to ascertain how the length of the term eventually granted was settled, along with the other terms of the lease. Perhaps of more consequence would be to see the basis on which the rental was finally settled. Valuers' reports would be of use and copies should be requested. A buyer will also want to know if the lessor originally sought to oppose the grant of the lease and why. The ground for possession would be of material interest to the buyer, especially if it related to a breach of covenant or for arrears of rent. Detailed enquiries should be directed to the seller's practitioner seeking as much information as possible about the circumstances of any recent statutory renewal. If the lease was granted after 1 January 1996 on assignment, an AGA may be involved. Enquiries should be made of the terms of this agreement. If industrial premises are being purchased, detailed environmental and contamination enquiries must be made of the seller.

16.3.2 The Commercial Property Standard Enquiries

An attempt has been made to draft some standard enquiries for commercial properties. The outcome of this effort is the Commercial Property Standard Enquiries (CPSEs).

Details of the CPSEs can be found at uk.practicallaw.com. The enquiries in the CPSEs are intended as a standard minimum for use in any commercial property transaction.

CPSE.1 is designed to cover all commercial property transactions and will (together with any additional enquiries relevant to the particular transaction) be sufficient if the transaction deals only with a freehold sold with vacant possession. Recent updates have been made to include enquiries relating to concealment of planning breaches, assets of community value and the Community Infrastructure Levy. The following supplemental enquiries are intended to be used in conjunction with CPSE.1. Which particular additional form or forms will be required will depend upon the individual circumstances of each transaction. The following supplemental forms are available:

- CPSE.2: where the property is sold subject to existing tenancies;
- CPSE.3: where a lease of a property is being granted;
- CPSE.4: where the property being sold is leasehold (ie the lease is being assigned or transferred);
- CPSE.5: enquiries before surrender of a rack rent commercial lease;
- CPSE.6: supplemental pre-contract enquiries for property subject to residential tenancies;
- CRC enquiries: these new enquiries are necessary to deal with issues arising under the Carbon Reduction Commitment Energy Efficiency Scheme 2010 (CRC). The CRC is a mandatory carbon emissions reporting and pricing scheme that may affect commercial property companies. The CRC came into force in April 2010 and aims to reduce significantly UK carbon emissions not covered by other pieces of legislation; and
- CPSE.7: general short-form pre-contract enquiries for all property transactions. Because the enquiries can be lengthy, they may not suit all transactions. Accordingly, a short-form set has been issued as CPSE 7. This form is not suitable for the purchase of development sites or transactions involving investment property subject to multiple tenancies or in other complex commercial transactions. CPSE.7 omits some of the questions raised in CPSE.1 (eg those relating to employees and commonhold) and simplifies many others (eg the Community Infrastructure Levy, stamp duty land tax (SDLT) and other tax questions).

16.3.3 Completion matters

On completion, the seller must hand over not merely the reversionary title deeds and documents, but also the lease(s) or tenancy agreement(s), as well as rental authorities. These authorities should be completed in letter format and signed by the seller and addressed to the lessees authorising them to pay all future rents to the buyer or as the buyer directs (standard pre-printed requisitions normally include a request that such authorities be made available on completion). Where the subject property constitutes a dwelling, s3 of the Landlord and Tenant Act 1985 compels the buyer to give written notice of the change of ownership to the lessee or tenant in occupation within two months of completion. Where a dwelling has been sold, s48 of the Landlord and Tenant Act 1987 compels the lessor buyer to provide the lessee in occupation with an address in England and Wales that can be used for the service of notices.

EXAMPLE

In the purchase of 18 Minchin Street, London, here is the likely format of a **completion statement** you will receive from the seller's solicitors showing apportionments of rent:

COMPLETION STATEMENT: 18 MINCHIN STREET LONDON W2
Allsop Property Company Ltd to Ezra Holdings Ltd

Purchase price		£700,000.00
DEDUCT deposit paid		
on exchange	£70,000.00	
		£630,000.00
DEDUCT rent by Webmaster Communications Limited from 30/08 to 24/12 at	£29,095.89	
£90,000 p.a. (118 days)		
DEDUCT rent by Lifestyle Mortgage and Insurance Brokers Ltd from 30/08 to 24/12 at	£50,109.59	£79,205.48
£155,000 p.a. (118 days)		
TOTAL payable on completion		£556,794.52

16.4 **Commercial property and key elements of tax law**

In this section VAT is considered, as well as SDLT and other taxes insofar as they relate to commercial property transactions.

CONDUCT POINT

Be careful about how you advise on taxation issues. All conveyancing practitioners should be aware of the implications of the decision in *Hurlingham Estates Ltd v Wilde & Partners* (1997) 147 NLJ 453. Lightman J made it clear that a solicitor will be liable in negligence for adverse Revenue implications for a client that arise from a transaction effected by the solicitor, even though the solicitor was not expressly instructed to consider the Revenue implications. This is also true even if the solicitor assumed that the client had previously sought the advice of an accountant. The consequence of this decision is to make it quite clear that if a solicitor feels unable to cover the Revenue implications of a commercial transaction, they should explain to the client, at the commencement of instructions, that this is so and that the client should separately seek professional advice on the tax implications of the proposed transaction.

16.4.1 **VAT: an introduction**

Value added tax (VAT) is a tax that is in effect a tax on turnover. VAT payments could arise both in a commercial lease and in a commercial property purchase. HM Revenue and Customs (HMRC) deals with VAT, which is currently payable at 20 per cent on chargeable items. A chargeable item is called a 'supply'. In the context of commercial property, if a lease is granted there can be the supply of a lease by the lessor to the lessee. If a commercial property is to be sold, then there can be a supply of the subject property by the seller to the buyer. If a lease is assigned or transferred, there can be a supply of the residue of the term granted by the lease by the **assignor**/transferor to the **assignee**/transferee.

The general rule is that property transactions such as transfers, conveyances, assignments or the granting of leases can all be exempt supplies; that is, they do not attract a VAT charge. However, this can be reversed by written election (see shortly). On the face of it, conveyancing transactions are exempt. Nevertheless, some transactions can be compulsorily standard-rated (ie paying the full rate of tax), some are zero-rated (ie subject to VAT but at 0 per cent) and the taxpayer always has the option to elect to tax.

Parties can register as taxable persons who can pay and receive VAT. HMRC sets a threshold at which they are obliged so to register (of the value of taxable supplies, usually the business turnover figures). In the context of commercial transactions, the tax can be payable either on the price paid for a commercial property or on the rent payable by the terms of a commercial lease. Thus, if the rent is £100 the VAT (at 20 per cent) is added to it in the sum of £20, making £120 payable by the lessee.

Where a person or company is required to pay VAT on a purchase price or rent, they should receive an invoice (a VAT invoice) showing how much VAT has been charged. This amount of VAT is called 'input tax'. That person or company may also charge VAT to someone else; this is called 'output tax'. VAT is payable quarterly (being a 'prescribed accounting period' by s25(1) Value Added Tax Act 1994). The taxpayer can, when accounting to HMRC for the output tax received, deduct input tax paid. The net balance is then actually paid, and if input tax exceeds output tax the full amount is recoverable (see s25(3) 1994 Act).

The rate of VAT presently at 20 per cent is called the standard rate. There is another rate, called the zero rate, where there is a taxable supply but the rate of tax is zero. Otherwise a supply can be exempt, namely not subject to VAT at all. So, the sale of a greenfield site for development is exempt (but there is an option to tax, see later). The surrender of a lease is exempt as is the assignment of a lease (but again, in both cases there is an option to tax). However, the charges levied by a solicitor or other professional instructed in a commercial transaction will involve fees together with standard-rate VAT. Similarly, construction services for the building of a commercial development are standard-rated.

16.4.2 **VAT and leases generally**

If a commercial lease is granted, the rule is that it is generally exempt from VAT (ie there is an exempt supply), but it is nevertheless subject to the option to tax, namely to make the letting taxable. The option to tax arises when the lessor decides voluntarily to give up the exemption and to opt for VAT liability at the standard rate (see s89 Value Added Tax Act 1994). Notice of the election must be given to HMRC within 30 days of its being exercised, and best practice dictates the use of customs form VAT 1614. The building or premises concerned will thereafter be a taxable supply instead of an exempt supply. If it is a taxable supply, on a lease of the subject premises, VAT will be chargeable to the lessee. An election must be for the whole of the subject premises; an election in respect of part is not possible. This is also true for assignments and surrenders. It is in effect an option to waive the standard exemption. The lessor must be registered for VAT; and, if there is such a registration, written notice must be given to HMRC within 30 days of the election having been made. As it will be for the lessees to pay the VAT on their rent, it is vital that at the same time they are advised of the VAT election. This election is personal to the elector. This means that if there are sub-lessees, the sub-lessor must also elect for VAT to be payable on the sub-lessees' rents.

Electing to charge VAT will only suit a lessor who wishes to recover VAT. Careful consideration should be given to the effect of charging VAT on the rent as many prospective lessees will be put off taking the premises where they are not registered for VAT and cannot therefore recover the VAT themselves.

There should always be a covenant in all leases to require payment of VAT in addition to the rent. On the assumption that there is an existing lease and it is silent as to the payment of VAT, the lessee will nevertheless have to pay VAT on the rent should the lessor decide to opt to tax. However, there is one vital point to note where you are acting for a lessor who intends to grant a new lease and also intends to opt to tax. You must advise the lessor not to make the election before the grant of the new lease. If the election precedes the grant, HMRC will deem the new rent to be *inclusive* of VAT. This pitfall can be avoided by electing immediately *after* the grant of the lease but including in the lease a covenant requiring the lessee to pay any VAT on all the rents. Finally, bear in mind that HMRC views any rent-free period, or periods that are granted as an inducement to a new lessee, as subject to VAT. VAT will be payable on the unpaid rent.

If VAT is payable on a rent, it will also be payable on any service charge under the terms of the same lease by which the rent is paid. In both cases, the lessor can issue mere demands (and not VAT invoices), and when the rents and service charges are actually paid, receipted VAT invoices should be issued. In this way, the lessor can delay accounting for VAT to HMRC until the lessor receives the actual payments. This has the benefit of delaying payment of tax, as well as ensuring that no VAT payments are made on supplies where monies have yet to reach the lessor, namely rent arrears.

16.4.3 VAT and buying/selling a commercial property

If the commercial property to be sold or purchased is not new (ie not less than three years old), there is an exempt supply of the property on sale. A building is said to be VATable when the lessor has made an election and collects rent and VAT on the rent payable by the lessee(s) of the subject premises. The option to tax arises when the lessor decides voluntarily to give up the standard exemption and to opt for VAT liability at the standard rate (see s89 1994 Act). Notice of the election must be given to HMRC within 30 days of its being exercised and best practice dictates the use of customs form VAT 1614. The building concerned will thereafter be a taxable supply instead of an exempt supply. If it is a taxable supply, on sale of the subject premises VAT will be chargeable to the buyer. An election must be for the whole of the subject premises as an election in respect of part is not possible.

When buying a commercial investment property, the buyer will want to know whether VAT will be payable on top of the proposed purchase price. The SCPCs provides for all sums payable under the contract to be exclusive of VAT, namely any VAT is added to the purchase price. So the buyer is to pay the seller on completion an additional amount equal to the VAT in exchange for a VAT invoice from the seller (SCPC 2.2). If the buyer wishes to avoid paying VAT, it will require a special condition to this effect. (In the fifth edition of the Standard Conditions, SC 1.4.1 states that the purchase price and any contents price are inclusive of any VAT.) The condition will say either that the purchase price is to be inclusive of any VAT or that the seller warrants that it has not elected to waive any exemption to VAT and will not do so on or before completion. This is especially important for buyers who make exempt supplies in the course of their businesses, such as banks, building societies and insurance companies, because they are unable to recover their VAT payments. In Part 2 of the contract Condition A1 covers VAT in that it can provide that this agreement does not constitute a taxable supply.

If a new freehold building (ie less than three years old) is sold, it is subject to the standard rate of VAT. Accordingly, if a client instructs you to sell a new commercial property, the seller will be making a supply that will be standard-rated. This being so, the consideration will attract VAT at the standard rate. However, the client will want to know whether the stated price includes or excludes the standard rate of VAT. Clearly, the seller will want the VAT added to the consideration. Unless there is evidence or documentation to the contrary, there will be a presumption that the stated consideration is to *include* VAT. Practitioners acting for a seller in these circumstances should ensure that there is a clear contractual term making the consideration exclusive of VAT so that the full price is paid to the seller with VAT on top of it. To omit such a clause in these circumstances would amount to a clear act of negligence. Therefore, as a matter of course, a VAT-exclusive clause should be included in all such contracts. The SCPCs provide for all sums payable under the contract to be exclusive of VAT; that is, any VAT is *added* to the purchase price but in the Standard Conditions (SC 1.4.1) VAT is inclusive (see SCPC 2).

16.4.4 VAT and the Standard Commercial Property Conditions of Sale

The third edition of the SCPCs is divided into two parts. Part 1 contains general conditions building on those in the first edition, while Part 2 contains new clauses and in particular detailed provisions covering VAT, capital allowances and reversionary interests in flats. In general, Part 1 applies unless specifically excluded, while Part 2 will only apply if expressly incorporated. Completing tick boxes on the back page of the agreement effects explicit incorporation (see SCPC 1.1.4(a) and (b)).

The standard position in Part 1 is that the seller warrants that the sale of the property does constitute a supply that is taxable for VAT purposes. Part 2 changes this because A1 states that the sale does constitute a supply that is taxable for VAT purposes. A1.3 requires the buyer to pay VAT on top of the purchase price in exchange for a proper VAT invoice. Secondly, Condition A2 covers a transfer of a going concern. In this case, the seller warrants that it is using the property for the business of letting to produce a rental income.

EXAMPLE

As in the previous example, the client is acquiring a commercial freehold property 18 Minchin Street, London (built in the 1950s) for £700,000. Is VAT payable in addition to the purchase price? The law states that on the sale of an 'old' commercial building (ie more than three years old) the transaction is exempt from VAT. However, the seller may elect to waive the exemption ('opt to tax') and thus charge VAT. It is therefore important to establish whether the seller intends to waive the exemption for VAT in this transaction. If so, 20 per cent VAT would be payable on top of the £700,000 purchase price.

16.4.5 Stamp duty land tax

SDLT is based on the taxation of transactions in place of deeds or documents that were the case for the old stamp duty regime. It is assessed directly against the buyer rather than the property being purchased.

The SDLT regime came into force on 1 December 2003. Leasehold transactions are caught by SDLT as to the consideration paid and the rent in the lease. The starting threshold for the payment of SDLT is £150,000 for commercial properties. Practitioners should note that there is guidance on the HMRC website regarding SDLT rates.

Transactions under the threshold will be taxed at 0 per cent but will still require a land transaction return to be completed for these transactions above a starting threshold of £40,000. For non-residential and mixed-use properties, the purchaser pays the following rates of SDLT:

- property price, premium or value up to £150,000 (annual rent no greater than £1,000) = zero
- properties between £150,001 and £250,000 = 2%
- properties over £250,000 = 5%

EXAMPLE

If you buy a freehold commercial property for £275,000, the SDLT you will owe is calculated as follows:

- 0% on the first £150,000 = £0
- 2% on the next £100,000 = £2,000
- 5% on the final £25,000 = £1,250
- Total SDLT = £3,250

The land transaction return Form SDLT1 is used in most transactions. SDLT2, 3 and 4 supplement SDLT1. SDLT2 is used where there are more than two sellers and/or two buyers. SDLT3 is used where land is involved and further space is required in addition to the space provided on SDLT1. Perhaps of greater importance in commercial property is Form SDLT4, which should be used for complex commercial transactions and leases.

SDLT includes a regime for the rental element of commercial leases. The charge will be at a rate of 1 per cent on the net present value (NPV) of the total rent payable over the term of the lease. Future rents will be discounted at 3.5 per cent per annum in order to arrive at the NPV. Leases where the NPV of the rent over the term of the lease does not exceed £150,000 will be exempt. HMRC has suggested that change in the regime could mean that some 60 per cent of all commercial leases

TABLE 16.1 SDLT on rent for commercial properties or land—new leases

Net present value of rent	SDLT rate
£0–£150,000	Zero
Over £150,000	1% of the value that exceeds £150,000
Over £5,000,000	2% of the value that exceeds £5,000,000

could avoid any SDLT on the rental element. On the HMRC website there is a facility to work out the SDLT liability for leasehold transactions. The rental element is represented in **Table 16.1**.

Once HMRC have received and processed a proper SDLT return and, where required, payment, they will issue a certificate of payment. The certificate, the SDLT5, is issued under s79 of the Finance Act 2003 and evidences that SDLT has been accounted on the particular transaction notified to HMRC. This must be sent to the **Land Registry** to enable an application to register to proceed.

16.4.5.1 Welsh land transaction tax

Since April 2018, land transaction tax (LTT) has replaced UK stamp duty land tax in Wales (for more details, see **Chapter 11**).

16.4.6 **Other taxes including the annual tax on enveloped dwellings**

If the lessor charges and receives a premium for the granting of a commercial lease, that premium will be potentially liable to tax as a capital gain. As premiums are uncommon in the context of commercial leases, this tax liability is unlikely to be of any real consequence. However, the lessor's profit rental income will be liable either to income tax or, if a company, corporation tax. HMRC also deems a premium paid on a lease for a term of less than 50 years to be partly taxable as income. There is no double charge to tax as the element deemed to be income will be excluded from **capital gains tax**. A premium paid on assignment will, potentially, attract capital gains tax as it is, of course, a 'disposal' that attracts this tax liability.

16.4.6.1 The annual tax on enveloped dwellings (ATED)

The ATED, formerly called the annual residential property tax, is a tax payable by companies that own high-value residential property. It is due on high-value residential property and will be payable each year. An ATED return is required if it is a dwelling and it is in the UK and it is owned partly or completely by a company (or collective investment vehicle, eg a unit trust). See the government website for further details on the criteria: https://www.gov.uk/guidance/annual-tax-on-enveloped-dwellings-the-basics.

The tax rates vary according to property value. The chargeable amounts for 1 April 2023 to 31 March 2024 are as follows:

Property value	Annual charge
More than £500,000 but not more than £1 million	£4,150
More than £1 million but not more than £2 million	£8,450
More than £2 million but not more than £5 million	£28,650
More than £5 million but not more than £10 million	£67,050
More than £10 million but not more than £20 million	£134,550
More than £20 million	£269,450

A dwelling for this tax may be all or part of a residential or mixed-use property. If a property consists of a number of self-contained flats, each flat will usually be valued separately. The tax is called annual tax on enveloped dwellings because the dwelling is said to be 'enveloped' as the ownership sits within a corporate 'wrapper' or 'envelope'.

16.4.6.2 Overseas entities and the Economic Crime (Transparency and Enforcement) Act 2022

Money laundering is often hidden behind opaque and complex offshore corporate structures, making it difficult to uncover illicit finance from abroad being laundered through UK property. Identifying who owns property becomes more difficult if it is registered to an overseas company whose ultimate beneficiaries are hidden from view. The Economic Crime (Transparency and Enforcement) Act 2022 came into force on 1 August 2022. It created the Register of Overseas Entities (ROE) at Companies House, making it more difficult for foreign companies, known as Overseas Entities (OEs) to launder dirty money through property in the UK and to increase transparency around property ownership. The Act provides that an OE with a legal or beneficial interest in UK-registered property is required to identify its beneficial owner(s) and register itself on the ROE by 31 January 2023. And, importantly for conveyancers, an OE acquiring UK land for the first time must ensure that it identifies its beneficial ownership and is registered on the ROE before making an application to the Land Registry to register its purchase. There is a continuing annual duty on OEs to keep the information on the ROE up to date. Failure to do so will be a criminal offence, and it will also mean that OEs will be unable to dispose of their land in the UK until the updating duty is complied with.

KEY POINT SUMMARY

- The sale contract should be based upon the Standard Commercial Property Conditions.
- If the sale is of a reversion subject to residential long leases, the sale cannot proceed without careful consideration of the effects of the Landlord and Tenant Act 1987, which may give the lessees in occupation a right of pre-emption. If the right exists, the contract will need to show that steps have been taken to comply with the Act.
- Where there is a substantial commercial rental income from the property, the contract will need to cover the question of rent arrears and the apportionment of rent at completion. SC 3.3.2(b) requires the seller to inform the buyer of any lease or tenancy termination after exchange but before completion, and to act as the buyer reasonably directs, with the buyer indemnifying the seller against any consequent loss or expense.
- Bear in mind that where the property constitutes a dwelling, s3 of the Landlord and Tenant Act 1985 compels the buyer to give written notice of the change of ownership to the lessee or tenant in occupation within two months of completion; and s48 of the Landlord and Tenant Act 1987 compels the lessor buyer to provide the lessee in occupation with an address within England and Wales that can be used for the service of notices.
- Do you need to make environmental enquiries and searches, including flooding matters and ground stability tests?
- Can you or should you use the Commercial Property Standard Enquiries? Would CPSE7—the short form—suit your transaction?
- If a commercial lease is granted, the rule is that it is generally exempt from VAT but is nevertheless subject to the option to tax, namely to make the letting VATable.
- In a commercial lease, where VAT is to be charged on the rent, the lessor must be registered for VAT; and, if there is such a registration, written notice must be given to HMRC within 30 days of the election having been made.
- If the election precedes the grant of a new commercial lease, HMRC will deem the new rent to be *inclusive* of VAT. If acting for the lessor, to avoid this problem make sure the lease contains a covenant by the lessee to pay VAT in addition to the rent.

- The election to tax is personal to the elector and is in respect of individual properties, namely on a property-by-property basis.
- On the assumption that there is an existing lease and it is silent as to the payment of VAT, the lessee will nevertheless have to pay VAT on the rent should the lessor decide to opt to tax. For certainty, always ensure that there is a covenant requiring the lessee to pay VAT on rent if required.
- If a commercial property that is not new (ie not less than three years old) is to be sold or purchased, there is an exempt supply of the property on sale and VAT will not be payable unless the seller opts to tax.
- If a new freehold building is to be sold, it will be subject to the standard rate of VAT. Accordingly, if a client instructs you to sell a new commercial property, the seller will be making a supply that will be standard-rated.
- Practitioners acting for sellers should always draft contracts so as to make all sums exclusive of VAT.
- The HMRC national advice service can be contacted on 0300 200 3700, where it will deal with general VAT enquiries.

CHAPTER 17
Security of Tenure under Part II of the Landlord and Tenant Act 1954 (Part A)

FUNCTIONING LEGAL KNOWLEDGE

This chapter covers the following functioning legal knowledge required to pass the SQE 1 assessments:

Security of tenure under a business lease

Landlord and Tenant Act 1954 (Part II):

- application of 1954 Act
- renewal **lease** by the tenant
- termination by the landlord

AUTHORITIES UNDERPINNING PRACTICE

The key authorities that underpin this area of practice are listed below. Note that for legislation you are linked to legislation.gov.uk.

Although much of the legislation on this government website is available in its amended form, the incorporation of new amendments into the text of legislation can be delayed. You should refer to legal databases to ensure you are referencing the most up-to-date legislation.

- Part II of the Landlord and Tenant Act 1954
https://www.legislation.gov.uk/uksi/1989/1548/contents/made
- Regulatory Reform (Business Tenancies) (England and Wales) Order 2003
https://www.legislation.gov.uk/uksi/2003/3096/contents/made

17.1 Introduction

Part II of the Landlord and Tenant Act 1954 (the Act) provides security of tenure for the majority of business tenants by giving to those tenants a statutory right to renew their lease or **tenancy**. The court will order a new lease but will require the tenant to pay a market rent prevailing at the time of renewal. In general terms, provided the tenant occupies the subject property for business purposes, that tenant can remain in the property at the end of the contractual lease and can seek to renew the letting. The landlord is obliged by statute to agree a renewal unless they can establish one or more of the grounds for eviction under s30(1) of the Act. See **Figures 17.1** and **17.2** later in the chapter.

CONDUCT POINT

There are strict time limits for service of the various notices under the Act and for the tenant's application to the court for a new tenancy. Failure to adhere to these time limits represents one of the most common examples of solicitors' negligence. Attention to detail and a fail-safe diary or computer entry system are therefore essential when dealing with business tenancy renewals.

The Act applies to 'any tenancy where the property comprised in the tenancy is or includes premises that are occupied by the tenant and are so occupied for the purposes of a business carried on by him or for those and other purposes' (s23(1)). Thus, to qualify for protection under the Act *a tenant must be occupying premises for the purposes of a business.* This wording is now considered.

17.2 Need for 'tenancy'

Only tenancies of business premises are protected under the Act. The key factor in determining whether an arrangement is a tenancy is whether the occupier has been granted exclusive possession of the property (*Street v Mountford* [1985] 2 All ER 289, HL). Exclusive possession by the occupier will connote a tenancy, and this has been confirmed in several cases involving commercial property. In *Esso Petroleum Ltd v Fumegrange Ltd* [1994] 2 EGLR 90, the Court of Appeal held that exclusive possession of a petrol station had not been granted because the licensor had reserved extensive rights over the property. These included control over the way in which the occupier's business was to be operated, as well as the physical layout of the site. It should be noted that a **reservation** of a simple right of entry or access onto the occupier's premises will be insufficient to negate exclusive possession (see *Addiscombe Garden Estates Ltd v Crabbe* [1957] 3 All ER 563, CA). In *National Car Parks Ltd v Trinity Development Co (Banbury) Ltd* [2000] EGCS 128, the court held that an agreement to occupy premises as a car park did not constitute a tenancy and was a mere **licence**. Here, the fact that the agreement allowed the licensor potentially to use the premises itself to park cars, and also laid down regulations as to the conduct of the licensee's business, was sufficient to deny exclusive possession.

A licence cannot be protected by the Act because it is not a tenancy. However, there are dangers for landlords who seek to avoid the Act by purporting to grant a licence to occupiers of their premises. The courts have construed many so-called licences to be mere fabrications and have held them instead to be tenancies. If the agreement has the hallmarks of a tenancy (exclusive possession, for a term and at a rent), then the courts will generally construe it as such, notwithstanding that the parties may call it a licence (see *Bruton v London & Quadrant Housing Trust Ltd* [1999] 3 WLR 150, HL).

EXAMPLE

Harry shares a business workshop with his landlord Colin. Harry's business is repairing motorcycles. Colin's business is repairing cars. As Harry does not have exclusive possession of the business premises, he cannot be a tenant and so has no protection under Part II of the Landlord and Tenant Act 1954.

17.2.1 Tenancies excluded from statutory protection

17.2.1.1 Fixed-term tenancies not exceeding six months (s43(3))

Although generally excluded, it should be noted that these short, fixed-term tenancies will be protected under the Act in two situations:

- if they contain provisions for renewing the term or extending it beyond six months (s43(3)(a)); or
- if the tenant (including any predecessor in the same business) has already been in occupation for a period exceeding 12 months (s43(3)(b)). For the tenant to have protection, such occupation must be under either a fixed-term or a periodic tenancy, namely not as licensee, tenant at will or trespasser. Note that any predecessor in the tenant's business need not necessarily have been a tenant and may have been occupying as a mere licensee, or even as freeholder.

The exception under s43(3)(b) allows a tenant starting up in business to be granted up to three successive tenancies of less than six months each. This is because by the time the third tenancy is granted, the tenant will not have been in occupation for 12 months.

17.2.1.2 Contracted out tenancies

Under s38A of the Act, the prospective landlord and tenant may agree to exclude from the tenancy the security of tenure provisions of the Act (ss24–28). The tenancy must be for a 'term of years certain' and the definition of the 'term' of the tenancy must not include any continuation, extension or holding-over period. Importantly, the agreement must satisfy three statutory requirements, failing which the agreement will be void with the consequence that the tenancy will be protected under the Act. For landlords, it is therefore vital that these requirements are observed. They are:

1 *Landlord's health warning.* Before the tenant enters into the tenancy (or, if earlier, before the tenant is contractually bound to do so), the landlord must serve on the tenant a 'health warning' notice. The notice should be served 14 days before the tenant commits itself to the lease. After receiving the health warning notice the tenant (or someone authorised by the tenant, eg their solicitor) must take the following action before entering into the tenancy (or, if earlier, becoming contractually bound to do so). The tenant (or authorised person) must sign a declaration that the tenant has received the health warning and accepts the consequences of contracting out of the Act. Provided the tenant receives the health warning at least 14 days before committing themselves to the lease, the tenant (or authorised person) merely signs a simple declaration (not requiring a witness), stating that the tenant has received the notice and accepts the consequences of contracting out of the Act.

2 *Tenant's declaration.* However, the landlord is permitted to serve the health warning notice less than 14 days before the tenant enters into the tenancy (or, if earlier, becomes contractually bound to do so). In this case, the tenant must sign a more formal statutory declaration in front of an independent solicitor (or someone else empowered to administer oaths). Thus the parties can effectively waive the 14-day period. Notwithstanding this, it is important to appreciate that however late the health warning is served, it must always be served before the tenant actually enters into the tenancy (or becomes contractually bound to do so). Failure to do so will make the agreement to contract out of the Act void.

3 *Reference in the lease.* The third requirement is that the lease must contain reference to: (a) the health warning; (b) the tenant's declaration or statutory declaration; and (c) the agreement to contract out. Typically, this will all be contained in a separate clause in the lease. Alternatively, a separate endorsement to this effect can be attached to the lease.

17.2.1.3 Other excluded tenancies

Examples of other excluded tenancies include tenancies at will (ie where someone occupies property with the permission of the owner but does not pay rent) and service tenancies (those granted to persons in connection with their office or employment).

17.3 Need for 'occupation'

In most cases it will be fairly clear whether the tenant is in occupation of the premises. The courts have held that the important factors to be taken into account are the tenant's physical occupation or presence, and the measure of control the tenant exercises over those who use the premises.

17.3.1 Sub-letting

Generally, if the tenant sub-lets or parts with possession of the premises it can no longer be said to be in occupation of the part (or whole) that has been sub-let. It would therefore not qualify for statutory protection in respect of the part (or whole) of the premises occupied by the sub-tenant.

17.4 Need for 'the purposes of a business'

To qualify for protection under the Act, the tenant is required to occupy the premises for the purposes of a business. The fact that they are occupied for business purposes does not necessarily mean that the tenant must carry on the business there. What is important is that the premises must be occupied for that purpose. A business carried on by one member of a group of companies of which the tenant company is a member is treated as a business of the tenant (s42(2)(a)). Similarly, where a tenancy is held on trust, the carrying on of a business by the beneficiaries under the trust is treated as being the business of the tenant (s41(1)).

17.4.1 Meaning of 'business'

The definition of 'business' in s23(2) includes a 'trade, profession or employment and includes any activity carried on by a body of persons, whether corporate or unincorporate'. It can be seen that the definition is narrower for an individual ('trade, profession or employment') than it is for a body of persons ('any activity').

EXAMPLE

A body of persons running a tennis club was held to be a business (*Addiscombe Garden Estates v Crabbe* [1958] 1 QB 513, CA), as was the administration of a hospital by a board of governors (*Hills (Patents) Ltd v University College Hospital Board of Governors* [1956] 1 QB 90, CA). Similarly, a local authority's maintenance of a park was classified as a business activity under the Act (*Wandsworth LBC v Singh* (1991) 62 P & CR 219, CA). However, an individual running a Sunday school has been held not to be within the definition of 'trade, profession or employment'. The provision of residential accommodation by way of a business venture has been classified as a business activity (*Lee-Verhulst (Investments) Ltd v Harwood Trust* [1973] QB 204).

17.4.2 Mixed use

If the premises are used partly for business and partly for residential purposes (eg a flat above a shop), the test is whether the business activity is a significant purpose of the occupation or whether it is merely incidental to the occupation as a residence. It is a question of degree in each case. An office block might have sleeping accommodation for staff on the top floor. Although residential in nature, the sleeping accommodation would only be incidental to the building's principal use as business premises. Conversely, one room in a dwellinghouse set aside exclusively for business purposes (eg a doctor's private consultation room at home) would not alter the fact that the significant purpose of the occupation of the property was residential.

EXAMPLE

In *Gurton v Parrot* [1991] 1 EGLR 98, a residential tenant's conversion of outbuildings into dog kennels was held to be merely incidental to the property's use as a dwellinghouse. Similarly, in *Wright v Mortimer* (1996) 28 HLR 719, CA, an art historian's use of his flat for writing was held to be merely incidental to his residential use. On the other hand, a seafood importer who received business visitors and kept files, a telephone and typewriter in his flat, and had no other business premises, was held to occupy the flat for business purposes (*Cheryl Investments Ltd v Saldanha* [1979] 1 All ER 5, CA).

If the lease prohibits business use generally (eg 'not to use the premises for business purposes'), the tenant cannot obtain protection from the Act simply by carrying on a business in breach of the **covenant** (s23(4)).

17.5 Key methods of termination under the Act

A business tenancy protected by the Act can be terminated only in one of the ways prescribed by the Act. Until that occurs, the tenancy simply continues on the same terms as the original tenancy (except for the termination provisions). The landlord or the tenant can seek an increased rent by applying to the court for an **interim rent** under s24A of the Act (see **18.2**).

The most widely used methods of termination are the landlord's s25 notice and the tenant's s26 request, which are considered later.

The other methods of termination are:

- a tenant's notice under s27(1) or (2) of the Act, where the tenancy is for a fixed term (these notices are used where the tenant does not wish the lease to continue or be renewed);
- a tenant's notice to quit in a periodic tenancy (provided the tenant has been in occupation for at least one month);
- surrender;
- **forfeiture**;
- forfeiture of a superior lease;
- notice to quit served by a mesne landlord on the superior landlord; and
- an agreement between the parties for a future tenancy under s28 of the Act.

17.5.1 Tenant's notices under s27

If the tenant has a fixed-term tenancy and does not wish it to continue, the tenant can terminate the lease by serving on the immediate landlord a statutory notice under s27 of the 1954 Act. There are two types of notice. A notice under s27(1) is served before the end of the contractual term, whereas a notice under s27(2) is served after the end of the contractual term where the tenant is holding over.

17.5.1.1 Before the end of the contractual term: tenant's notice under s27(1)

A tenant who has been in occupation under a business tenancy for at least one month and who does not wish to renew its fixed-term tenancy can serve a notice in writing on its immediate landlord under s27(1). This notice must be served not later than three months before the end of the fixed term. The tenancy will then come to an end on the expiry of the contractual term. Section 27(1) applies only to 'a term of years certain', namely a fixed term. This would exclude periodic tenancies but would include a fixed term of less than one year. It has been held that 'a term of years certain' would not include a term of 12 months and thereafter from year to year determinable on the landlord giving 12 months' notice.

EXAMPLE

There is no prescribed form, but a typical notice might read as follows:

To [name of landlord]
of [address of landlord]
From [name of tenant]
of [address of tenant]

1. *I am the tenant of [address of property] under a lease dated [date of lease] ('the Lease') made between [original parties to lease].*
2. *The Lease expires on [contractual expiry date].*

> 3. *I hereby give you notice under section 27(1) of the Landlord and Tenant Act 1954 ('the Act') that I do not wish my tenancy to be continued under the provisions of Part II of the Act.*
>
> *Dated:*
> *Signed:*
> *[signature of tenant, or on behalf of tenant]*

A tenant who has served a s27(1) notice is not permitted to serve a s26 request (s26(4)). A s27(1) notice will not affect any sub-tenancy protected by the Act.

What is the position if the tenant vacates the premises before the contractual expiry date? Is a s27(1) notice needed? In *Esselte AB v Pearl Assurance plc* [1997] 02 EG 124, it was held that a s27(1) notice is strictly not necessary if the tenant has ceased to occupy the premises for business purposes on or before the contractual expiry date. This is because the tenancy is no longer one to which the 1954 Act applies (ie not in occupation for the purposes of a business) and so cannot be continued under s24.

The 2004 reforms amend the Act to reflect the decision in *Esselte AB v Pearl Assurance plc* [1997] 02 EG 124. Section 27(1A) provides, in effect, that a fixed-term tenancy will not continue under the Act if the tenant was not in occupation at the contractual expiry date. However, in cases of doubt as to whether the tenant has fully quit the premises, it is still best practice for the tenant to serve a s27(1) notice.

17.5.1.2 After the end of the contractual term: tenant's notice under s27(2)

A notice under s27(2) differs slightly from a s27(1) notice. It is served by a tenant who is holding over after the contractual expiry date has passed and who does not wish to renew the tenancy. As with a s27(1) notice, the tenant must have been in occupation for at least one month. It is served on the immediate landlord who must be given at least three months' notice expiring on any day. This is a change from the position before 1 June 2004 where the three months' notice had to expire on a quarter day.

> **EXAMPLE**
>
> There is no prescribed form, but a typical notice might read as follows:
>
> *To [name of landlord]*
> *of [address of landlord]*
> *From [name of tenant]*
> *of [address of tenant]*
>
> 1. *I am the tenant of [address of property] under a lease dated [date of lease] ('the Lease') made between [original parties to lease].*
> 2. *The Lease expired on [contractual expiry date] and my tenancy continues under section 24 of the Landlord and Tenant Act 1954 ('the Act').*
> 3. *I hereby give you notice under section 27(2) of the Act that my tenancy will come to an end on [date tenancy to end] by virtue of this notice.*
>
> *Dated:*
> *Signed:*
> *[signature of tenant, or on behalf of tenant]*

A tenant who has served a s27(2) notice is not permitted to serve a s26 request (s26(4)). A s27(2) notice will not affect any sub-tenancy protected by the Act. If the tenant vacates the premises after the end of the contractual term, it cannot rely on the effect of *Esselte AB v Pearl Assurance plc* [1997] 02 EG 124 and the new s27(1A). This is because s27(2) provides that where a fixed term continues under s24, the tenancy will not end merely because the tenant ceases to occupy the premises. The tenant must therefore serve a s27(2) notice to bring the tenancy to an end.

Under the new s27(3), provision is made for the appropriate apportionment of rent to be made in the tenant's favour as at the expiry of a s27(2) notice. The tenant may therefore recover any overpayment of rent.

17.5.2 Landlord's notice under s25

If the tenant is protected under the Act and the landlord requires the premises back at the end of the lease, the landlord must serve a s25 notice on the tenant specifying the grounds on which the landlord is claiming possession. This is known as a 'hostile notice'. The specified grounds for possession are contained in s30(1) of the Act. Even if the landlord is content for the tenant to remain in possession under a negotiated new lease, the landlord must still serve a s25 notice to end the existing lease. This is known as a 'non-hostile notice'. The landlord cannot serve a s25 notice if the tenant has already served a s26 request or a s27 notice.

The s25 notice is effective only if it is in a prescribed form. Moreover, there are strict time limits for service in that the notice must be given not less than six months or more than 12 months before the termination date specified in the notice. As will be seen, the termination date cannot be earlier than the contractual expiry date, and may well be later. If the time limits are not observed, the notice will be invalid and of no effect. If the landlord client suffers loss as a result of an invalid notice, a negligence claim against the solicitors is likely to ensue.

17.5.2.1 Prescribed form and content of s25 notice

The current prescribed form must be used. A form 'substantially to the like effect' can be used, but this is not to be recommended. To ensure that the most current form is used, the safest practice is to use a printed form from law stationers or a computer software form. If firms use their own word-processed forms there is always a danger that errors or omissions could occur, leading to possible negligence claims. The s25 notice must:

- specify the date at which the tenancy is to end (s25(1)). This termination date must not be earlier than the date on which the tenancy could have been terminated at common law. Thus for a normal fixed term without a break clause, the specified termination date cannot be earlier than the last day of the contractual term. And for a fixed-term lease with a break clause (as well as a periodic tenancy), the specified termination date cannot be earlier than the date on which the landlord could have ended the tenancy by common law notice;
- state whether the landlord would oppose the tenant's application to the court for a new tenancy and, if so, on which statutory grounds (s25(6) and (7)). Thus, the landlord must decide whether the notice is 'hostile' or 'non-hostile'. The statutory grounds of opposition are considered at **18.3**. The notice cannot be amended once it has been served so the landlord should specify all the grounds on which it wishes to rely.
- if the s25 notice states that the landlord would not oppose the tenant's application for a new tenancy, it must set out the landlord's proposals as to: (a) the property to be comprised in the new tenancy (either the whole or part of the property comprised in the current tenancy); (b) the new rent; and (c) the other terms of the new tenancy (s25(8)). This is a new provision introduced by the 2004 reforms;
- be given and signed by, or on behalf of, the landlord. If there is more than one landlord, all their names must be given. If there are joint tenants, the notice must be served on all of them unless the **joint tenancy** is held by a partnership. In this case, s41A of the Act permits the landlord to serve only those tenants who are partners involved in running the business;
- relate to the whole of the demised premises not part only. This applies even where the tenant has sub-let part of the premises. Where, after the grant of the tenancy, the **reversion** becomes vested in different landlords, the landlords should either serve a notice jointly or serve separate notices that can be read together;
- be served on any sub-tenant where the tenant has sub-let the whole of the premises. This is provided the sub-tenancy satisfies s23 (see also 17.8 regarding s40).

17.5.2.2 Omission of prescribed information

If the prescribed information is omitted from the s25 notice, is it still valid? The test, as laid down by Barry J in *Barclays Bank Ltd v Ascott* [1961] 1 WLR 717, is whether the notice gives 'the proper information to the tenant which will enable the tenant to deal in a proper way with the situation, whatever it may be, referred to in the statement of the notice'. Accordingly, if the form is not materially different from the prescribed form then it will generally be considered valid.

17.5.2.3 Error or defect in s25 notice

If the notice contains an error or is incorrectly completed, is it still valid? The test was laid down by the House of Lords in *Mannai Investment Co Ltd v Eagle Star Life Assurance Ltd* [1997] 3 All ER 352. Essentially, the court has to decide, first, whether the error in the notice is obvious or evident and, secondly, whether, despite the error, the notice read in its context is sufficiently clear to leave a reasonable recipient in no reasonable doubt as to the terms of the notice. Although each case will turn on its own facts, it may be useful to consider examples of where defects have and have not invalidated a notice.

EXAMPLE

Examples of defects that have invalidated a s25 notice:

- failure to name all joint landlords in the notice;
- naming the wrong person as landlord;
- an **assignor** serving a notice after the reversion had been assigned.

Examples of defects that have not invalidated a s25 notice:

- the notice was not signed but the covering letter made it apparent that the notice was served on behalf of the landlord;
- the notice stated the wrong termination date but the covering letter made it apparent what date was intended;
- failure to date the notice;
- failure to refer to a tiny part of the premises.

If the landlord discovers that a s25 notice it has served is defective in some way (eg it contains an error or has been incorrectly served), best practice is to serve a fresh notice without prejudice to the validity of the original notice. Then if the original notice is subsequently held to be invalid, the second notice will become effective.

17.5.2.4 Time limits for service of s25 notice

The notice must be given not more than 12 months or less than six months before the date of termination specified in the notice (s25(2)). Moreover, this date of termination cannot be earlier than the date on which the tenancy can be terminated at common law. There are thus different considerations for a normal fixed term, a fixed term with a break clause and a periodic tenancy. These are considered later. In computing time limits under the Act, the corresponding date rule is used, and 'month' means calendar month (s5, s22(1) and Sch 2, para 4(1) Interpretation Act 1975). This means that the relevant period will end on the corresponding date in the appropriate subsequent month.

EXAMPLE

Two months starting on 2 May will end on 2 July; but two months starting on 31 July will end on 30 September and two months starting on 31 December will end on 28 (or 29) February. These time limits are strictly enforced by the courts and it is therefore vitally important for practitioners to abide by them.

17.5.2.5 Fixed-term tenancies without a break clause

In the usual case of a fixed-term lease, the earliest time a landlord can serve the notice is one year before the end of the contractual term. For example, if the lease is due to end on 30 September 2025, the landlord cannot serve the notice earlier than 30 September 2024 (and for the avoidance of doubt it is probably safer to wait until the next day, 1 October 2024).

If the landlord delays serving notice until less than six months remain of the fixed term, it must still give the tenant at least six months' notice. In this situation, the landlord would have to specify a termination date in the notice later than the contractual expiry date.

EXAMPLE

A lease is due to expire on 30 September 2025. If the landlord delays giving notice until after 30 March 2025, the termination date they specify in the notice will inevitably need to be later than the contractual expiry date (30 September 2025). Even if the landlord delays serving notice until after the contractual expiry date has passed (ie when the lease is continuing under s24), the tenant must still be given a minimum of six months' notice.

17.5.2.6 Periodic tenancies

The notice required to end a periodic tenancy at common law is at least one full period of the lease expiring on the last day of a completed period of the tenancy (ie on a rent day). The landlord serving a s25 notice must ensure that the date of termination specified in the notice is not earlier than the date at which the tenancy could have been terminated by notice to quit (*Commercial Properties Ltd v Wood* [1968] 1 QB 15, CA). However, the s25 notice must be given not more than 12 months or less than six months before the date of termination specified in the notice (s25(2)).

17.5.2.7 Tenant's and landlord's applications to the court for a new tenancy

Section 24(1) of the Act, as amended, enables either the tenant or the landlord to apply to the court for an order for the grant of a new tenancy. The application can be made only after the service of a landlord's s25 notice or a tenant's s26 request (the latter is considered at **17.5.3**) and must be made within the time limits referred to next. Neither party may make an application if the other has already made an application under s24(1) and the application has been served. Nor can either party make an application under s24(1) if the landlord has already made an application under the new s29(2) for an order for the termination of the current tenancy and the application has been served.

17.5.2.8 Time limits

Section 29A provides that an application to the court by either party under s24(1) must be made on or before the date specified in the landlord's s25 notice or immediately before the date specified in the tenant's s26 request. These are the latest dates by which the application can be made (unless there is an agreement to extend: see shortly). The deadline is strictly enforced and so, for example, if the tenant fails to apply within the required time the tenancy will come to an end on the date specified in the s25 notice or immediately before the date specified in the s26 request, as the case may be. As such, the tenant's right to apply for a new tenancy will be lost and the tenant's solicitor is likely to be sued in negligence. A fail-safe diary or computer entry system is therefore essential.

Even if the landlord has indicated that they are willing to grant a new tenancy and terms are nearly agreed, the tenant must still apply to the court as a 'fallback'. Without the backup of the court application, the landlord could simply change their mind and there would be nothing the tenant could do about it (save possibly a claim in estoppel) or that the landlord has waived their rights.

Where the tenant has made a s26 request, the landlord or the tenant may not apply to the court until the landlord has served the required counter-notice or the two-month period for service of the counter-notice has expired, whichever occurs first (s29A(3)). Without this provision, a court application might be made at a time when it was not known whether the landlord opposed renewal and, if so, on what grounds. Once the landlord's counter-notice has been served, either party may apply to the court without waiting for the two months to elapse. The position in respect of a s25 notice is much simpler. If the landlord has served a s25 notice, there is no two-month waiting period and either party may apply to the court immediately.

17.5.2.9 Agreement to extend time limit

Section 29B allows the parties to agree to extend the latest time for applying to the court, provided they do so before the current time limit expires. The agreement must be made in writing. The parties may agree further postponements from time to time provided the agreement is made before the end of the period of postponement specified in the current agreement (s29B(2)). The effect of such an agreement is that the s25 notice or s26 request is treated as terminating the tenancy at the end of the period specified in the agreement (s29B(4)). This provision, introduced in the 2004 reforms, has assisted in reducing the number of court applications.

EXAMPLE

Elijah's firm acts for Cambo Ltd acquiring the freehold reversion of 18 Clover Street, London W2 for £700,000 subject to and with the benefit of two occupational business leases. Completion of the freehold purchase has recently taken place and the client is anxious to renew one of the occupational business leases (ground floor lease) as soon as possible in order to secure a higher market rent than is currently being received (the last rent review was four years ago). The ground floor lease will expire in 13 months' time. Elijah would advise his client to serve a non-hostile s25 notice on the tenant of the ground floor lease specifying the last day of the contractual term as the termination date in the notice. However, the s25 notice must be served between six and 12 months before the termination date specified in the notice so the client cannot serve the notice until 12 months before the contractual expiry date, namely in one month's time. Elijah should prepare the s25 notice in readiness for service at the appropriate time.

17.5.3 Tenant's request under s26

This method of termination is not available to periodic tenants and those with fixed terms of one year or less. However, such tenants still have security of tenure and can apply for a new tenancy if the landlord has served them with a s25 notice. Accordingly, to be able to serve a s26 request the tenant must have been granted a term of years certain exceeding one year (whether or not continued by s24), or a term of years certain and thereafter from year to year (s26(1)).

A s26 request must be served on the tenant's 'competent' landlord, or its agent, otherwise it will be invalid. The tenant's competent landlord may not necessarily be the same as the tenant's immediate landlord (see **17.7** for a discussion of competent landlord). A s26 request cannot be served if the landlord has already served a s25 notice or the tenant has already served a s27 notice (see **17.5.1**). Once the tenant has served a valid s26 request it cannot later withdraw it and serve another amended one.

17.5.3.1 Situations in which a tenant would be advised to serve a s26 request

If a tenant has security of tenure, then the tenancy will continue under s24 until it is terminated by one of the ways under the Act. This gives rise to the question why, if the tenant can continue in occupation under s24, paying the existing rent, should it want to end the lease by serving a s26 request? Why not wait until the landlord serves a s25 notice and in the meantime carry on paying rent that is probably less than the market rent under any new lease? The following are situations in which a tenant may be advised to serve a s26 request:

- *Tenant's tactical pre-emptive strike.* In a normal rising market, the tenant will wish to pay the current rent as long as possible because it will be lower than the market rent. In these circumstances, a prudent landlord would end the lease as early as possible by serving a s25 notice one year before the expiry date (the termination date in the notice would be the expiry date of the contractual term, ie 12 months hence). However, if the landlord is dilatory and forgets to serve a s25 notice, the tenant could serve a s26 request, say, six months before the expiry date, in which the tenant specifies a date 12 months ahead as the termination date. In this way, the tenant would get six months longer paying the old rent.

EXAMPLE

A lease has a contractual expiry date of 31 December. If by the middle of the previous June the landlord has not served a s25 notice, the tenant could serve a s26 request specifying a termination date 12 months ahead, namely in June of the following year. That would be six months after the earliest date the landlord could have ended the lease.

- *Proposed improvements.* If the tenant intends to spend money improving the premises, it may prefer the certainty of a new fixed-term lease before doing so.
- *Proposed sale.* If the tenant intends to assign the lease, a prospective buyer will probably want the certainty of a new fixed-term lease being in place.
- *Fall in market rent.* If the market rent has fallen (eg during a recession) and is less than the existing rent under the lease, the tenant will want a new lease with a lower market rent in place as soon as possible. The landlord, of course, will be happy for the old (higher) rent to continue.

17.5.3.2 Interim rent

Interim rent is considered at **18.2**. As a consequence of the 2004 reforms, tenants should be aware that interim rent is now payable from the earliest date that could have been specified for commencement of the new tenancy in the s26 request. Thus, a tenant who serves a s26 request but states a commencement date for the new tenancy 12 months after service, when the contractual termination date is only six months away (and so they could have served six months' notice), will find that the interim rent will be payable from the earliest date that they could have specified. In a rising market, a well-advised landlord could therefore reduce the effectiveness of the tenant's pre-emptive strike by applying for an interim rent payable from this earlier date.

17.5.3.3 Prescribed form and content of s26 request

The current prescribed form must be used. A form 'substantially to the like effect' can be used, but this is not to be recommended. The s26 request must:

- specify a date for the commencement of the new tenancy (the existing tenancy will end immediately before this date). This commencement date must not be more than 12 months or less than six months after the making of the request. Nor must it be earlier than the date on which the tenancy could have been terminated at common law. Thus, for a normal fixed term without a break clause, the specified termination date cannot be earlier than the last day of the contractual term. And for a fixed-term lease with a break clause, the specified termination date cannot be earlier than the date upon which the tenant could have ended the tenancy by common law notice;
- set out the tenant's proposals for the new lease, namely:
  - the property to be comprised in the new tenancy. This can be either the whole or part of the property in the current tenancy (compare this with a s25 notice, in which the whole of the property must be specified),
  - the new rent (valuation advice should be taken before doing so),
  - the other terms of the new tenancy.

These proposals must be genuine and the tenant must have a real intention of taking up the new tenancy. Thus a request served merely as a precautionary measure will be invalid;

- be given and signed by, or on behalf of, the tenant. If there is more than one tenant, all their names must be given unless the joint tenancy is held by a partnership. In this case, s41A of the Act allows only those tenants who are partners carrying on the business to be named in the request. If there are joint landlords, the notice must be served on all of them.

17.5.3.4 Time limits for service of s26 request

As already mentioned, the date specified in the s26 request as the date for the commencement of the new tenancy must not be more than 12 months or less than six months after the request is served on the landlord. Accordingly, the earliest time a tenant can serve a request is one year before the contractual expiry date. In the case of a 'tenant's pre-emptive strike' (see **17.5.3**), the tenant will often specify a commencement date 12 months ahead, having given the request between 12 and six months before the contractual expiry date.

17.5.3.5 The landlord's counter-notice

Upon receiving a tenant's s26 request the landlord has two months in which to notify the tenant if they intend to oppose the tenant's application to the court for a new tenancy (s26(6)). There is no prescribed form of 'counter-notice' so a clear letter will suffice, but the landlord must state on which grounds in s30 of the Act the landlord opposes the application (see **18.3**). The landlord should be certain of their grounds because the grounds cannot be amended later. If the landlord fails to serve a counter-notice within the two months, they will lose their right to oppose the new tenancy. If the reversion is assigned after the counter-notice has been given, the incoming landlord steps into the shoes of the outgoing landlord and can rely on the grounds specified in the counter-notice. Needless to say, there have been many cases of negligence against landlord's solicitors who have overlooked this two-month deadline.

EXAMPLE

A typical form of counter-notice might read as follows:

> *To [name of tenant]*
> *of [address of tenant]*
>
> *I [name of landlord] of [address of landlord] received on [date of receipt] your request under section 26 of the Landlord and Tenant Act 1954 Part II ('the Act') for a new tenancy of [description of property] ('the Property').*
>
> *I hereby give you notice that I will oppose your application to the court for a new tenancy of the Property on the following ground(s) contained in section 30(1) of the Act, namely paragraph(s) [insert paragraph letter(s)].*
>
> *Dated:*
> *Signed:*
> *[signature of landlord, or on behalf of landlord]*

17.6 'The holding'

On an application for a renewal of the lease the tenant will only be entitled to a renewal of 'the holding' as defined by the Act in s23(3). The holding is defined as:

> . . . the property comprised in the tenancy, there being excluded any part thereof which is occupied neither by the tenant nor by a person employed by the tenant and so employed for the purposes of a business by reason of which the tenancy is one to which this Part of this Act applies.

It follows that the holding will not include the following, in respect of which the tenant cannot claim a new lease:

- any part of the premises presently sub-let by the tenant, unless the tenant can show that it remains in occupation of that part for business purposes;
- any part of the premises occupied by a third party;
- any part of the premises that is unoccupied;
- any part of the premises occupied by the tenant's employees in connection with another of the tenant's businesses.

17.7 'Competent landlord'

A tenant's request for a new tenancy under s26 must be served on the 'competent landlord' as defined by s44(1) of the Act. Similarly, the competent landlord must serve a landlord's s25 notice. There can only be one competent landlord at any given time, and their identity may change during the course of the renewal procedure. If this occurs, the new competent landlord must be made a party to any proceedings under the Act. The time for determining the competent landlord is the date of service of the s25 notice or s26 request.

17.7.1 Sub-leases

Where the tenant's immediate landlord is the freeholder, establishing the identity of the competent landlord will be easy (as it will obviously be the freeholder). However, in the case of **sub-leases** it is necessary to consider s44(1) of the Act. This provides that where a landlord is a tenant themselves, they will be the competent landlord to their immediate tenant only if their own tenancy will not come to an end within 14 months. If it will end within 14 months, the competent landlord will be the next landlord up the chain of tenancies whose tenancy satisfies this criterion (or the freeholder if you reach the top). This is illustrated by Examples 1 and 2 in **Figure 17.1** involving a sub-lease. In each case, consider who is the sub-tenant's competent landlord.

In Example 1, because T has sub-let the whole, T is not 'in occupation', will not have the protection of the Act and T's lease will not continue under s24 (ie it ends on the contractual expiry date). Thus, once T's lease (L–T) has less than 14 months to run, it will certainly come to an end within 14 months. ST's competent landlord will be L (freeholder) in any event.

EXAMPLE 1	EXAMPLE 2
L	L
Fixed-term head-lease	Fixed-term head-lease
T	T
Sub-lease of whole	Sub-lease of part
ST	ST
Example 1: L (freeholder) lets premises to T on fixed term; T sub-lets whole of premises to ST	Example 2: L (freeholder) lets premises to T on fixed term; T sub-lets part of premises to ST

FIGURE 17.1 Sub-leases: establishing the competent landlord

In Example 2, T occupies that part of the premises they have not sub-let to ST. Accordingly, T is protected by the Act ('in occupation') and T's lease (L–T) will continue under the Act (s24). Thus, even during the last 14 months of T's lease it will not come to an end within 14 months because it continues under the Act. ST's competent landlord will be T.

Importantly, however, the situation in Example 2 is reversed if L serves T with a s25 notice, or T serves L with a s26 request or s27 notice. In this case, T's lease will come to an end within 14 months because it is being terminated by one of the ways prescribed by the Act. In this case, ST's competent landlord will be L (freeholder).

In Example 2, for ST of part where T remains in occupation of the remainder, it is crucial for ST to know, in respect of T's lease (L–T), whether T has been served with a s25 notice (by L), or whether T have themselves served a s27 notice or s26 request (on L). To establish the position, ST can serve a notice on T under s40 of the Act. Section 40 notices are considered at **17.8**.

The following should also be considered where there is a sub-lease or sub-leases. If the immediate landlord is the competent landlord and the immediate landlord's own lease has less than 16 months to run from the date of service or receipt, they are obliged to send a copy of the s25 notice or s26 request to their own landlord (Sch 6, para 7 Landlord and Tenant Act 1954). The superior landlord, if they become the competent landlord within two months of service of the s25 notice, may serve notice withdrawing the s25 notice (ibid, Sch 6, para 6). The superior landlord may then choose whether to serve their own s25 notice on the sub-tenant.

Similarly, where the superior landlord is not themselves the freeholder, they must send a copy to their landlord, who has the same rights as already described. The superior/competent landlord will bind the intermediate landlord(s) in relation to s25 notices that they give to the sub-tenant. Moreover, the terms of any new tenancy that the superior/competent landlord agrees with the sub-tenant are binding on the intermediate landlord(s). However, the latter must give its/their consent (such consent not to be unreasonably withheld), failing which the superior/competent landlord will be liable to pay compensation for any loss arising from the making of the agreement (ibid, Sch 6, para 4).

EXAMPLE

Your firm acts for Charlotte Enterprises Ltd ('Charlotte'), a public relations company that occupies 20a Broad Street, Oxford ('the Premises'), a suite of offices on the first and second floors of 20 Broad Street, a three-storey building in the centre of Oxford. Charlotte has a lease of the Premises from the present landlord Stiletto Shoes Ltd ('Stiletto'). The lease expires in six months' time. Stiletto has a lease of the whole of 20 Broad Street from the present freehold reversioner, Aragon Investments Ltd ('Aragon'). This lease was granted for a term of 25 years and expires in six months and ten days. Stiletto occupies and trades from the ground-floor shop premises. So the parties involved in this matter are Aragon Investments Limited ('A'), the freeholder, Stiletto Shoes Limited ('S'), the head tenant, and C, the sub-tenant and our client. You will consider the following:

- Making the first move: the tenant could consider making the first move on the lease renewal procedure. However, the **lessee** should only do so if certain conditions prevail in the local lettings market. If it is apparent that market rents in the locality of the subject property have risen, then the lessee could make an application to the **lessor** for a new tenancy as a pre-emptive strike stating 12 months hence as the end date. If the lessee does so, then that way the lessee will get six months at the existing or old rent but for a period extending beyond and after the contractual lease expiry date. Indeed, if market rents have actually fallen, C will want the new lease in place as soon as possible to take advantage of a lower rent. In the circumstances, your advice to C is to serve a s26 request stating six months hence as the lease end date.
- Who is the competent landlord? S's lease has less than 14 months to run but S is 'in occupation' and so S's lease continues under the Act until terminated in accordance with the Act (eg A serves on S a s25 notice or S serves on A Gorton s26 request, in either case terminating

S's lease within 14 months). C can find out whether S's lease has been terminated in accordance with the Act by serving on S a s40 notice (see **17.8**). The identity of the competent landlord can change more than once during the course of any litigation and renewal procedure. When acting for a tenant serving a s40 notice on a landlord, you should request in the covering letter a copy of any s25 notice received by the landlord terminating its tenancy. You can then serve s40 notices and similar covering letters on the superior landlord(s) until you reach the competent landlord for the anticipated renewal period.

17.8 Section 40 notices

The identity of the competent landlord can change more than once during the course of the litigation and renewal procedure. In Example 2 in **Figure 17.1**, the identity of the competent landlord will depend on whether notices or requests have been given to terminate T's lease (L–T) under the Act. To request information about superior leases and sub-leases, and whether notices or requests have been given, landlords and tenants can serve on each other a notice under s40 of the Act. Ideally, the s40 notice should be served before or simultaneously with the notices or requests under ss25, 26 and 27. A tenant can also serve a s40 notice on any person being a **mortgagee** in possession. A s40 notice may not be served earlier than two years before the date on which, apart from the Act, the tenancy would end by effluxion of time, or could be brought to an end by notice to quit given by the landlord (s40(6)).

17.8.1 Good practice

As a matter of good practice, the only time a s40 notice can safely be dispensed with is where you are certain that the landlord is the freeholder and the tenant occupies the whole of the premises (perhaps a tenant should also resist serving a s40 notice where they intend to serve a s26 request and do not wish to prompt their landlord into serving a s25 notice). Only a tenant who is entitled to serve a s26 request may to serve a s40 notice; thus a periodic tenant cannot serve one.

17.8.2 Action by recipient of s40 notice

A tenant who receives a s40 notice must indicate within one month whether they occupy the premises or any part of them wholly or partly for business purposes. The tenant must also indicate whether they have sub-let; and, if so, must provide information about the sub-letting, including whether there has been a contracting-out and whether a s25 notice has been served or a s26 request made. The tenant must state the identity of any known reversioner. Conversely, a landlord who receives a s40 notice must indicate within one month whether they own the freehold; and, if not, must give the identity of their immediate landlord and when their own tenancy will expire. A landlord must also state whether there is a mortgagee in possession and, if so, its name and address. Where there is a superior lease, the landlord must state whether a s25 notice has been served or a s26 request has been made. The landlord must also state the identity of any known reversioner. There is a statutory duty on both landlord and tenant to update the information given for a period of six months from the date of service of the s40 notice, where it ceases to be correct (s40(5)).

A landlord may learn from a tenant in response to a s40 notice that the premises have been sub-let. If the landlord has served a s25 notice on the tenant, the landlord will now be the competent landlord of the sub-tenant. In these circumstances, generally it will be good practice for the landlord to serve a s25 notice on the sub-tenant to prevent the sub-tenant making a s26 request.

Figure 17.2 shows a lease renewal flow chart.

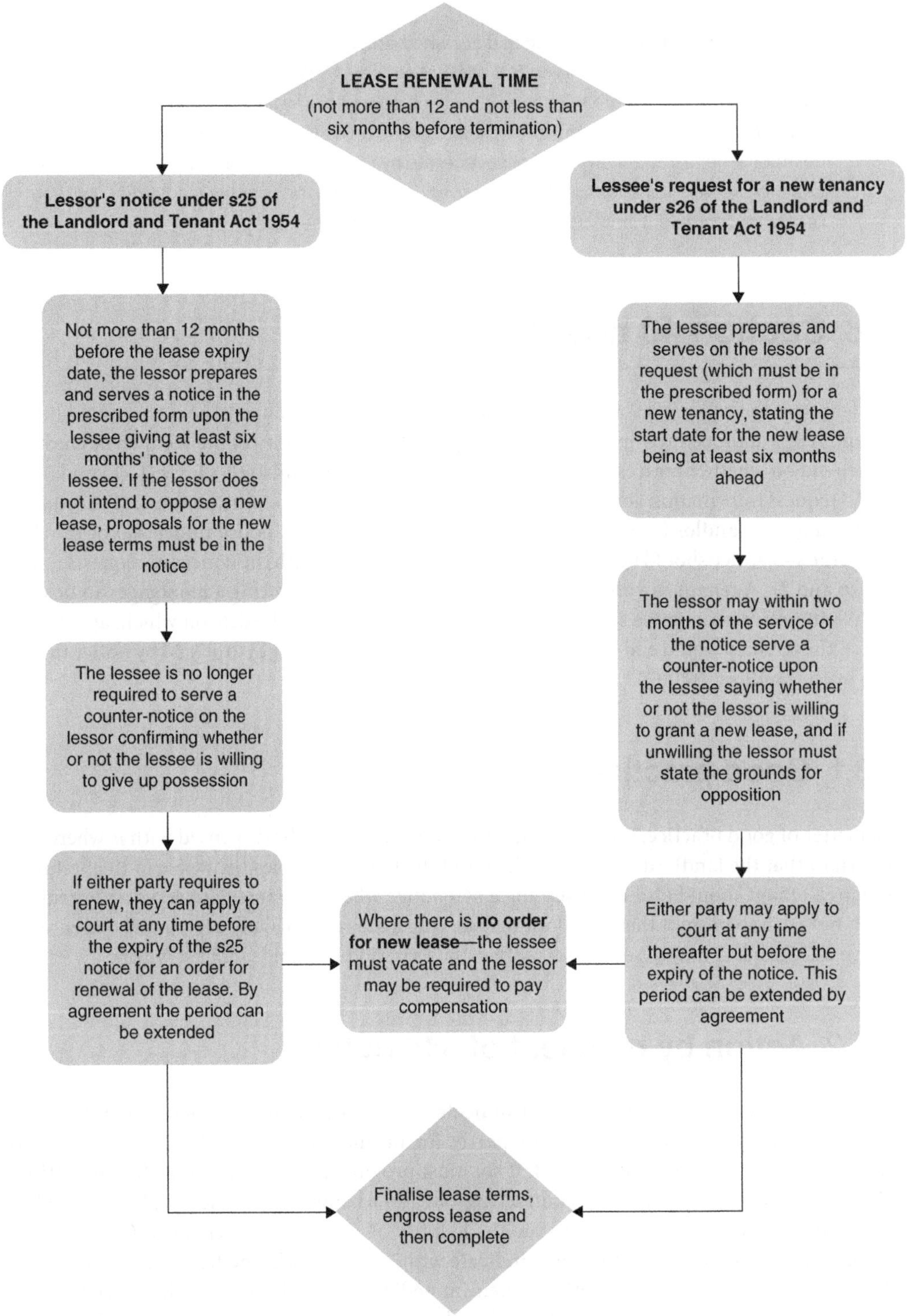

FIGURE 17.2 Lease renewal flow chart

KEY POINT SUMMARY

- The 1954 Act affords statutory protection to 'a tenant who occupies premises for the purposes of a business'.
- The tenant's statutory protection is twofold: the tenancy automatically continues at the end of the contractual tenancy; and the tenant can apply to the court for a statutory renewal of the tenancy.

- Certain tenancies are excluded from statutory protection, for example fixed-term tenancies not exceeding six months and contracted-out tenancies.
- For an agreement to contract out of the security-of-tenure provisions to be valid, the landlord must first serve a 'health warning' on the tenant who, in turn, must sign a declaration that they have received it.
- Tenancies protected by the Act can be terminated only by one of the methods prescribed by the Act.
- The most common methods of termination are by landlord's s25 notice or tenant's s26 request.
- Section 25 notices and s26 requests must be in a prescribed form and contain prescribed information. There are strict deadlines for service (see **17.5.2** and **17.5.3**).
- The s25 notice/s26 request must be served by/on the 'competent landlord'. Consider serving a s40 notice to establish the identity of the competent landlord.
- If you want the tenant to leave at the end of the lease, serve a hostile s25 notice and be sure of your statutory grounds for opposing a new lease.
- Be sure you are the 'competent landlord' for the tenant in question. It may be necessary to serve a notice under s40 to be sure.
- The s25 notice must be given not more than 12 months or less than six months before the date of termination specified in the notice; this termination date must not be earlier than the date on which the tenancy could have been terminated at common law (eg the contractual expiry date of a fixed term).
- If you are happy for the tenant to continue in occupation under a new lease and wish the new lease to be in place as soon as possible, serve a non-hostile s25 notice one year before the contractual expiry date, specifying the contractual expiry date as the termination date in the notice.
- Ensure that any s25 notice is in the prescribed form and contains the prescribed content.
- If you receive a tenant's s26 request and you want the tenant to leave, you must serve a counter-notice within two months specifying your statutory grounds for opposing a new lease.
- Serve by registered post or recorded delivery (in which case, service is deemed to be the date of postage).
- If you receive a landlord's s25 notice and you want to renew your lease, ensure that you apply to the court for a new lease on or before the date specified in the s25 notice.
- If you have not received a s25 notice by the time there is less than 12 months to go on the lease, consider a 'pre-emptive strike' by serving a s26 request and specifying a commencement date for the new lease 12 months hence.
- Serve the s26 notice on your 'competent landlord'. It may be necessary to serve a notice under s40 to be sure.
- Ensure that your s26 request is in the prescribed form and contains the prescribed content.
- If you serve a s26 request, be sure to apply to the court for a new lease before the date specified in the s26 request.
- Serve by registered post or recorded delivery (in which case, service is deemed to be the date of postage).

CHAPTER 18
Security of Tenure under Part II of the Landlord and Tenant Act 1954 (Part B)

FUNCTIONING LEGAL KNOWLEDGE

This chapter covers the following functioning legal knowledge required to pass the SQE 1 assessments:

Security of tenure under a business lease

Landlord and Tenant Act 1954 (Part II):

- landlord's grounds of opposition
- terms of new **lease**
- availability of compensation

AUTHORITIES UNDERPINNING PRACTICE

The key authorities that underpin this area of practice are listed below. Note that for legislation you are linked to legislation.gov.uk.

Although much of the legislation on this government website is available in its amended form, the incorporation of new amendments into the text of legislation can be delayed. You should refer to legal databases to ensure you are referencing the most up-to-date legislation.

- Part II of the Landlord and Tenant Act 1954
  https://www.legislation.gov.uk/uksi/1989/1548/contents/made
- Regulatory Reform (Business Tenancies) (England and Wales) Order 2003
  https://www.legislation.gov.uk/uksi/2003/3096/contents/made
- Landlord and Tenant (Covenants) Act 1995
  https://www.legislation.gov.uk/ukpga/1995/30/contents
- Costs of Leases Act 1958
  https://www.legislation.gov.uk/ukpga/Eliz2/6-7/52/contents

18.1 Introduction

In this second chapter on security of tenure under a business lease and Part II of the Landlord and Tenant Act 1954 (the Act), other significant issues for landlord and tenant in this area are considered including the process of applying to the court for an **interim rent**, the landlord's statutory grounds of opposition to a new business lease, the tenant's right to compensation for failure to obtain a new business lease and the likely terms of any new business lease.

18.2 Interim rent applications

18.2.1 Landlord's application

After an application to the court for a new lease, the current **tenancy** continues at the old contractual rent until three months after the conclusion of the proceedings (s64). This is clearly disadvantageous to a landlord seeking a higher market rent under the new lease, and it is also an incentive for the tenant to extend the proceedings for as long as possible. To remedy this unreasonable state of affairs, the Law of Property Act 1969 inserted a new s24A into the Act to allow the competent landlord to apply to the court for an interim rent to be fixed until the current tenancy comes to an end. In the case of a sub-tenancy where the head tenancy is also being continued under s24, the competent landlord will be the head landlord. Thus, rather curiously, the head landlord will be applying for an interim rent that is payable to the intermediate landlord.

18.2.2 Tenant's application

Under the 2004 reforms, both landlords and tenants now have the right to make applications for interim rent. The reason for allowing the tenant to apply as well is because there may be market conditions under which rents are falling and, in this situation, it is only fair to allow tenants to benefit from such market conditions.

A new s24A was introduced on 1 June 2004. It states that provided either a s25 notice has been served or a s26 request has been made, both landlords and tenants may apply for an interim rent while the tenancy is continuing under s24. However, no application may be made later than six months after the termination of the contractual tenancy. To avoid duplication of proceedings, neither party may apply if the other party has already done so unless that application has been withdrawn.

Under s24B, the interim rent is payable from:

1 the earliest date that could have been specified for termination of the tenancy, where a s25 notice has been served (s24B(2)); or

2 the earliest date that could have been specified for commencement of the new tenancy, where a s26 request has been made (s24B(3)).

This is intended to rule out the tactical use of s25 notices and s26 requests (eg the tenant's pre-emptive strike: see **17.5.3**).

18.2.3 Good practice on interim rent

In a normal rising market the landlord will generally apply for an interim rent as early as possible, namely as soon as the s25 notice or s26 request has been given or received. Conversely, in a falling market the landlord will have no need for an interim rent if the contractual rent is higher than the prevailing market rent. Here, it is the tenant who would be advised to apply for an interim rent. Another instance when it should be unnecessary for a landlord to apply for an interim rent will be where the rent was reviewed immediately before the contractual expiry date (a 'penultimate day rent review'); in this case, the tenant should already be paying the market rent.

The tenant will be required to start paying interim rent as soon as the court determines it. Interest will also be payable from this date unless the lease provides that interest will be payable from a period after the rent becomes due, such as 14 days. Interim rent continues to be payable until the date on which the current tenancy comes to an end.

EXAMPLE

Lyra, a landlord of a warehouse in Cardiff, has recently served a non-hostile s25 notice on her business tenant Tammy whose 25-year tenancy comes to an end in 11 months' time. Lyra is happy to enter into negotiations with Tammy for a renewal of her tenancy. As Tammy's rent was last reviewed four years ago and market rents have risen sharply in recent years, Lyra should be advised to apply to the court for an interim rent to be determined during the renewal process.

CONDUCT POINT

Failure to apply to the court for an interim rent determination may amount to a breach of the SRA Code of Conduct. You must act in the best interests of each client and you must provide a proper standard of service to your clients.

18.3 Landlord's statutory grounds of opposition

There are seven statutory grounds in s30(1) of the 1954 Act that entitle a landlord to resist a tenant's application for a new lease. If the landlord is successful in proving one or more of those grounds, then the tenant's application should fail. It should be noted that some grounds are subject to the court's discretion. The landlord must state the relevant ground(s) in its s25 notice or counter-notice to the tenant's s26 request. No later amendments or additions to the grounds are allowed so it is important that the landlord specifies the correct grounds at this early stage. However, the landlord's stated grounds must be genuine; if the grounds are false and made fraudulently, the notice may be rendered invalid and unenforceable. A subsequent purchaser of the landlord's interest will also be bound by the original landlord's choice of ground(s).

In summary, the grounds of opposition are:

(a) tenant's failure to carry out repairing obligations;
(b) tenant's persistent delay in paying rent;
(c) tenant's substantial breaches of other obligations;
(d) suitable alternative accommodation is available for the tenant;
(e) on sub-letting of part, the landlord requires the whole property for subsequent letting;
(f) the landlord intends to demolish or reconstruct the premises;
(g) the landlord intends to occupy the holding.

18.3.1 Discretionary grounds

Grounds (a), (b), (c) and (e) are discretionary. Thus, even if the landlord establishes the ground, the court may decide to order a new tenancy in any event, for example because of the tenant's good conduct. Examples of situations where the court may decide to use its discretion are considered next under the individual grounds. The remaining grounds—(d), (f) and (g)—are mandatory, so that if the landlord establishes the ground the court must refuse to order a new tenancy.

The specific grounds are now considered and, to assist in interpretation, the precise wording of the grounds is set out, followed by commentary and reference to cases.

18.3.1.1 Ground (a): tenant's failure to carry out repairing obligations

(a) where under the current tenancy the tenant has any obligations as respects the repair and maintenance of the holding, that the tenant ought not to be granted a new tenancy in view of the state of repair of the holding, being a state resulting from the tenant's failure to comply with the said obligations . . .

Ground (a) only applies to failure to repair the tenant's 'holding' as defined by the Act (see **17.6**). Thus, it would not apply to a part of the demised premises in disrepair that is occupied by a sub-tenant. Moreover, a substantial breach of **covenant** on the tenant's part may on its own be insufficient to establish the ground. The landlord must go further and show that the breach is serious enough that the 'tenant ought not to be granted a new tenancy'. Because of the ground's discretionary nature, the court may grant a new tenancy despite the breach. The grant could be on the basis of an **undertaking** by the tenant to remedy the breach. In exercising its discretion, the court will consider whether a new tenancy would be unfair to the landlord having regard to the tenant's past performances and conduct. It will also consider the reasons for the tenant's breach of covenant to repair.

If the landlord intends to rely on this ground, it (or its surveyor) should first serve on the tenant a schedule of dilapidations with a request that the repairs be carried out (on the assumption that there is a lease-repairing covenant). The landlord may also consider **forfeiture** of the lease as an alternative to ground (a). A tenant faced with opposition under ground (a) should consider giving the landlord an undertaking to carry out the repairs within a set time. A court may take such an undertaking into account when exercising its discretion but may also seek evidence that the tenant has sufficient funds to carry out the works. If the tenant is refused a new lease under ground (a), the tenant is not entitled to compensation.

18.3.1.2 Ground (b): tenant's persistent delay in paying rent

> (b) that the tenant ought not to be granted a new tenancy in view of his persistent delay in paying rent which has become due . . .

The word 'persistent' is significant, as it clearly means more than one incident of delay. The court will consider the frequency and extent of the delays, the steps the landlord had to take to secure payment and how the landlord may be protected against delay in any future tenancy. The ground is discretionary so that even if persistent delay is proven the court may decide to order a new tenancy if the tenant can offer a satisfactory explanation for the delay. The word 'rent' may include other payments due under the lease if these are reserved as rent, for example **service charges**. The tenant seeking to resist an opposition under ground (b) should ensure that no further arrears accrue and, if appropriate, suggest means of guaranteeing future payments (eg a rent deposit or guarantor). If the tenant is refused a new lease under ground (b), the tenant is not entitled to compensation.

18.3.1.3 Ground (c): tenant's substantial breaches of other obligations

> (c) that the tenant ought not to be granted a new tenancy in view of other substantial breaches by him of his obligations under the current tenancy, or for any other reason connected with the tenant's use or management of the holding . . .

This is another discretionary ground. It concerns the tenant's substantial breaches (note the use of the word 'substantial') of other obligations in the lease (ie other than repair or rent), and it also extends to reasons linked generally with the tenant's use or management of the holding. Thus, a court can refuse to grant a new lease if the tenant is at fault in some way, even though the tenant has performed all their obligations under the lease. The court must have regard to all relevant circumstances, including whether the landlord's interest has been prejudiced, the general conduct of the tenant and any proposals for remedying the breach.

Whether a breach is 'substantial' is a question of fact in each case. For example, in *Youssefi v Mussellwhite* [2014] EWCA Civ 885 the tenant's failure to allow access to the property and its failure to open a business were found to be substantial breaches of the lease.

It is not necessary for the breaches to relate to 'the holding' and so substantial breaches relating to any sub-let part of the premises may be included. If the tenant is refused a new lease under ground (c), the tenant is not entitled to compensation.

18.3.1.4 Ground (d): suitable alternative accommodation is available for the tenant

> (d) that the landlord has offered and is willing to provide or secure the provision of alternative accommodation for the tenant, that the terms on which the alternative accommodation is available are reasonable having regard to the terms of the current

> tenancy and to all other relevant circumstances, and that the accommodation and the time at which it will be available are suitable for the tenant's requirements (including the requirement to preserve goodwill) having regard to the nature and class of his business and to the situation and extent of, and facilities afforded by, the holding . . .

This ground is not discretionary, so if the landlord can provide suitable alternative accommodation based on these criteria the court must dismiss the tenant's application for a new tenancy. The relevant date to assess the reasonableness of the terms and the suitability of the alternative accommodation is the date of the hearing. Alternative accommodation in the future may also be sufficient for the landlord: if they can establish that it will be available at a later date (ie even after the termination date in the s25 notice or s26 request), they may still be able to succeed on ground (d) (see s31(2); see also 'near miss' cases at **18.3.2**). If the tenant is refused a new lease under ground (d), the tenant is not entitled to compensation.

18.3.1.5 Ground (e): on sub-letting of part, the landlord requires the whole property for subsequent letting

> (e) where the current tenancy was created by the sub-letting of part only of the property comprised in a superior tenancy and the landlord is the owner of an interest in **reversion** expectant on the termination of that superior tenancy, that the aggregate of the rents reasonably obtainable on separate lettings of the holding and the remainder of that property would be substantially less than the rent reasonably obtainable on a letting of that property as a whole, that on the termination of the current tenancy the landlord requires possession of the holding for the purpose of letting or otherwise disposing of the said property as a whole, and that in view thereof the tenant ought not to be granted a new tenancy . . .

Ground (e) is another discretionary ground and is the least used of all the grounds (indeed, there are no reported cases on how the discretion is to be exercised). It applies only where there is a sub-letting of part and the competent landlord of the sub-tenant is the superior landlord, for example not the sub-tenant's immediate landlord. As previously explained, the intermediate lease will, in these circumstances, have less than 14 months to run.

The landlord must show two things:

- the rent obtainable on separate lettings of the whole building would be substantially less than the rent obtainable on a letting of the whole. It should be noted that the rent has to be substantially less, not merely less; and
- on the termination of the sub-tenancy the landlord requires possession of the sub-let part to let or otherwise dispose of the property as a whole. The landlord may have difficulty in establishing this unless the intermediate lease is due to end before the sub-tenancy is terminated (on the basis that they cannot re-let the whole if the intermediate tenant is still in occupation).

In exercising its discretion, a court would have regard to whether the landlord originally consented to the sub-letting. Section 31(2) of the Act also applies to ground (e), namely if the landlord can establish the ground at a later date (see 'near miss' cases at **18.3.2**). If the tenant is refused a new lease under ground (e), the tenant is entitled to compensation (see **18.5**).

18.3.1.6 Ground (f): the landlord intends to demolish or reconstruct the premises

> (f) that on the termination of the current tenancy the landlord intends to demolish or reconstruct the premises comprised in the holding or a substantial part of those premises or to carry out substantial work of construction on the holding or part thereof and that he could not reasonably do so without obtaining possession of the holding . . .

This is the most frequently used ground. To rely on it, the landlord must show on the termination of the tenancy the following three elements:

- the landlord's intention;
- to demolish or reconstruct the premises in the holding (or a substantial part thereof) or to carry out substantial work of construction on the holding (or part thereof); and
- that they could not reasonably do so without obtaining possession of the holding.

Each of these three elements is now considered.

Landlord's intention

The landlord's intention to carry out the work must be more than a simple desire to bring it about. The intention must be firm and settled. It must have 'moved out of the zone of contemplation—out of the sphere of the tentative, the provisional and the exploratory—into the valley of decision' (per Asquith LJ in *Cunliffe v Goodman* [1950] 2 KB 237, and subsequently approved by Viscount Simonds in *Betty's Cafes Ltd v Phillips Furnishing Stores Ltd* [1959] AC 20, HL). Further, as a question of fact, there must be a reasonable prospect that the landlord's plan will succeed, although they do not need to prove that it will be a commercial success. Even if the landlord can show the requisite intention to carry out the works, any ulterior motive of the landlord may defeat the ground.

EXAMPLE

In *S Franses Ltd v The Cavendish Hotel (London) Ltd* [2018] UKSC 62, the tenant successfully appealed to the Supreme Court on the basis that the landlord's proposed works were devised solely for the purpose of evicting the tenant and with no other benefit for the landlord. The court held that it was not sufficient for the landlord to have an intention to undertake the works only if the tenant did not voluntarily vacate—in other words, for the landlord's intention to be conditional. This would not be a firm and settled intention. In the light of this decision, tenants whose renewals are being opposed under ground (f) should ask for full disclosure of their landlord's development plans. Any evidence that, but for the tenant, the development would be carried out in another way, may help the tenant defeat the ground.

The time when the landlord's intention must be established is the date of the court hearing. The fact that the landlord (or their predecessor) had no such intention at the time of serving the s25 notice (or counter-notice to s26 request) is irrelevant. Provided the landlord can prove the ground as a matter of fact, the court will not examine the landlord's motives for using the ground. For example, in *Fisher v Taylors Furnishing Stores Ltd* [1956] 2 QB 78, it did not matter that the landlord's primary object was to occupy the reconstructed premises themselves.

The necessary intention is a question of fact in each case, but the landlord's position will be strengthened if, by the time of the hearing, they have taken appropriate steps. These would include instructing professionals, obtaining quotations, preparing plans and drawings, securing any necessary **planning permissions**, arranging finance and, for a company landlord, passing a board resolution. The less the landlord has to do by the time they get to court, the better. Where planning permission has been applied for but not obtained by the date of the hearing, the test the court will use is whether there is a reasonable prospect that permission will be granted.

The works must be carried out 'on the termination of the current tenancy'. The Court of Appeal has held this to include within a reasonable time from the date of the termination of the tenancy (*London Hilton Jewellers Ltd v Hilton International Hotels Ltd* [1990] 1 EGLR 112). For practical purposes, 'termination of the current tenancy' would include any continuation tenancy under s64 of the Act, as the landlord would clearly be entitled to possession before the works were carried out. A reasonable time will, of course, be a question of fact in each case.

Demolish, reconstruct or carry out substantial work of construction

In addition to establishing an intention, the landlord must also show that the proposed works fall within the express wording of ground (f). This will depend on the nature and extent of the works and is a question of fact in each case. The key words used are 'demolish', 'reconstruct' and 'substantial work of construction'. 'Demolish' is easily understood and there must be some property on the holding that is capable of being demolished, such as a building or wall. If part of the premises are to be demolished, then they must be 'substantial', which is a question of fact. 'Reconstruct' has been held to involve rebuilding and a substantial interference with the structure of the building. The work need not be confined necessarily to the outside of the premises or to load-bearing walls.

'Substantial work of construction' implies a new building or adding to what was already there. It connotes more than mere refurbishment or improvement.

EXAMPLE

In *Barth v Pritchard* [1990] 1 EGLR 109, CA, an intention to rewire, re-roof, redecorate, install central heating and reposition a staircase was held to be insufficient. Yet in *Joel v Swaddle* [1957] 1 WLR 1094, a proposal to convert a shop with two storage rooms into part of a large amusement arcade came within the ground. Other successful works of 'construction' have been the laying of pipes, wires, cables and drains, and the laying of a road.

On the question of what amounts to a reconstruction of a substantial part of the holding, the court in *Joel v Swaddle* said the proper approach was to look at the position as a whole. The result after carrying out the proposed work should be compared with the condition and state of the premises before the work was begun.

Landlord could not reasonably carry out the work without obtaining possession of the holding

The landlord must show that they need legal possession of the holding, not merely physical possession. In other words, they must show that they need to terminate the tenancy in order to carry out the work. If the landlord can do the work simply by exercising their right of entry under the terms of the lease, ground (f) will not be established (this right is often reserved by landlords to enable them to execute improvements and alterations; see *Heath v Drown* [1973] AC 496, HL).

Tenant's defences under s31A

Even if the landlord can show that they require possession to carry out work, the tenant may be assisted by s31A of the Act (inserted by s7(1) Law of Property Act 1969). This effectively prevents the landlord from using ground (f) in circumstances where the proposed work would be over quickly or where the work will affect only part of the premises. Section 31A provides that a court cannot hold that the landlord could not reasonably carry out the demolition or other work without obtaining possession if either of the following occurs:

1 The tenant agrees to the inclusion in the terms of the new tenancy of terms giving the landlord access and other facilities for carrying out the work intended and, given that access and those facilities, the landlord could reasonably carry out the work without obtaining possession of the holding and without interfering to a substantial extent or for a substantial time with the use of the holding for the purposes of the business carried on by the tenant. The tenant may decide to rely on this defence where the landlord has failed to reserve adequate rights in the lease to allow them to carry out the work. The word 'interfering' refers to interference with the tenant's use of the holding for its business purposes, not the business itself or the goodwill. Thus, a tenant intending to leave while the works are being carried out and then return with its goodwill unaffected cannot use s31A.

2 The tenant is willing to accept a tenancy of an economically separable part of the holding and either para (a) is satisfied with respect to that part or possession of the remainder of the holding would be reasonably sufficient to enable the landlord to carry out the intended work.

Here, a part of the holding will be an economically separable part if, and only if, the aggregate of the rents that, after completion of the intended work, would be reasonably obtainable on separate lettings of that part and the remainder of the premises affected by or resulting from the work would not be substantially less than the rent that would then be reasonably obtainable on a letting of those premises as a whole (s31A(2)). If the tenant establishes defence (b), the order for the new tenancy will be only of the economically separable part (s32(1A)).

Section 31(2) of the Act applies to ground (f), namely the landlord has a second chance if they can establish the ground at a later date (see 'near miss' cases at **18.3.2**). However, ground (f) must be established within one year of the termination date specified in the s25 notice or s26 request. If the tenant is refused a new lease under ground (f), the tenant is entitled to compensation (see **18.4**).

18.3.1.7 Ground (g): the landlord intends to occupy the holding

> (g) that on the termination of the current tenancy the landlord intends to occupy the holding for the purposes, or partly for the purposes, of a business to be carried on by him therein, or as his residence . . .

This is another frequently used ground that has three important elements: the five-year rule, the landlord's intention and the occupation of the holding. These are now considered.

The five-year rule

The five-year rule is an integral part of ground (g) and is set out in s30(2) of the Act. It provides that the landlord cannot rely on ground (g) if the landlord's interest 'was purchased or created after the beginning of the period of five years which ends with the termination of the current tenancy'. So to rely on ground (g) the landlord effectively must have owned the reversion for at least five years before the termination date specified in the s25 notice or s26 request. The word 'purchased' means 'bought for money', and the time at which the purchase occurs is the date of **exchange of contracts**. The landlord must have been the 'competent' landlord for the five years prior to the end of the tenancy. This means that the landlord must either have owned the freehold or had a leasehold interest with at least 14 months to run.

Purpose of rule

The purpose of this rule is to prevent persons from buying the landlord's interest towards the end of the tenancy simply in order to gain possession for themselves. The rule applies only where the premises have been let on a tenancy or series of tenancies within the Act's protection throughout the five-year period.

EXAMPLE

If three years before the end of a tenancy a purchaser buys the reversion (subject to the tenancy), the five-year restriction would prevent them from using ground (g). However, if the same purchaser bought the freehold with vacant possession and then subsequently granted a lease, the five-year restriction would not apply.

Circumventing the rule

A landlord requiring possession can circumvent the five-year rule if they can prove ground (f) instead, namely an intention to demolish or reconstruct the premises. The court will not examine the landlord's motives for using ground (f), so they could lawfully move in after the construction works have been completed. In addition, the future application of the five-year rule can be avoided if the current landlord is a company. Here, if the purchaser acquires the company by share acquisition it will not be purchasing the 'landlord's interest'.

Landlord's intention

The landlord must intend to occupy the premises either for business purposes or as their residence. As with ground (f), the landlord must be able to show by the date of the hearing a firm and settled intention. The matters already considered are therefore equally applicable here. One relevant factor will be the likely prospect of the landlord succeeding in their plans to occupy.

EXAMPLE

If planning permission were to be refused for the landlord's intended business use, this could make the necessary intention harder to establish. However, the courts have held that likely failure of the landlord's proposed business is not a relevant consideration; nor is whether it is commercially sensible.

The occupation of the holding

The landlord must intend to occupy the holding for the purposes, or partly for the purposes, of a business to be carried on by them in the premises, or as their residence. Section 42(3) enables a landlord that is a company in a group of companies to rely on ground (g) where another member of the group is to occupy the premises. Section 41(2) enables a landlord who is a trustee to rely on ground (g) where there is an intention to occupy by a beneficiary under the trust. Under the 2004 reforms, ground (g) is extended to a wider category of landlords. Section 30(1A) provides that where a landlord has a controlling interest in a company, then a reference in ground (g) to the landlord is a reference either to the landlord or to the company. Similarly, s30(1B) provides that where the landlord is a company, and a person has a controlling interest in that company, then a reference in ground (g) to the landlord is a reference either to the landlord or that person.

If the tenant is refused a new lease under ground (g), the tenant is entitled to compensation (see **18.3**).

18.3.2 'Near miss' cases

If the landlord fails to establish ground (d), (e) or (f) (alternative accommodation, uneconomic **sub-lease** or intention to demolish or reconstruct) at the date of the hearing, they may still be saved by s31(2) of the Act. If the landlord can show that they would have been able to establish one of these grounds had the termination date in the s25 notice or s26 request been up to 12 months later, the court must refuse the tenant's application for a new tenancy. In this case, the tenant can ask the court to substitute that later date for the original termination date in the s25 notice or s26 request and the tenancy will continue until the later date.

EXAMPLE

Your firm acts for Cambo Ltd acquiring the freehold reversion of 18 Clover Street, London W2 for £700,000 subject to and with the benefit of two occupational business leases. Completion of the freehold purchase has recently taken place. The tenant of the business lease of the first and second floors has a history of late payment and is in breach of its repairing obligations. Your client would like to evict the tenant as soon as possible and let the premises to another interested tenant with a better covenant. The lease of the first and second floors ends in six months' time. You would advise your client to serve a hostile s25 notice on the tenant, specifying the last day of the contractual term as the termination date in the notice. This can be served immediately as the lease only has six months to run. The grounds of opposition will be ground (b) (persistent delay in paying rent) and ground (a) (breach of repairing obligations). Your client should be advised that both grounds are discretionary and so the court may allow the tenant to renew in any event, for example if the tenant can convince the court that it will mend its ways. In respect of the repairs, the court may accept an undertaking from the tenant to carry out the repairs within a reasonable period. If your client is successful in obtaining possession based on ground (b) or (a), then your client will have no liability to pay compensation to the tenant for disturbance (see **18.3**). As an alternative, your client could consider seeking forfeiture of the lease for breach of the tenant's covenants. In respect of the repairs breach, a notice under s146 of the Law of Property Act 1925 will be required to be served on the tenant, accompanied by a schedule of dilapidations.

18.4 Tenant's right to compensation

The tenant can claim financial compensation from the landlord if the landlord succeeds in establishing one or more of the 'non-fault' grounds (e), (f) or (g). This is often referred to as 'compensation for disturbance'. The tenant's right to compensation on quitting the premises is contained in s37(1) of the Act. The basis for compensation is that the tenant is being denied a new tenancy through no fault of its own. Conversely, if one of the 'fault' grounds (a), (b) or (c) is established, then the tenant properly will have no right to compensation. Similarly, there will be no right to compensation if the landlord can provide suitable alternative accommodation under ground (d) (on the basis that the tenant has suffered no loss).

It should be noted that s37(1) allows the tenant compensation on quitting the holding where the landlord in their s25 notice (or counter-notice to a s26 request) has specified ground (e), (f) or (g) in the notice and the tenant has either:

- not applied to the court for a new tenancy; or
- made and then withdrawn an application for a new tenancy; or
- applied to the court for a new tenancy but has been defeated on one or more of ground (e), (f) or (g).

Where the landlord has opposed on both fault and non-fault grounds and has been successful, the tenant must, in order to claim compensation, apply to the court for a certificate confirming that the landlord was successful only on ground (e), (f) or (g) and on no other ground (s37(4)). This is normally done at the hearing of the application for the new lease and the certificate is then incorporated into the court order. The landlord's stated grounds must be genuine; if the grounds are false and made fraudulently, such as by stating a fault ground in an attempt to avoid paying compensation, the notice may be rendered invalid and unenforceable.

18.4.1 Amount of compensation

The amount of compensation is calculated by multiplying the rateable value of the holding (as at the date of service of the s25 notice or s26 request) by the 'appropriate multiplier' set from time to time by the Secretary of State. The current multiplier at the time of writing is 1, as prescribed by the Landlord and Tenant Act 1954 (Appropriate Multiplier) Order 1990 (SI 1990/363), which came into force on 1 April 1990 (before that date the multiplier was 3). The rateable value to be used is taken from the valuation list in force at the date of service of the landlord's s25 notice or s26(6) counter-notice (s37(5)(a)).

18.4.2 Double compensation

Double compensation is payable where the tenant or their predecessors in the same business have been in occupation for at least 14 years prior to the termination of the current tenancy (s37(3)). The date of termination is either the date of termination specified in the s25 notice or the date specified in the s26 request as being the date from which the new tenancy is to start (s37(7)). In these circumstances, double compensation is calculated by multiplying twice the rateable value by the appropriate multiplier (presently 1). Where the tenant has occupied for nearly 14 years, the timing of a s26 request or s25 notice may be crucial in determining whether double compensation is payable.

18.4.3 Excluding compensation by agreement

The landlord and tenant may agree (eg in the lease) to exclude or modify the tenant's right to compensation for failure to obtain a new tenancy (s38(3)). However, s38(2) provides that such agreement will be void where the tenant or their predecessors in the same business have been in occupation for five years or more prior to the date the tenant quits the premises. A prospective tenant would be wise to resist attempts by the landlord to 'contract out' of compensation as

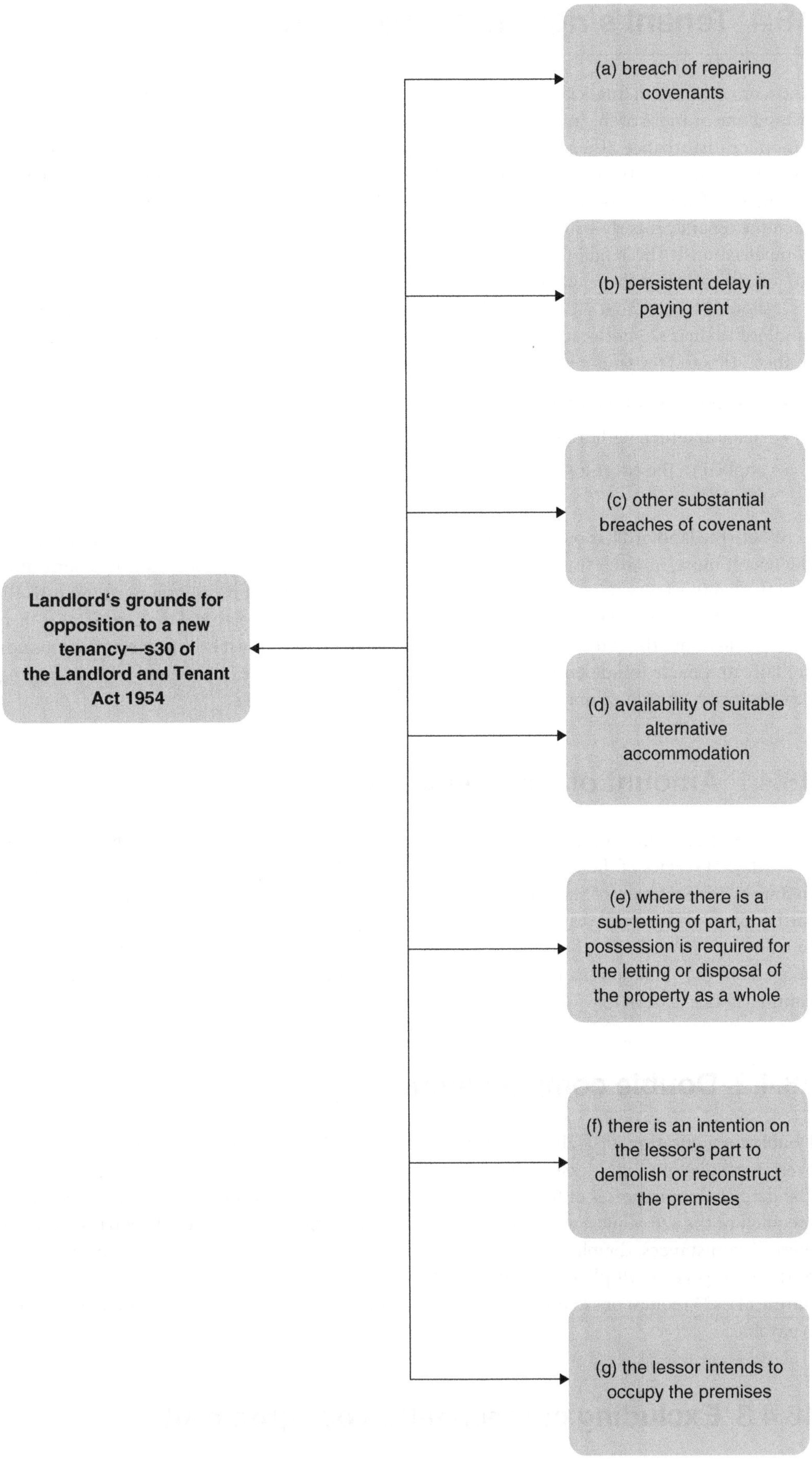

FIGURE 18.1 Landlord's statutory grounds for opposing new lease

such a provision may adversely affect the marketability of the lease during the last five years of the term.

Compensation is also available in special circumstances, such as a failure to be granted a new tenancy on the grounds of public interest or national security (see ss57–60).

18.5 The terms of the new tenancy

If the tenant properly applies to the court after following all the correct procedures, the court will order a new lease where: (a) the landlord fails to establish an opposition ground under s30; or (b) the landlord has not opposed the tenant's application. In (b), it is rare for the matter to get to court, as the parties' solicitors, after a period of negotiation, will normally be able to agree on the terms of the new lease. The tenant's application in this situation is simply a back-up in case the negotiations break down, and if the parties reach agreement on the terms of the new lease the tenant can simply instruct the court to close its file on the matter.

When conducting negotiations, it is important to know the powers of the court, and in particular the lease terms that the court would be likely to impose. You are clearly in a far stronger position if you can argue for the inclusion of a particular clause on the basis that the court would order it. Accordingly, this section will concentrate on the terms a court would be likely to impose in a renewed tenancy. If the parties agree some terms but not others, the court will rule on the unresolved matters leaving the agreed terms to stand.

18.5.1 Premises

Generally, the new lease will be of 'the holding' (s32), which is all the property comprised in the existing tenancy excluding any part not occupied by the tenant (eg a sub-let part). The parties may agree as to the extent of the premises to be comprised in the new lease.

18.5.2 Duration

The parties are free to agree whatever length of term they like, but in default of agreement the maximum fixed term that the court can order is 15 years (s33). The court has a wide discretion and may order such term as it considers reasonable in all the circumstances (subject to the 15-year maximum). The court also has the power to order a periodic tenancy (although this is rare). In the absence of agreement between the parties, the new tenancy will commence when the current tenancy ends under s64, namely three months after the application has finally been disposed of. The court should also specify an end date for the new tenancy.

The court will consider such matters as:

- duration of the current tenancy;
- length of time the tenant has held over under the current tenancy;
- comparative hardship caused to either party;
- landlord's future plans for the property. The court may decide to order a short term where, although the landlord at the date of the hearing is unable to show sufficient intention under ground (f) (demolition/reconstruction), the court is satisfied that they will do so in the near future. The court may include a break clause in the lease which would allow the landlord to end the lease early to carry out future development plans;
- any other factors relevant to the particular case.

18.5.3 Rent

Rent is usually the most contentious matter between the parties. Section 34(1) provides that the rent shall be that at which 'having regard to the terms of the tenancy (other than those relating to rent), the holding might reasonably be expected to be let in the open market by a willing **lessor**'. In assessing the rent, the court will usually hear evidence from surveyors or valuers and consider comparable rents in the area ('comparables'). If relevant comparables are not available, the court will consider generally any increases of rent in the locality.

As the other terms of the tenancy will have a bearing on the rent, such other terms are normally agreed before the rent. The courts have approved this as being the most sensible approach. The tenant's user covenant in the new lease will be especially relevant when determining the new rent. Landlords often seek a wider use clause so as to command a higher rent (on the basis that a wider use is more attractive to a tenant thus increasing the rent a tenant in the open market would be willing to pay). In general, the courts have been reluctant to permit a relaxation of the user covenant for this purpose.

18.5.4 Disregards when assessing rent

Under s34(1), the court when assessing the rent must disregard certain factors that would otherwise work against the tenant. These 'disregards' are similar to those found in a typical rent review clause in a business lease. For further reference on rent review and cases interpreting these disregards, see Chapter 2 of *A Practical Approach to Commercial Conveyancing and Property* by Abbey and Richards (Oxford University Press, 2016).

The 'disregards' in s34(1) are:

- occupation: 'any effect on rent of the fact that the tenant has or his predecessors in **title** have been in occupation of the holding'. Thus, the landlord cannot argue for a higher rent on the basis that a tenant in occupation would pay more rent to avoid the expense of moving elsewhere;
- goodwill: 'any goodwill attached to the holding by reason of the carrying on thereat of the business of the tenant (whether by him or by a predecessor of his in that business)'. If the tenant has through their own efforts generated goodwill in their business, then they should not be penalised for it by having to pay a higher rent;
- improvements: 'any effect on rent of an improvement . . . carried out by a person who at the time it was carried out was the tenant . . . otherwise than in pursuance of an obligation to his immediate landlord'. This effectively avoids the tenant paying for the improvements twice over; once when the tenant carries them out and again through a consequential uplift in the rent. The words 'otherwise than in pursuance of an obligation to his immediate landlord' (s34(2)) mean that improvements to the premises that the tenant was obliged to carry out (eg under the terms of the lease) will not be disregarded. In other words, such obligatory improvements will be taken into account when assessing the rent.

18.5.5 Rent review in new tenancy

The court is permitted, if it thinks fit, to include a provision in the new lease for varying the rent; that is, a rent review clause (s34(3)). This applies irrespective of whether a rent review clause was included in the current lease. However, a court will normally include a review clause if one is present in the current lease. The scope and frequency of the rent review is entirely at the court's discretion. Upward-only reviews are common but tenants have successfully argued for the inclusion of downward reviews if market rents have fallen.

18.5.6 Other terms of the new tenancy

In default of agreement, the other terms of the lease 'may be determined by the court; and in determining those terms the court shall have regard to the terms of the current tenancy and to all relevant circumstances' (s35(1)). This includes the operation of the provisions of the Landlord and Tenant (Covenants) Act 1995 (see **18.4.9**). Accordingly, if either party wishes to introduce terms that were not included in the current lease, they must justify this by showing that it is fair and reasonable in all the circumstances.

18.5.7 Help for tenant in the case of *O'May*

It is usually the landlord who seeks to introduce new terms under the guise of 'modernising' the lease. Predictably, these new terms are usually more onerous on the tenant. Such modernisation provisions should be resisted by the tenant, who is assisted by the House of Lords decision in *O'May v City of London Real Property Co Ltd* [1983] 2 AC 726. In *O'May*, Lord Hailsham gave the following guidance:

> the court must begin by considering the terms of the current tenancy, that the burden of persuading the court to impose a change in those terms against the will of either party must rest on the party proposing the change and the change proposed must in the circumstances of the case be fair and reasonable and should take into account, amongst other things, the comparatively weak negotiating position of a sitting tenant requiring renewal, particularly in conditions of scarcity, and the general purpose of the Act which is to protect the business interests of the tenant so far as they are affected by the approaching termination of the current lease, in particular as regards his security of tenure.

The landlord in *O'May* failed to show that a proposed new term requiring the tenant to pay a service charge was reasonable, even though the tenant was offered a reduction in rent. The court could see that the landlord's true intention was to shift the burden of maintenance and repair of the building onto the tenant, and this was unjustified.

18.5.8 Guarantors

The court is able to require the tenant to provide guarantors for the new tenancy. This is likely to occur where the tenant has a poor record of paying rent or performing other covenants, or where the tenant is a recent **assignee** or newly formed company.

18.5.9 Effect of the Landlord and Tenant (Covenants) Act 1995

18.5.9.1 Alienation covenant in new lease

One area in which the courts may be sympathetic to a landlord seeking to introduce new terms is with regard to the tenant's **alienation** covenant. If the current lease was granted before 1 January 1996, the old privity of contract rules meant that the original tenant was bound for the entire duration of the lease even after they had assigned it. The change to the privity of contract rule introduced by the Landlord and Tenant (Covenants) Act 1995 (the 1995 Act) benefited tenants, in that for leases granted on or after 1 January 1996 the tenant was released from liability after **assignment**. A renewed lease today is therefore a 'new lease' under the 1995 Act, and the landlord's position will be worse than it was under the current lease (assuming the current lease was granted before 1 January 1996).

To reflect the changes introduced by the 1995 Act, new leases generally contain more restrictive alienation obligations on the tenant, for example preconditions to be satisfied before assignment and the use of **authorised guarantee agreements** (AGAs). Accordingly, to counteract the landlord's loss of privity, the courts will generally permit a modernisation of the alienation covenant in the renewed lease to reflect current practice on the grant of new leases. This is reinforced by Sch 1, para 4 to the 1995 Act, which amends s35 of the 1954 Act to provide that the reference to 'all relevant circumstances' includes the operation of the provisions of the 1995 Act (s35(2)).

EXAMPLE

In *Wallis Fashion Group Ltd v CGU Life Assurance Ltd* [2000] 27 EG 145, the landlord argued that the renewal lease should entitle the landlord to an automatic AGA from the assigning tenant. However, Neuberger J held that although there could be an AGA condition, it should be qualified by the words 'where reasonable'. This decision is important for tenants who can now properly resist any claim by the landlord for an automatic AGA. An AGA is appropriate only if it is reasonable in all the circumstances.

Alternatively, the landlord's loss of privity under the 1995 Act may be counterbalanced by changes to other terms in the lease, including the level of rent. To underline the point, the 1995 Act amends s34 of the 1954 Act by inserting a new s34(4) as follows:

> It is hereby declared that the matters which are to be taken into account by the court in determining the rent include any effect on rent of the operation of the provisions of the Landlord and Tenant (Covenants) Act 1995.

18.5.10 **Costs of the new tenancy**

The question of whether the tenant agrees to pay the landlord's costs in connection with the new lease will depend on the parties' relative bargaining strengths. However, the tenant should endeavour to resist this as it is highly unlikely that the tenant will be forced to do so by the court. Section 1 of the Costs of Leases Act 1958, provides that, unless the parties otherwise agree in writing, each party should be responsible for its own costs.

18.5.11 **Court order for new tenancy**

If the court orders a new tenancy, it will not commence until three months after the proceedings are 'finally disposed of' (s64). The landlord and tenant should execute a lease and counterpart lease, respectively (s36(1)).

EXAMPLE

Lyra, a landlord of a warehouse in Cardiff, has entered into negotiations with Tammy for a renewal of her 25-year tenancy which expires shortly. If negotiations break down between them and the terms of the new tenancy have to be determined by the court, then the maximum fixed term the court can order is 15 years. In assessing the rent, the court will consider comparable rents in the area and disregard the matters in s34 of the 1954 Act (tenant's occupation, goodwill and voluntary improvements). If Lyra wishes to impose new or 'modernised' terms in the renewed tenancy, the court will have to determine whether it is fair and reasonable in all the circumstances. However, the court will generally permit a modernisation of the alienation covenant in the renewed lease to reflect current practice on the grant of new leases. Lyra and Tammy should each pay their own legal costs.

KEY POINT SUMMARY

- Four of the seven grounds are discretionary. They are the tenant's 'fault' grounds—(a) tenant's failure to repair; (b) tenant's delay in paying rent; and (c) tenant's breaches of other obligations—and ground (e) on sub-letting of part, where the superior landlord requires the whole property for subsequent letting.
- You cannot amend your grounds at a later date, so be sure of them when the notices are served.
- Grounds (f) (demolish/reconstruct) and (g) (landlord's occupation) are the most frequently used grounds. They require a firm and settled intention on the landlord's part, to be established at the date of the hearing.
- Ground (f) (demolish/reconstruct) will not be established if the tenant is willing to accept a new tenancy of part of the holding or under the new lease the landlord is allowed access to carry out the works.

- Ground (g) (landlord's occupation) will not be established if the landlord acquired the reversion less than five years before the end of the current tenancy.
- Ground (d), (e) or (f) may be proven under the 'near miss' rule if the landlord can show they could have established them within 12 months.
- The landlord can oppose the tenant's application for a new lease by relying on one or more of the statutory grounds for opposition in s30.
- The competent landlord should consider applying to the court for an interim rent to be assessed. If market rents have fallen, the tenant should consider doing so.
- The landlord must pay the tenant compensation for disturbance if they establish one or more of the 'non fault' grounds ((e), (f) or (g)).
- The amount of compensation is the rateable value of the holding times 1. However, the landlord must pay double compensation if the tenant or predecessors in the same business have occupied for at least 14 years.
- The parties may exclude compensation by agreement unless the tenant or predecessor in the same business has been in occupation for five years or more.
- The parties' advisors should appreciate the terms a court is likely to order in the lease. This puts them in a stronger negotiating position. In particular:
- the court will order a new lease of 'the holding' which generally excludes sub-let parts;
- the maximum fixed term the court can order is 15 years. The duration of the current tenancy will be an important consideration but there are other factors too;
- in assessing the rent, the court will consider comparable rents in the area and disregard the matters in s34 of the 1954 Act (tenant's occupation, goodwill and voluntary improvements).
- If the landlord wishes to impose new terms in the renewed tenancy, the landlord will have to show that it is fair and reasonable in all the circumstances (see *O'May v City of London Real Property Co Ltd* [1983] 2 AC 726).
- The court will take into account the effect of the Landlord and Tenant (Covenants) Act 1995 (ie landlord's loss of privity) when fixing the rent and other terms (eg alienation provisions).
- Tenants are within their rights to resist a landlord's demand for an automatic AGA; accept an AGA only where reasonable.

APPENDIX 1
Guides and Useful Websites

Here is a list of web links to the guides and useful webpages mentioned in this manual.

- Energy Performance Certificate (EPC)
  https://www.gov.uk/buy-sell-your-home/energy-performance-certificates
- Law Society's Conveyancing Quality Scheme (CQS)
  https://www.lawsociety.org.uk/topics/firm-accreditations/conveyancing-quality-scheme/
- Land Registry Portal
  https://www.gov.uk/government/collections/how-to-use-the-land-registry-portal
- Capital gains tax allowance
  https://www.gov.uk/capital-gains-tax/allowances
- Stamp duty land tax
  https://www.gov.uk/stamp-duty-land-tax/residential-property-rates
- Welsh land transaction tax rates and bands
  https://gov.wales/land-transaction-tax-rates-and-bands
- SRA Code of Conduct for Solicitors 2019
  https://www.sra.org.uk/solicitors/standards-regulations/code-conduct-solicitors/
- SRA Transparency Rules
  https://www.lawsociety.org.uk/support-services/risk-compliance/price-and-service-transparency/
- Law Society's anti-money laundering guidance
  https://www.lawsociety.org.uk/support-services/risk-compliance/anti-money-laundering/?ctype=advice
- National Conveyancing Protocol
  https://www.lawsociety.org.uk/topics/property/conveyancing-protocol
- Standard Conditions of Sale
  https://www.lawsociety.org.uk/topics/property/standard-conditions-of-sale
- NLIS channels
  https://www.nlis.org.uk/what-is-nlis
- Law Society Practice Note on Consumer Protection Regulation in Conveyancing
  https://www.lawsociety.org.uk/support-services/advice/practice-notes/consumer-protection-regulations-in-conveyancing
- Coal mining search
  https://www.groundstability.com
- Law Society's best practice guidance on coal mining searches
  https://www.lawsociety.org.uk/topics/property/con29-forms
- Terramfirma: CON29M report producer
  https://www.terrafirmasearch.co.uk/coal/
- Land Registry MapSearch service
  https://www.gov.uk/guidance/mapsearch
- Companies House
  https://www.gov.uk/government/organisations/companies-house
- Law Society's Practice Note on Flood Risk
  http://www.lawsociety.org.uk/advice/practice-notes/flood-risk/
- Environment Agency
  https://www.gov.uk/government/publications/flood-risk-maps-for-surface-water-how-to-use-the-map

- Chancelcheck
  http://www.clsl.co.uk
- Groundsure—Cheshire salt search report
  https://www.groundsure.com/cheshire-salt-search
- Cornwall Consultants Ltd—tin mining search
  https://cornwallminingconsultants.co.uk/services/mining-searches/
- Law Society's transaction forms
  https://www.lawsociety.org.uk/topics/property/transaction-forms
- Countrywide Legal Indemnities
  http://www.countrywidelegal.co.uk/
- *UK Finance Mortgage Lenders' Handbook*
  https://lendershandbook.ukfinance.org.uk/lenders-handbook/
- Lifetime ISA
  https://www.gov.uk/lifetime-isa/
- *Council of Mortgage Lenders' Handbook*
  http://www.cml.org.uk/lenders-handbook
- BSA mortgage instructions
  https://www.bsa.org.uk/information/mortgage-instructions
- Law Society's certificate of title
  https://www.lawsociety.org.uk/support-services/advice/articles/approved-certificate-of-title/
- Law Society mortgage fraud
  https://www.lawsociety.org.uk/support-services/advice/practice-notes/mortgage-fraud/
- Formulae for exchanging contracts by telephone
  https://www.lawsociety.org.uk/topics/property/formulae-for-exchanging-contracts-by-telephone
- Land Registry transfer forms
  https://www.gov.uk/government/publications/registered-titles-whole-transfer-tr1
- Registered titles part transfer
  https://www.gov.uk/government/publications/registered-titles-part-transfer-tp1
- Land Registry Practice Guide 8 (execution of deeds)
  https://www.gov.uk/government/publications/execution-of-deeds/practice-guide-8-execution-of-deeds
- Official searches and outline applications
  https://www.gov.uk/government/publications/official-searches-and-outline-applications/practice-guide-12-official-searches-and-outline-applications#types-of-official-search
- Law Society's code for completion by post
  https://www.lawsociety.org.uk/support-services/advice/articles/code-for-completion-by-post
- WebFiling facility at Companies House
  https://www.gov.uk/government/organisations/companies-house/about/about-our-services#webfiling
- HM Revenue and Customs calculator for SDLT
  http://www.hmrc.gov.uk/tools/sdlt/land-and-property.htm
- Business tax: stamp duty and other taxes on property
  https://www.gov.uk/business-tax/stamp-taxes
- Law Society's interest rates
  http://www.lawsociety.org.uk/advice/articles/law-society-interest-rate/
- Apply to the land registration tribunal
  https://www.gov.uk/apply-land-registration-tribunal/apply-to-the-tribunal
- National House Building Council
  http://www.nhbc.co.uk

- Land Registry Practice Guide (No 64)
  https://www.gov.uk/government/publications/prescribed-clauses-leases
- Law Society's leasehold forms
  https://www.lawsociety.org.uk/topics/property/leasehold-forms
- Royal Institution of Chartered Surveyors
  https://consultations.rics.org/
- Carbon Reduction Commitment Energy Efficiency Scheme 2010
  https://www.gov.uk/government/collections/crc-energy-efficiency-scheme
- HMRC stamp duty land tax calculator
  https://www.gov.uk/stamp-duty-land-tax-calculators

APPENDIX 2
Specimen Land Registry Official Copy Entries

Land Registry

Official copy of register of title

Title number DN649563 | **Edition date 28.02.2024**

- This official copy shows the entries in the register of title on 28 February 2024 at 11:50:13.
- This date must be quoted as the "search from date" in any official search application based on this copy.
- The date at the beginning of an entry is the date on which the entry was made in the register.
- Issued on 28 February 2024.
- Under s.67 of the Land Registration Act 2002, this copy is admissible in evidence to the same extent as the original.
- For information about the register of title see Land Registry website www.landregistry.gov.uk or Land Registry Public Guide *1 - A guide to the information we keep and how you can obtain it.*
- This title is dealt with by Land Registry Plymouth Office.

A: Property register

This register describes the land and estate comprised in the title.

DEVON : SOUTH HAMS
DEVON : EXETER
CITY OF PLYMOUTH

1 (28.02.2024) The Freehold land shown edged with red on the plan of the above Title filed at the Registry and being 14 Heather Close, Waverley(WY15 9PB).

B: Proprietorship register

This register specifies the class of title and identifies the owner. It contains any entries that affect the right of disposal.

Title absolute

1 (28.02.2024) PROPRIETOR: Christopher Hunt of 14 Heather Close, Waverley (WY15 9PB).

2 (28.02.2024) The price stated to have been paid on 12 February 2024 was £125,000.

3 (28.02.2024) RESTRICTION: No disposition of the registered estate by the proprietor of the registered estate is to be registered without a written consent signed by the proprietor for the time being of the Charge dated 12 February 2024 in favour of Limitless Mortgages UK Ltd referred to in the Charges Register.

Title number DN649563

C: Charges register

This register contains any charges and other matters that affect the land.

1 (28.02.2024) REGISTERED CHARGE dated 12 February 2024.

2 (28.02.2024) Proprietor: LIMITLESS MORTGAGES UK LTD (Co. Regn. No. 7654321) of Poplar House, 104 Barge Street, Leatherhead, Surrey KT23 8BZ.

End of register

Land Registry
Current title plan

Title number **DN649563**
Ordnance Survey map reference **TL2426SW**
Scale **1:1250**
Administrative area **Devon: South Hams**

This official copy issued on 28 February 2024 shows the state of this title plan, on 28 February 2024 at 11:50:13 admissible in evidence to the same extent as the original (s.67 Land Registration Act 2002).
This title plan shows the general position, not the exact line, of the boundaries. It may be subject to distortions in scale. Measurements scaled from this plan may not match measurements between the same points on the ground. See Land Registry Public Guide 7 – Title Plans.
This title is dealt with by Land Registry Plymouth Office

APPENDIX 3
TR1

HM Land Registry
Transfer of whole of registered title(s)

TR1

Any parts of the form that are not typed should be completed in black ink and in block capitals.

If you need more room than is provided for in a panel, and your software allows, you can expand any panel in the form. Alternatively use continuation sheet CS and attach it to this form.

For information on how HM Land Registry processes your personal information, see our Personal Information Charter.

Leave blank if not yet registered.	1 Title number(s) of the property: CL362638
Insert address including postcode (if any) or other description of the property, for example 'land adjoining 2 Acacia Avenue'.	2 Property: 19 Minster Yard Blakey Cornshire BL4 5EH
Remember to date this deed with the day of completion, but not before it has been signed and witnessed.	3 Date:
Give full name(s) of **all** the persons transferring the property. Complete as appropriate where the transferor is a company. Enter the overseas entity ID issued by Companies House for the transferor pursuant to the Economic Crime (Transparency and Enforcement) Act 2022. If the ID is not required, you may instead state 'not required'. Further details on overseas entities can be found in practice guide 78: overseas entities.	4 Transferor: Shilpa Jennings For UK incorporated companies/LLPs Registered number of company or limited liability partnership including any prefix: For overseas entities (a) Territory of incorporation or formation: (b) Overseas entity ID issued by Companies House, including any prefix: (c) Where the entity is a company with a place of business in the United Kingdom, the registered number, if any, issued by Companies House, including any prefix:

Give full name(s) of **all** the persons to be shown as registered proprietors. Complete as appropriate where the transferee is a company. Also, for an overseas company, unless an arrangement with HM Land Registry exists, lodge either a certificate in Form 7 in Schedule 3 to the Land Registration Rules 2003 or a certified copy of the constitution in English or Welsh, or other evidence permitted by rule 183 of the Land Registration Rules 2003. Enter the overseas entity ID issued by Companies House for the transferee pursuant to the Economic Crime (Transparency and Enforcement) Act 2022. If the ID is not required, you may instead state 'not required'. Further details on overseas entities can be found in practice guide 78: overseas entities.	5 Transferee for entry in the register: Lydia Alice Walmsley For UK incorporated companies/LLPs Registered number of company or limited liability partnership including any prefix: For overseas entities (a) Territory of incorporation or formation: (b) Overseas entity ID issued by Companies House, including any prefix: (c) Where the entity is a company with a place of business in the United Kingdom, the registered number, if any, issued by Companies House, including any prefix:
Each transferee may give up to three addresses for service, one of which must be a postal address whether or not in the UK (including the postcode, if any). The others can be any combination of a postal address, a UK DX box number or an email address.	6 Transferee's intended address(es) for service for entry in the register: 19 Minster Yard Blakey Cornshire BL4 5EH
	7 The transferor transfers the property to the transferee
Place 'X' in the appropriate box. State the currency unit if other than sterling. If none of the boxes apply, insert an appropriate memorandum in panel 11.	8 Consideration ☒ The transferor has received from the transferee for the property the following sum (in words and figures): One Hundred Thousand Pounds (£100,000.00) ☐ The transfer is not for money or anything that has a monetary value ☐ Insert other receipt as appropriate:
Place 'X' in any box that applies. Add any modifications.	9 The transferor transfers with ☒ full title guarantee ☐ limited title guarantee

Where the transferee is more than one person, place 'X' in the appropriate box.

Complete as necessary.

The registrar will enter a Form A restriction in the register *unless*:
- an 'X' is placed:
  - in the first box, or
  - in the third box and the details of the trust or of the trust instrument show that the transferees are to hold the property on trust for themselves alone as joint tenants, *or*
- it is clear from completion of a form JO lodged with this application that the transferees are to hold the property on trust for themselves alone as joint tenants.

Please refer to *Joint property ownership* and practice guide *24: private trusts of land* for further guidance. These are both available on the GOV.UK website.

10 Declaration of trust. The transferee is more than one person and

☐ they are to hold the property on trust for themselves as joint tenants

☐ they are to hold the property on trust for themselves as tenants in common in equal shares

☐ they are to hold the property on trust:

Insert here any required or permitted statement, certificate or application and any agreed covenants, declarations and so on.

11 Additional provisions

The transferor must execute this transfer as a deed using the space opposite. If there is more than one transferor, all must execute. Forms of execution are given in Schedule 9 to the Land Registration Rules 2003. If the transfer contains transferee's covenants or declarations or contains an application by the transferee (such as for a restriction), it must also be executed by the transferee.

If there is more than one transferee and panel 10 has been completed, each transferee must also execute this transfer to comply with the requirements in section 53(1)(b) of the Law of Property Act 1925 relating to the declaration of a trust of land. Please refer to *Joint property ownership* and practice guide 24: *private trusts of land* for further guidance.

Examples of the correct form of execution are set out in practice guide 8: execution of deeds. Execution as a deed usually means that a witness must also sign, and add their name and address.

Remember to date this deed in panel 3.

12	Execution
	Signed as a deed by Shilpa Jennings In the presence of:

WARNING
If you dishonestly enter information or make a statement that you know is, or might be, untrue or misleading, and intend by doing so to make a gain for yourself or another person, or to cause loss or the risk of loss to another person, you may commit the offence of fraud under section 1 of the Fraud Act 2006, the maximum penalty for which is 10 years' imprisonment or an unlimited fine, or both.

Failure to complete this form with proper care may result in a loss of protection under the Land Registration Act 2002 if, as a result, a mistake is made in the register.

Under section 66 of the Land Registration Act 2002 most documents (including this form) kept by the registrar relating to an application to the registrar or referred to in the register are open to public inspection and copying. If you believe a document contains prejudicial information, you may apply for that part of the document to be made exempt using Form EX1, under rule 136 of the Land Registration Rules 2003.

Glossary

Administrator *See* **Personal Representative**.

Alienation The act of disposing of one's property; that is passing it from one owner to another, particularly in relation to leasehold property.

Assent A disposition by personal representatives, by which property is vested in the person entitled under the deceased's will or on intestacy.

Assignee The incoming tenant on an assignment of a lease.

Assignment A transfer of property, particularly in relation to the transfer of a lease.

Assignor The outgoing tenant on an assignment of a lease.

Authorised guarantee agreement An agreement by the assignor with the landlord on an assignment of the lease that the assignor will guarantee the liabilities of their immediate successor in title; that is the assignee.

Bridging loan A short-term loan that finances the purchase of a property while the client is selling an existing property.

Building regulations Standards for the design and construction of buildings to ensure the health and safety of people in or about those buildings.

Business lease A lease of business or commercial premises. Can be used interchangeably with Commercial lease.

Capital gains tax Tax on the gain (or profit) when the client sells something that's increased in value, such as property. The gain on the sale of a principal private dwelling-house is exempt.

Caveat emptor Let the buyer beware.

Charge An encumbrance securing the payment of money.

Commercial lease A lease of business or commercial premises. Can be used interchangeably with **Business lease**.

Commons registration search A search made by a buyer to check whether land is common land entitling community members to access the land by foot and use it for certain purposes, for example grazing, village fetes.

Completion date The date agreed in the contract when the balance of the purchase money is paid to the seller and the buyer moves in.

Completion statement A statement provided by the seller's solicitor to the buyer's solicitor before completion setting out the amount required to complete the purchase.

Confidentiality A solicitor's duty to protect confidential information relating to the solicitor's relationship with their clients.

Conflict of interest A situation where a solicitor's separate duties to act in the best interests of two or more clients in the same or a related matter conflict. A conflict may also occur where a solicitor's own interest conflicts with the client's.

Contract race A situation that occurs when the seller issues more than one contract to two or more prospective buyers. Subject to professional conduct rules.

Conveyance An instrument which transfers an unregistered freehold title from one owner to another.

Co-ownership A form of ownership in which two or more people are entitled to possession of property at the same time.

Covenant A promise made by deed.

Covenantee The person who makes a covenant, and who takes the benefit of the covenant and has a right to enforce the promise.

Covenantor The person who makes a covenant, and who has the burden of performing the promise.

Deducing title The process whereby the seller demonstrates to the buyer that the seller owns the property and can transfer it to the buyer.

Deed A document which is signed in the presence of a witness as a deed and is then delivered.

Deposit A sum in part payment made by the buyer to the seller on exchange of contracts, which is normally 10 per cent of the purchase price.

Dominant tenement A piece of land which is benefited by some right (*see* **Easement**).

Easement A right enjoyed over one piece of land (the 'servient tenement') for the benefit of another piece of land (the 'dominant tenement'), for example rights of way, rights of drainage, rights of light.

Encumbrance A liability burdening property, for example a restrictive covenant.

Energy Performance Certificate A certificate showing a property's energy efficiency.

Enfranchisement The statutory right of leaseholders to acquire the superior title, for example freehold, or to extend their lease term.

Epitome of title In unregistered land, a schedule with copy documents attached prepared by the seller listing all the material deeds or events that form the chain of title.

Equity of redemption The mortgagor's interest in the property during the life of the mortgage.

Estate An interest in land which entitles its owner to exercise proprietary rights over that land for a prescribed period. The two legal estates in land are freehold and leasehold.

Estate contract A contract to sell or grant an estate in land.

Exchange of contracts The crucial stage in the conveyancing transaction when the parties become legally bound to buy and sell the property.

Executor *See* **Personal representative**.

First registration The process of converting unregistered land to registered land following a disposition of unregistered land. The new registered title is given a unique title number.

Flying freehold A freehold property which is not attached to the ground, such as a first-floor flat. It is unattractive to lenders because of the difficulty of enforcing covenants and it is the reason why flats are normally leasehold.

Forfeiture A landlord's remedy, normally for breach of covenant, in which the landlord is permitted to terminate the lease and recover possession of the property.

Freehold estate The first legal estate in land which gives the owner a right to possession of the land indefinitely (*compare* **Leasehold estate**).

Indemnity covenant In conveyancing, a covenant typically given by a buyer to a seller indemnifying the seller against any future breaches of existing covenants on the title. Subsequent transactions can lead to a chain of indemnity covenants building up.

Index map Information on all land that is registered or being registered with the Land Registry. A search of the index map is made when buying unregistered land to check that it is not in fact registered.

Instrument A legal document whereby a right is created or confirmed or a fact recorded.

Interim rent Rent paid by a commercial business tenant whilst a tenancy of a property continues beyond the expiry of the contractual term; a situation commonly known as 'holding over'.

Intestacy The condition of dying without having made a will.

Investigating title The process whereby the buyer ensures that the seller owns the property and can transfer it to the buyer.

Joint tenancy The form of co-ownership in which each owner is entitled to the whole property, rather than to an individual share in it. The right of survivorship applies so that upon death, the surviving tenant(s) becomes solely entitled to the whole property.

Land charges search A search made in unregistered land against the names of past and current title owners to check for undisclosed encumbrances, for example restrictive covenants.

Land Registry A government department which guarantees title to registered estates and interests in land. It records the ownership rights of freehold properties, and leasehold properties where the lease has been granted for a term exceeding seven years.

Land transaction tax (LTT) A tax replacing stamp duty land tax in Wales from April 2018 and collected by the Welsh Revenue Authority.

Lease The instrument creating the leasehold estate.

Lessee Tenant under a lease.

Leasehold estate The second legal estate in land which gives the person entitled exclusive possession of the land for a period of time, usually in consideration of the payment of rent (*compare* **Freehold estate**).

Lessor Landlord under a lease.

Licence Permission to use land or to do something, such as when a lessor grants a lessee permission to assign a lease (known as a 'licence to assign').

License to assign (*see* **Licence**).

Local authority search An essential search for all buyers which uncovers information about the property held in the Local Land Charges Register and other council records.

Local land charges Generally financial charges or restrictions on the use of land which are governmental in character and imposed by public authorities under statutory powers, for example a Tree Preservation Order.

Mortgage The grant of an interest in land as security for the payment of a debt or the discharge of an obligation.

Mortgagee The person to whom a mortgage is granted and the interest in the mortgage granted, otherwise known as a lender.

Mortgagor The person who creates the mortgage and conveys an interest in their land as security for the payment of a debt, otherwise known as a borrower.

Notice to complete If completion does not take place on the contractually agreed completion date, the party not in breach can serve on the defaulting party a notice to complete, making 'time of the essence'. This is usually ten working days after service (depending on the contract conditions).

Official copies of register Evidence of a registered title issued by the Land Registry. Official copies are the equivalent of title deeds in unregistered land.

Official search A search of a registered title which confers a 'priority period'.

Overreaching A statutory procedure which enables a purchaser to take the legal estate free from certain equitable interests provided the purchase money is paid to at least two trustees or a trust corporation.

Overriding interest An interest to which a registered title is subject, even though it does not appear on the register. It is binding both on the registered proprietor and all who acquire later interests in the land. The categories of overriding interest are set out in Sch 3 to the Land Registration Act 2002.

Permitted development Rights which allow the improvement or extension of homes without the need to apply for express planning permission. Subject to size and volume limits.

Personal representative Person authorised to administer the estate of a dead person. There are two types: executors who are appointed by will and administrators who are appointed by the court in cases of intestacy, or where there is no executor willing or able to act.

Planning permission Formal consent from a local authority for the erection or alteration of buildings or similar development, or change of use.

Preliminary enquiries Pre-contract enquires concerning the property raised by the buyer to be answered by the seller. Sometimes known as a Property Information Form.

Priority period A period of protection given by a search certificate which effectively freezes the register so that no other dealing can take priority over the current purchase transaction. The priority period for an official search of a registered title is 30 working days within which the buyer must complete and apply for registration of the purchase.

Profit à prendre The right to take something from land belonging to another, such as sand or wood.

Purchase deed A generic term for a deed that transfers the legal estate in the property from the seller to the buyer. Applies to both registered and unregistered land.

Redemption statement A statement by a mortgagee detailing the amount required to discharge the debt secured by the mortgage.

Registered land Land registered in a central registry maintained by the Land Registry. Over 85 per cent of land in England and Wales is registered land (*compare* **Unregistered land**).

Registered proprietor The person registered as the owner of a legal estate in registered land.

Requisitions on title Questions or queries raised by the buyer's solicitor concerning the seller's title.

Reservation A method of creating an easement or profit à prendre, whereby a grantor retains rights over the land which they convey to the grantee.

Reversion The right remaining in a grantor after they have granted some interest shorter in duration than their own, for example a freeholder owning the reversion in a lease.

Service charge A yearly financial sum payable by each household on a development, or within a flat in an apartment block, to pay for the upkeep of an area or a service that communally benefits the contributing units. This may typically be the insurance of an apartment building, cleaning and lighting communal hallways and gardening in external areas.

Servient tenement A piece of land which is burdened by some right (*see* **Easement**).

Severance The procedure by which a joint tenant converts their relationship with the other co-owners into that of a tenant in common, so that they have an undivided share in the property and are no longer affected by the right of survivorship.

Stamp duty land tax (SDLT) A tax payable when you buy property in England over a certain price.

Standard Conditions of Sale A set of Law Society-produced contract conditions to which the vast majority of residential sale contracts are subject.

Sub-lease A lease granted by landlords who are themselves tenants of a superior estate owner, for example the owner of a freehold estate. Otherwise known as an under lease.

Survey A health inspection of a property that is carried out by a chartered surveyor on behalf a buyer or mortgagee before exchange of contracts.

Tenancy Another name for a lease. Both terms can be used interchangeably.

Tenancy in common The form of co-ownership in which each owner has an undivided share in the property, which passes with their estate on death. The right of survivorship does not apply (*compare* **Joint tenancy**).

Time of the essence A contractual requirement for an obligation to be performed within the timescale specified. Generally, a failure to do so will result in a breach of contract which cannot be remedied (which may also attract damages for breach), and which will entitle the innocent party to terminate the contract.

Title A person's right to property or the evidence of that right.

Transfer The purchase deed used to pass the legal estate in registered land from one owner to another.

Trust of land A trust in which some or all of the trust property is land. The term was introduced by the Trusts of Land and Appointment of Trustees Act 1996.

Underlease A lease granted by a landlord who is them self a tenant of a superior estate owner, for example a freeholder. Otherwise known as a sublease.

Undertaking A promise made by a solicitor to do something which is enforceable against the solicitor by the courts. Failure to comply with an undertaking is likely to be professional misconduct leading to disciplinary action by the Solicitors Regulation Authority.

Unregistered land Land which is not registered at the Land Registry, the title to which is evidenced by deeds (*compare* **Registered land**).

Index

T

U

V

W